Process
Quality
Control

Process
Quality
Control

Troubleshooting and
Interpretation
of Data

Ellis R. Ott

Professor Emeritus, Rutgers,
The State University of New Jersey

McGraw-Hill Book Company

New York   St. Louis   San Francisco   Auckland   Düsseldorf
Johannesburg   Kuala Lumpur   London   Mexico   Montreal
New Delhi   Panama   Paris   São Paulo   Singapore
Sydney   Tokyo   Toronto

Library of Congress Cataloging in Publication Data

Ott, Ellis Raymond   date
  Process quality control.

  Bibliography: p.
  Includes index.
  1. Quality control—Statistical methods. I. Title.
TS156.O86   658.5'6   75–4648
ISBN 0-07-047923-2

    567890 DODO   8432

The editors for this book were Jeremy Robinson
and Lila Gardner, the designer was Naomi Auerbach,
and the production supervisor was George Oechsner.
It was set in Times New Roman.

It was printed and bound by R. R. Donnelley, Inc.

To Virginia, with love and appreciation

Contents

Case Histories

Preface

Every manufacturing operation has problems. Some are painfully obvious; others require ingenuity and hard work to identify. Every production engineer and supervisor has to be a troubleshooter. Anyone hoping to become a production engineer or supervisor must learn about process-improvement and troubleshooting that uses systematic data obtained from the process. There are two approaches to reducing trouble: learn to prevent it and learn to cure it when it develops. This book has something to say on each approach.

Some methods are presented for identifying opportunities for process improvements and for locating important differences. The knowledge that such differences do exist and the pinpointing of them are vital information. Experience has shown that those familiar with the process can then find ways to make improvements and corrections, if they can first be convinced that the differences actually do exist. This is one reason for the emphasis on graphical presentations.

Methods, examples, and broader case histories will relate to a wide variety of experiences. The case histories are real experiences, typical of ever-recurring problems. Many persons find it meaningful to read about an experience relating specifically to his own problem. However, the reader is encouraged to give even more attention to case histories in those industries not even apparently relevant to his own. He may be surprised to find how often they bring up ideas and suggestions applicable to his own problems.

Some readers will want to browse through the first three introductory chapters. The material will be familiar, though presenting some new ideas. Many readers will want to study them more carefully. They present some basic methods of obtaining and diagnosing data. The book also presents some useful statistical methods and concepts having important practical applications. Derivations of a mathematical nature are included occasionally when they seem to support applications.

Many books emphasize control charts and acceptance sampling plans. Such books are important, and their readers will find broad new avenues in this book extending them into important areas of investigation. Some books emphasize management aspects. Many emphasize experimental design and analysis, especially on technical investigations in agriculture, the biological sciences, and chemical engineering. Some elements of these different areas have been included and related here, but emphasis in this book is on combining a number of approaches to troubleshooting and process improvement in manufacturing, including basic methods and principles of statistical quality control and experimental designs.

Some books emphasize the testing of hypotheses, but usually the problem confronting a production problem solver is entirely different: discovering hypotheses that warrant testing, (see Chap. 4, especially). Troubleshooting cannot be entirely formalized, and there is no substitute for being inquisitive and exercising ingenuity. Many problems can be resolved without recourse to formal data collection. The ideas presented here are intended to support and extend the science of processes, not to replace them; the support and cooperation of technical and production personnel are to be cultivated by troubleshooters.

The business of providing product to the consumer requires many major functions. Production itself has major subdivisions: design and specify, purchase and acquire, manufacture, package, inspect and ensure quality. Each of these critical functions observes Murphy's first law: *If anything can go wrong, it will.* Although troubleshooting and process improvement projects are as old as civilization itself, today they are still usually left to individuals who are relatively untrained in the area and who regard it as a chore. It is our intent here to gather together and organize some procedures rather universally applicable to troubleshooting. This procedure usually employs data collection and/or logic in addition to the process science and know-how.

A fortunate series of events led me from a university life into industrial quality control early in World War II, then back into a progressive state university with permission to build a graduate program in applied statistics. Hundreds of students there, many from neighboring industries, delighted their professor with choice sets of data—data from real, in-plant problems and operations. Many of these students became colleagues and personal friends. All of them contributed and exchanged experiences and ideas on industrial problems. William C. Frey, Edwin S. Shecter, Carl Mentch, Edward

G. Schilling, Frank W. Wehrfritz are among the "old-timers." Living nearby were many pioneers in quality control, all of whom were so very generous in giving advice in many ways: Walter A. Shewhart, Harold F. Dodge, Paul S. Olmstead, Enoch B. Ferrell shared their ideas, their time, and their support. It was a rich heritage. References are made to numerous articles from publications of the American Society for Quality Control, especially from *Indusrtial Quality Control*. It pleases me to acknowledge their permission to use various excerpts from them. Most recently, the patient, and delightful technical and editorial assistance of Allegra Rodgers, a neighboring Texan and former "student," has been invaluable. And if Virginia, an amazingly versatile wife, had not given such steady support throughout the project, completion of this manuscript would have been impossible or long delayed—in spite of her exceptionally able typing. To all these, and to so many others unnamed here, who have contributed so many ideas and given so much support, it is a pleasure to give thanks.

It will please me if this book can pass along some of the heritage which came my way by contributing ideas and principles which will lead you to new levels of competence.

ELLIS R. OTT

Lake Marble Falls, Texas

Process Quality Control

1
Variables Data: An Introduction

1-1 Introduction—an Experience with Data

My first industrial experience with data pertained to the thickness of mica pieces being supplied by a vendor. The pieces had a design pattern of punched holes. They were carefully arranged to hold various grids, plates, and other radio tube components in their proper places. But the failure of mica pieces to conform to thickness specifications for radio tubes presented a problem. In particular, there were too many thin pieces being found in many different types of mica. The vendor was aware of the problem but was quite sure that there was nothing he could do to resolve it. "The world supply of first-grade mica has been cut off by a world war; only an inferior quality is obtainable. My workers split the mica blocks quite properly to the specified dimensions.[1] Because of the poor mica quality," he insisted, "these pieces subsequently split in handling and produce two thin pieces." He was sorry, but there was nothing he could do about it! Now there are some general principles to be recognized by troubleshooters:

[1] Purchase specifications were 8.5 to 15 thousandths (0.0085 to 0.015 in.) with an industry-accepted allowance of 5% over and 5% under these dimensions. Very thin pieces did not give enough support to the assemblage. Very thick pieces were difficult to assemble. (It should be noted that specifications which designate such an allowance outside the stated "specifications" are quite unusual.)

1

RULE 1:   Don't expect many people to advance the idea that the problem is their own fault.   Rather it is the fault of raw materials and components, a wornout machine, or something else beyond their own control. *"It's not my fault!"*

RULE 2:   Get some *data* on the problem; do not spend too much time in initial planning.   (An exception is when data collection requires a long time or is very expensive; very careful planning is then important.)

RULE 3:   *Always graph* your data in some simple way—*always*.   In this case, the engineer took mica samples from a recent shipment and measured the thickness of 200 pieces.[1]   The resulting data shown in Table 1-1 are presented in Fig. 1-1 as a histogram.

Discussion: Figure 1-1 shows some important things:

1.   A substantial number[2] of mica pieces are too thin and some are too thick when compared to the upper and lower specifications limits (USL and LSL).

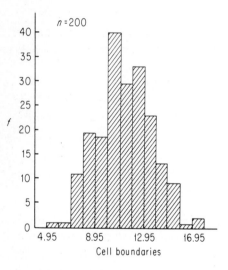

Fig. 1-1   Thickness of mica pieces shown as a histogram. (Data from Table 1-1.)

2.   The center of the two specifications is $0.5(8.5 + 15) = 11.75$ thousandths; the peak of the thickness distribution is to the left of 11.75 at 10.25 thousandths.   If the splitting blades were adjusted to increase the thickness by about 0.5 thousandth, then: the peak would be moved near the center of specifications; the number of thin pieces would be reduced slightly more than the number of thick pieces would be increased.   The adjusted process would produce fewer nonconforming pieces but would still produce more outside than the 5% allowable deviation on each side.

[1] After some years experience with problem solving, I would now ask for only about 50 measurements—certainly not more than 100.   An exception would arise when an overwhelming mass of data is required, usually for psychological reasons.

[2] A count shows that 24 of the 200 pieces are under 8.5 thousandths in. and 7 over 15 thousandths.

3. It is conceivable that a few of the mica pieces split during handling, as the vendor believed. However, if more than an occasional one were splitting, a bimodal[1] pattern would be formed. Consequently, it is neither logical nor productive to attribute the problem of thin micas to the splitting process.

What might the vendor investigate to reduce the variability in his own splitting process?

Answer: He has more than one operator hand-splitting this particular type of mica piece. Differences between these operators are almost certainly contributing to variation in the process.

Also, differences in thickness from an individual operator would be expected to develop over a period of a few hours because *changes* in knife sharpness and *operator fatigue* could produce important changes.

At his suggestion, we helped institute quality control charts on individual operators. These charts helped reduce variability in the process and produce micas conforming to specifications.

In our larger study of the mica thickness problem, we examined samples from several different mica types; we found many pieces too thin and relatively few pieces too thick with each type. What then?

Economic factors often exert an influence on manufacturing processes, either consciously or unconsciously. In this splitting operation, the vendor bought the mica by the pound but sold it by the piece. One can imagine a possible reluctance to direct the mica-splitting process to produce any greater thickness than absolutely necessary.

A more formal discussion of data display will be presented in following sections. Mechanics of grouping the data in Table 1-1 and of constructing Fig. 1-1 will also be explained in Secs. 1-3 and 1-4.

1-2 Variability

In every manufacturing operation there is variability. The variability becomes evident whenever a quality characteristic of the product is measured. There are two basically different reasons for variability, and it is very important to distinguish between them.

Variability Inherent in the Process

It is important to learn how much of the product variability is actually inherent in the process. Is the variation a result of *random* effects of components and raw materials? Is it from small mechanical linkage variations in a machine producing random variation in the product? Is it from slight variations in an operator's performance? Many factors influence a process and each contributes to the inherent variation affecting the resulting product.

[1] See Fig. 1-4.

There is also variation in test equipment and test procedures—whether used to measure a physical dimension, an electronic or a chemical characteristic, or any other characteristic. This inherent variation in testing is a factor contributing to the observed measurement of product characteristics—sometimes an important factor.[1]

There *is* variation in a process even when all adjustable factors known to affect the process have been set and held constant during its operations.

Also there is a *pattern* to the inherent variation of a specific stable process, and there are different basic characteristic patterns of data from different processes. However, the most frequent and useful one is called the *normal distribution*; its idealized mathematical form is shown in Fig. 1-2; it is discussed further in Sec. 1-8.

The mica thickness data in Fig. 1-1 have a general resemblance to the normal distribution of Fig. 1-2. A majority of observations are clustered around a

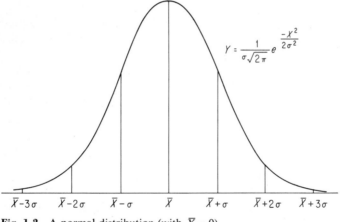

$$Y = \frac{1}{\sigma\sqrt{2\pi}}e^{\frac{-X^2}{2\sigma^2}}$$

| $\bar{X}-3\sigma$ | $\bar{X}-2\sigma$ | $\bar{X}-\sigma$ | $\bar{X}$ | $\bar{X}+\sigma$ | $\bar{X}+2\sigma$ | $\bar{X}+3\sigma$ |

Fig. 1-2   A normal distribution (with $\bar{X}=0$).

central value, there are tails on each end, and it is relatively symmetrical about a vertical line drawn at about 11.2 thousandths.

There are other basic patterns of variability; they are referred to as *non-normal* distributions. The *log normal* is fairly common when making acoustical measurements and certain measurements of electronic products. If the logarithms of the measurements are plotted, the resulting pattern is a normal distribution—hence its name. A sketch of a log normal pattern is shown in Fig. 1-3: it has a longer tail to the right.

In my industrial experience, the basic log normal distribution does not exist as frequently as some analysts believe. Many apparently basic log normal distributions of data are *not* the consequence of a *stable log normal*

[1] See Case History 2-4.

process but of *two basically normal distributions* with a large percentage produced at one level. The net result can produce a bimodal distribution as in Fig. 1-4, which presents a false appearance of being inherently log normal.

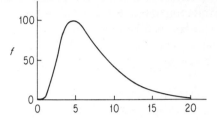

Fig. 1-3 A log-normal distribution.

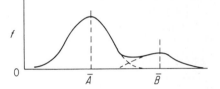

Fig. 1-4 A bimodal distribution composed of two normal distributions.

The production troubleshooter needs help in identifying the *nature* of the causes producing variation. If different operators or machines are performing the same operation, it is important to learn whether some are performing better or worse than others. Specific differences, when discovered, will often lead to ideas for improvement when those performing differently—either better or worse—are compared. Some causes may be common to all machines and operators. In reducing process variability caused by them, the troubleshooter may need to identify a variety of small improvements which can be extended over all machines and operators.

Variability from Assignable Causes

Secondly, there are other important causes of variability which Dr. Walter Shewhart called *assignable* causes.[1]

This type of variation often contributes in large part to the overall variability of the process. Evidence of this type of variation offers important opportunities for improving the uniformity of product. The process average may change gradually as a result of gradual changes in temperature, tool wear, or operator fatigue. Or the process may be unnecessarily variable

---

[1] Walter A. Shewhart, *Economic Control of Quality of Manufactured Product*, D. Van Nostrand Company, Inc., New York, 1931.

because two operators or machines are performing at different averages. Variability resulting from two or more processes operating at different levels, or of a single source operating with an unstable average, are typical of production processes. *They are the rule*, not the exception to the rule.

This second type of variability must be studied by various techniques of data analysis which will be presented in this book. Then after responsible factors have been identified and corrected, a continuing control[1] of the process will be needed.

1-3   Organizing Data

Certain concepts and methods about the analysis and interpretation of data appear to be simple. Yet they are not easily acquired and assimilated. The discussion of methods extends over our first two chapters. Some patience will be needed. After some concepts and methodologies have been considered, the weaving of them together with actual experiences (case histories) will begin to make sense.

The data presented in Table 1-1 are measurements of small pieces of mica

TABLE 1-1   Mica Thickness, Thousandths of an Inch

8.0	12.5	12.5	14.0	13.5	12.0	14.0	12.0	10.0	14.5
10.0	10.5	8.0	15.0	9.0	13.0	11.0	10.0	14.0	11.0
12.0	10.5	13.5	11.5	12.0	15.5	14.0	7.5	11.5	11.0
12.0	12.5	15.5	13.5	12.5	17.0	8.0	11.0	11.5	17.0
11.5	9.0	9.5	11.5	12.5	14.0	11.5	13.0	13.0	15.0
8.0	13.0	15.0	9.5	12.5	15.0	13.5	12.0	11.0	11.0
11.5	11.5	10.0	12.5	9.0	13.0	11.5	16.0	10.5	9.0
9.5	14.5	10.0	5.0	13.5	7.5	11.0	9.0	10.5	14.0
9.5	13.5	9.0	8.0	12.5	12.0	9.5	10.0	7.5	10.5
10.5	12.5	14.5	13.0	12.5	12.0	13.0	8.5	10.5	10.5
13.0	10.0	11.0	8.5	10.5	7.0	10.0	12.0	12.0	10.5
13.5	10.5	10.5	7.5	8.0	12.5	10.5	14.5	12.0	8.0
11.0	8.0	11.5	10.0	8.5	10.5	12.0	10.5	11.0	10.5
14.5	13.0	8.5	11.0	13.5	8.5	11.0	11.0	10.0	12.5
12.0	7.0	8.0	13.5	13.0	6.0	10.0	10.0	12.0	14.5
13.0	8.0	10.0	9.0	13.0	15.0	10.0	13.5	11.5	7.5
11.0	7.0	7.5	15.5	13.0	15.5	11.5	10.5	9.5	9.5
10.5	7.0	10.0	12.5	9.5	10.0	10.0	12.0	8.5	10.0
9.5	9.5	12.5	7.0	9.5	12.0	10.0	10.0	8.5	12.0
11.5	11.5	8.0	10.5	14.5	8.5	10.0	12.5	12.5	11.0

SOURCE: Lewis M. Reagan, Ellis R. Ott, and Daniel T. Sigley, *College Algebra*, rev. ed., chap. 18, Rinehart and Company, Inc., New York, 1940. (Reprinted by permission of Holt, Rinehart & Winston, Inc.)

[1] See Chaps. 2, 8, and 15.

delivered as one shipment. These readings were made with a dial indicator gage on a sample of $n = 200$ pieces of one mica type. (Table 1-1 is the data source for Fig. 1-1.)

The observations in Table 1-1 could also be displayed individually along a horizontal scale. Such a display would show extremes and any indication of clustering. When n is large, we often decide to present the data in the condensed form of a *grouped frequency distribution* or *histogram* (Table 1-2). A histogram is a picture.

TABLE 1-2   Data: Mica Thickness as a Tally Sheet
Data of Table 1-1 Grouped into Cells Whose Boundaries and Midpoints Are Shown in Columns at the Left

Cell boundaries	Cell midpoint	Tally	Observed frequency	Percent frequency
4.75				
	5.25	/	1	0.5
5.75				
	6.25	/	1	0.5
6.75				
	7.25	/	11	5.5
7.75				
	8.25	////	19	9.5
8.75				
	9.25	///	18	9.0
9.75				
	10.25		40	20.0
10.75				
	11.25	////	29	14.5
11.75				
	12.25	///	33	16.5
12.75				
	13.25	///	23	11.5
13.75				
	14.25	///	13	6.5
14.75				
	15.25	////	9	4.5
15.75				
	16.25	/	1	0.5
16.75				
	17.25	//	2	1.0
17.75				
			$n = 200$	100%

Table 1-2 was prepared[1] by selecting *cell boundaries* to form equal intervals of width $m = 1$ called *cells*. A tally mark was then entered in the proper cell corresponding to each measurement in the table. The number of measurements which fall in a particular cell is called the *frequency* (f_i) for that *i*th cell; also f_i/n is called the *relative frequency*, and $100\, f_i/n$ is the *percent frequency*. An immediate observation from Table 1-2 is that mica pieces vary from a thickness of about 5 thousandths at one extreme to 17 at the other. Also the frequency of measurements is greatest near the center, 10 or 11 thousandths, and tails off to low frequencies on each end.

1-4   Grouping Data When n Is Large—Histograms

Cells—How Many and How Wide?

Table 1-1 has been presented in Table 1-2 as a *tally sheet*. Many times there are advantages in recording the data *initially* on a blank tally sheet instead of listing the numbers as in Table 1-1. In preparing a histogram, it is usually best:

1.   To make the *cell intervals* equal, of width m.

2.   To choose the *cell boundaries* halfway between two possible observations. This simplifies classification. For example, in Table 1-1 observations were recorded to the nearest half (0.5); cell boundaries were chosen beginning with 4.75, i.e., halfway between 4.5 and 5.0.

3.   The *number of cells*[2] should preferably be between 13 and 20. However, when the number of observations is less than say 200, then as few as 10 cells may be of use. The number of cells k is a direct consequence of the cell width: $k = \Delta/m$. In Table 1-1, a large[3] observation is 17.0; a small one is 6.0. Their difference Δ is read "delta."

$$\Delta = 17.0 - 6.0 = 11.0$$

Now if the cell width m is chosen to be $m = 1$, we expect at least $\Delta/m = 11$ cells; if chosen to be $m = 0.5$, we expect the data to extend over at least $11/0.5 = 22$ cells. The tally (Table 1-2) was prepared with $m = 1$, resulting in 13 cells. (See Exercise 1-1 for $m = 0.5$.)

4.   *Choose cell boundaries which will simplify the tallying.* The choice of 4.75, 5.75, 6.75, etc. as cell boundaries when grouping the data of Table 1-1 results in classifying all numbers beginning with a 5 into the same cell; its midpoint is 5.25, halfway between 5.0 and 5.5. Similarly, all readings beginning with a 6 are grouped into the cell whose midpoint is 6.25, etc. This makes tallying quite simple.

[1] A discussion of the grouping procedure is given in Sec. 1-4.

[2] American Society for Testing Materials, *ASTM Manual on Presentation of Data*, pp. 6–10, Philadelphia, 1937.

[3] Whether these are actually the largest and smallest is not critical.

5. The *midpoint of a cell* is the average of its two boundaries.   Midpoints begin with

$$0.5(4.75 + 5.75) = 5.25$$

then increase successively by the cell width *m*.

6.   A histogram representing a set of data makes it possible to compute two different numbers (See Table 1-3) and gives objective and useful information about the *location* and *shape* of the frequency distribution.   These computed numbers are especially important in data analysis.   The number $\bar{X}$ is[1] an *estimate* of the central location of the process.   The number $\hat{\sigma}$ is an *estimate* of the variation; some interpretations of $\hat{\sigma}$ will be discussed in Sec. 1-8. Both $\bar{X}$ and $\hat{\sigma}$ can be computed easily from the data after they have been organized as a histogram; the computations are shown in Table 1-3.

1-5   The Arithmetic Average or Mean—Central Value

There are $n = 200$ measurements of mica thickness recorded in Table 1-1. The *arithmetic average* of this sample could be found by adding the 200 numbers and then dividing by 200.   We do this when n is small and sometimes when using a machine computer.   The average $\bar{X}$ obtained in this way is 11.1525; it compares closely with 11.165 obtained in Table 1-3.

More generally, let the n measurements be

$$X_1, X_2, X_3, \ldots, X_n \tag{1-1}$$

A shorthand notation is commonly used to represent sums of numbers.   The capital Greek letter *sigma*, written $\sum$, indicates summation.   Then the average $\bar{X}$ of the n numbers in Eq. (1-1) is written symbolically[2] as

$$\bar{X} = \frac{\sum_{i=1}^{n} X_i}{n} \tag{1-2}$$

---

[1] Read "X bar" for the symbol $\bar{X}$; and read "sigma hat" for $\hat{\sigma}$.

[2] The expression $\sum_{i=1}^{n} X_i$ is read "the summation of X_i from $i = 1$ to n."   The letter i (or j or whatever letter is used) is called the *index of summation*.   The numbers written above and below, or following $\sum$ indicate that the index i is to be given successively each integral value from 1 to n, inclusive.

The expression

$$\sum_{i=1}^{10} X_i^2$$

represents the sum

$$X_1^2 + X_2^2 + X_3^2 + \cdots + X_{10}^2$$

and

$$\sum_{i=1}^{n} (X_i - \bar{X})^2 = (X_1 - \bar{X})^2 + (X_2 - \bar{X})^2 + (X_3 - \bar{X})^2 + \cdots + (X_n - \bar{X})^2$$

Both these expressions are used frequently in data analysis.

TABLE 1-3   Mica Thickness
Computation of $\bar{X}$ and $\hat{\sigma}$; Data of Table 1-1

Cell boundaries	Cell midpts	Tally	f_i	d_i	$f_i d_i$	$f_i d_i^2$	$\sum f_i$	$\sum \%$
	5.25	/	1	−5	−5	25	1	0.5
5.75								
	6.25	/	1	−4	−4	16	2	1.0
6.75								
	7.25	ⅢⅢ Ⅲ /	11	−3	−33	99	13	6.5
7.75								
	8.25	ⅢⅢ ⅢⅢ ⅢⅢ ////	19	−2	−38	76	32	16.0
8.75								
	9.25	ⅢⅢ ⅢⅢ ⅢⅢ ///	18	−1	−18	18	50	25.0
9.75								
	$A = 10.25$	ⅢⅢ ⅢⅢ ⅢⅢ ⅢⅢ ⅢⅢ ⅢⅢ ⅢⅢ ⅢⅢ	40	0	0	0	90	45.0
10.75								
	11.25	ⅢⅢ ⅢⅢ ⅢⅢ ⅢⅢ ⅢⅢ ////	29	+1	29	29	119	59.5
11.75								
	12.25	ⅢⅢ ⅢⅢ ⅢⅢ ⅢⅢ ⅢⅢ ⅢⅢ ///	33	+2	66	132	152	76.0
12.75								
	13.25	ⅢⅢ ⅢⅢ ⅢⅢ ⅢⅢ ///	23	+3	69	207	175	87.5
13.75								
	14.25	ⅢⅢ ⅢⅢ ///	13	+4	52	208	188	94.0
14.75								
	15.25	ⅢⅢ ////	9	+5	45	225	197	98.5
15.75								
	16.25	/	1	+6	6	36	198	99.0
16.75								
	17.25	//	2	+7	14	98	200	100.0
17.75								
		$n =$	200		+183	1169		

$$E_1 = \qquad E_2 =$$
$$0.915 \quad 5.845$$

$$E_1 = \frac{\sum f_i d_i}{n} = 0.915 \qquad E_2 = \frac{\sum f_i d_i^2}{n} = 5.845$$

$$\bar{X} = A + mE_1 = 10.25 + (1)(0.915) = 11.165 \qquad (1\text{-}3)$$

$$\hat{\sigma} = m\sqrt{E_2 - E_1^2} = (1)\sqrt{5.845 - 0.837} = 2.238 \qquad (1\text{-}4b)$$

Simplified Computation Procedure to Find
$\overline{X}$ with Grouped Data

1. Begin by selecting an arbitrary cell midpoint A as origin; the computation is simplified when A is chosen near the center of the distribution. In Table 1-3, we have chosen $A = 10.25$.

2. Fill in the d_i column beginning with a zero opposite the chosen A cell; this is the *origin*. The d_i indicate the *deviation in cells* from A. Number increasing cell midpoints consecutively with $+1$, $+2$, $+3$, etc., and number decreasing cell midpoints with -1, -2, -3, etc.

3. Complete the $f_i d_i$ column by multiplying corresponding f_i and d_i.

4. Add the numbers in the $f_i d_i$ column to obtain $\sum f_i d_i = 183$, and divide by $n = 200$ to obtain $\dfrac{\sum f_i d_i}{n} = 0.915$. The expression $\dfrac{\sum f_i d_i}{n}$ will be written as E_1 for simplicity.

5. Return to the original scale by computing

$$\overline{X} = A + mE_1$$
$$= 10.25 + (1)(0.915) = 11.165 \tag{1-3}$$

This value 11.165 has been obtained after assigning all measurements within a cell to have the value of the midpoint of that cell. The result compares closely with the arithmetic average 11.1525 computed by adding all individual measurements and dividing by 200.

Median

A *second* measure of the center of a distribution is the *median*. When there is an odd number of observations, the middle one is called the median. When there is an even number, the median is defined to be halfway between the two central values, i.e., their arithmetic average. In brief, half of the observations are greater than the median and half are smaller.

1-6   Measures of Variation

Computing a Standard Deviation, large n

Figure 1-5 shows two distributions having the same average. It is very clear that the average alone does not represent a distribution adequately. The distribution in (2) spreads out more than the one in (1). Thus some measure is needed to describe the *spread* or *variability* of a frequency distribution. The variability of the distribution in (2) appears to be about twice that in (1).

A useful *measure* of variability called the *standard deviation* σ may be computed from Table 1-3 for variables data for large n.[1] We shall present

---

[1] There is no sharp delineation between "large" and "small" values of n. However, less than 20 or 25 is usually considered "small"; larger than 40 or 50 is considered "large."

the calculation and then discuss some uses and interpretations of $\hat{\sigma}$. This is the small Greek letter sigma with a "hat" to indicate that it is an *estimate* of the *unknown measure of population variability*.

The computation of $\hat{\sigma}$ for smaller values of n is often obtained[1] from the formula

$$\hat{\sigma} = \sqrt{\frac{\sum (X - \bar{X})^2}{n - 1}} = \sqrt{\frac{n \sum X_i^2 - (\sum X_i)^2}{n(n - 1)}} \qquad (1\text{-}4a)$$

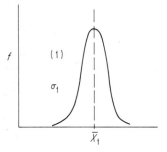

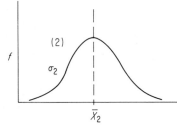

Fig. 1-5 Two normal distributions with $\bar{X}_1 = \bar{X}_2$ but $\sigma_2 > \sigma_1$.

The computation of $\hat{\sigma}$ in Table 1-3 requires one more column than for $\bar{X}$: it is labeled $f_i d_i^2$. It is obtained by multiplying each number in the d_i column by the corresponding number in the $f_i d_i$ column. Then compute

$$E_2 = \frac{\sum f_i d_i^2}{n} = \frac{1,169}{200} = 5.845$$

and compute $\hat{\sigma}$ from Eq. (1-4b):

$$\hat{\sigma} = m\sqrt{E_2 - E_1^2} = (1)\sqrt{5.008}$$
$$= 2.238 \qquad (1\text{-}4b)$$

This computation procedure is a great simplification over other procedures when n is large. When n is small, see Chap. 10. Some interpretations and uses of $\hat{\sigma}$ will be given in subsequent sections.

Note: The procedures of Table 1-3 not only provide values of $\bar{X}$ and $\hat{\sigma}$ but also provide a display of the data. If the histogram shows a definite

---
[1] Also see Sec. 10-3.

bimodal shape, for example, any interpretations of either $\overline{X}$ or $\hat{\sigma}$ must be made carefully.

One advantage of plotting a histogram is to check on whether the data appear to come from a single source or from perhaps two or more sources having different averages. As stated previously, the mica manufacturer believed that many of the mica pieces were splitting during handling. Then he should expect a definite bimodal shape in Table 1-3. The data *do not* lend support to his belief.

The mica-splitting data (Tables 1-1, 1-2, 1-3) were obtained by measuring the thickness of mica pieces at our incoming inspection department. The data almost surely came from a process representing production over some time period of different workers on different knife splitters; it just is not reasonable to expect all conditions to be the same. The data represent *what was actually* shipped to us—not necessarily what the production process was capable of producing.

Some Coding of Data[1]

The computations of $\overline{X}$ and $\hat{\sigma}$ in Table 1-3 have used some important properties and methods of coding (transforming) data. Consider again the n measurements in Eq. (1-1).

$$X_1, X_2, X_3, \ldots, X_n \tag{1-1}$$

■ What happens to their average $\overline{X}$ and standard deviation $\hat{\sigma}$ if we translate the origin by *adding* a constant c to each?

$$X_1 + c, X_2 + c, X_3 + c, \ldots, X_n + c \tag{1-5}$$

1. The *average* of this new set of numbers will be the original average increased by c:

$$\text{New average} = \frac{\sum (X_i + c)}{n} = \frac{\sum X_i + nc}{n} = \overline{X} + c$$

2. The *standard deviation* of this new set of numbers in Eq. (1-5) is not changed by a translation of origin; their standard deviation is still $\hat{\sigma}$.

■ What happens to the average $\overline{X}$ and standard deviation $\hat{\sigma}$ if we multiply each number in Eq. (1-1) by a constant c?

$$cX_1, cX_2, cX_3, \ldots, cX_n \tag{1-6}$$

1. The average of these numbers will be the original average multiplied by c:

$$\text{New average} = \frac{\sum cX_i}{n} = \frac{c \sum X_i}{n} = c\overline{X}$$

[1] This procedure may be omitted. Simple algebra is sufficient to prove the following relations pertaining to *standard deviations*; simple but tedious. The proofs are omitted.

2.   The standard deviation of these numbers will be the original multiplied by c; that is,

$$new \ \hat{\sigma} = c\hat{\sigma}$$

1-7   Plotting on Normal Probability Paper

This graphical method of presenting data is often helpful in checking on the stability of the source producing the data.   The *accumulated percents* of mica-thickness data are shown in Table 1-3, right-hand column.   These have been plotted on normal probability paper in Fig. 1-6.   There are 13 cells in Table 1-3; a convenient scale has been chosen on the base line (Fig. 1-6) to accommodate the 13 cells.   The upper cell boundaries have been printed on the base scale; the chart shows the accumulated percent frequencies to the upper cell boundaries.

Normal probability paper is scaled in such a way that a truly *normal curve* will be represented by a straight line.   A line can be drawn using a clear plastic ruler to approximate the points; it is not unusual for one or two points on each end to deviate slightly, as in Fig. 1-6, even if the source of the data is essentially a normal curve.   The data line up rather surprisingly well.

The *median* and the *standard deviation* of the data can be estimated from the straight-line graph on normal probability paper:

The Median Is Simply the 50 % Point: A perpendicular line has been dropped from the intersection of the plotted line and the 50% horizontal line.   This cuts the base line at the median: its estimate is

$$10.75 + 0.4 = 11.15$$

This is in close agreement with the computed $\overline{X} = 11.165$.

Estimating the *Standard Deviation* Involves More Arithmetic: One method is to determine where horizontal lines corresponding to the accumulated

$$16\% \text{ and } 84\%$$

cut the line.   These numbers correspond to areas under the normal curve to the left of ordinates drawn at $\overline{X} - \hat{\sigma}$ and $\overline{X} + \hat{\sigma}$, that is, they differ by an estimated $2\hat{\sigma}$.   See Eq. (1-10) of the following Sec. 1-8.

In Fig. 1-6, corresponding vertical lines appear to cut the base line at

$$84\% \text{ point:} \quad 13.75 - 0.2 \cong 13.55$$
$$16\% \text{ point:} \quad 8.75 + 0.2 \cong \ 8.95$$
$$2\hat{\sigma} \cong \ 4.60$$
$$\hat{\sigma} \cong \ 2.30^{[1]}$$

This agrees reasonably well with the previously computed value

$$\hat{\sigma} = 2.238 \text{ in Table 1-3}$$

---

[1] The symbol $\cong$ means "approximately equal to."

Interpretation: The only possible evidence of mica pieces splitting into two during handling is the pair of points at the lower left end of the line. But splitting is certainly not a major factor—rather, the process average should be increased by about 0.6 thousandths ($11.75 - 11.15 = 0.6$) since the center of specifications is at

$$\tfrac{1}{2}(8.5 + 15.0) = 11.75 \text{ thousandths}$$

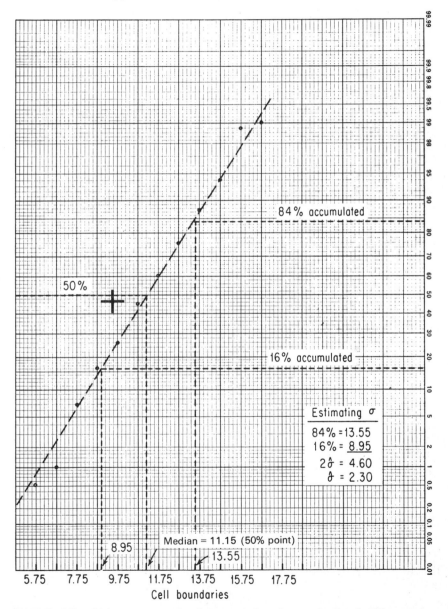

Fig. 1-6   Mica thickness; accumulated percents plotted on normal probability paper. (Data from Table 1-3).

EXAMPLE 1-1: Depth-of-cut data are shown as a histogram in Table 1-4 with accumulated frequencies on the right (data from Table 1-9).

TABLE 1-4   Data: Depth of Cut

Data from Table 1-9 Displayed on a Tally Sheet

Cell boundaries	Cell interval	Tally	f	$\sum f$	$\sum\%$
	1610–11	//	2	125	100%
1609.5					
	1608–09		0	123	98.4
1607.5					
	1606–07	////	4	123	98.4
1605.5					
	1604–05	//	2	119	95.2
1603.5					
	1602–03	／Ж //	7	117	93.6
1601.5					
	1600–01	／Ж ／Ж /	11	110	88.0
1599.5					
	1598–99	／Ж ／Ж ／Ж /	16	99	79.2
1597.5					
	1596–97	／Ж ／Ж ／Ж ／Ж ／Ж ////	29	83	66.4
1595.5					
	1594–95	／Ж ／Ж ／Ж ／Ж ／Ж ///	28	54	43.2
1593.5					
	1592–93	／Ж ／Ж ／Ж /	16	26	20.8
1591.5					
	1590–91	／Ж	5	10	8.0
1589.5					
	1588–89	///	3	5	4.0
1587.5					
	1586–87		0	2	1.6
1585.5					
	1584–85	/	1	2	1.6
1583.5					
	1582–83	/	1	1	0.8

These accumulated frequencies have been plotted on normal probability paper in Fig. 1-7.   The points give evidence of fitting *two* line segments; a single line does not fit them well.   There is a *run* of length 5 below the initial line.   Although it is possible mechanically to compute an $\bar{X}$ and a $\hat{\sigma}$, we should be hesitant to do so.   These data represent *two* different processes.

This set of data is discussed again in Chap. 2, Case History 2-1.

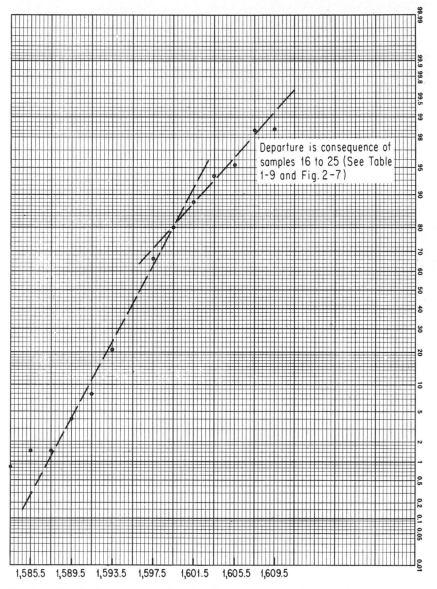

Departure is consequence of samples 16 to 25 (See Table 1-9 and Fig. 2-7)

Fig. 1-7 Depth of cut on normal probability paper. (Data from Table 1-4).

1-8 Predictions Regarding Sampling Variation; the Normal Curve

This topic is of primary importance in process maintenance and improvement.

Consider pieces of mica being split by one operator. The operator produces many thousands a day. We can imagine that this process will continue for many months or years. The number produced is large—so large that we can consider it to be an infinite universe. In production operations, we are concerned not only with the mica pieces which are actually produced *and* examined but with those which were produced and *not* examined. We are also concerned with those which are yet to be produced. We want to make inferences about them. This is possible provided the process is stable.

We can think of the process as operating at some *fixed stable level* and with some *fixed stable standard deviation*. We shall refer to these two concepts by the Greek letters[1] μ and σ, respectively. The actual values of μ and σ can never be learned in practice; they are abstract concepts. Yet they can be estimated as closely as we please by computing $\overline{X}$ and $\hat{\sigma}$ from large enough samples. How large the sample must be is answered in the following discussions (Sec. 1-11).

If we have two operators splitting micas, it is not unusual to find differences in their output either in average thickness or in variability of product. If they are found to have equal averages and standard deviations, then they can be considered to be a single population source.

It is important to know how much variation can be predicted in a succession of samples from a stable[2] process. What can be predicted about a second sample of 200 mica pieces which we might have obtained from the shipment which provided the data in Table 1-1? It would be surprising if the newly computed $\overline{X}$ were exactly *11.165* thousandths as it was for the first sample; it would be equally surprising if the computed $\hat{\sigma}$ were exactly 2.238 again. The following two theorems relate to the amount of variation expected among sample averages $\overline{X}_i$ and standard deviations $\hat{\sigma}_i$ of samples of n each drawn from a stable process (or which might be so drawn).

The k averages

$$\overline{X}_1, \overline{X}_2, \overline{X}_3, \ldots, \overline{X}_k$$

of the k samples will vary and will themselves form a frequency distribution. The sample averages will vary "considerably less" than individuals vary.

THEOREM 1: *The standard deviation $\hat{\sigma}_{\overline{x}}$ of averages of samples of size n drawn from a process will be related to the standard deviation of individual observations by the relation:*

$$\hat{\sigma}_{\overline{x}} = \hat{\sigma}/\sqrt{n} \tag{1-7}$$

[1] μ is pronounced "mew." It designates *an assumed true, but unknown, process average.*
  When *n* items of a random sample from a process are measured/tested, their average $\overline{X}$ designates *an estimate* of μ: $\overline{X} = \hat{\mu}$.
  Another important concept is that of *a desired or specified average:* It is commonly designated by the symbol $\overline{X}'$ (read "X bar prime").
  The symbol σ' (read "sigma prime") is sometimes used to designate a *desired or specified measure of process variability.*
[2] Unstable processes are unpredictable. Few processes are stable for very long periods of time whether in a laboratory or in production.

This theorem says that averages of $n = 4$, for example, are predicted to vary half as much as individuals and that averages of $n = 100$ are predicted to vary one-tenth as much as individuals.

From each of the k samples, we can also compute a standard deviation

$$\hat{\sigma}_1, \hat{\sigma}_2, \hat{\sigma}_3, \ldots, \hat{\sigma}_k$$

These also form a distribution. What can be predicted about the variation among these standard deviations computed from samples of size n?

THEOREM 2: *The standard deviation of sample standard deviations will be related to the standard deviation of individual measurements ($\hat{\sigma}$) by the relation:*

$$\hat{\sigma}_\sigma \cong \frac{\hat{\sigma}}{\sqrt{2n}} \tag{1-8}$$

These two theorems are important in the study of industrial processes. The basic theorems about the predicted variation in $\sigma_{\bar{x}}$ and σ_σ relate to idealized mathematical distributions. In applying them to real data, we must obtain estimates $\hat{\sigma}_{\bar{x}}$ and $\hat{\sigma}_\sigma$; these estimates are given in Eqs. (1-7) and (1-8).

Distributions of sample averages from parent universes (populations) of different shapes are similar.

Consider averages of samples of size n drawn from a parent population or process. It had been known that sample averages were essentially *normally* distributed:

1. When n was "large," certainly when n approached infinity.
2. Usually regardless of the shape of the parent population, normally distributed or not.

In the late 1920s, Dr. Walter A. Shewhart conducted some basic and industrially important chip drawings. Numbers were written on small metal-rimmed tags, placed in a brown kitchen bowl, and experimental drawings (with replacement of chips) made from it. Among other things he wanted to see if there were predictable patterns (shapes) to distributions of averages of size n drawn from some simple populations. He recognized the portent of using *small* samples for industrial applications provided more was known about small samplings from a stable universe, such as drawing numbered chips from a bowl. Three different sets of chips were used: one represented a rectangular universe; another, a right-triangular distribution universe; and the third, a normal distribution. In each experiment, many sample averages were obtained using $n = 3$, 4, and 5. One important consequence is given in Theorem 3.

THEOREM 3: *Even with samples as small as $n = 4$, the distribution of averages of random samples drawn from almost any shaped parent population[1] will be essentially normal.*

[1] With a finite variance.

Figure 1-8 portrays the relationship of the distribution of sample averages to their parent universes even for samples as small as $n = 4$. For sample sizes larger than $n = 4$, the shape of the curve of averages also tends to normality.

The normal curve is symmetrical and bell-shaped; it has an equation whose idealized form is

$$Y = \frac{1}{\sigma\sqrt{2\pi}} \, e^{[-(X-\mu)^2/2\sigma^2]} \tag{1-9}$$

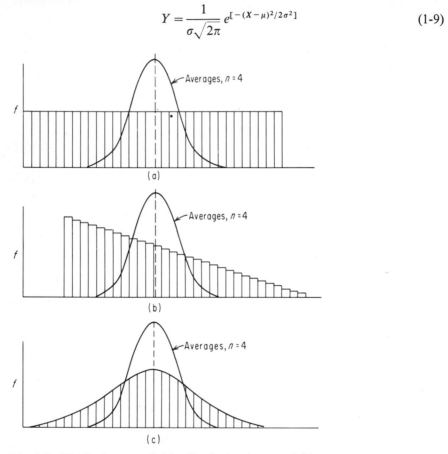

Fig. 1-8   Distributions sampled by Shewhart.   Averages (with *n* as small as 4) from these different parent populations tend to be normally distributed (Theorem 3).
(*a*) Rectangular parent population; (*b*) right-triangular parent population; (*c*) normal parent population.

The term *normal* is a technical term; it is not synonymous with *usual* nor the opposite of abnormal.

Areas under the normal curve (Fig. 1-2) can be calculated, but the calculations are tedious.   Values are given in Table A-1.   However, there are a few important area relationships which are used so frequently that they should be memorized: the following are obtained from Table A-1:

Between	*Percent of area under normal curve*	
$\mu - 3\sigma$ and $\mu + 3\sigma$	99.73 $\cong$ 99.7, that is, "almost all"	
$\mu - 2\sigma$ and $\mu + 2\sigma$	95.44 $\cong$ 95	
$\mu - \sigma$ and $\mu + \sigma$	68.26 $\cong$ 68	(1-10)

In practice, of course, we do not know either μ or σ; they are replaced by their estimates $\bar{X}$ and $\hat{\sigma}$, computed from a representative sample of the population.

In other words, about 95 % of all production from a well-controlled (stable) process can be expected to lie within a range of $\pm 2\sigma$ about the process average, and almost all—99.7%—within a range of $\pm 3\sigma$ about the average.

EXAMPLE 1-2: *Two applications*

1. *Within what region can we predict that mica thickness will vary in the shipment from which the sample of Table 1-1 came?*

To obtain the answer, we assume a stable process producing normally distributed thicknesses.

ANSWER A: In Table 1-3, we computed $\bar{X} = 11.165$ and $\hat{\sigma} = 2.238$. From relation (1-10), we expect almost all (about 99.7%) to be between

$$\bar{X} + 3\hat{\sigma} = 11.165 + 3(2.238) = 17.88 \text{ thousandths}$$

and $\bar{X} - 3\hat{\sigma} = 11.165 - 3(2.238) = 4.45 \text{ thousandths}$

Also from relation (1-10), we expect about 95% to be between:

$$\bar{X} + 2\hat{\sigma} = 15.64 \text{ and } \bar{X} - 2\hat{\sigma} = 6.69$$

ANSWER B: In Table 1-1, we find one thinnest piece to be 5.0; also, two thickest ones to be 17.0 This is good agreement with the $\pm 3\sigma$ prediction of ANSWER A.

2. *What percent of nonconforming mica pieces do we expect to find in the entire shipment of which the data in Table 1-1 comprise a sample?*

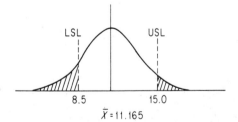

Fig. 1-9 Estimating percent of a normal curve outside given specifications. (Related to data of Table 1-1.)

ANSWER: The specifications on the mica thickness were 8.5 to 15.0 thousandths in. We can compute the distance from $\bar{X} = 11.165$ to each of the specifications expressed in standard deviations

$$d_1 = \frac{\bar{X} - \text{LSL}}{\hat{\sigma}} = \frac{11.165 - 8.5}{2.238} = 1.19 \tag{1-11a}$$

From Appendix Table A-1, we find the corresponding percent below 8.5 (that is, below $\bar{X} - 1.19\hat{\sigma}$) to be 11.7%. (The actual count from Table 1-1 is 24, that is, 12%.) Also,

$$d_2 = \frac{\text{USL} - \bar{X}}{\hat{\sigma}} = 1.71 \qquad (1\text{-}11b)$$

Again from Table A-1, we find the expected percent above 15 (that is, above $\bar{X} + 1.71\hat{\sigma}$) to be about 4.4%. (The actual count is 7, that is, 3.5%.)

Discussion: There are different possible explanations for the excessive variability of the mica-splitting operation: variation in the mica hardness, variation in each of the operators who split the blocks of mica using a small bench knife, and any variations between operators.

An important method of future process surveillance was recommended— a Shewhart control chart which is discussed in Chap. 2.

EXAMPLE 1-3: *Using the mica-thickness data.* The average and standard deviation were computed from the sample of 200 measurements to be

$$\bar{X} = 11.165 \text{ thousandths and } \hat{\sigma} = 2.238 \text{ thousandths}$$

■ Then from *Theorem 2* for a series of averages of samples of $n = 200$ from this same process, assumed stable,

$$\hat{\sigma}_{\bar{x}} = \frac{\hat{\sigma}}{\sqrt{200}} = \frac{2.238}{14.14} = 0.158$$

An estimate of the variation of averages to be expected in random, representative samples of $n = 200$ from a process with $\hat{\sigma} = 2.238$ and average $\bar{X} = 11.165''$ is then[1]

$$\bar{X} \pm 2\hat{\sigma}_{\bar{x}} = 11.165 \pm 2(0.158) = 11.165 \pm 0.316 \text{ thousandths}$$

(with about 95% confidence)

$$\bar{X} \pm 3\hat{\sigma}_{\bar{x}} = 11.165 \pm 0.474 \text{ thousandths}$$

(with about 99.7% confidence)

■ Also from *Theorem 1*, we can estimate the location of the assumed *true* but *unknown* average μ of the mica-splitting process. This converse use of Theorem 1 is applicable when n is as large as 30. A modification, not discussed in this text, is required for smaller sample sizes. For $n = 200$

$$\bar{X} - 2\hat{\sigma}_{\bar{x}} = 11.165 - 0.316 \cong 10.85$$

and $\qquad \bar{X} + 2\hat{\sigma}_{\bar{x}} = 11.165 + 0.316 \cong 11.48$

that is, $10.85 < \mu < 11.48$ thousandths (with about 95% confidence). Also, we can estimate the location of the unknown average μ to be between

$$\bar{X} - 3\hat{\sigma}_{\bar{x}} = 11.165 - 0.474 \cong 10.69$$

and $\qquad \bar{X} + 3\hat{\sigma}_{\bar{x}} = 11.165 + 0.474 \cong 11.64$

that is, $10.69 < \mu < 11.64$ with 99.7% confidence.

In Fig. 1-10, we see the increase in interval required to change the confidence in our estimate from 95.5% to 99.7%.

---

[1]See Eq. (1-10) and *Theorem 1*.

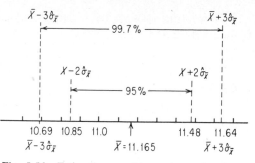

Fig. 1-10 Estimating confidence intervals of unknown process average.

1-9 Series of Small Samples from a Production Process

The amount of variation expected in $\bar{X}$ and $\hat{\sigma}$ from a succession of samples from an industrial process can be predicted only when the process average and variability are stable.[1] In the following discussion we assume that the process is stable and make predictions about the expected variation in samples obtained randomly from it.

1-10 Change in Sample Size: Predictions about $\bar{X}$ and $\hat{\sigma}$

We might have taken a smaller sample from the mica shipment. For example, the measurements in the top five rows constitute a sample of $n = 50$ from the mica-splitting process which produced the shipment. We expect large random samples to provide more accurate estimates of the true process average and standard deviation than smaller samples. Smaller samples, however, often provide answers which are entirely adequate. The two theorems of this chapter give useful information pertaining to sample size.

The computed values $\bar{X}$ and $\hat{\sigma}$ from Table 1-3 were

$$\bar{X} = 11.165 \quad \text{and} \quad \hat{\sigma} = 2.238 \quad \text{with } n = 200$$

(These values are the ones computed from the sample of 200; we shall now assume them to be the true values of an assumed stable process average and standard deviation—a very risky assumption in practice.)

The values, $\bar{X}$ and $\hat{\sigma}$, of the top 50 measurements from Table 1-1 are computed below from a histogram.

[1] Actually, of course, the lack of basic stability in a process average is the usual situation; it is the major reason for troubleshooting and process-improvement studies. Methods of using a succession of small samples in studying lack of stability in a process will be considered in Chap. 2 and subsequently.

First, what can we predict about $\bar{X}$ and $\hat{\sigma}$ of samples of size $n = 50$ drawn from a population with

$$\mu = 11.165 \quad \text{and} \quad \sigma = 2.238$$

Variation of X

From Eq. (1-10) and Theorem 1 the expected average of a sample of $n = 50$, assuming stability, is in the region

$$\mu \pm 3\sigma_{\bar{x}} = 11.165 \pm 3\left(\frac{2.238}{\sqrt{50}}\right) \quad (99.7\% \text{ confidence})$$

$$= 11.165 \pm 0.951$$

that is
$$11.165 - 0.951 < \bar{X} < 11.165 + 0.951$$

and
$$10.214 < \bar{X} < 12.116 \quad (99.7\% \text{ confidence})$$

The sample average from Table 1-5, $\bar{X} = 12.13$, falls just outside this interval. We conclude the data of Table 1-1 are not a single homogeneous universe. (See Sec. 2-5.)

Variation of $\hat{\sigma}$

The expected value of $\hat{\sigma}$ for samples of $n = 50$, assuming stability, is in the region

$$\sigma \pm 3\sigma_{\sigma} = 2.238 \pm 3\left(\frac{2.238}{\sqrt{100}}\right) \quad (99.7\% \text{ confidence})$$

$$= 2.238 \pm 3(0.224)$$

$$= 2.238 \pm 0.672$$

Therefore,
$$1.566 < \hat{\sigma} < 2.910$$

The sample standard deviation computed in Table 1-5, $\hat{\sigma} = 2.216$, falls within this 99.7% confidence interval.

1-11   How Large a Sample Is Needed to Estimate a Process Average?

There are many things to consider when answering this question. In fact, the question itself requires modification before answering. Is the test destructive, nondestructive, or semi-destructive? How expensive is it to obtain and test a sample of n units? How close an answer is needed? How much variation among measurements is expected? What level of confidence is adequate? All these questions must be considered.

Discussion: We begin by returning to the discussion of variation expected

TABLE 1-5   Computing $\bar{X}$ and $\hat{\sigma}$ from a Sample
Data Used Are the Top 50 Measurements in Table 1-1

Cell boundaries	Cell midpoint	Tally	f	d	fd	fd^2
	17.25	//	2	6	12	72
16.75						
	16.25		0	5	0	0
15.75						
	15.25	////	4	4	16	64
14.75						
	14.25	⤭ /	6	3	18	54
13.75						
	13.25	⤭ /	6	2	12	24
12.75						
	12.25	⤭ ⤭	10	1	10	10
11.75						
	$A = 11.25$	⤭ ⤭	10	0	0	0
10.75						
	10.25	⤭	5	−1	−5	5
9.75						
	9.25	///	3	−2	−6	12
8.75						
	8.25	///	3	−3	−9	27
7.75						
	7.25	/	1	−4	−4	16
			$n = 50$		+44	284
				$E_1 =$	0.88	5.68 $= E_2$

$$\bar{X} = A + mE_1$$
$$= 11.25 + 0.88 = 12.13$$
$$\hat{\sigma} = m\sqrt{E_2 - E_1^2} = \sqrt{5.68 - (0.88)^2} = \sqrt{4.91}$$
$$= 2.216$$

in averages of random samples of n items about the true but unknown process average μ.   The expected variation of sample averages about μ[1] is

$$\pm 2 \frac{\sigma}{\sqrt{n}} \qquad \text{(confidence about 95\%)}$$

and

$$\pm 3 \frac{\sigma}{\sqrt{n}} \qquad \text{(confidence 99.7\%)}$$

[1] See Sec. 1-8, Theorems 1 and 3; also Eq. (1-10).

Now let the allowable deviation (error) in estimating μ be $\pm\Delta$ (read "delta"); also let an estimate or guess of σ be $\hat{\sigma}$; then

$$\Delta \cong \frac{2\hat{\sigma}}{\sqrt{n}} \quad \text{and} \quad n \cong \left(\frac{2\hat{\sigma}}{\Delta}\right)^2 \quad \text{(about 95\% confidence)} \quad (1\text{-}12a)$$

also $\quad \Delta \cong \dfrac{3\hat{\sigma}}{\sqrt{n}} \quad \text{and} \quad n \cong \left(\dfrac{3\hat{\sigma}}{\Delta}\right)^2 \quad \text{(99.7\% confidence)} \quad (1\text{-}12b)$

Confidence levels other than the two shown in Eq. (1-12) can be used by referring to Table A-1. When our estimate or guess of a required sample size n is even as small as $n = 4$, then *Theorem* 3 applies.

EXAMPLE 1-4: The mica manufacturer wants to estimate the true process average of one of his operators (data of Table 1-1). How large a random sample will he need?

■ In this simple nondestructive testing situation, cost associated with simple size selection and test are of little concern.

■ What is a reasonable choice of Δ? Since specifications are 8.5 to 15 thousandths, an allowance of $\pm\Delta = \pm 0.001$ seems reasonable to use in estimating a sample size.

■ What is an estimate of σ? No information is available here for any one operator; we do have an estimate of overall variation, $\hat{\sigma} = 2.238$ from Table 1-3. This estimate probably includes variation resulting from several operators and thus is larger than for any one. However, the best available estimate is from Eq. (1-4b): $\hat{\sigma} = 2.238$. Then from Eq. (1-12a) $n = \left(\dfrac{4.476}{1}\right)^2 \cong 20$, (about 95\% confidence).

Decision: A sample size of $n = 20$ to 25 should be adequate to approximate the process average μ. However, a somewhat larger sample might be selected since it would cost but little more and might be accepted more readily by other persons associated with the project.

1-12   Sampling and a Second Method of Computing $\hat{\sigma}$

The method of this section is basic to many procedures for studying production processes.

The data in Table 1-1 represent a sample of 200 thickness measurements from pieces of mica delivered in one shipment. We have also considered a smaller sample from the shipment and used it to make inferences about the average and variability of the entire shipment.

There are definite advantages in subdividing sample data already in hand into smaller samples, such as breaking the mica sample of 200 into 40 samples of $n = 5$. Table 1-6 shows the data of Table 1-1 displayed in 40 sets of five each. The decision to choose five vertically aligned samples is an arbitrary one; there is no known physical significance to the order of manufacture in this set. Where there is a known order—either of manufacture or measurement—such an order should be preserved in representing the data, as in Fig. 1-11.

TABLE 1-6 Mica Thickness Data in Subgroups of $n = 5$ with Their Averages and Ranges
Data of Table 1-1

	8.0	12.5	12.5	14.0	13.5	12.0	14.0	12.0	10.0	14.5
	10.0	10.5	8.0	15.0	9.0	13.0	11.0	10.0	14.0	11.0
	12.0	10.5	13.5	11.5	12.0	15.5	14.0	7.5	11.5	11.0
	12.0	12.5	15.5	13.5	12.5	17.0	8.0	11.0	11.5	17.0
	11.5	9.0	9.5	11.5	12.5	14.0	11.5	13.0	13.0	15.0
$\bar{X}$:	10.7	11.0	11.9	13.1	11.9	14.3	11.7	10.7	12.0	13.7
R:	4.0	3.5	7.5	3.5	4.5	5.0	6.0	5.5	4.0	6.0
	8.0	13.0	15.0	9.5	12.5	15.0	13.5	12.0	11.0	11.0
	11.5	11.5	10.0	12.5	9.0	13.0	11.5	16.0	10.5	9.0
	9.5	14.5	10.0	5.0	13.5	7.5	11.0	9.0	10.5	14.0
	9.5	13.5	9.0	8.0	12.5	12.0	9.5	10.0	7.5	10.5
	10.5	12.5	14.5	13.0	12.5	12.0	13.0	8.5	10.5	10.5
$\bar{X}$:	9.8	13.0	11.7	9.6	12.0	11.9	11.7	11.1	10.0	11.0
R:	3.5	3.0	6.0	8.0	4.5	7.5	4.0	7.5	3.5	5.0
	13.0	10.0	11.0	8.5	10.5	7.0	10.0	12.0	12.0	10.5
	13.5	10.5	10.5	7.5	8.0	12.5	10.5	14.5	12.0	8.0
	11.0	8.0	11.5	10.0	8.5	10.5	12.0	10.5	11.0	10.5
	14.5	13.0	8.5	11.0	13.5	8.5	11.0	11.0	10.0	12.5
	12.0	7.0	8.0	13.5	13.0	6.0	10.0	10.0	12.0	14.5
$\bar{X}$:	12.8	9.7	9.9	10.1	10.7	8.9	10.7	11.6	11.4	11.2
R:	3.5	6.0	3.5	6.0	5.5	6.5	2.0	4.5	2.0	6.5
	13.0	8.0	10.0	9.0	13.0	15.0	10.0	13.5	11.5	7.5
	11.0	7.0	7.5	15.5	13.0	15.5	11.5	10.5	9.5	9.5
	10.5	7.0	10.0	12.5	9.5	10.0	10.0	12.0	8.5	10.0
	9.5	9.5	12.5	7.0	9.5	12.0	10.0	10.0	8.5	12.0
	11.5	11.5	8.0	10.5	14.5	8.5	10.0	12.5	12.5	11.0
$\bar{X}$:	11.1	8.6	9.6	10.9	11.9	12.2	10.3	11.7	10.1	10.0
R:	3.5	4.5	5.0	8.5	5.0	7.0	1.5	3.5	4.0	4.5

We have computed two numbers from each of these 40 subsamples: the average $\bar{X}$ and range, R, are shown directly below each sample. The range of a sample is simply:

$$R = \text{the largest observation minus the smallest}$$

The range is a measure of the variation within each small sample; the *average* of the ranges is designated by a bar over the R, that is, $\bar{R}$, and one reads " R bar." There is an amazingly simple and useful relationship (theorem)[1]

[1] Acheson J. Duncan, The Use of Ranges in Comparing Variabilities, *Ind. Qual. Control*, vol. 11, no. 5, pp. 18ff, February, 1955. E. S. Pearson, A Further Note on the Distribution of Range in Samples from a Normal Population, *Biom.*, vol. 24, p. 404, 1932.

between the *average range*, $\bar{R}$, and the *standard deviation* σ of the process of which these $k = 40$ groups of $n = 5$ are subsamples. The theorem is very important in industrial applications.

THEOREM 4: *Consider k small random samples* ($k > 20$, usually) *of size n drawn from a normally distributed stable process. Compute the ranges for the k samples and their average $\bar{R}$. Then the standard deviation (σ) of the stable process is estimated by*

$$\hat{\sigma} = \bar{R}/d_2 \qquad (1\text{-}13)$$

where d_2 is a constant depending upon the subsample size, n.

Some frequently used values of d_2 are given in Table 1-7.

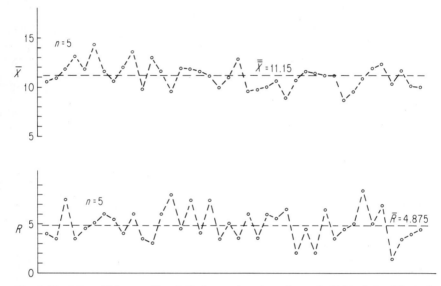

Fig. 1-11 Mica thickness, $\bar{X}$ and R charts; data in order as in Table 1-6. (Control limits are shown on same data in Fig. 2-5.)

TABLE 1-7 Values of the Constant d_2 for Small n
(See also Table A-4)

n	d_2
2	1.13
3	1.69
4	2.06
5	2.33
6	2.53

In other words, an estimate of the standard deviation of the process can be obtained either from the grouped method of Table 1-3 or directly from $\bar{R}$ in Eq. (1-13). For additional discussion, see Secs. 2-5 and 10-6.

EXAMPLE 1-5: *Data of Table* 1-6: The ranges ($n = 5$) have been plotted in Fig. 1-11b; the average of the 40 ranges is $\bar{R} = 4.875$. Then from Eq. (1-13) and Table 1-7

$$\hat{\sigma} = (4.875)/2.33 = 2.09$$

This estimate of σ is somewhat smaller than the value 2.238 obtained in Table 1-3. There are several possible reasons why the two estimates of σ are not exactly equal:

1. Theorem 1 is based on the concept of a process whose average is stable; this is a condition seldom justified in real life. Almost every process, even those which are stable for most practical purposes, show gradual trends and abrupt shifts in average when analyzed carefully by control-chart methods.[1]

2. The predicted variation of $\hat{\sigma}$ computed from samples of 200 from a stable population with known standard deviation, $\sigma_1 = 2.238$, is, from Theorem 2 and Eq. (1-10),

$$2.238 - \frac{3\sigma_1}{\sqrt{400}} < \hat{\sigma} < 2.238 + \frac{3\sigma_1}{\sqrt{400}} \quad (99.7\% \text{ confidence})$$

or $2.238 - 0.336 < \hat{\sigma} < 2.238 + 0.336$

and $\quad\quad\quad\quad 1.902 < \hat{\sigma} < 2.574 \quad (99.7\% \text{ confidence})$

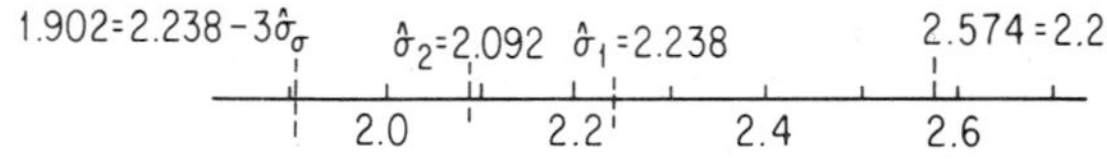

Fig. 1-12   Location of $\hat{\sigma}_2$ with respect to $\hat{\sigma}_1 - 3\sigma_\sigma$ and $\hat{\sigma}_1 + 3\hat{\sigma}_\sigma$.

We see then that this second estimate, $\hat{\sigma}_2 = \bar{R}/d_2 = 2.09$, lies within the region predicted for computed values of repeat samplings of $n = 200$ from the mica-splitting process. Thus, the difference between the first and second estimates is small when compared to repeat sampling variation from the same stable process.

1-13   Some Important Remarks about the Two Estimates

$$\hat{\sigma}_2 = \bar{R}/d_2 \quad \text{and} \quad \hat{\sigma}_1 = m\sqrt{E_2 - E_1^2}$$

Figure 1-13 portrays a situation typified by machining a hole in the end of a shaft. The shifting average of the process is represented in the figure by a succession of small curves at 8 A.M., 8:30 A.M., etc. The short-term variation of the process is considered to be unchanging. The shift in average may be steady or irregular. Consider successive small samples, say of $n = 5$, taken from the process at 30-min intervals beginning at 8 A.M.

The variability σ of the grinding process *over a short time interval* is measured by

$$\hat{\sigma}_2 = \bar{R}/d_2 = \bar{R}/2.33$$

---

[1] *Note:* The methods of Chap. 2 consider practical methods of examining data from a process for excessive variation in its average and variability.

This is a measure of the inherent capability *provided it were operating at a stable average*; this stability is possible only if ways can be found to remove those factors causing evident changes in the process average. (These include such possible factors as tool wear or slippage of chuck fastenings.)

The shaded area to the right of Fig. 1-13 represents the accumulated measurements of individuals from samples of five obtained successively beginning at 8 A.M. The variability of these accumulated sample measurements is *not* measured by $\hat{\sigma}_2 = \bar{R}/d_2$, but from the method of Table 1-3

$$\hat{\sigma}_1 = m\sqrt{E_2 - E_1^2}$$

This latter is an estimate of the variation in the accumulated *total* production from 8 A.M. to 4:30 P.M.

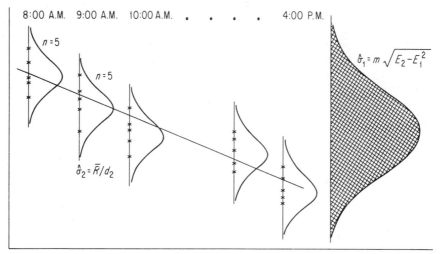

Fig. 1-13 Schematic of a tobogganing production process. A gradually diminishing average diameter having a normal distribution (with spread $6\hat{\sigma}_2 = 6\bar{R}/d_2$) at any given time. The product accumulated over a period of time will be much more widely spread, often appearing to be almost normal, and with spread

$$6\hat{\sigma}_1 = 6m\sqrt{E_2 - E_1^2} = 6m\sqrt{\frac{\sum fd^2}{n} - \left(\frac{\sum fd}{n}\right)^2}$$

Evidently $6\hat{\sigma}_1$ will be substantially larger than $6\hat{\sigma}_2$.

In Fig. 1-13, the value of $\hat{\sigma}_1 = m\sqrt{E_2 - E_1^2}$ appears to be about twice $\hat{\sigma}_2 = \bar{R}/d_2$, since the spread of the accumulated shaded area is about twice that of each smaller distribution.

A comparison of the two estimates from the same set of data

$$\hat{\sigma}_1 = m\sqrt{E_2 - E_1^2} \quad \text{and} \quad \hat{\sigma}_2 = \bar{R}/d_2$$

is frequently helpful in troubleshooting. If they differ substantially, the process average is suspected of instability.[1] The second, $\hat{\sigma}_2$, estimates the

---

[1] More discussion of testing for stability is given in Sec. 2-5.

within subgroup variability of individuals.   The first, $\hat{\sigma}_1$, estimates the variability of individuals produced over the period of sampling.   If the process is stable, we expect the two estimates to be in fairly close agreement.

The following pertinent discussion is from the ASTM *Manual on Presentation of Data*:[1]

Breaking up data into rational subgroups. One of the essential features of the method . . . is classifying the total set of test observations under consideration into subgroups or samples, within which variations may be considered to be due to non-assignable chance causes only, but between which there may be differences due to assignable causes whose presence is suspected or considered possible.

This part of the problem is obviously not statistical in character but depends on technical knowledge and familiarity with the conditions under which the material sampled was produced and the conditions under which the data were taken.

The production person has a problem in deciding what constitutes a reasonable procedure for obtaining rational subgroups from a process.   Experience and knowledge of the process will suggest certain possible sources which should be kept separate: Product from different machines, operators, or shifts; from different heads or positions on the same machine; from different molds or cavities in the same mold; from different time periods.   Such problems will be considered throughout this book.

1-14 Summary

An orderly collection and plotting of a moderate data sample will frequently suggest trouble, and if not solutions, then sources of trouble which warrant further investigation.   This chapter considers a case history of 200 samples taken from a mass repetitive process.

From this sample, methods of calculating various statistical parameters are set forth; the standard deviation, average (mean), and range.   In a discussion of basic probability distributions a foundation is laid for comparing what is expected to happen with what is actually happening.

This chapter introduces concepts about samples from a process or other population source.   It presents methods of estimating the central tendency of the process μ and its inherent process capability σ.   The importance of an estimate computed from a large sample is compared with that computed from a set of k small samples from the same process.   These concepts are basic in troubleshooting.   They are also basic to the methods of Chap. 2.

1-15 Practice Exercises

The following exercises are suggestions which may be used in association with the indicated sets of data.   Working with sets of data is helpful in understanding the basic concepts which have been discussed.   If you have real

[1] American Society for Testing Materials, *op. cit.*, p. 48.

sets of data from your own experience, however, you are urged to use these same methods with them.

1. *a.* Make a tally sheet for the data in Table 1-1 using cell width $m = 0.5$ thousandth (inch).
    b. From the tally, choose an A, then compute $\bar{X}$ and $\hat{\sigma}$; make a casual comparison with the previous results using $m = 1$ in Table 1-3. (They should agree closely but not exactly.)
2. The top half of the data in Table 1-1 is also a sample, $n = 100$, of the mica-splitting process.
    a. Compute $\bar{X}$ and $\hat{\sigma}$ from Eqs. (1-3) and (1-4b) for this top half.
    b. Also, compute $\hat{\sigma} = \bar{R}/d_2$ from Eq. (1-13) using $k = 20$ vertical sets of $n = 5$.
    c. Compare $\hat{\sigma}$ obtained in (b) with that obtained in Ex. 1-b and Table 1-5.
    d. Also compute $\hat{\sigma}$ from Eq. (1-13) using horizontal subgroups, $n = 5$.
3. The first four columns of Table 1-1 comprise a sample, $n = 80$, of the mica-splitting process.
    a. Compute $\bar{X}$ and $\hat{\sigma}$ from Eqs. (1-3) and (1-4b).
    b. Compute $\hat{\sigma} = \bar{R}/d_2$ from Eq. (1-13) using $k = 20$ sets of $n = 4$, grouped horizontally. Are the results of (a) and (b) similar?
4. Prepare a histogram for the "depth-of-cut" data of Table 1-9. (We suggest that you make your tally marks in one color for the first 16 rows of samples and in a contrasting color for the last 9 rows. Then note the contrast in location of the two sets.)
    a. Compute $\bar{X}$ and $\hat{\sigma}$ from Eqs. (1-3) and (1-4b).
    b. Compute $\hat{\sigma}_2$ from Eq. (1-13) using ranges from the rows of samples, $n = 5$.
    c. Compute $\hat{\sigma}_1$ from the histogram of the first 16 rows or all 25. *Note:* See Case History 2-1 for some discussion.
5. Prepare suitable histograms of the sets of data referred to in the exercises below. Find $\bar{X}$ and $\hat{\sigma}$ for each set. (Also, compare $\hat{\sigma}$ obtained from the histogram with $\hat{\sigma} = \bar{R}/d_2$ from a suitable range chart, using any grouping you choose or may be assigned.)
    a. The 77 measurements in Table 1-8 on an electrical characteristic.
    b. The 125 measurements in Table 1-9; depth of cut.
    c. Consider again the process which produced the data in Table 1-1. If we assume that the average of the process could be increased to be at the center of the specifications, what percent would be expected to be under the LSL and what percent over the USL? Assume no change in σ.

TABLE 1-8   Electrical Characteristics (in Decibels) of Final Assemblies from 11 Strips of Ceramic: Case History 13-1

	1	2	3	4	5	6	7	8	9	10	11
	16.5	15.7	17.3	16.9	15.5	13.5	16.5	16.5	14.5	16.9	16.5
	17.2	17.6	15.8	15.8	16.6	13.5	14.3	16.9	14.9	16.5	16.7
	16.6	16.3	16.8	16.9	15.9	16.0	16.9	16.8	15.6	17.1	16.3
	15.0	14.6	17.2	16.8	16.5	15.9	14.6	16.1	16.8	15.8	14.0
	14.4	14.9	16.2	16.6	16.1	13.7	17.5	16.9	12.9	15.7	14.9
	16.5	15.2	16.9	16.0	16.2	15.2	15.5	15.0	16.6	13.0	15.6
	15.5	16.1	14.9	16.6	15.7	15.9	16.1	16.1	10.9	15.0	16.8
$\bar{X} = $	16.0	15.8	16.4	16.5	16.1	15.0	15.9	16.3	14.6	15.7	15.8
$R = $	2.8	3.0	2.4	1.1	1.1	2.5	3.2	1.9	5.9	4.1	2.8

SOURCE: Ellis R. Ott, Variables Control Charts in Production Research, *Ind. Qual. Control*, vol. 6, no. 3, p. 30, 1949. (Reprinted by permission of the editor.)

TABLE 1-9 Air-Receiver Magnetic Assembly: Case History 2-1

Measurements (Depth of Cut): in Inches on Each of Five Items in a Sample Taken at 15-min Intervals during Production

Sample no.			$(n = 5)$		
1	.1600	.1595	.1596	.1597	.1597
2	.1597	.1595	.1595	.1595	.1600
3	.1592	.1597	.1597	.1595	.1602
4	.1595	.1597	.1592	.1592	.1591
5	.1596	.1593	.1596	.1595	.1594
6	.1598	.1605	.1602	.1593	.1595
7	.1597	.1602	.1595	.1590	.1597
8	.1592	.1596	.1596	.1600	.1599
9	.1594	.1597	.1593	.1599	.1595
10	.1595	.1602	.1595	.1589	.1595
11	.1594	.1583	.1596	.1598	.1598
12	.1595	.1597	.1600	.1593	.1594
13	.1597	.1595	.1593	.1594	.1592
14	.1593	.1597	.1599	.1585	.1595
15	.1597	.1591	.1588	.1606	.1591
16	.1591	.1594	.1589	.1596	.1597
17	.1592	.1600	.1598	.1598	.1597
18	.1600	.1605	.1599	.1603	.1593
19	.1599	.1601	.1597	.1596	.1593
20	.1595	.1595	.1606	.1606	.1598
21	.1599	.1597	.1599	.1595	.1610
22	.1596	.1611	.1595	.1597	.1595
23	.1598	.1602	.1594	.1600	.1597
24	.1593	.1606	.1603	.1599	.1600
25	.1593	.1598	.1597	.1601	.1601

6. If the specifications are as listed below, find the expected percentages produced by the process which produced the corresponding samples:
   a. In Table 1-8, below LSL = 14.5 dB and above 17 dB.
   b. In Table 1-9, below LSL = 0.159 in. and above USL = 0.160 in.
   c. Prepare a histogram for the data of Table 14.3, using data for any one pad. Then prepare a graph on normal probability paper as in Sec. 1-7. These data, on any one pad, were presumed to represent a stable process. Does the graph tend to agree?
      Repeat the above procedure using the $\bar{X}$ values in column 5. Discuss and compare with the graph for a single pad.
7. Prepare a graph on normal-probability paper for all the data of Table 1-8.
   a. Is there seeming evidence of more than one principal parent universe?
   b. Estimate σ from the normal-probability graph. Compare it with $\hat{\sigma} = \bar{R}/d_2$. Do they disagree "substantially," that is, are they "in the same ball park"?

2

Ideas from Time Sequences of Observations

An adequate science of control for management should take into account the fact that measurements of phenomena in both social and natural science for the most part obey neither deterministic nor statistical laws, until assignable causes of variability have been found and removed . . .

W. A. SHEWHART[1]

2-1 Introduction

A gradual change in a critical adjustment or condition in a process is expected to produce a gradual change in the data pattern.   An abrupt change in the process is expected to produce an abrupt change in the data pattern.   We need ways of identifying the *presence* and *nature* of these patterns.   The fairly standard practice of examining any regular data reports simply by looking at them is grossly inadequate.   Such reports are far more valuable when analyzed by methods discussed in the following sections.

There is no single way for a medical doctor to diagnose the ailment of a patient.   He considers information from a thermometer, a stethoscope, pulse rates, chemical and biological analyses, x-rays, and many other tests.

Neither is there just one way to obtain or diagnose data from the operation of a process.   Simple processes are often adjusted without reference to any data.   But data from even the simplest process will provide unsuspected information on its behavior.   In order to benefit from data coming either regularly or in a special study from a temperamental process, it is important to follow one important and basic rule:

[1] W. A. Shewhart, Statistical Quality Control, *Trans. ASME*, Ten-Year Management Report, May, 1942.

34

Plot the data[1] in a time sequence.

Different general methods are employed to diagnose the behavior of time-sequence data after plotting. Two important ones will be discussed in this chapter.

1. Use of certain *run* criteria (Sec. 2-4).
2. Control charts with control limits and various other criteria (Sec. 2-5) signaling the presence of assignable causes.

EXAMPLE 2-1: *A look at some data.* In a graduate course, primarily of students in statistics but including graduate students from the natural and social sciences, my first assignment for each student has been to "obtain a time sequence of *k* subgroups from some process," asking them if possible, to "choose a process considered to be stable." A young lady[2] elected to complete her assignment by measuring times for sand to run through a 3-min egg timer in successive tests. The time was measured by a stop watch. Data are shown in Fig. 2-1. Does this set of data appear to represent a stable (random) process? Also, is it a "3-min egg timer"?

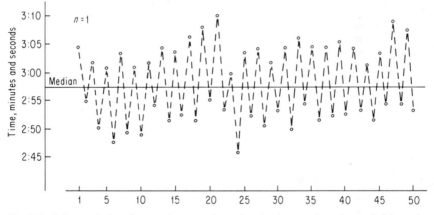

Fig. 2-1 Measured time for sand to run through a 3-min egg timer (recorded in order of observation). (*Courtesy of Mrs. Elaine Amoresano Rose.*)

SOME CASUAL OBSERVATIONS:

■ The median of the 50 observations is about $2\frac{1}{2}$ s below 3 min. This is a slight bias (inaccuracy) but should not affect the taste quality of boiled eggs.

■ Almost no point is "close" to the median! Half of the points lie about 10 s above the median and the other half 5 to 10 s below.

■ The points are alternately high and low—a perfect "sawtooth" pattern *indicating two causes* operating alternately to produce the pattern. This agrees with the preceding observation.

[1] It is standard practice to scan a data report, then file it, and forget it. We suggest instead that you plot important data and usually dispose of the report. Or, perhaps record the data initially in graphical form.

[2] Mrs. Elaine Amoresano Rose, former graduate student in Applied and Mathematical Statistics, Rutgers Statistics Center.

■ There appears to be a steady increase from the eighth to the twentieth point on each side of the egg timer.

■ Beginning with the twenty-third observation, there is an abrupt drop, both on the "slow half" and the "fast half." After the drop, the process operates near the initial level.

DISCUSSION—EGG TIMER DATA:

An egg timer is surely a simple machine; one would hardly predict nonrandomness in successive trials with it. However, once the peculiar patterns are seen, what are possible explanations?

■ *The sawtooth:* The egg timer had two halves. Elaine recognized this as an obvious "probable" explanation for the sawtooth pattern; she then made a few more measurements to identify the "fast" and "slow" sides of the timer.

■ *The abrupt shift downward* (*twenty-third point*). There are three possibilities:

1. *the egg timer;* the *sand* may be affected by *humidity* and *temperature.* Elaine said she took a break after the twenty-third experiment. Perhaps she laid the timer in the sun or on a warm stove. A change in heat or humidity of the sand may be the explanation for the drop at the twenty-fourth experiment.

2. the *stop watch* used in timing. There is no obvious reason to think that its performance might have produced the sawtooth pattern, but thought should be given to the possibility. It does seem possible that a change in the temperature of the watch might have occurred during the break. Or, was the watch rewound, possibly?

3. *the operator observer.* Was there an unconscious systematic parallax effect introduced by the operator herself? Or some other operator effect?

Thus when studying *any process* to determine the cause for peculiarities in the data, one must consider in general: (1) the manufacturing process, (2) the measuring process, and (3) the way the data are taken and recorded.

SUMMARY REGARDING EGG TIMER DATA IN FIG. 2-1.

Figure 2-1 shows the presence of two types of nonrandomness, neither of which was foreseen by the experimenter. Nonrandomness *will almost always* occur; such occurrence is *the rule and not the exception.*

An egg timer is a very simple system in comparison with the real-life scientific systems we must learn to diagnose and operate. The unsuspected behaviors of large-scale scientific systems are much more complicated; yet

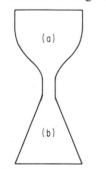

they can be investigated in the same manner as the egg timer. Data from the process showed differences: between the two sides of the egg timer, *and* a change with time. Sometimes the causes of unusual data patterns can be identified easily. It is logical here to surmise that a slight difference exists in the shape of the two sides (*a*) and (*b*); often the identification is more elusive. Knowing that nonrandomness exists is most important information to the experimenter. However, this knowledge must be supported by follow-up investigations to *identify the causes* of any non-randomness which are of practical interest.

Fig. 2-2   An egg timer.

Note: This set of data, Fig. 2-1, will be discussed further in Sec. 2-4. The very powerful graphical display and the "look test" provide the important information.   But more formal methods are usually needed, and two important direct methods of analysis are discussed later in the chapter. The methods are *run analysis* and *control charts*.   We shall first consider two general approaches to process troubleshooting.

2-2   Data from a Scientific or Production Process

It is standard practice to study a scientific process by changing different variables suspected of contributing to the variation of the process.   The resulting data are then analyzed in some fashion to determine whether the changes made in these variables have had an effect which appears significant either scientifically or economically.

A less-utilized but important method is to *hold constant all variables* which are suspected of contributing to variations of the process, and then decide whether the *resulting pattern* of observations actually represents a stable, uniform process—i.e., whether the process is "well-behaved" or whether there is evidence of previously unknown nonstability (statistical nonrandomness).   Different patterns indicate different causes of nonrandomness and often suggest the type of factors which have influenced the behavior of the process—even though neither their existence nor identity may have been suspected.   This unsuspected nonrandom behavior occurs frequently, and recognition of its existence may prompt studies to identify the unknown factors, that is, *lead to scientific discovery.*

Whenever a sequence of observations in order of time can be obtained from a process, an analysis of its data pattern can provide important clues regarding variables or factors which may be affecting the behavior of the process.

What's in a Name?

Many classifications of persons obtain data from a process important to them and want the data to provide useful information.   No common name can be applied to these different types of persons without risk of injuring "nationalistic" sensibilities.   Chemists do not want to be called "engineers"; production managers want to maintain their separateness from theoreticians, and vice-versa; not all professional statisticians consider it an honor to be called one.   A common denominator of all the many groups associated with scientific and industrial processes is the need to *obtain, analyze,* and *interpret real-life data.*   Being called a "data analyst" arouses only modest enthusiasm.   We shall attempt to produce a minimum of injured nationalism by using different terms as the occasion seems to warrant.   We shall probably use the term "engineer" or "scientist" most frequently, where the term may relate to development, manufacturing and production, research, sales, purchasing, or others.

2-3   Signals and risks

Dr. Paul Olmstead[1] remarks:

—To the extent that we as engineers have been able to associate physical data with assignable causes, these causes may be classified by the types of physical data that they produce, namely:
1. Gross error or blunder (shift in an individual).
2. Shift in average or level.
3. Shift in spread or variability.
4. Gradual change in average or level (trend).
5. A regular pattern of change in level (cycle).

When combinations of two or more assignable causes occur frequently in a process, they will then produce combinations of data patterns. Learning that something in the system is affecting it, either to its advantage or disadvantage, is important information. The province and ability of specialists —engineers, scientists, production experts—are to find compensating corrections and adjustments. Their know-how results both from formal training and practical experience. However, experience has shown that they welcome suggestions. Certain patterns of data have origins which can be associated with causes; origins are suggested at times by data patterns.

When analyzing process data, we need criteria which will signal the presence of important process changes of behavior but which will not signal the presence of rather minor process changes. Or, when we are studying the effects of different conditions in a research and development study, we want criteria which will identify those different conditions (factors) which may contribute substantially either to potential improvements or to difficulties. If we tried to establish signals which never were in error when indicating the presence of important changes, then those signals would sometimes *fail to signal* the presence of important conditions. It is *not possible to have perfection*.

The facts are that we must take risks in any scientific study just as in all other aspects of life. There are two kinds of risks: (1) that we shall institute investigations which are unwarranted either economically or scientifically; this is called the alpha risk (α risk), the sin of *commission*, and (2) that we shall miss important opportunities to investigate; this is called the beta risk (β risk), the *sin of omission*.

We aspire to sets of decision criteria which will provide a reasonable compromise between the α and β risks. A reduction in the α risk will increase the β risk unless compensations of some kind are provided. The risk situation is directly analogous to the person contemplating the acceptance of a new position, of beginning a new business, of hiring a new employee, or of buying a stock on the Stock Exchange.

[1] Paul S. Olmstead, How to Detect the Type of an Assignable Cause, *Ind. Qual. Control*, vol. 9, no. 3, p. 32 and vol. 9, no. 4, p. 22. (Reprinted by permission of the author and editor.)

What risks are proper? There is no single answer, of course. When a process is stable, we want our system of signals to indicate stability; when there is *enough* change to be of possible scientific interest, the signaling system should *usually* indicate the presence of assignable causes. Statisticians usually establish unduly low risks for α, often $\alpha = .05$ or $\alpha = .01$. They are reluctant to advise engineering, production, or other scientists to investigate conditions unless they are almost certain of identifying an important factor or condition. However, the scientist is the one who has to decide the approximate level of compromise between "looking unnecessarily for the presence of assignable causes" and "missing opportunities for important improvements." A scientist in research will often want to pursue possibilities corresponding to appreciably *larger* values of α and *lower* values of β, especially in exploratory studies; and may later want to specify *smaller* values of α when publishing the results of important research. Values of $\alpha = .10$ and even larger are often sensible to accept when making a decision whether to investigate possible process improvement. In diagnosis for troubleshooting, we expect to make some unnecessary investigations. It is prudent to investigate many times knowing that we may fail to identify a cause in the process. Perhaps $\alpha = .10$ or $\alpha = .25$ is economically practical. Not even the best professional baseball player bats as high as .500 or .600.

The relationship of these risks to some procedures of data analysis will be discussed in the following sections. Some methods of *runs* are considered first. Then methods of *control charts* are presented in the following chapter.

Some Signals to Observe

When it has been decided to study a process by obtaining data from its performance, then the data should be plotted in some appropriate form and in the order it is being gathered. Every set of k subgroups offers two opportunities:

1. To *test the hypothesis* that the data represent *random variation* from stable sources. Was the source of data apparently stable or is there evidence of nonrandomness?

2. To infer the *nature* of the source(s) responsible for any nonrandomness (from the data pattern), that is, to infer previously unsuspected hypotheses.

Two major types of criteria are discussed in Secs. 2-4 and 2-5.

2-4 Run Criteria

Introduction

When someone repeatedly tosses a coin and produces a run of six heads in succession, we realize that something is unusual. *It could* happen; the probability is $(.5)^6 = .015$. We would then usually ask to see both sides of the coin because these would be very unlikely runs from an ordinary coin having a head and a tail. When we then question the coin's integrity, our *risk* of being unreasonably suspicious is $\alpha = .015$.

A *median* line is one with half of the points above and half below.   (Probability that a single observation falls above is $P_a = .5$ and that it falls below is $P_b = .5$, when k is even.)   The use of runs is formalized in the following sections; it is a most useful procedure to suggest clues from an analysis of ordered data from a process.

When exactly three consecutive points are above the median, this is a *run above the median* of length 3.   In Fig. 2-3 consecutive runs *above and below*

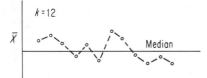

Fig. 2-3   Twelve averages showing six runs above and below the median.

the median are of length: 3, 1, 1, 1, 2, and 4.   The total number of runs is $N_R = 6$.   We usually count the number directly from the figure once the median line has been drawn.   Locating the median when k is larger can be expedited by adjusting a clear, plastic ruler or the edge of a card.

EXAMPLE 2-2:   The data plotted in Fig. 2-4 represent $k = 24$ averages (gross weights of ice cream) in order of production.   Data represent $\bar{X}$ values, $n = 4$, in Table 2-5.

The median is between 204.00 and 204.25.   The *total number of runs above and below the median* is $N_R = 8$.

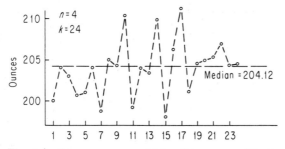

Fig. 2-4   Gross average weights of ice cream fill at 10-min intervals. (Data from Table 2-5.) (*Courtesy David Lipman.*)

The runs are of length

$$7, 3, 3, 1, 1, 2, 1, \text{ and } 6, \text{ respectively}$$

Before presenting a formal direct run analysis, let us consider the first run; it is of length 7.   It is just as improbable for a stable process to produce the first seven observations on the same side of the median as for a coin to flip seven heads (tails) at the start of a demonstration. *We do not believe that the process represented in Fig.* 2-4 *was stable* over the first 4-h period of manufacture. This is not surprising; it is *unlikely that any industrial process* will function at an entirely stable level over a 4-h period. Whether the magnitude of the changes here is economically important is a different matter. Now let us consider a direct analysis using *runs*.

Some Interpretations of Runs

Too many runs above and below the median indicate the following possible engineering reasons:

1. Samples being drawn alternately from two different populations (sources), resulting in a "sawtooth" effect. These occur fairly frequently in *portions* of a set of data. Their explanation is usually found to be two different sources—analysts, machines, raw materials—which enter the process alternately or nearly alternately.

2. Three or four different sources which enter the process in a cyclical manner.

"Too few" runs are quite common. Their explanations inlcude:

1. A general shift in the process average.
2. An abrupt shift in the process average.
3. A slow cyclical change in averages.

Sources of variation in a process can usually be determined (identified) by the engineer, chemist, or production supervisor when he is aware that they exist.

Formal Criteria: Total Number of Runs about the Median

The total number of runs in the data of Fig. 2-4 is $N_R = 8$. How many such runs are expected in a set of n or k random points? In answering the question, it is sufficient to consider even numbers only, that is, numbers of the form $k = 2m$. The *average expected number is*

$$\overline{N}_R = \frac{k + 2}{2} = m + 1 \tag{2-1}$$

and the *standard deviation* of the sampling distribution of N_R is

$$\sigma = \sqrt{\frac{m(m - 1)}{2m - 1}} \tag{2-2}$$

Relation (2-1) is used so frequently that it helps to remember it. An aid to memory is the following:

1. The *minimum* possible number of runs is 2.
2. The *maximum* possible number is k.
3. The *expected* number is the average of these two. This is an aid to memory, not a proof.[1]

---

[1] Churchill Eisenhart and Freda S. Swed, Tables for Testing Randomness of Grouping in a Sequence of Alternatives, *Ann. Math. Stat.*, vol. 14, pp. 66–87, 1943.

Of course, the number of runs actually observed will often be more or less than $\bar{N}_R = m + 1$. By how much? The answer is obtained easily from Table A-2; it lists significantly small critical values and significantly large critical values corresponding to risks $\alpha = .05$ and $.01$.

EXAMPLE 2-3: *Use of Table A*-2: In Fig. 2-4 with $k = 24$, the expected number of runs is $0.5(24 + 2) = 13$. The number we observe is only 8. From Table A-2, small critical values of N_R corresponding to $k = 24$ are seen to be 8 and 7 for $\alpha = .05$ and $.01$, respectively.

Thus the count of 8 runs is less than expected with a 5% risk, but not significantly less with a 1% risk. This evidence of a nonstable (nonrandom) process behavior agrees with the presence of a run of length 7 below the median. We would ordinarily investigate the process expecting to identify sources of assignable causes.

Expected Number of Runs of Exactly Length s

A set of data may display the expected total number of runs but may have an unusual distribution of long and short runs. Table A-3 has two columns. The first one lists the *expected number of runs* $\bar{N}_{R,s}$ of *exactly length s*; the second lists the expected number of runs, $\bar{N}_{R \geq s}$, that is, of length greater than or equal to s.

From the second column, for example, it can be seen that when $k = 2^6 = 64$, only one run of *length 6 or longer* is expected. When $k = 2^5 = 32$, only one-half a run of length 6 or longer is expected (i.e., a run of length 6 or longer is expected about half the time).

EXAMPLE 2-4: Consider again the ice-cream fill data of Fig. 2-4, $k = 24$. The number of runs of exactly length $s = 1$, for example, is 6.8 as shown in Table 2-1. The number expected from the approximation, Table A-3, is $24/4 = 6$; the number

TABLE 2-1   A Comparison of the Expected Number of Runs and the Observed Number
Data of Fig. 2-4 Where $n = 24$

s	Expected number of runs of exactly length s	Number observed	Expected number of runs of length $\geq s$	Number observed
1	6.8	3	13.0	8
2	3.4	1	6.2	5
3	1.6	2	2.8	4
4	0.7	0	1.2	2
5	0.3	0	0.5	2
6	0.1	1	0.2	2
7	0.1	1	0.1	1

Note: Values for expected number of runs in this table have been computed from the exact formulae in Table A-3. This is not usually advisable since the computation is laborious and the approximate values are sufficiently close for most practical purposes.

actually in the data is 3.   Other comparisons of the number expected with the number observed are given in this table.   It indicates two long runs: the first is a run of 7 below average; then a run of 6 high weights at the end.   This pattern suggests an increase in filling weight during the study; it is not clear whether the increase was gradual or abrupt.

EXAMPLE 2-5: The sawtooth pattern of the egg timer, Fig. 2-1. From Table A-2 the critical values for the total expected numbers of runs N_R above and below the median for $k = 50$ are

$$17 \leq N_R \leq 34$$

The observed number is 50.   This is much larger than the critical value of 34 corresponding to $\alpha = .01$.   We conclude (again) that the data are not random.   The pattern produced by the egg timer is a perfect sawtooth indicating two alternating sources.   The sources are evidently the two sides of the egg timer.

The Longest Run-up or Run-down

In Fig. 2-4, there are four *increases* in $\overline{X}$ beginning with sample 18 and concluding with 22.   This four-stage increase is preceded and followed by a decrease; this is said to be a *run-up of length exactly* 4.

It is easy to recognize a long run-up or run-down once the data have been plotted.   A long run-up or run-down is typical of a substantial shift in the process average.   Expected values of both long and short extreme lengths in a random display of k observations are sometimes of value when analyzing a set of data.   A few critical values have been given in Table 2-2.

TABLE 2-2   Critical Extreme Length of a Run-up or a Run-down in a Random Set of k Observations

k	$\alpha = .01$ Small critical value	$\alpha = .01$ Large critical value	$\alpha = .05$ Small critical value	$\alpha = .05$ Large critical value
10	0	6	1	5
20	1	6	1	5
40	1	7	1	6
60	1	7	2	6
100	2	7	2	6
200	2	7	2	7

SOURCE: These tabular values were sent me by Paul S. Olmstead based on his article: Distribution of Sample Arrangements for Runs-Up and Runs-Down, *Ann. Math. Stat.*, vol. 17, pp. 24–33, March 1946.   (They are reproduced by permission of the author.)

It is easy to see and remember that a run-up of length 6 or 7 is quite unusual for sets of data even as large as $k = 200$.   Even a run of 5 may warrant investigating.

Summary—Run Analysis

Important criteria which indicate the presence of assignable causes by unusual runs in a set of k subgroups of n each have been described.   They are applicable either to sets of data representing k individual observations ($n = 1$) or to k averages ($n > 1$); or, to k percents defective found by inspecting k lots of an item.

The ultimate importance of any criterion in analyzing data is its usefulness in identifying factors which are important to the behavior of the process. The application of runs ranks high in this respect.

RUN CRITERIA

1. *Total number* of runs N_R about the median:[1]

   a. Expected number is $\overline{N}_R = \dfrac{k + 2}{2}$

   b. The fewest and largest number of expected runs are given in Table A-2 for certain risks, α.

2. A run *above or below the median of length* greater than six is evidence of an assignable cause warranting investigation, even when k is as large as 200.

3. The *distribution* of runs of length s about the median (See Table A-3).   A set of data may display about the expected total number of runs yet have too many or too few short runs (or long ones).

4. A long run-up or run-down usually indicates a gradual shift in the process average.   A run-up or run-down of length five or six is usually longer than expected.

2-5   Shewhart Control Charts for Variables

Introduction

The Shewhart control chart is a well-known, powerful method of checking on the stability of a process.   It was conceived as a device to help production in its routine hour-by-hour adjustments; its value in this regard is unequaled. It is applicable to quality characteristics, either of a variable or attribute type. The control chart provides a graphical time sequence of data from the process itself.   This permits then the application of run analyses to study the historical

---

[1] Sometimes we apply the criteria of runs to the *average* line instead of the median; we do this as tentative criteria.

behavior patterns of a process. Further, the control chart provides *additional* signals to the current behavior of the process; the upper and lower control limits (UCL and LCL) are limits to the maximum expected variation of the process. The mechanics of preparing variable and attribute control charts will be presented. Their application to troubleshooting is a second reason for their importance.

Mechanics of Preparing Control Charts (Variables)

The control chart is a method of studying a process from a sequence of small random samples from the process. The basic idea of the procedure is to collect small samples of size n (usually at regular time intervals) from the process being studied. Samples of size $n = 4$ or 5 are usually best. It will sometimes be expedient to use $n = 1$, 2, or 3; sample sizes larger than 6 or 7 are not recommended. A quality characteristic of each unit of the sample is then measured, and the measurements are (usually) recorded *but are always charted*.

The importance of *rational subgroups* must be emphasized when specifying the source of the $n = 4$ or 5 items in a sample. Since our aim is to actually locate the trouble, as well as to determine whether or not it exists, we must break down the data in a logical fashion. "The man who is successful in dividing his data initially into *rational* subgroups based upon rational hypotheses is therefore inherently better off in the long run than the one who is not thus successful."[1]

In starting a control chart, it is necessary to collect some data to provide preliminary information determining central lines on average $\overline{X}$ and ranges R. It is usually recommended that $k = 20$ to $k = 25$ subgroups of n each be obtained, but $k < 20$ may be used initially to avoid delay. (Modifications may be made to adjust for unequal subgroup sizes.) The formal routine of preparing the control chart once the k data subgroups have been obtained are as follows:

STEP 1: Compute the average $\overline{X}$ and the range R of each sample. Plot the k points on the $\overline{X}$ chart and R chart being sure to preserve the order in which they were produced. (It is important to write the sample size on every chart and in a regular place, usually in the upper left-hand side as in Fig. 2-5*a*, 2-5*b*.)

STEP 2: Compute the two averages, $\overline{X}$ and $\overline{R}$; draw them as lines.

STEP 3: Compute the following 3-sigma control limits for the R chart and draw them as lines

$$UCL(R) = D_4 \overline{R}$$
$$LCL(R) = D_3 \overline{R}$$

[1] Walter A. Shewhart, *Economic Control of Quality of Manufactured Product*, p. 299, D. Van Nostrand Company, Inc., New York, 1931.

Observe whether any ranges fall above $D_4\bar{R}$ or below $D_3\bar{R}$. If not, accept the concept (tentatively) that the variation of the process is homogeneous, and proceed to Step 4.[1]

Note: The distribution of R is not symmetrical—it is "skewed" with a tail for larger values. Although we want values of $(\bar{R} + 3\hat{\sigma}_R)$, values of $3\hat{\sigma}_R$ are not obtained simply. The easiest calculation is to use the D_4 factors given in Table 2-3, where $D_4\bar{R} = \bar{R} + 3\hat{\sigma}_R$.

TABLE 2-3   Factors to Use with $\bar{X},R$ Control Charts for Variables

Choose n to Be Less Than Seven When Feasible; These Factors Assume Sampling from a Normal Universe; See also Table A-4

n	D_3	D_4	A_2	d_2
2	0	3.27	1.88	1.13
3	0	2.57	1.02	1.69
4	0	2.28	0.73	2.06
5	0	2.11	0.58	2.33
6	0	2.00	0.48	2.53
7	0.08	1.92	0.42	2.70
8	0.14	1.86	0.37	2.85
9	0.18	1.82	0.34	2.97
10	0.22	1.78	0.31	3.08

STEP 4: Compute $A_2\bar{R}$, and obtain 3-sigma control limits on $\bar{X}$:

$$\text{UCL}(\bar{X}): \bar{\bar{X}} + A_2\bar{R} = \bar{\bar{X}} + 3\hat{\sigma}_{\bar{x}}$$
$$\text{LCL}(\bar{X}): \bar{\bar{X}} - A_2\bar{R} = \bar{\bar{X}} - 3\hat{\sigma}_{\bar{x}}$$

where $\hat{\sigma}_{\bar{x}} = \hat{\sigma}/\sqrt{n}$
$\hat{\sigma} = \bar{R}/d_2$

STEP 5: Draw dotted lines corresponding to $\text{UCL}(\bar{X})$ and $\text{LCL}(\bar{X})$.

STEP 6: Consider whether there is evidence of assignable causes (see following discussion). If any point falls outside UCL and LCL, we call this an "outage" which indicates the existence of an *assignable cause*.

---

[1] When the R chart has a single outage, we sometimes do two things: (*a*) check the sample for a maverick, and (*b*) exclude the outage subgroup and recompute $\bar{R}$. Usually this recomputing is not worth the effort.

When the R chart has several outages, the variability of the process is unstable, and it will not be reasonable to compute a $\hat{\sigma}$. The process needs attention.

Other examples treating an R chart with outages are discussed in other sections of this book.

Some Discussion

The recommendation to use 3-sigma control limits was made by Dr. Shewhart after extensive study of data from production processes. It was found that almost every set of production data having as many as 25 or 30 subsets will show outages. Further, the nature of the assignable causes signaled by the outages using 3-sigma limits was usually important and identifiable by process personnel.

Upper and lower control 3-sigma limits on $\overline{X}$ are lines to judge "excessive" variation of *averages* of samples of size n

$$\overline{X} \pm 3\hat{\sigma}_{\bar{x}} = \overline{X} \pm \frac{3\hat{\sigma}}{\sqrt{n}} = \overline{X} \pm \frac{3\overline{R}}{d_2\sqrt{n}}$$

However, computation is simplified by using the A_2 factor from Table 2-3

$$\text{UCL}(\overline{X}) = \overline{X} + A_2\overline{R}$$

where $A_2 = \dfrac{3}{d_2\sqrt{n}}$

It was also found from experience that it was practical to investigate production sources signaled by certain *run criteria* in data. These run criteria are recommended as adjuncts to outages.

The choice of a reasonable or *rational* subgroup is important but not always easy to make in practice. Items produced on the same machine, at about the same time, and with the same operator will often be a sensible choice—but not always. A machine may have only one head or several; a mold may have one cavity or several. A decision will have to be made whether to limit the sample to just one head or cavity or allow all heads or cavities to be included. Initially, the decision may be to include several heads or cavities and then change to individuals if large differences are found.

Sample sizes of 4 or 5 are usually best. They are large enough to signal important changes in a process; they are not large enough usually to signal smaller less important changes. Some discussion of the sensitivity of sample size is given in connection with operating-characteristic curves.

Example of Control-chart Limits,
Mica-thickness Data

In Fig. 1-11, charts of $\overline{X}$ and R points, $n = 5$, were made for the mica-thickness data of Table 1-6. We assumed there that the range chart represented a stable process; under that assumption, we computed

$$\hat{\sigma} = \overline{R}/d_2 = 2.09$$

We may now use the procedure outlined above to compute 3-sigma control limits on each chart and to consider different criteria to check on stability of the process.

Control-chart Limits

STEP 1:   See Table 1-6: an $\overline{X}$ and R have been computed for each subgroup.

STEP 2: $\overline{\overline{X}} = 11.15$ and $\overline{R} = 4.875$

STEP 3: $\text{UCL}(R) = D_4 \overline{R} = (2.11)(4.875) = 10.29$
$\qquad\quad \text{LCL}(R) = D_3 \overline{R} = 0$

All points fall below $\text{UCL}(R)$; see Fig. 2-5b.

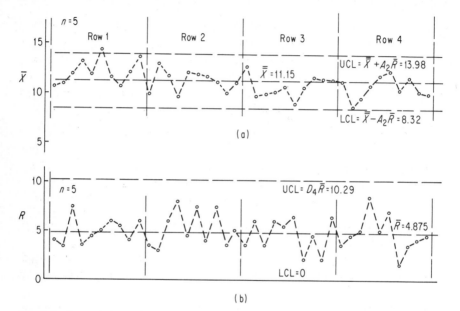

Fig. 2-5   Control chart of mica thickness data with limits.   (Data from Table 1-6.)

STEP 4: $\overline{\overline{X}} + A_2 \overline{R} = 11.15 + (0.58)(4.875)$
$\qquad\qquad\qquad\; = 11.15 + 2.83 = 13.98$
$\qquad\; \overline{\overline{X}} - A_2 \overline{R} = 11.15 - 2.83 = 8.32$

STEP 5:   See Fig. 2-5a, control limits are plotted.

STEP 6:   Based on criteria below.

Discussion: R chart (*Fig. 2-5b*)

There is no point above $\text{UCL}(R)$, nor any above (or close to) $\overline{R} + 2\sigma_R$. Neither is there a long run on either side of $\overline{R}$; there is one run of length 4 below and one of length 4 above.   Runs of length 4 are expected.

Conclusion: The chart suggests no unreasonable process variability; all points are below the upper control limit.

Discussion: $\overline{X}$ chart (Fig. 2-5a)

Point 6 ($\overline{X} = 14.3$) is above $\text{UCL}(X)$; the outage indicates a difference in the process average.   Also, of the eight points 3 to 10, inclusive, there are seven points above $\overline{\overline{X}}$.   This run criterion indicates that the average of the first group of about 10 points is somewhat higher than the average of the entire set of data.   The difference is not large; but it does indicate that something in the manufacturing or measuring process was "not quite" stable.

This set of data was chosen initially in order to discuss a process which was much more stable than ordinary.   It is almost impossible to find $k = 20$ or more data subsets from an industrial process without an indication of instability.   In process improvement and troubleshooting, these bits of evidence can be important.

Summary: Some Criteria for Statistical Control (Stability)

Routine Production: Criteria for Action: On the production floor, definite and uncomplicated signals and procedures to be used by production personnel work best.   Recommended control-chart criteria to use as evidence of assignable causes requiring process adjustment or possible investigations are:
1.   One point outside lines at

$$\bar{X} \pm A_2 \bar{R} = \bar{X} \pm 3\hat{\sigma}_{\bar{x}} \qquad (\alpha \cong 3/1{,}000)$$

A process shift of as much as 1σ is not immediately detected by a point falling outside 3-sigma limits; the probability is about $1/6$ for $n = 4$ (see Fig. 2-8).
2.   Two consecutive points (on the same side) outside either

$$\bar{X} + 2\hat{\sigma}_{\bar{x}} \quad \text{or} \quad \bar{X} - 2\hat{\sigma}_{\bar{x}} \qquad (\alpha \cong 1/800)$$

3.   A run of seven consecutive points above (or below) the process average or median. $(\alpha \cong 1/64)$

The first criterion is the one in ordinary usage; these last two should be used when it is important not to miss shifts in the average and there is someone to supervise the process adjustments.

Process Improvement and Troubleshooting: Since we are now anxious to investigate opportunities to learn more about the process or to adjust it, it is sensible to accept greater risks of making investigations or adjustments which may be futile perhaps as often as 10% of the time (allow a risk of $\alpha = .10$). Besides the three criteria just listed above, some or all of the following may be practical for you:
1.   One point outside $\bar{X} \pm 2\hat{\sigma}_{\bar{x}} \qquad (\alpha \cong .05)$
2.   A run of the last five points (consecutive) on the same side of $\bar{X}$.[1]
$(\alpha \cong .06)$
    (Note: the risk associated with any run of the last n points, $n > 5$, is less than for five.)
3.   Six of the last seven points (6/7) on the same side. $(\alpha \cong .10)$
Risk for n out of the last $(n + 1)$, $n > 7$, is less than .10.
4.   Eight of the last ten points (8/10) on the same side. $(\alpha \cong .10)$
5.   The last three points outside $\bar{X} \pm \hat{\sigma}_{\bar{x}}$ (on the same side). $(\alpha \cong .01)$
6.   The last two points outside $\bar{X} \pm 1.5\hat{\sigma}_{\bar{x}}$ (on the same side). $(\alpha \cong .01)$

---

[1] Probabilities associated with runs here and below are based on runs about the median of the data but are only slightly different when applied to runs about their mean (arithmetic average).

There are different types of assignable causes, and some will be signaled by one of these criteria sooner than by another. Any signal which results in process improvement is helpful. It provides signals to those with the process know-how to investigate and gradually allows some of the art of manufacturing to be replaced by science.

CASE HISTORY 2-1   Depth of Cut

While walking through a department in a hearing-aid plant rather early one morning, I stopped to watch a small assembly operation. A worker was performing a series of operations; she would pick a diaphragm from a pile, place it as a cover on a small brass piece (see Fig. 2-6), and then place the assembly in an electronic meter where she observed a reading. If the reading

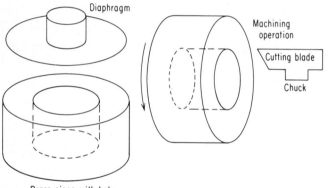

Fig. 2-6 Machining a hole in a brass piece, with diaphragm assembly.

were within certain limits, she would send the assembly on to the next stage in production. If not, she removed the diaphragm, tried another, and repeated the testing. After five or six such trials,[1] she said she usually found satisfactory mates.

I had a discussion with the engineer. Why was this selective assembly necessary? He explained that the lathe being used to cut the hole was too old to provide the necessary precision—there was too much variation in the depth of cut. "However," he said, "management has now become con-

---

[1] This is a fairly typical selective-assembly operation. They are characteristically expensive, although they may be a necessary temporary evil: (1) they are expensive in operator assembly and test time, (2) there always comes a day when acceptable mating parts are impossible to find, but assembly "must be continued," (3) it serves as an excuse for delaying corrective action on the process producing the components.

vinced that a new lathe is a necessity, and one is on order [$18,000]." This was not an entirely satisfying explanation. "Could we get 20 or 25 sets of measurements at 15-min intervals as a special project today?" I asked. "Well, yes." Plans were made to have one inspector work this into her day's assignments. I returned to look at the data about 4 P.M.

The individual measurements which had been collected were given in Table 1-9; they are repeated, with the additional $\overline{X}$ and R columns, in Table 2-4. (A histogram displays them in Table 1-4; also see the plot on normal probability paper in Fig. 1-7.)

TABLE 2-4 Data: Air Receiver Magnetic Assembly (depth of cut)
Taken at 15-min Intervals in Order of Production

						$\overline{X}$	Range R
1	160.0	159.5	159.6	159.7	159.7	159.7	0.5
2	159.7	159.5	159.5	159.5	160.0	159.6	0.5
3	159.2	159.7	159.7	159.5	160.2	159.7	1.0
4	159.5	159.7	159.2	159.2	159.1	159.3	0.6
5	159.6	159.3	159.6	159.5	159.4	159.5	0.3
6	159.8	160.5	160.2	159.3	159.5	159.9	1.2
7	159.7	160.2	159.5	159.0	159.7	159.6	1.2
8	159.2	159.6	159.6	160.0	159.9	159.7	0.8
9	159.4	159.7	159.3	159.9	159.5	159.6	0.6
10	159.5	160.2	159.5	158.9	159.5	159.5	1.3
11	159.4	158.3	159.6	159.8	159.8	159.4	1.5
12	159.5	159.7	160.0	159.3	159.4	159.6	0.7
13	159.7	159.5	159.3	159.4	159.2	159.4	0.5
14	159.3	159.7	159.9	158.5	159.5	159.4	1.4
15	159.7	159.1	158.8	160.6	159.1	159.5	1.8
16	159.1	159.4	158.9	159.6	159.7	159.5	0.8
17	159.2	160.0	159.8	159.8	159.7	159.7	0.8
18	160.0	160.5	159.9	160.3	159.3	160.0	1.2
19	159.9	160.1	159.7	159.6	159.3	159.7	0.8
20	159.5	159.5	160.6	160.6	159.8	159.9	1.1
21	159.9	159.7	159.9	159.5	161.0	160.0	1.5
22	159.6	161.1	159.5	159.7	159.5	159.9	1.6
23	159.8	160.2	159.4	160.0	159.7	159.8	0.8
24	159.3	160.6	160.3	159.9	160.0	160.0	1.3
25	159.3	159.8	159.7	160.1	160.1	159 8	0 8

$$\overline{\overline{X}} = 159.67 \qquad \overline{R} = 0.98$$

The steps below relate to the previous numbering in preparing a control chart:
1.   The averages and ranges have been plotted in Fig. 2-7.
2.   The average $\bar{X} = 159.67$ mils and $\bar{R} = 0.98$ mils have been computed and lines drawn in Fig. 2-7.
3.   UCL$(R) = D_4 \bar{R} = (2.11)(0.98) = 2.07.$
Since all range points fall below 2.07, we proceed to (4).
4.   UCL$(\bar{X}) = 159.67 + (0.58)(0.98) = 160.24.$
      LCL$(\bar{X}) = 159.67 - 0.57 = 159.10.$
5.   See Fig. 2-7 for UCL and LCL.

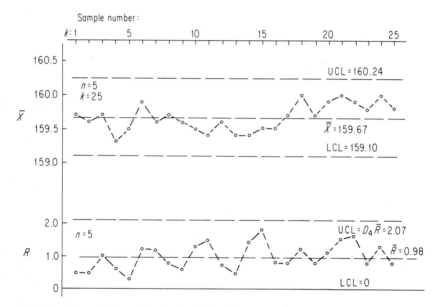

Fig. 2-7   Control chart (historical) of $\bar{X}$ and R on depth of cut (Case History 2-1). (Data from Table 2-4.)

6.   *Possible evidence of assignable causes:*
     a. Runs: Either the run of eight points below $\bar{X}$ or the following run of nine points above $\bar{X}$ is evidence of a process operating at a level other than $\bar{X}$.   See discussion in (7) below.
     b. Are there any points outside $\bar{X} \pm 3\hat{\sigma}_{\bar{x}} = \bar{X} \pm A_2 \bar{R}$?   No.   Any pair of consecutive points above $\bar{X} \pm 2\hat{\sigma}_{\bar{x}}$?   No, but three points in the last eight points are "close."
     c. Observations have been plotted on cumulative normal probability paper, see Fig. 1-7 and Sec. 1-7.

7. The run evidence is conclusive that some fairly abrupt drop in $\overline{X}$ occurred at the ninth or tenth point and $\overline{X}$ increased at the seventeenth or eighteenth point (from production of about 2 P.M.). After looking at the data, I asked the foreman what had happened at about 2 P.M. "Nothing, no change." "Did you change the cutting tool?" "No." "Change inspectors?" "No."

The foreman finally looked at the lathe and thought "perhaps" the chuck governing the depth of cut might have slipped. Such a slip might well explain the increase in depth of cut (at the seventeenth or eighteenth sample) but *not* the smaller values at the ninth and tenth samples. He got quite interested in the control-chart procedure and decided to continue the charting while waiting for the new lathe to arrive. He learned to recognize patterns resulting from a chip broken out of the cutting tool—an abrupt drop; the gradual downward effect of tool wear; effects from changing stock rod. It was an interesting experience.

Eventually the new lathe arrived, but I found it had been removed a few weeks later and the old lathe back in use. "What happened?" The foreman explained that with the control chart as a guide, the old lathe was shown to be producing more uniform depth of cut than they could get from the new one.

2-6 Probabilities Associated with an $\overline{X}$ Control Chart; Operating-characteristic Curves

Identifying Presence of Assignable Causes

Troubleshooting is successful when it gives us ideas of *when* the trouble began and *what* may be causing it. It is important to have different sources which suggest sensible ideas about when and what to investigate. Specialists in data analysis can learn to cooperate with the engineer scientist in suggesting the general type of trouble to consider. Data presented in the form of control-chart criteria, patterns of runs, the presence of outliers in the data; these will often suggest areas of investigation (hypotheses). The suggested hypotheses will ordinarily evolve from joint discussions between the scientist and the specialist in data analysis. The objective is to identify the physical sources producing the unusual data effects and to decide whether the cost of the cure is economically justified. The role of identifying causes rests principally with the process specialists.

The role of the Shewhart control chart in signaling production to make standard *adjustments* on a process is an important one. It also has the role of signaling opportune times to *investigate* the system. The risks of signals occurring just by chance (without the presence of an assignable cause) are quite small. When a process is stable, the probabilities (α) that the following criteria *will signal erroneously* a shift are small. They are:

1. That a single point will fall outside 3-sigma limits just by chance: about three chances in a thousand, that is $\alpha \cong .003$.

2. That a single point will fall outside 2-sigma limits just by chance: about one time in 20, that is, $\alpha \cong .05$.

3. That the last two points will both fall outside 2-sigma limits on the same side just by chance: about[1] one time in 800, that is, $\alpha \cong .001$.

Thus, the two-consecutive-points criterion is evidence of a change in the process at essentially the same probability level as a single point outside 3-sigma limits.

Operating-characteristic Curves of $\bar{X}$ Charts

When working to improve a process, our concern is not so much that we shall investigate a process without justification; rather it is that we shall miss a worthwhile opportunity to discover something important. As a rule of thumb, we may assume that a shift in process average of *one standard* deviation (one sigma) is of practical interest in troubleshooting. Just how sensitive is an $\bar{X}$ chart in detecting a shift of 1σ? Or in detecting a shift of 1.5σ? Or in detecting a shift of $z\sigma$? The operating-characteristic curves (OC curves) of Figs. 2-8 and 2-10 provide some answers.[2]

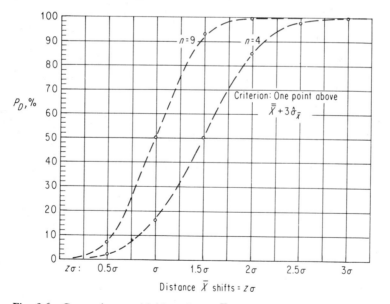

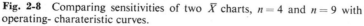

Fig. 2-8   Comparing sensitivities of two $\bar{X}$ charts, $n=4$ and $n=9$ with operating- charateristic curves.

[1] The probability that the first point will be outside is approximately 1/20; the probability that the next point will then be outside on the *same* side is essentially 1/40; thus the probability that two consecutive points will be outside, on the basis of chance alone, is about $(1/20)(1/40) = 1/800$.

[2] The method of deriving OC curves is outlined below.

The two OC curves in Fig. 2-8 have been computed for averages of $n = 4$ and $n = 9$; the criterion for detecting a shift of $z\sigma$ in average is one point above $\overline{X} + A_2 \overline{R} = \overline{X} + 3\sigma_{\bar{x}}$. The abscissa represents the amount of shift in $\overline{X}$; the probabilities P_D of detecting such shifts are shown on the vertical scale.

Consider first the OC curve for n = 4:

- A shift of σ has a small probability of being detected: $P_D \cong 16$ or 17%.
- A shift of 1.5σ has a 50% chance of being detected.
- A shift of 2σ has $P_D \cong 85\%$.
- Shifts of more than 3σ are almost certain to be detected.

Consider now the OC curve for n = 9:

- Except for very small and very large shifts in $\overline{X}$, samples of $n = 9$ are much more sensitive than with $n = 4$.
- A shift of 1σ has a 50% chance of being detected.
- A shift of 1.5σ has a 92 or 93% chance of detection.

Discussion: Samples of $n = 9$ are appreciably more sensitive than samples of $n = 4$ in detecting shifts in average. Every scientist knows this, almost by instinct.

This may suggest the idea that we should use samples of nine rather than the recommended practice of $n = 4$ or 5. And sometimes in nonroutine process-improvement projects, one may elect to do this. Even then, however, we tend to hold to the smaller samples and take them more frequently. During ordinary production, experience has shown that assignable causes which produce a point out of 3-sigma limits with samples of $n = 4$ or 5 can usually be identified by an engineer or production supervisor provided he investigates promptly. If they are not detected on the first sample, then usually on the second or third, or by one of the earlier run criteria of this chapter.

Samples as large as $n = 9$ or 10 frequently indicate causes which do not warrant the time and effort required to investigate them during regular production.

Some Computations Associated with OC Curves[1]

The following discussion will consider samples of $n = 4$. Figure 2-9 represents four locations of a production process.

In position 1, the "outer" curve (the wider one) represents the process centered at $\overline{X}$; the "inside" curve portrays the distribution of samples of $n = 4$, which is just one-half the spread of the process itself $\left(\sigma_{\bar{x}} = \sigma/\sqrt{n}\right)$.

---

[1] This section may be omitted without seriously affecting the understanding of subsequent sections.

In position 2, the process has shifted $1.5\sigma = 3\sigma_{\bar{x}}$ and 50% of the shaded distribution of averages is now above $\bar{X} + A_2 \bar{R}$. $(P_D = 50\%)$

In position 4, the process has shifted $3\sigma = 6\sigma_{\bar{x}}$; "all" the distribution of averages is above the original control limit. That is, $P_D \cong 100\%$.

In the general position 3, the process has shifted $z\sigma = 2z\sigma_{\bar{x}}$. The distance of the new process average below the original control limit is $(3 - 2z)\sigma_{\bar{x}}$.

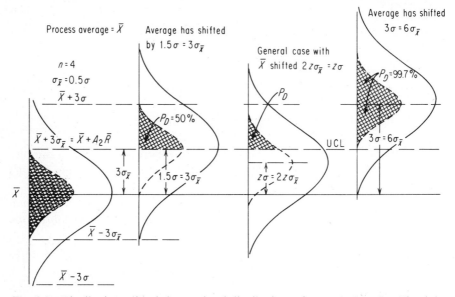

Fig. 2-9 Distributions with their associated distributions of averages $(n = 4)$. The three figures on the right represent a process with averages increased by 1.5σ, $z\sigma$, and 3σ, respectively. The probabilities P_D that a single $\bar{X}$ point will fall above the upper control limit, after the shift in process, are indicated by the shaded areas.

The area of the shaded tail above $\bar{X} + A_2 \bar{R}$ may be obtained from Table A-1. The distribution of samples even as small as $n = 4$ are essentially normally distributed, even when the process distribution is nonnormal as discussed in Sec. 1-8, Theorems 1 and 3.

Some OC Curves Associated with Other Criteria

Figure 2-10 shows the increased sensitivity when using 2-sigma decision limits over 3-sigma limits in troubleshooting projects. Both the one-point and two-point criteria of plans 2 and 3 are more sensitive to change than plan 1 with 3-sigma limits. These plans are often to be used when looking for ways to improve a process.

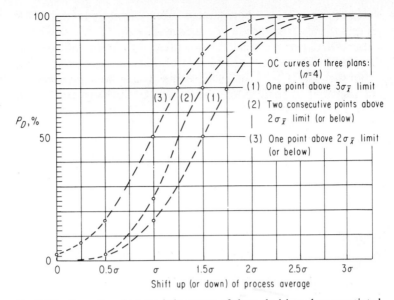

Fig. 2-10   Operating-characteristic curves of three decision plans associated with an $\bar{X}$ control chart, $n = 4$.

CASE HISTORY 2-2   *Excessive Variation in Chemical Concentration*

Figure 2-11 shows some measurements (coded) of the chemical *concentration* obtained by sampling from a continuous production line in a large chemical company; samples were obtained at hourly intervals over a period of two weeks.   During this period, every effort was made to hold the manufacturing conditions at the same levels; whatever variation there was in the process was unintentional and was considered inherent to the process. Although the process average was excellent, the variation being experienced

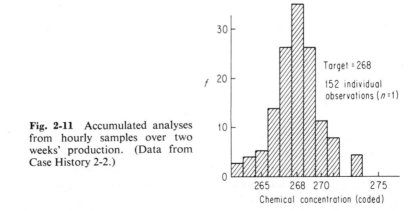

Fig. 2-11   Accumulated analyses from hourly samples over two weeks' production. (Data from Case History 2-2.)

was greater than could be tolerated in subsequent vital steps of the chemical process. This distribution of concentration was presented (by the scientists) as conclusive evidence that the process could not be held to closer variation than 263 to 273.

But such a picture (histogram) of the process *does not necessarily* represent the *potential capability* of the process. Perhaps unsuspected changes occurred during the two weeks, caused by factors which could be controlled once their presence was recognized.

In Fig. 2-12 we show the data (used to prepare Fig. 2-11) as averages of four consecutive readings, i.e., covering a 4-h production period. Each point on

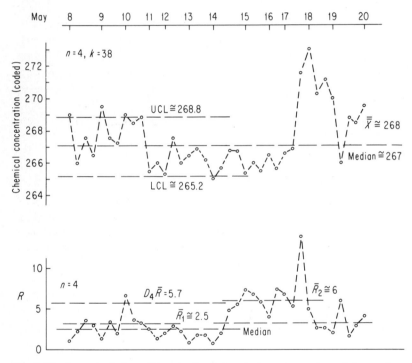

Fig. 2-12 A control chart (historical) of chemical concentration of data taken about once an hour over a two-week period. (Sample averages and ranges of four consecutive analyses.)

the $\bar{X}$ chart represents the average of four consecutive readings, and each point on the R chart represents the range of these four readings. This is a record over time. We see conclusive evidences of certain important changes having taken place during these two weeks—changes whose existence were not recognized by the very competent chemists who were guiding the process.

The R chart increases abruptly about May 14. Its earlier average is $\bar{R} \cong 2.5$, and the later average about $\bar{R} = 6$. Something happened quite abruptly to affect the 4-h average of the process.

On the $\bar{X}$ chart: the median overall is just about 267.   The total number of runs above and below the median is 11, which is convincing evidence of a nonstable process average (risk less than .01; the critical value is 12).   Although no more evidence is needed, one can draw tentative control limits on the $\bar{X}$ chart and see some further evidence of a nonstable average.   Control limits drawn over the first half of the data (which averages about 267) are

$$\bar{X} \pm A_2 \bar{R} \cong 267 \pm (0.73)(2.5)$$
$$\text{UCL} \cong 268.8 \qquad \text{and} \qquad \text{LCL} \cong 265.2$$

These lines have been drawn in Fig. 2-12.   Even during this first week, there are outages on the upper control chart limit on May 8, 9, and 10 and below the LCL during the next three or four days.   There was an abrupt drop in average on May 11.

We could compute control-chart limits on both the R chart and $\bar{X}$ chart over the entire set of data; this would not mean much because of the obvious shifting in R and $\bar{X}$.   The process has been affected by several assignable causes.   It was agreed by production that points should be plotted on the control chart when available (every 4 h, or so) and evidences of assignable causes investigated to improve the process.

This particular process history is typical of those in every industry.   Samples of size $n = 1$ are relatively common in industries where measurements are on finished batches, samples from continuous processes, complicated items (missiles, electronic test equipment), or monthly sales records, as examples.   Grouping the data into subgroups of $n = 3$, 4, or 5 for analysis will usually be beneficial.   It is usually best if there is a rationale for the grouping.   But even an arbitrary grouping will often be of supplemental value to a histogram.

Recognition of the existence of important changes in any process is a necessary prerequisite to a serious study of causes affecting that process.

CASE HISTORY 2-3   *Filling Vanilla Ice Cream Containers*

A plant was manufacturing French-style vanilla ice cream.   The ice cream was marketed in 2.5-gal containers.   Specified gross weight tolerances were: 200 ± 4 oz.   Four containers were taken from production at 10-min intervals in a special production study.   The gross weights for $k = 24$ subgroups of $n = 4$ containers are shown in Table 2-5.   What are appropriate ways[1] of presenting these observations for analysis?

Computation of control limits

The 24 sample averages and ranges are shown in Table 2-5; they have been plotted in Fig. 2-13.

$$\bar{X} = 203.95, \bar{R} = 5.917; \text{ also the median, } \tilde{X} = 204.12$$
$$\text{For } n = 4, \text{ UCL}(R) = D_4 \bar{R} = (2.28)(5.917) = 13.49$$

---

[1] Runs about the median for averages $\bar{X}$ from this set of data were considered in Sec. 2-4.

TABLE 2-5   Data: Gross Weight of Ice Cream Fill in 2.5-gal Containers

Samples of $n = 4$ in Order of Production at 10-min Intervals

Subgroup number					R	$\bar{X}$
1	202	201	198	199	4	200.00
2	200	202	212	202	12	204.00
3	202	201	208	201	7	203.00
4	201	200	200	202	2	200.75
5	210	196	200	198	14	201.00
6	202	206	205	203	4	204.00
7	198	196	202	199	6	198.75
8	206	204	204	206	2	205.00
9	206	204	203	204	3	204.25
10	208	214	213	207	7	210.50
11	198	201	199	198	3	199.00
12	204	204	202	206	4	204.00
13	203	204	204	203	1	203.50
14	214	212	206	208	8	210.00
15	192	198	204	198	12	198.00
16	207	208	206	204	4	206.25
17	205	214	215	212	10	211.50
18	204	208	196	196	12	201.00
19	205	204	205	204	1	204.50
20	202	202	208	208	6	205.00
21	204	206	209	202	7	205.25
22	206	206	206	210	4	207.00
23	204	202	204	207	5	204.25
24	206	205	204	202	4	204.25
						$\bar{\bar{X}} = 203.95$

SOURCE: Data by courtesy of David Lipman, then a graduate student at the Rutgers University Statistics Center.

The fifth range point 14 exceeds the UCL.   We recommend the exclusion of this range point; it represents more variation than expected from a stable, controlled process.   Then we compute the range average and get $\bar{R} = 5.57$.

Then $$\text{UCL} = D_4 \bar{R} = (2.28)(5.57) = 12.70$$

When we compare the short-term inherent process variability of $6\hat{\sigma}_2 = 6(5.57)/2.06 = 16.2$ oz with the specification tolerance of ± 4 oz $= 8$ oz, we find the short-term process is twice as variable as specifications allow.   In other words, the inherent process variability is not economically adequate even if the process average were stable at $\bar{\bar{X}} = 200$ oz.

Since the 23 remaining range points fall below this revised UCL(R), we also proceed to calculate control limits on $\overline{X}$.   For $n = 4$

$$\text{UCL}(\overline{X}): \overline{\overline{X}} + A_2\overline{R} = 203.95 + (0.73)(5.57)$$
$$= 203.95 + 4.07 = 208.02$$
$$\text{LCL}(\overline{X}): \overline{\overline{X}} - A_2\overline{R} = 203.95 - 4.07 = 199.88$$

See Fig. 2-13.

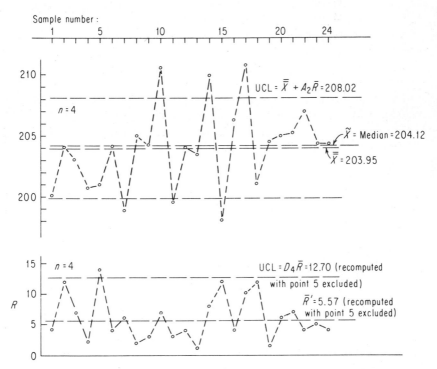

Fig. 2-13 A control chart (historical) of filling weights of ice cream containers.   (Data from Table 2-5.)

EVIDENCE FROM THE $\overline{X}$ CONTROL CHART

Before these data were obtained, it was known that the variability of the filled 2.5-gal ice cream containers was more than desired.   In every such process where there is excessive variability, there are two possibilities:

1.   Excessive average short-term variation represented by $6\hat{\sigma}_2 = 6\overline{R}/d_2$ as discussed above.   Even with an R chart in control and an $\overline{X}$ chart in control, the process just is not constructed to meet the desired specifications.

2.   A *process average not controlled*.   The two general methods of this chapter (runs and control charts) are applicable to consider this question of average process stability.

a. The control chart for $\overline{X}$ in Fig. 2-13 provides evidence that the process average was affected by *assignable causes* on several occasions:

b. Three separate points above UCL: points 10, 14, 17

c. Three separate points below LCL: points 7, 11, 15

d. Consider (1), the group of four points 7, 8, 9, 10 (over a 30-min period):

then (2), the group of four points 11, 12, 13, 14 (over 30 min).

then (3), the group of three points 15, 16, 17 (over 20 min) and;

then (4), the group of five points 18, 19, 20, 21, 22 (over 40 min).

The pattern of these sequences *suggests* that the process average would creep upward over a 25- to 30-minute period, then was probably adjusted downward; then the adjustment cycle was repeated for a total of four such cycles.   This is a supposition (hypothesis) worth investigation.

The total number of runs about the median is 8; since the small critical value is 8 for $\alpha = .05$, this is statistically significant at that risk.

The long run of 7 below the median at the beginning and the run of 6 at the end are additional evidence of a nonstable process.

TABLE 2-6 Gross Weight of Ice Cream Fill in 2.5-gal Containers
Individual Fill Weights Grouped in a Histogram

Cell interval	f	d	fd	fd^2	
215–216	1	6	6	36	
213–214	4	5	20	100	
211–212	3	4	12	48	
209–210	3	3	9	27	
207–208	10	2	20	40	
205–206	17	1	17	17	USL $= 204$
203–204	21	0	0	0	
201–202	18	-1	-18	18	
199–200	7	-2	-14	28	
197–198	7	-3	-21	63	
195–196	4	-4	-16	64	
193–194	0	-5	0	0	
191–192	1	-6	-6	36	
$n =$ 96			$+9$	477	
		$E_1 =$	0.094	4.969	$= E_2$

$\overline{\overline{X}} = 203.5 + (2)(0.094) = 203.69$

$\hat{\sigma}_1 = (2)\sqrt{4.969 - (0.094)^2} = 4.46.$

SUMMARY OF EVIDENCE: The process average was quite variable; the 24 samples averaged 2% higher than specified. Even so, there is some danger of underfilled containers.

The inherent process variability is not economically acceptable even if process average is stabilized at $\overline{X} = 200$ oz.

EVIDENCE FROM HISTOGRAM ANALYSIS

The individual fill weights are shown in Table 2-6. Several containers were overfilled; there is some underfill. The histogram does not provide information about process stability or about process capability.

We can go through the routine of computing $\overline{X}$ and $\hat{\sigma}_1$ as in Table 1-3, although this cannot be expected to add to the analysis

$$\overline{X} = A + mE_1 = 203.5 + 2(0.094)$$
$$= 203.69$$
$$\hat{\sigma}_1 = m\sqrt{E_2 - E_1^2} = (2)\sqrt{4.96}$$
$$= 4.46$$

This is much larger than $\hat{\sigma}_2 = \overline{R}/d_2 = 2.70$. This will almost always be the case when the control chart shows lack of control as discussed in Sec. 1-13.

SUMMARY—CASE HISTORY 2-3

■ The control chart shows the process was not operating at any fixed level; a series of process changes occurred during the 4-h study.

The average overfill of the 96 filled containers was about 2%; also, 38/96 = 39.6% of the containers were filled in excess of the USL of 204 oz (Table 2-6).

■ The *inherent process capability* is estimated as follows

$$\hat{\sigma}_2 = \overline{R}/d_2 = 5.57/2.06 = 2.70$$
and $\qquad 6\hat{\sigma}_2 = 16.20$ oz

This means that the innate variability of the process is about twice what is specified.

■ Two major types of investigation will be needed to reduce the process variability to the stated specifications:

1. *What are the important assignable causes producing the shifting process average shown by the $\overline{X}$ control chart?* Once identified, how can improvements be effected? The control chart can be continued and watched by production personnel to learn how to control this average; investigations by such personnel made right at the time an assignable cause is signaled can usually identify the cause. Identifications are necessary to develop remedies.

2. *What are possible ways of reducing the inherent variability ($\hat{\sigma} = \overline{R}/d_2$) of the process?* Sometimes relationships between recorded adjustments made in the process and changes in the *Range chart* can be helpful. For example, there is a *suggestion* that the process variation increased for about 40 min (points 14 to 18) on the R chart. This suggestion would usually be

disregarded in routine production; however, when trying to improve the process, it would warrant investigation.   A serious process-improvement project will almost surely require a more elaborately designed study.   Such studies are discussed in Chaps. 5, 11, 12, 13, and 15.

CASE HISTORY 2-4   An Adjustment Procedure for Test Equipment

SUMMARY

The procedure of using items of production as standards to compare test-set performance indirectly with a primary standard (such as a bridge resistance in electrical testing) is discussed.   The procedure is not limited to the electronic example described below; the *control chart of differences is recommended* also in analytical chemistry laboratories and in other analytical laboratories.

INTRODUCTION

In measuring certain electrical characteristics of electronic tubes, it was necessary to have a simple, efficient method of adjusting (calibrating) the test sets which are in continuous use by production inspectors on the factory floor.   No fundamental standard could be carried from one test set to another.   The usual procedure in the tube industry had been to attempt comparisons between individual test sets and a standard bridge by the intermediate use of "standard" tubes.   The bridge itself was calibrated by a laborious method; the same technique was not considered practical for the different test sets located in the factory.

A serious lack of confidence had developed in the reliability of the factory test sets which were being used in a radio tube company.   Large quantities of tubes were involved, and the situation was serious.   Inaccurate or unstable test sets could approve some nonconforming tubes from the daily production; also, they could reject other tubes at one inspection which conformed to specifications on a retest.   The tube engineers chided the test-set engineers for poor engineering practice.   Conversely, of course, those responsible for the test sets said: "It's not our fault."   They argued that the tubes were unstable and were to blame for the excessive variations in measurements.   It became a matter of honor and neither group made serious efforts to substantiate their position or exerted effort to improve the performance either of the tubes or the test equipment.   Large quantities of tubes were being tested daily; it became urgent to devise a more effective criterion to make adjustments.

The comparison procedure used previously to adjust the test sets was to select five "standard" tubes which had been aged to ensure reasonable stability and whose readings were within or near specification limits.   The transconductance G_m of the five standard tubes was read on the bridge and the readings recorded on form sheets, one for each test set.   The tubes were then taken to each of the floor test sets where the tubes were read again and the readings recorded on its form sheet.   From a series of these form sheets, the responsible persons attempted to see some signals or patterns to guide the adjustment and maintenance of the test equipment. Whether it was the adjustment procedure on test equipment which was ineffective or the instability of tubes could not be established.

A MODIFIED APPROACH

It was generally agreed that there might be appreciable variation in a test set over a period of a few days and that voltage conditions could gradually produce increasing errors in a set. Also, changes in temperature and humidity were expected to produce fluctuations. It was also known that internal variations within a tube would produce appreciable variations in G_m readings at unpredictable times. Consequently, it was decided to use a control chart with averages and ranges *in some way.*

After some discussion, the original comparison technique between the bridge and the test sets with five standard tubes was modified to permit a control-chart procedure.

The bridge was accepted as a working plant standard since there were data to indicate that it varied by only a fraction of a percent from day to day.

In the modified procedure, each of five standard tubes was read on the bridge and then on each floor test set, as before; the readings were recorded on a modification of the original form sheet (see Table 2-7). The difference

$$\Delta_i = S_i - B_i$$

between the set reading and the bridge reading for each tube was then determined, and the average $\bar{\Delta}$ and the range R of these five differences were computed. Plus and minus signs were used to indicate whether the set read higher or lower than the bridge.

TABLE 2-7   Computations Basic to a Control-chart Test Set Calibration

Standard tube no.	Reading on bridge (B)	Reading on test set (S)	Difference $\Delta = S - B$
1	1820	1960	$+140$
2	2590	2660	$+\ 70$
3	2370	2360	$-\ 10$
4	2030	1930	-100
5	1760	1840	$+\ 80$
			$\bar{\Delta} = +\ 36$
			$R = \ \ 240$

SOURCE: Ellis R. Ott, An Indirect Calibration of an Electronic Test Set, *Ind. Qual. Control*, January, 1947. (Reproduced by consent of the editor.)

In the initial program a control chart of these differences was recorded at one test set; readings of the standard tubes were taken on it every two hours. Within a few days, control charts of the same type were posted at other test sets. An example of one of the control charts is shown in Fig. 2-14. After a short experience, several things became apparent. Certain test sets were

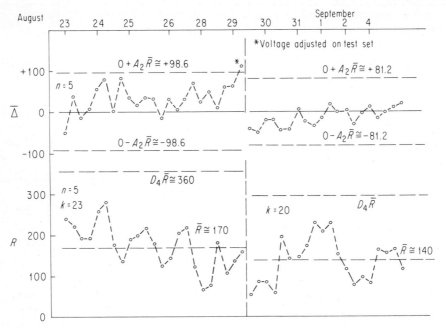

Fig. 2-14 A control-chart guide to test set adjustments. The central line has been set at a desired value of $\bar{\Delta} = 0$. Besides the one outage on August 29, there are other evidences of nonrandomness about $\bar{\Delta} = 0$ on the chart of averages and on the R charts; too few runs on each part of the R chart and on the August record on the $\bar{\Delta}$ chart.

quite variable; it was not possible to keep them in satisfactory adjustment. But a much improved performance of some was obtained easily by making minor systematic adjustments with the control charts as guides.

One of the early interests was in comparing the performance of the test sets under control charts guidance with the previous performance. Data from previous months were available to make control charts and a two-week period in June was selected to compare *before* and *after*. A comparison of variabilities of six test sets in June with a period in August (a few days after the start of the control charts) and then with a later two-week period in November is shown in Table 2-8.

Note: The average $\bar{\Delta}$ indicates the amount of bias (inaccuracy); the desired average is $\bar{\Delta} = 0$. Small values of $\bar{R}$ indicate less variability.

The immediate improvements effected in August are apparent: the average differences (bias) are reduced on every test set; the variability $\bar{R}$ is reduced on

**TABLE 2-8   A Performance Comparison of Six Test
Sets over Three Time Periods**

Set no.	June 1–15 $\bar{\Delta}$	$\bar{R}$	Aug. 15–30 $\bar{\Delta}$	$\bar{R}$	Nov. 1–15 $\bar{\Delta}$	$\bar{R}$
1	−63	181	−6	72	17	74
3	−86	164	−1	68	−1	68
5	−62	216	−12	61	−13	61
6	−47	202	9	74	7	75
7	−136	138	16	86	17	140
8	−92	186	2	81	3	92

SOURCE: Ellis R. Ott, An Indirect Calibration of an
Electronic Test Set, *Ind. Qual. Control*, January, 1947.
(Reproduced with the consent of the editor.)

several sets.   It was soon discovered that set 7 was in need of a major
overhauling.

No allowable limits of variation of the test sets with respect to the bridge
had been established, but it was agreed that it would be a decided improvement to maintain the average of five tubes within 5% of the bridge readings.
Table 2-8 showed that the variation had been in excess of 10% during the first
two weeks in June.   It was found during the first weeks of the experiment
that the average of five tubes could be held within 4% of the bridge for most
sets, and even closer agreements were obtained subsequently.   Three-sigma
control-chart limits were projected in advance on both $\bar{\Delta}$ and R charts and
used as criteria for adjustment.   Figure 2-14 shows a test set averaging about
40 units high during the last week in August.   The voltage adjustment at the
end of August centered it nicely.

It was surprising to find such large values of the range in Table 2-8.   On
the basis of logic, it was possible to explain this variability by any one of the
following explanations which revert to the original "tube versus test set"
controversy:

EXPLANATION 1:   *The five standard tubes were stable*

The variations in readings arose from the inability of a test set to duplicate
its own readings.   This assumption now had some support; $\bar{R}$ for set 7 in
November was significantly larger than for other sets.

Causes which produced a shift in the $\bar{\Delta}$ chart or in the R chart of one test set
but not in others were assignable to the test set.

EXPLANATION 2:   *The test sets were reliable*

The variations in readings resulted from internal variations within the
standard tubes.   The most obvious variations in all test sets would require
the replacement of one of the five standard tubes by a new one.   A reserve

pool of standard tubes was kept for the purpose. A need for replacement was evidenced by an upward trend of several different R charts. Such a trend could not necessarily be attributed to the standard tubes, but analysis of recent bridge readings from the form sheets on individual tubes would show whether a particular tube was the assignable cause.

EXPLANATION 3:   *A combination of assumptions 1 and 2*

It was most convenient to have data from at least three test sets in order to compare their behavior. The test-set engineers started control charts from data used in previous calibrations. They posted control charts at each test set, learned to predict and prevent serious difficulties as trends developed on the charts, and were able to make substantial improvements in test-set performance.

The advantages of control charts using differences in any similar indirect calibration program are essentially the same as the advantages of any control chart over the scanning of a series of figures.

The control chart of differences is applicable to a wide variety of calibration techniques in any industry where a sample of the manufacturer's product can be used as an intermediary. Reliable data is an important commodity.

3

Attribute or Go No-Go Data

3-1 Introduction

In every industry there are important quality characteristics which cannot be measured, or which are difficult or costly to measure. In these many cases, evidence from mechanical gages, electrical meters used as gages, or visual inspection may show that some units of production conform to specifications or desired standards and that some do not conform. Units which have cracks, missing components, appearance defects or other visual imperfections, or which are gaged for dimensional characteristics and fail to conform to specifications may be recorded as *rejects*, *defectives*, or *nonconforming* items.[1] They may be of a mechanical, electronic, or chemical nature. The *number* or *percentage* of such units is referred to as *attribute data*; each unit is recorded simply as having or not having the attribute.

Process improvement and troubleshooting with attribute data have received relatively little attention in the literature. In this book, methods of analyzing such data receive major consideration; they are of major economic importance in the great majority of manufacturing operations. (See especially Chap. 5.)

[1] Some nonconforming items may be sold as "seconds"; others reworked and retested; others scrapped and destroyed.

3-2   Three Important Problems

The ordinary manufacturing process will produce some defective[1] units. When random samples of the same size are drawn from a stable process, we expect variation in the number of defectives in the samples.   Three important problems (questions) need consideration:

1.   What *variation* is expected when samples of size *n* are drawn from a stable process?

2.   Is the process *stable* in producing defectives?   This question of stability is important in process-improvement projects.

3.   How *large* a sample is needed to estimate the *percent defective* in a warehouse or in some other type of population?

Discussion of the Three Questions

What can be predicted about the sampling variation of the *number* of defectives found in random samples of size *n* from a stable process?   There are two possibilities to consider: *first*, the percent[2] defective is assumed known.   This situation rarely occurs in real-life situations.   *Second*, the process percent defective is not known but is estimated from *k* samples, $k \geq 1$, where each sample usually consists of more than one unit.   The samples may or may not all be of the same size.   This is the usual problem we face in practice.

Binomial Theorem

Assume that the process is stable and that the probability of each manufactured unit being defective is known to be *p*.   Then the *probability of exactly x defectives* in a random sample of *n* units is known from the Binomial Theorem.   It is

$$\Pr(x) = \frac{n!}{x!(n-x)!} p^x q^{n-x} \tag{3-1}$$

where *p* is the probability of a unit being defective and $q = 1 - p$ is the probability of it being nondefective.   It can be proved that the *expected number* of defectives in the sample is *np*: there will be variation in the number which actually occur.

EXAMPLE 3-1:   When $n = 10$ and $p = q = .5$, for example, this corresponds to tossing 10 ordinary coins[3] and counting the number of heads or tails on any single toss of the 10.

Probabilities have been computed and are shown in Table 3-1 and plotted in Fig. 3-1. The expected or most probable number of defectives in a sample of 10 with $p = q = .5$ is $np = 5$.   Also, it is almost as likely to have 4 or 6 heads as to have 5 and about *half* as likely to have 3 or 7 heads as 5.

[1] If a unit of production has at least one defect or flaw, then the unit is called *defective* or *nonconforming*.   In this book, the two terms are often used interchangeably.

[2] The percent defective *P* equals 100*p* where *p* is the *fraction defective* in the process.

[3] Or of tossing a single coin 10 times.

TABLE 3-1 Probabilities $\Pr(x)$ of Exactly x Heads in 10 Tosses of an Ordinary Coin

$\Pr(0) = \Pr(10) =$		$(.5)^{10} = 0.001$
$\Pr(1) = \Pr(9)$	$=$	$10(.5)^{10} = 0.010$
$\Pr(2) = \Pr(8)$	$=$	$45(.5)^{10} = 0.044$
$\Pr(3) = \Pr(7)$	$=$	$120(.5)^{10} = 0.117$
$\Pr(4) = \Pr(6)$	$=$	$210(.5)^{10} = 0.205$
$\Pr(5)$		$= 252(.5)^{10} = 0.246$

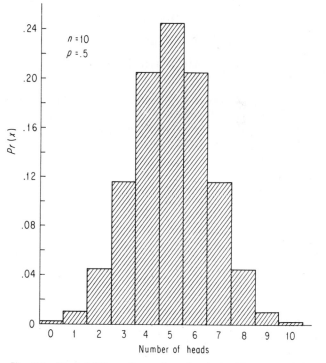

Fig. 3-1 Probabilities of exactly x heads in 10 tosses of an ordinary coin ($n = 10$, $p = \frac{1}{2}$).

The sum of all probabilities from $\Pr(0)$ to $\Pr(10)$ is *one*, i.e., certainty. The combined probability of 0, 1, or 2 heads can be represented by the symbol: $\Pr(x \leq 2)$. Also, $\Pr(x \geq 8)$ represents the probability of eight or more. Neither of these probabilities is large:

$$\Pr(x \leq 2) = \Pr(x \geq 8) = .055$$

These represent the two tails or extremes in Fig. 3-1. We can state for example:
When we make a single toss of 10 coins, we predict that we shall observe between three and seven heads inclusive, and our risk of being wrong is about

$$.055 + .055 = 0.11 \text{ or } 11\%$$

We expect to be right about 90% of the time.

Binomial Probability Tables for Selected Values of n

Decimal values of probabilities are tedious to compute from Eq. (3-1) even for small values of n. Consequently, a table of Binomial Probabilities is included (Table A-5) for selected values of n and p. Values in the table columns headed by x are probabilities of exactly x defective units in a sample of n when the probability of occurrence of a defective is p on each item. For certain other probabilities see Sec. 3-4.

Values in the table columns headed by c are *accumulated* values; they represent $\Pr(x \leq c)$. For example, the probability of 3 or fewer heads (tails) when $n = 10$, $p = .5$ is

$$\Pr(\leq 3) = \Pr(0) + \Pr(1) + \Pr(2) + \Pr(3)$$

Probabilities[1] in Table 3-1 can also be read in Table A-5 for $n = 10$, $p = .5$.

> **EXAMPLE 3-2:** Assume a stable process has been producing 3% defectives; when we inspect a sample of $n = 75$ units, we find six defectives.
>
> QUESTION: Is finding as many as six defectives consistent with an assumption that the process is still at the 3% level?
>
> ANSWER: Values of $\Pr(x)$ are shown in Table 3-2 and again in Fig. 3-2. The probability of finding as many as six is seen to be small; it is represented by the symbol
>
> $$\Pr(x \geq 6) = 1 - \Pr(x \leq 5) = \Pr(6) + \Pr(7) + \Pr(8)$$

TABLE 3-2   Probabilities of x Occurrences in $n = 75$ Trials and $p = .03$

$\Pr(0) = .101$
$\Pr(1) = .236$
$\Pr(2) = .270$
$\Pr(3) = .203$
$\Pr(4) = .113$
$\Pr(5) = .049$
$\Pr(6) = .018$
$\Pr(7) = .005$
$\Pr(8) = .001$

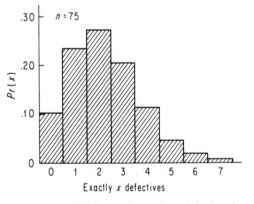

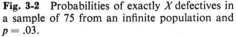

Fig. 3-2 Probabilities of exactly X defectives in a sample of 75 from an infinite population and $p = .03$.

Also $\Pr(c) = \Pr(x \leq c)$ is given in Table A-5 in the column for c.

Each individual probability above may have a rounding discrepancy of ± 0.0005. Also cumulative probabilities may have a rounding discrepancy; such discrepancies will be common but of little importance.

---

[1] A decimal point is to be placed in front of each 3-digit entry in Table A-5.

Thus it is very unlikely that the process is still at its former level of 3%. There is only a 2.5% risk that an investigation would be unwarranted. If a process average greater than 3% is economically important, then an investigation of the process should be made.

When we obtain k samples of size n_i from a process, we count the number of defectives in each sample found by inspection or test. Let the numbers be

$$d_1, d_2, d_3, \ldots, d_k$$

Then the percent defective in the process, which is assumed to be stable, or in a population assumed to be homogeneous, is *estimated* by dividing the total number of defectives found by the total number inspected

$$\hat{p} = \frac{\sum d_i}{\sum n_i} \quad \text{and} \quad \hat{P} = 100\hat{p} \tag{3-2}$$

We do not expect these *estimates*[1] of the process average to be exactly equal to it, nor shall we ever know exactly the "true" value of P.

A Measure of Variability for the Binomial Distribution

When n is *large* and p and q are each larger than say 5% and

$$np \geq 5 \text{ or } 6 \quad \text{and} \quad nq \geq 5 \text{ or } 6 \tag{3-3}$$

then the binomial distribution closely approximates the continuous normal curve (Fig. 1-2). The values in Eq. (3-3) are guideposts and not exact requirements.

The computation of a $\hat{\sigma}$ for the binomial (attribute data) can be a much simpler operation than when computing one for variables (Table 1-3). After the value of $\hat{p}$ is obtained as in Eq. (3-2), the computation is made from the following formulas.[2]

$$\hat{\sigma}_p = \sqrt{\frac{p(1-p)}{n}} \quad \text{for fraction defective} \tag{3-4}$$

$$\hat{\sigma}_P = \sqrt{\frac{P(100-P)}{n}} \quad \text{for percent defective} \tag{3-5}$$

$$\hat{\sigma}_{np} = \sqrt{np(1-p)} \quad \text{for number defective} \tag{3-6}$$

Thus knowing only the process level p and the sample size n, we compute standard deviations directly from the appropriate formula above.

EXAMPLE 3-3: A stable process is producing 10% nonconforming items. Samplings of size $n = 50$ are taken at random from it. What is the standard deviation of the sampling?

---

[1] We usually will not show the "hat" over either p or P.
[2] This is proved in texts on mathematical statistics; the method of proof is an extension of the method used in Table 3-3, as an example.

First answer: Any one of the following, depending upon the interest.

$$\hat{\sigma}_p = \sqrt{\frac{(.10)(.90)}{50}} = 0.0424 \qquad \hat{\sigma}_P = 4.24\% \qquad \hat{\sigma}_{np} = 2.12$$

Second answer: The answer can also be obtained as in Table 1-3; this second procedure is much too laborious and is not done in practice.   We shall compute $\hat{\sigma}_{np}$ to illustrate the procedure.

Consider 1,000 samplings of size $n = 50$ from the process.   The expected frequencies of x defectives is $f_x = 1,000 \cdot \text{Pr}(x)$ where $\text{Pr}(x)$ is obtained from Table A-5 for $n = 50$. They are shown in Table 3-3, and the procedure yields the answer $\hat{\sigma}_{np} = 2.10$.   The slight difference from the first answer of 2.12 is a consequence of rounding in Table A-5.

TABLE 3-3   Computing σ_{np} from Theoretical Values of $\text{Pr}(x)$ Obtained from Table A-5 for $n = 50$, $p = .10$ Using the Method of Grouped Data, Table 1-3

x	$f_x =$ 1,000 $\text{Pr}(x)$	d	fd	fd^2
12	2	7	14	98
11	6	6	36	216
10	15	5	75	375
9	33	4	132	528
8	64	3	192	576
7	108	2	216	432
6	154	1	154	154
5	185	0	0	0
4	181	−1	−181	181
3	139	−2	−278	556
2	78	−3	−234	702
1	29	−4	−116	464
0	5	−5	−25	125

$$n = 999 \quad \sum fd = -15 \qquad 4,407 = \sum fd^2$$

$$E_1 = \sum fd/n = -0.015$$
$$E_2 = \sum fd^2/n = 4.407$$
$$\sigma_{np} = m\sqrt{E_2 - E_1^2}$$
$$= \sqrt{4.407} = 2.10$$

Question 1.   *Expected Variation*

Assuming a stable process with $\bar{p} = .10$, the expected variation in the number of defectives in samples of $n = 50$ can be represented in terms of np and $\hat{\sigma}_{np}$. Just as in Eq. (1-10) for the normal curve, when the conditions of Eq. (3-3) are applicable, the amount of variation is predicted to be between

$$np - 3\sigma_{np} \quad \text{and} \quad np + 3\sigma_{np} \quad (99.7\%)$$
$$np - 2\sigma_{np} \quad \text{and} \quad np + 2\sigma_{np} \quad (95.4\%) \qquad (3\text{-}7)$$
$$np - \sigma_{np} \quad \text{and} \quad np + \sigma_{np} \quad (68.3\%)$$

Thus in Example 3-3 with $n = 50$ and $p = .10$, the average number expected is $np = 5$ and the standard deviation is $\hat{\sigma}_{np} = 2.12$. From Eq. (3-7), we can predict the variation in samples to be from

$$5 - 6.36 \text{ to } 5 + 6.36 \quad \text{i.e., 0 to 11 inclusive } (99.7\%)$$
$$\text{or} \quad 5 - 4.24 \text{ to } 5 + 4.24 \quad \text{i.e., 1 to 9 inclusive } (95.4\%)$$

Just as easily, the expected sampling variation in p or P can be obtained from Eq. (3-4) and (3-5) with (3-7).

Question 2.   But Is the Process Stable?

A simple and effective answer is available when we have k samples of n each by making a control chart for fraction or percent defective. This chart is entirely analogous to a control chart for variables.

In routine production, control limits are usually drawn using 3-sigma limits. Points outside these limits (outages) are considered evidence of assignable causes. Also evidence from *runs* (Chap. 2) is used jointly with that from outages, especially in process improvement studies, when 2-sigma limits are usually the basis for investigations.

We expect "almost all" points which represent samplings from a *stable process* to fall inside 3-sigma lines. If they *do not*, we say "The process is *not* in control" and there is only a small risk of the conclusion being incorrect. If they *do* all fall inside, we say "The process *is* in statistical control" or "The process appears stable"; this is not the same as saying "It *is* stable." There is an analogy: a person is accused of a crime. The evidence may (1) convict him of guilt, and we realize there is some small chance that justice miscarried, or (2) fail to convict him, but this is not the same as believing him to be innocent.

EXAMPLE 3-4:   (Data of Table 5-18, machine 1 only.)   Final inspection of small glass bottles was showing an unsatisfactory reject rate. A sampling study of bottles was made over several days to obtain evidence regarding stability and to identify possible major sources of rejects. A partial record of the number of rejects, found in samples of $n = 120$ bottles taken three times per day from one machine, has been plotted in Fig. 3-3. The total number of rejects in the 21 samples was 147; the total number inspected was $7(3)(120) = 2,520$. Then $P = 0.0583$ or 5.83%. When considering daily production by shifts, the sample inspected was $n = 8(15) = 120$. Then

$$\hat{\sigma}_P = \sqrt{\frac{(5.83)(94.17)}{120}} = \sqrt{4.575\%} = 2.14\%$$

The upper 3-sigma limit is: $5.83\% + 3(2.14) = 12.25\%$. The lower limit is taken to be zero.

DISCUSSION: Was the process stable during the investigation?

Outages: There is one on August 17.

Runs: The entire set of data is suggestive of a process with a gradually increasing P. This apparent increase is not entirely supported by a long run.   The run of five above at the end (and its two preceding points exactly on the median and average) is "suggestive support" (Table A-3); and the six below the median out of the first seven strengthens the notion of increasingly defective process.

Both the outage and the general pattern indicate an uptrend.

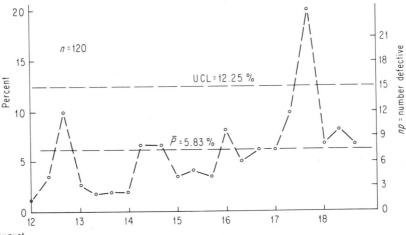

Fig. 3-3   A control-chart record of defective glass bottles found in samples of 120 per shift over a seven-day period (see Example 3-4).

Question 3.   How Large a Sample?

How many are needed to estimate the percent defective in a warehouse or in some other population or universe?   A recent newspaper article presented forecasts of a scientific survey of a national presidential election on the basis of 1,400 individual voter interviews.   The survey was conducted to determine the expected voting pattern of 60 to 80 million voters.   The chosen sample size is not determined on a percentage basis.

The question of sample size was discussed in Sec. 1-11 for variables data. The procedure with attributes is much the same but differs in detail.

From a statistical viewpoint, we must first adopt estimates of three quantities:

1.   The *magnitude* of allowable error Δ in the estimate we will obtain for P.   Do we want the answer to be accurate within 1%?   Or within 3%? *Some* tentative estimate must be made.

2.   What is a rough guess as to the value of P?   We shall designate it here by $\hat{P}$.

3.   With what assurance do we want to determine the region within which P is to be established?   Usually about 95 or 90% assurance is reasonable. These two assurances correspond to $\pm 2\hat{\sigma}$ and $\pm 1.65\hat{\sigma}$.

Answer: The basic equations to determine sample size in estimating P in a population, allowing for a possible error of $\pm\Delta$, are

$$\pm\Delta = \pm3\hat\sigma_p \qquad \text{if we insist on } 99.7\% \text{ confidence}$$
$$\pm\Delta = \pm2\hat\sigma_p \qquad \text{if about } 95\% \text{ confidence is acceptable}$$
$$\pm\Delta = \pm1.65\hat\sigma_p \qquad \text{if we accept about a } 90\% \text{ confidence level}$$

The second of these equations may be rewritten as

$$\Delta = 2\sqrt{\frac{\hat P(100 - \hat P)}{n}}$$

which simplifies to

$$n = \frac{4\hat P(100 - \hat P)}{\Delta^2} \qquad (95\% \text{ confidence}) \tag{3-8a}$$

Similarly from the third and first equations above, we have

$$n = \frac{(1.65)^2\hat P(100 - \hat P)}{\Delta^2} \qquad (90\% \text{ confidence}) \tag{3-8b}$$

$$n = \frac{9\hat P(100 - \hat P)}{\Delta^2} \qquad (99.7\%) \tag{3-8c}$$

Other factors are very important, too, in planning a sampling to estimate a percent defective within a population. We must plan the sampling procedure so that whatever sample is chosen it is as nearly *representative* as possible. How expensive is it to obtain items from the process or other population for the sample? What is the cost of providing test equipment and operators? We would be reluctant to choose as large a sample when the testing is destructive as when it is nondestructive. These factors may be as important as the statistical ones involved in Eq. (3-8). However, values obtained from Eq. (3-8) will provide a basis for comparing the reasonableness of whatever sample size is eventually chosen.

EXAMPLE 3-5: How large a sample is needed to estimate the percent P of defective glass bottles in a second warehouse similar to the one discussed in Example 3-4? Preliminary data suggest that $\hat P \cong 5\%$ or 6%. Now it would hardly be reasonable to ask for an estimate correct to 0.5%, but possibly to 1% or 2%. If we choose $\Delta = 1\%$, a confidence of 95%, and $\hat P = 5\%$, then

$$n = \frac{4(5)(95)}{1} = 1,900$$

If we were to increase Δ to 2%, then

$$n = \frac{4(5)(95)}{4} = 475$$

DECISION: A representative sample of 1,900 is probably unnecessary, too expensive, and too impractical.   A reasonable compromise might be to inspect about 475 initially.   Then whatever percent defective is found, compute $P \pm 2\hat{\sigma}_P$.   Be sure to keep a record of all different *types* of defects found; a sample of 475 will probably provide more than enough information to decide what further samplings or other steps need be taken.

3-3   On How to Sample

There Are Different Reasons for Sampling

Estimating the percent P in a warehouse or from a process are examples just discussed.   Now, we shall discuss the frequency and size of samples necessary to *monitor* a production process.   This is a major question of process control.

■ When daily production from any one shift is less than say 500, *and* 100 % inspection is already in progress, it may be sensible to initiate a control chart with the entire production as the sample[1].   The control limits UCL and LCL can be computed and drawn on the chart for an *average n* as a basis for monitoring daily production.   The control limits can be adjusted (recomputed) for any point corresponding to a substantially larger or smaller sample; this would be warranted only for points near the computed limits for average n.   A factor of 2 is a reasonable basis for recomputing.

■ When a daily shift production is more than say 500 or when evidence suggests process trouble, smaller random samples—checked by a special inspector—can provide valuable information.   Samples of $n = 50$ or 100 can provide much useful information; sometimes even smaller ones will be adequate as a starter.   The special inspector will not only record whether each item is defective but will inspect for *all* defect categories and will record the major types of defects and the number of each.   See Case Histories 15-1, 15-2, and Sec. 8-13.

■ How large a sample is necessary when starting a control chart with attributes?   In Case History 3-1, a chart was plotted daily from records of 100 % inspection.   In Fig. 3-4 we see that variation of daily production defectives during January was as much as 4 or 5 % and more above and below average.   If a variation of $\Delta = 2\%$ about $p = 5.6\%$ were now accepted as a reasonable variation to signal a daily shift, and we choose 3-sigma limits to use in production, then from Eq. (3-8c) it follows that

$$n = \frac{9(5.6)(94.4)}{4} = 1,189 \cong 1,200$$

But a sample of about 1,200 would be adequate for a *total* day's production.   When samples are to be inspected hourly, then $n = 1,200/8 = 150$ becomes a reasonable choice.   If samples were to be inspected bihourly, then $n =$

---

[1] The entire production will be considered the population at times; but it is usually more profitable to consider it as a sample of what the process *may produce in the future*, if it is a stable process.

1,200/4 = 300 would be indicated from a statistical viewpoint.   However, a decision to choose a smaller sample would be better than no sampling.

The question of whether a sampling system should be instituted, and the details of both size and frequency of samples, should consider the potential savings compared to the cost of sampling.

Conclusion: If the potential economic advantages favor the start of a sampling plan, then initial samples of no larger than 150 are indicated. This would provide a feedback of information to aid production.   The sample size can later be changed—either smaller or larger—as suggested by experience with this specific process.

There is another reason for sampling in production.   Consider a shipment of items—either outgoing or incoming.   How large a random sample shall we inspect and how many defectives shall we allow in the sample and still approve the lot?   This is the problem of *acceptance sampling* (see Chap. 8).

3-4   Attribute Data Which Approximates a Poisson Distribution

In Table A-5, binomial tables are provided for selected values up to $n = 100$. In this section we consider

$$n \text{ to be ``large,''} \quad p \text{ to be ``small,''} \text{ and } np < 20 \text{ or } 30 \qquad (3\text{-}9)$$

EXAMPLE 3-6:   A spinning frame spins monofilament rayon yarn[1]; it has over a hundred spinarets.   There are occasional spinning stoppages at an individual spinaret because of yarn breakage.   A worker then corrects the breakage and restarts the spinaret.   An observer records the number of stoppages on an entire spinning frame during a series of 15-min periods.   The record over 20 time periods shows the following number of stoppages:

6, 2, 1, ..., etc., with an average of four per period.

This type of data is attribute or countable data.   However, it differs from our preceding attribute data in the following ways:

1.   There is no way of knowing the "sample size n"; the number of *possible* breaks is "very large" since each spinaret may have several stoppages during the same time period.   Although we do not know n, we know it is potentially "large," at least conceptually.

2.   There is no way of knowing the "probability p" of a single breakage; we *do* know that it is "small."

3.   We do not have estimates on either n or p, but we have a good estimate of their *product*: in fact, the average number of stoppages per period is $np = 4$.

There are many processes from which we obtain attribute data which satisfies these three criteria: n is "large" and p is "small" (both usually unknown) but their product np is known.   Data of this sort are called *Poisson* type— named after a soldier who studied the number of deaths caused by the kick of a mule among different Prussian army units.

[1] See Case History 5-3.

How Much Variation Is Predicted in Samples from a Poisson Distribution?

The question can be answered in two ways, both useful to know:

1. By Computing $\hat{\sigma}_{np}$. From Eq. (3-6), with $\hat{\sigma}_{np} = \sqrt{np(1-p)}$ we have, for the Poisson with p small, and therefore $(1-p) \cong 1$

$$\hat{\sigma}_{np} \cong \sqrt{np} \tag{3-10}$$

Discussion: In the artificial data of Example 3-6, we are given $np = 4$. Then from Eq. (3-10), $\hat{\sigma} = \sqrt{4} = 2$. Consequently, variation expected from this Poisson type of process, assumed stable, can be expected to extend from

$$4 - 2\hat{\sigma} \text{ to } 4 + 2\hat{\sigma} \qquad \text{(about 95\% confidence)}$$

i.e., from 0 to 8.

2. From Poisson Curves (Table A-6). These very useful curves give probabilities of *c or fewer* defects for different values of np. The value of $\Pr(\leq 8)$, for the previous example, is estimated by first locating the point $np = 4$ on the base line; follow the vertical line up to the curve for $c = 8$. Then using a plastic ruler locate $\Pr(\leq 8)$ on the left-hand vertical scale; it is slightly more than 0.98.

Discussion: Processes and events representable by Poisson distributions are quite common.

CASE HISTORY 3-1   Defective Glass Stems in a Picture Tube for a Color TV Set[1]

A 100% inspection was made following the molding process on machine A. A record of lot number, and then the number defective, and the percent defective for each lot are shown in Fig. 3-4 at the bottom. A chart of daily P values is shown on the same vertical line above the computed P values below. The inspector (only one) was instructed to note operating conditions and any problems observed. It was learned that he was able to explain why things were bad more often than why things were good.

Two types of visual defects predominated:

1. *Cracked throat*, the major problem, caused by stems sticking in a mold, probably from "cold" fires.

2. *Bubbles*, caused by "hot" fires.

All reject types have been combined for this present analysis and discussion. The control limits in Fig. 3-4 have been computed for $\bar{n} = 66{,}080/26 \cong 2{,}540$ and $\bar{P} = 100(3{,}703/66{,}080) = 5.60\%$.

DISCUSSION

The day-to-day variation is large; the percent of rejects was substantially better than the month's average on at least eleven different days. When possible reasons for these better performances were explored, not much specific evidence could be produced:

[1] Courtesy of Carl Mentch, General Electric Company.

■ It is not surprising to have excessive rejects on the day after New Year's nor at the startup of the process.

■ It was believed that the fires were out of adjustment on January 9, producing almost 20 % rejects.   Fires were adjusted on the tenth, and improved performance was evident on the next four days (January 10 through 14).

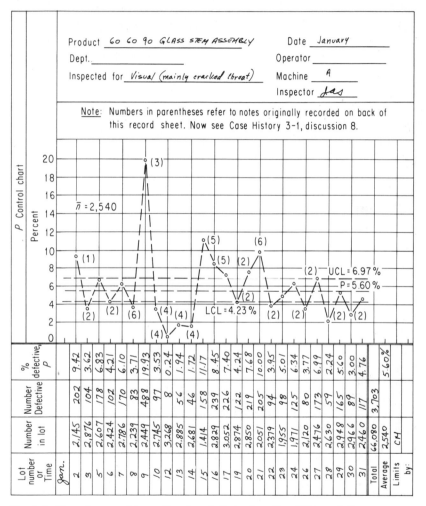

Fig. 3-4   Form to record inspection by attributes (see Case History 3-1).

■ On January 15, rejects jumped again (to 11 %).   An investigation showed stems sticking in mold 4.   This condition was improved somewhat over the next three days.

■ On January 21, fire position 6 on the machine was found to be too hot. An adjustment was made early on January 22, and the process showed an improvement in overall average and with less erratic performance for the remainder of January.

■ When this study was begun, the stem machine was considered to be in need of a major overhaul. This chart shows that either the machine easily lost its adjustment or possibly it was overadjusted. At any rate, the machine was shut down and completely rebuilt during February, and then started up again.

■ Since the methods used to adjust the machine during January were not very effective, perhaps it would now be helpful to inspect a sample of stems hourly or bihourly and post the findings. This systematic feedback of information to production would be expected to do several things: prevent a machine operating unnoticed all day at a high reject rate; signal both better and worse performance allowing production and engineering to establish reasons for the difference in performance.

Sometimes, large variations as in Fig. 3-4 are found to be a consequence of differences in inspectors. Since only one inspector was involved here, it is doubtful that his variation from day to day was a major contribution to the variation.

■ Calculation of control limits in Fig. 3-4 for average $n \cong 2,540$, attribute data. From Eq. (3-5)

$$\hat{\sigma}_P = \sqrt{\frac{(5.60)(94.40)}{2,540}} = 0.456\%$$

and

$$3\hat{\sigma}_P = 1.37\%$$

$$\text{UCL} = \bar{P} + 3\hat{\sigma}_P = 6.97\%$$

$$\text{LCL} = \bar{P} - 3\hat{\sigma}_P = 4.23\%$$

■ Notes and their numbers as recorded originally by inspector on back of Fig. 3-4.

1. Day after New Year's shutdown.
2. Reason that these points were out of control is unknown.
3. Four fires known to be out of adjustment.
4. Fires readjusted to bogie settings on 10th.
5. Stems sticking in 4 mold.
6. Fire position 6 too hot.

CASE HISTORY 3-2   Incoming Inspection of a TV Component[1]

A relatively inexpensive glass component (a mount) was molded at one plant of a company. After a 100% inspection, it was transported to a second plant of the same company. After a 100% inspection at the receiving plant, it was sealed into a TV picture tube.

[1] Courtesy of Carl Mentch, General Electric Company.

The two principal reasons for the second 100% inspection were:

1.   The transportation was a possible source of defective mounts, but a defective mount was easily repaired.

2.   Defective mounts were the principal cause of defective picture tubes. A defective picture tube was an expensive item and was nonrepairable.

The supplier plant was notified immediately by phone of any problems found at the receiver plant.   Also, a monthly report of performance was given the supplier plant by type of defect and this was passed along to production.   (All defects have been combined in Fig. 3-5.)   In the course of a year,

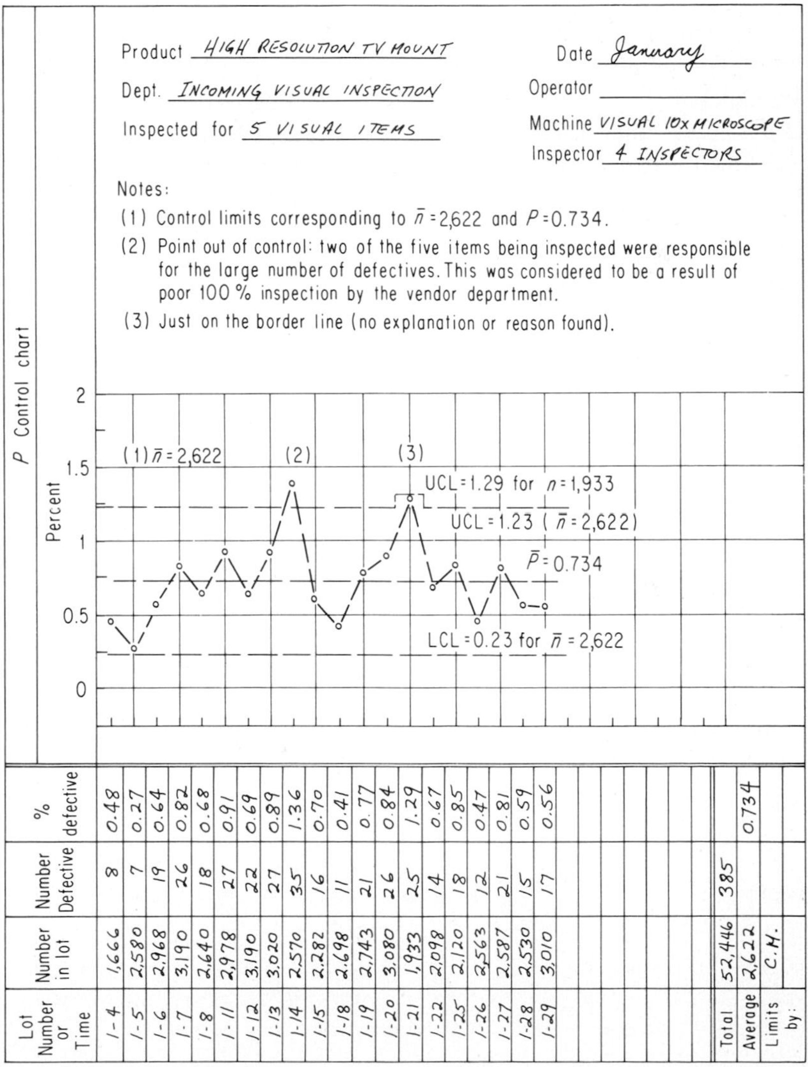

Product *HIGH RESOLUTION TV MOUNT*   Date *January*

Dept. *INCOMING VISUAL INSPECTION*   Operator _____

Inspected for *5 VISUAL ITEMS*   Machine *VISUAL 10x MICROSCOPE*

                                             Inspector *4 INSPECTORS*

Notes:

(1) Control limits corresponding to $\bar{n}$ = 2,622 and P = 0.734.

(2) Point out of control: two of the five items being inspected were responsible for the large number of defectives. This was considered to be a result of poor 100% inspection by the vendor department.

(3) Just on the border line (no explanation or reason found).

P Control chart / Percent

(1) $\bar{n}$ = 2,622   (2)   (3)

UCL = 1.29 for n = 1,933

UCL = 1.23 ($\bar{n}$ = 2,622)

$\bar{P}$ = 0.734

LCL = 0.23 for $\bar{n}$ = 2,622

Lot Number or Time	% defective	Number Defective	Number in lot
1-4	0.48	8	1,666
1-5	0.27	7	2,580
1-6	0.64	19	2,968
1-7	0.82	26	3,190
1-8	0.68	18	2,640
1-11	0.91	27	2,978
1-12	0.69	22	3,190
1-13	0.89	27	3,020
1-14	1.36	35	2,570
1-15	0.70	16	2,282
1-18	0.41	11	2,698
1-19	0.77	21	2,743
1-20	0.84	26	3,080
1-21	1.29	25	1,933
1-22	0.67	14	2,098
1-25	0.85	18	2,120
1-26	0.47	12	2,563
1-27	0.81	21	2,587
1-28	0.59	15	2,530
1-29	0.56	17	3,010
Total	0.734	385	52,446
Average			2,622
Limits by:			C.H.

Fig. 3-5   A control chart using attribute data: visual inspection of a TV component.

this operation dropped from over 5% to less than 1% defective.   The system was considered to be successful.

Discussion of numbered notes on the chart:

1.   The sample size of 2,580 on January 5 is smaller than $\bar{n} = 2,622$.   No recomputation was made since it would only lower the LCL.   No investigation was made.

2.   The number of mounts inspected on January 14 was 2,570.   This is less than $n = 2,622$ by so little that a recomputation is not warranted; it would not affect the decision that the day's lot was significantly worse than average.   The record of defects showed two particular items to be the reason for the increase.   An investigation established that inadequate 100% inspection by the supplier was the cause, and not the transportation.

3.   The number inspected on January 21 was 1,933; when the UCL is recomputed, it is found to be 1.29%.   On this date, $P = 1,293$; although this is "less" than UCL = 1,294%, it indicates a high probability that there is a findable cause.   (Actually, no substantial investigation was made.)

COMPUTATION OF MODIFIED CONTROL LIMITS ON FIG. 3-5, $n = 2,622$

$$\hat{\sigma}_P = \sqrt{\frac{(0.734)(99.266)}{2622}} = 0.1665\% \quad \text{and} \quad 3\hat{\sigma}_P = 0.500\%$$

$$UCL = 1.234\%$$
$$LCL = 0.234\%$$

4

Some Basic Ideas and Methods of Troubleshooting

4-1 Introduction

In Chaps. 2 and 3, a scientific process was studied by attempting to hold constant all variables which are thought to affect the process. Then data obtained in a time sequence from the process were examined for the presence of unknown causes (nonrandomness) by the number and length of runs and control charts. Experience in every industry has shown that its processes have opportunities for economic improvement to be discovered by this approach.

When evidence of nonrandomness has been observed, the assignable causes can sometimes be explained by standard engineering or production methods of investigation. Sometimes the method of investigation is to vary one factor or different factors suspected of affecting the quality of the process or the product. This should be done in a preplanned experimental pattern. This experimentation was formerly the responsibility of persons involved in research and development. More recently, process improvement and trouble shooting responsibilities have become the province of those engineers and supervisors who are intimately associated with the day-to-day operation of the plant processes. Effective methods of planning investigations have been developed and applied during the last two decades. Their adoption began in the electrical, mechanical, and chemical industries. However, the principles and methods are universal; applications into other industries may differ in detail.

The following sections will outline some procedures of designing and analyzing data from investigations (experiments). Examples from different sciences and industries will be presented to illustrate useful methods. We emphasize attribute data in Chap. 5 and variables data in Chaps. 10 and 11.

4-2   Some Types of Independent and Dependent Variables

Introductory courses in science introduce us to methods of experimentation. Time, temperature, rate of flow, pressure, and concentration are examples of variables often expected to have important effects in chemical reactions. Voltage, power output, resistance, and mechanical spacing are important in electronics and many laws involving them have been determined empirically. These laws have been obtained from many laboratory studies over long periods of time by many different experimenters. These laws are often known by the names of the scientists who first proposed and studied them. We have special confidence in a law when some background of theory has been developed to support it, but we often find it very useful even when its only support is empirical.

In order to teach methods of experimentation in science courses, students are often assigned the study of possible effects of different factors. Different levels of temperature may be selected and the resultant quality responses determined. Hopefully, the quality response will behave like a *dependent* variable. After performing the experimental study, a previously determined relationship (law) may be shown to the student to compare with his experimental data.

As specialized studies in a science are continued, we may be assigned the project to determine which factors have major influence on a specific quality characteristic. Two general approaches are possible:

1.   Recognized Causative Variables (Factors)

We study the effects of many variables known to have been important in similar studies (temperature, light intensity, voltage, power output, as examples). This procedure is often successful, especially in well-equipped research laboratories and pilot plants. This is often considered basic to the "scientific method."

Frequently, however, those scientific factors which are expected to permit predictions regarding the new process are found to be grossly inadequate. This inadequacy is especially common when a process is transferred from the laboratory or pilot plant to production. The predicted results may be obtained at some times but not at others, although no known changes have been introduced. In these cases, the methods of Chaps. 2 and 3 are especially relevant to check on stability.

2. Block-type Factors[1]

Sometimes the results vary from machine to machine and from operator to operator: The following fundamental " law" has resulted from empirical studies in many types of industry; it is presented with only slight " tongue in cheek ":

Consider k different machines assigned to the same basic operation:

■ When there are three or four machines, one will be substantially better or worse than the others.

■ When there are as many as five or six machines, at least one will be substantially better and one substantially worse than the others.

There are other important block-type factors. We might study possible effects in production from *components* purchased from different vendors[2]; or differences between k *machines* intended to produce the same items or materials; or differences between *operators* or *shifts* of operators. This type of experimentation is often called "troubleshooting" or problem solving; its purpose is to improve *either the product or the process, or both.*

A troubleshooting project often begins by studying possible differences in the quality output of different machines, or machine heads, or operators or other types of variables discussed below. Then when important differences have been established, experience has shown that careful study of the sources of better and worse performance by the scientist and supervisor will usually provide important *reasons* for those differences.

A key to making adjustments and improvements is in *knowing that actual differences do exist* and in being able to *pinpoint the sources* of the differences.

It is sometimes argued that *any* important change or difference will be evident to an experienced engineer or supervisor; *this is not the case.* Certainly many important changes and improvements are recognized without resort to analytical studies, *but* the presence and identity of many economically important factors are not recognized without them. Several case histories are presented throughout the following chapters which illustrate this very important principle.

---

[1] There is no term in common usage to designate what we mean by "*block-type*" factors. Other terms which might be used are *bunch type* or *chunky type*. The idea is that of an *omnibus type* of factor which will usually require subsequent investigation to establish methods of adjustment or other corrective action. A block-type factor deliberately confounds several factors; some may be known and others unknown.

[2] See Case History 5-9.

Summary on Variables

Types of Independent Variables (Factors) in a Study:
1.   Continuous variables with a known or suspected association or effect on the process: temperature, humidity, time of reaction, voltage.   Sometimes these variables can be set and held to different prescribed levels during a study—sometimes not.
2.   Discrete block-type factors.   Several examples will be given relating to this type: different heads or cavities on a machine, different operators, different times of day, different vendors.   Once it has been determined that important differences between "blocks" do exist, it can almost always lead to identification of specific adjustable causes and to subsequent process improvement.

Types of Quality Characteristics (Response Variables, Dependent Variables, Factors):
1.   Measurable, variable factors: the brightness of a TV picture, the yield of a chemical process, the breaking strength of synthetic fibers, the thickness of a sheet of plastic, the life (in hours) of a 6-V battery.
2.   Attribute or classification data (go no-go): the light bulb will or will not operate, the content of a bottle is or is not underfilled.   There are occasions where the use of attribute data is recommended even though variables data are possible.   In Chap. 7 the important, practical methods of narrow-limit gaging (NL-Gaging) are discussed.
Experimentation with variables response data is common in scientific investigations.   Our discussion of experimentation in Chaps. 11, 12, 13 will consider variables data.   In practice, however, important investigations frequently begin with quality characteristics causing rejects of a go no-go nature.   See Chap. 5 for discussions involving their use.

4-3   Some Strategies in Problem Finding, Problem Solving, and Troubleshooting

There are different strategies in approaching real-life experiences.   The procedures presented here have been tested by many persons and in many types of engineering and production problems.   Their effective use will sometimes be straightforward, but will always benefit from ingenuity in combining the art and science of troubleshooting.

It is traditional to study cause-and-effect relationships.   However, there are big advantages frequently to studies which only identify blocks, regions, or chunks as the source of difference or difficulty.   The pinpointing of specific cause and effect is thus postponed.   The blocks may be different areas of the manufacturing plant, or different subassemblies of the manufactured product.   Several examples are discussed in the following chapters and in case histories.

Two important principles need to be emphasized:

Basic Principle 1: Plan to Learn Something
Initially—Not Everything

This is important especially in those many industrial situations where more data are rather easily attainable.

It is not possible to specify all the important rules to observe in carrying out a scientific investigation, but a second very important rule to observe, if at all possible, is:

Basic Principle 2: Be Present at the Time
and Place the Data Are Being Obtained, at
Least for the Beginning of the Investigation

■ It often provides opportunities to observe possible error-sources in the data acquisition.   Compensations may be possible by improving the data-recording forms, or by changing the type of measuring instrumentation.

■ Observance of the data being obtained may suggest causative relationships which can be suggested, questioned, or evaluated only at the time of the study.

■ Observing the possibility of different effects due to operators, machines, shifts, vendors and other block-type variables can be very rewarding.

CASE HISTORY 4-1   Black Patches on Aluminum Ingots[1]

INTRODUCTORY INVESTIGATIONS

While conducting some model investigations in different types of factories, an occasion to investigate a problem of excessive black-oxidized patches on aluminum ingots came into our jurisdiction.   A general meeting was first held in the office of the plant manager.   At this meeting the general purpose of two projects, including this specific one, was described.   This problem had existed several months and competent metallurgists had considered such problems as contaminants in aluminum pigs and differences in furnace conditions.

Our study group had just two weeks to work on the problem; clearly, we could not expect to become better metallurgists than those competent ones already available.   Rather than investigate the possible effects of such traditional independent variables as furnace conditions (temperature and time, etc.) we considered what block-type variables might produce differences in the final ingots.

PLANNING THE STUDY

The ingots were cast in 10 different molds.   A traveling crane carried a ladle of molten aluminum to a mold; aluminum was poured into the mold, where it was allowed to solidify before removal by a hoist.   The plant layout in Fig. 4-1 shows the general location of the 10 molds (M), the electric

[1] Ellis R. Ott, United Nations Technical Assistance Programme, report no. TAA/IND/ 18, March 25, 1958.

furnace and track, doors (D), two walls, and two windows (W). It was considered that the location of these doors, windows, and walls might possibly affect the oxidation of black patches. The location of the patches was vaguely considered to be predominantly on the bottom of ingots.

It was decided to record the occurrence and location of the black patches on ingots from a selected sample of molds, one from each in the order M_1,

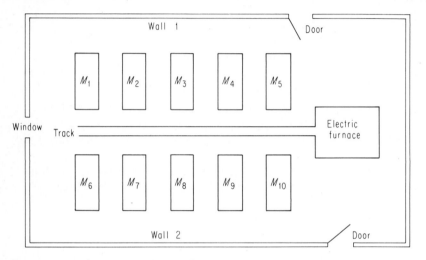

Fig. 4-1   Plant layout of molds and furnace.

M_{10}, M_3, M_6, M_5, M_8. Then the procedure was repeated once with these same six molds.

■ This selection of ingots would indicate whether the location of black patches would occur and reoccur on some molds and not on others, whether it occurred in about the same location on all molds, and whether it would *reoccur* in about the same location on the same mold. If the reoccurrence of black patches was predictable, then the problem was *not* contamination in the molten aluminum or in furnace conditions, but would relate to some condition of the molds. If the black patches did not reoccur in the same areas but their locations appeared random, then the problem might be of a metallurgical nature. The problem might be contamination in the molten aluminum or in changing conditions of the molds.

■ A comparison of "inside locations" (M_3 and M_8) with "outside locations" (M_1, M_5, M_6, M_{10}) might also indicate possible effects related to distances from furnace, doors, and windows.

How were the location and intensity of black oxidation to be measured? There is no standard procedure: (a) Often a diagram can be prepared and the location of defects sketched or marked on it; Fig. 4-2 shows the blank diagrams which were prepared in advance on sheets of papers. (b) Included on each form was the order of casting to be followed.

Note: While getting organized, it was learned that the 10 molds had electrical heating in their walls and bottoms (the tops were open). The metallurgists agreed that differences in heating might have an effect, and it would be possible to measure the temperatures at different locations in a mold with a contact thermometer. Prior to pouring, the temperatures at designated locations of the mold were measured and recorded on the form (Fig. 4-2).

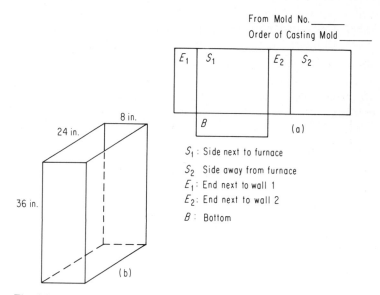

Fig. 4-2   (*a*) Form to record black patch areas on molds; (*b*) representation of a mold.

It was about six hours after the initial planning meeting that the data forms had been drawn, the plan formalized, and the first ingot poured. Then after solidifying, the ingot was withdrawn, its identity marked, and the procedure was continued.

OBTAINING DATA

Now if possible, be present when the study begins—long enough, at least to observe *some data*. We examined the ingot from M_1; yes, there was a smallish 3-in. irregular circle of oxide—*not* on the bottom, but on the side S_1. The location and size of the oxide were recorded as planned.

No clues were immediately available; the wall temperature in the area of the black patch was no different from the temperatures at locations lacking the oxide. Was there anything special about the condition of the mold wall at the origin of the black oxide? An immediate investigation "suggested" the *possibility* that the white-oxide dressing with which the molds were treated weekly "looked a bit different." It was of unlikely importance, but its existence was noted.

The casting of the first round of ingots was continued as planned; some of the ingots had black patches; some did not. Their location was indicated on the prepared forms. It was time to repeat molds beginning with M_1. When the second M_1 ingot was examined it showed a black patch in the *same* general location as the first M_1 ingot! And this was the general repeat pattern for the six molds. A careful examination in the area producing a black patch usually suggested a slight differing appearance: nothing obvious or very convincing.

It was the practice to dress the molds with white oxide every few days. When it was time to make a third casting on M_1, a redressing was applied (by brush) to the specific area of origin of the black patch.

ANALYSIS: Then the next casting was made. Consequence? *No black patch*. It was found that this same procedure would repeatedly identify areas in other molds which needed redressing to prevent black oxidized patches.

4-4 Summary

The basic logic and method of this study are important. Repeat observations on selected single units of your process will demonstrate one of two things: either the performance of the unit will repeat; or, it will not.

It was established in this case history that the black patches came repeatedly from specific geometric areas within molds. The reason for the problem was thus unrelated to contaminants or other metallurgical properties of aluminum pigs, or to distances or relationships to the furnace or windows and walls. Temperature differences within a mold could have been a possible explanation. Being present and able to inspect the first mold illustrates the importance of the previously stated Principle 2.

It is not always that the correction of a process can be identified so readily; but the opportunity was provided for simple data to suggest ideas. In this case history, the retreatment of molds provided a complete solution to the problem.

■ In some studies, the purpose of data collection is to provide organized information on relationships between variables. In many other instances, such as this one, the purpose is simply to find ways to eliminate a serious problem; the data themselves or a formal analysis of them are of little or no interest. It was the logic and informal analysis which was effective.

■ In troubleshooting and process improvement studies, we can plan programs of data acquisition which offer opportunities for detecting types of important differences and repeat performances. The opportunity to notice possible differences or relations, such as the location of black patches and their origin within molds, comes much more surely to one who watches "data in the process of acquisition" than to one sitting comfortably in an office chair.

These ideas will be extended in subsequent case histories.

5
Troubleshooting
with Attribute Data

5-1 Introduction

Perhaps the presence of an assignable cause has been signaled by a control chart. Or perhaps it is known that there are too many rejects, too much rework, or too many stoppages. These are important attribute problems. Perhaps organized studies are needed to determine which of several factors—materials, operators, machines, vendors, processings—have important effects upon quality characteristics. In this chapter, methods of analysis are discussed with respect to the quality characteristics of an attribute nature.

Not much has been written about process improvement and troubleshooting of quality characteristics of an attribute nature. Yet in almost every industrial process there are important problems where the economically important characteristics of the product are attributes: an electric light bulb will give light or it will not; an alarm clock will or will not ring; the life of a battery is or is not below standard. There are times when it is expedient to gage a quality characteristic (go no-go) even though it is possible to measure its characteristic as a variable. This chapter discusses some effective *designed studies* using enumerative or attribute data and methods of analysis and interpretation of resulting data.

Explanations of *why* a process is in trouble are often based on subjective judgment. How can we proceed to get objective evidence in the face of all plausable stories as to why this is not the time or place to get it? Data of attribute type often imply the possibility of personal carelessness. Not everyone understands that perfection is unattainable; a certain onus usually attaches to imperfection. Thus it is important to find ways of enlisting the active support and participation of the department supervisors, the mechanics, and possibly some of the operators. This will require initiative and ingenuity.

In many plants, little is known about differences in machine performance. Just as two autos of the same design may perform differently, so do two or three machines of the same make. Or, a slight difference in a hand operation which is not noticed (or is considered to be inconsequential) may have an important effect on the final performance of a kitchen mixer or a nickel-cadmium battery. Experience indicates that there will be important differences in as few as two or three machines; or in a like number of operators, shifts, or days. Several case histories are presented in this chapter to illustrate important principles of investigation. In each, it is the intent to find *areas of differences*. Independent variables or factors are often chosen to be block-type variables.[1] Once the presence and localized nature of important differences are identified, ways can usually be found by engineers or production personnel to improve operations.

Data from the case histories have been presented in graphical form for a variety of reasons. One compelling reason is that the experiment or study is valuable only when persons in a position to make use of the results are convinced that the conclusions are sensible. These persons have had long familiarity and understanding of graphical presentations; they respond favorably to them. Another reason is that the graphical form shows relationships and *suggests possibilities* of importance not otherwise recognized.

5-2   Ideas from Sequences of Observations over Time

The methods of Chap. 2 are applicable to sequences of attribute data as well as to variables data. Control charts with control limits, runs above and below the median; these procedures suggest ideas about the presence and nature of unusual performance. As each successive point is obtained and plotted, the chart is watched for evidence of economically important assignable causes in the process even while it is operating under conditions considered to be stable.[2]

If the process is stable (in statistical control), each new point is expected to fall within the control limits. Suppose the new point falls outside the established 3-sigma control limits. Since this is a very improbable event

---

[1] See Chap. 4.
[2] See Chap. 3.

when the process is actually stable, such an occurrence is recognized as a signal that *some* change has occurred in the process. We investigate the process to establish the nature of the assignable cause. The risk of an unwarranted investigation from such a signal is very small—about three in a thousand.

In troubleshooting, it is often important to make an investigation of the process with a somewhat greater chance (*risk*) of an unwarranted investigation than three in a thousand; lines drawn at $\bar{p} \pm 2\hat{\sigma}_p$ will be more sensitive to the presence of assignable causes. A somewhat larger risk of making an unwarranted investigation of the process is associated with a point outside 2-sigma limits; it is about one chance in 20 (about a 5% risk). *However, there is now a smaller risk (β) of missing an important opportunity to investigate,* especially important in a process-improvement study.

5-3   Decision[1] Lines Applicable to k Points Simultaneously

Introduction

When each point on a Shewhart control chart is *not* appraised at the time it is plotted for a possible shift in process average, there is a conceptual difference in probabilities to consider. For example, consider decision lines drawn at $\bar{p} \pm 2\hat{\sigma}_p$. The risk associated with them is indeed about 5% if we apply them as criteria to a single point just observed. But if applied to an *accumulated* set of 20 points, about one out of twenty is expected to be outside of them even when there has been no change in the process. Evidently then, decision lines to study $k = 20$ points simultaneously, with a 5% risk of unnecessary investigation, must be at *some* distance beyond $\bar{p} \pm 2\hat{\sigma}_p$.

Troubleshooting is usually interested in whether one or more sources—perhaps machines, operators, shifts, or days—can be identified as performing significantly differently from the average of the group of k sources. The analysis will be over the k *sources simultaneously*, with risk α.

In the examples and case histories considered here, the data to be analyzed will not usually relate to a previously established standard. For example, the data of Case History 5-1 represent the percent of rejects from 11 different spot-welding machine-operator combinations. In this *typical* troubleshooting Case History, there is *no given standard* to use as a basis for comparison of the 11 machine-operator combinations. They will be compared to their own group average.

---

[1] Even one point outside *decision lines* will be evidence of nonrandomness among a set of k points being considered simultaneously. Some persons prefer to use the term "control limits." Many practitioners feel strongly that only those lines drawn at ± 3 sigma about the average should be called control limits. At any rate, we shall use the term *decision lines* in the sense defined above.

Data in Fig. 5-1, pertaining to the percent winners in horse racing, are basically a different type; *there is a given standard.* If track position is not important, then it is expected that one-eighth of all races will be won in each of the eight positions.

This graphical analysis of k groups simultaneously is called the *analysis of means*[1] and is abbreviated ANOM.

Probabilities Associated with k · Comparisons, Standard Given[2]

Values of a factor Z_α to provide proper limits are given in Table 5-1 (or A-7) for values of $\alpha = 10\%, 5\%$, and 1%. *Upper and lower decision lines* to judge the extent of maximum expected random variation of points about a given group standard $\bar{p}$, or percent defective $\bar{P}$, of k samples are:

$$\text{UDL}(\alpha) = \bar{p} + Z_\alpha \hat{\sigma}_P \qquad \text{UDL}(\alpha) = \bar{P} + Z_\alpha \hat{\sigma}_P$$
$$\text{LDL}(\alpha) = \bar{p} - Z_\alpha \hat{\sigma}_P \qquad \text{LDL}(\alpha) = \bar{P} - Z_\alpha \hat{\sigma}_P \tag{5-1}$$

If even one of the k points falls outside these decision lines, it indicates (statistically) different behavior from the overall group average.

The following derivation of entries in Tables A-7 and 5-1 may help the reader understand the problem involved in analyzing sets of data. The analysis assumes that samples of size n are drawn from a process whose known average is $\bar{p}$; *and* n and $\bar{p}$ are such that the distribution of p_i in samples of size n is essentially normal. (Approximately, $n\bar{p} > 4$ or 5; see Eq. (3-3) Chap. 3.) We now propose to select k independent random samples of n each from the process and consider all k values p_i simultaneously. Within what interval

$$\bar{p} - Z_\alpha \hat{\sigma}_p \qquad \text{and} \qquad \bar{p} + Z_\alpha \hat{\sigma}_p$$

will all k sample fractions p_i lie, with risk α or confidence $(1 - \alpha)$?

Appropriate values of Z_α, corresponding to selected levels α and the above assumptions, can be derived as follows. Let Pr represent the unknown probability that any *one* sample p_i from the process will lie between the lines to be drawn from Eq. (5-1). Then the probability that *all* k of the sample p_i will lie within the interval in (5-1) is Pr^k. If at least one point lies outside these decision lines, this is to be evidence of *nonrandom variability* of the k samples; that is, some of the sample p_i are different, risk α. The value of Z_α can be computed as follows: set

$$\text{Pr}^k = 1 - \alpha \tag{5-2}$$

[1] Ellis R. Ott and Sidney S. Lewis: Analysis of Means Applied to Per-Cent Defective Data, *Rutgers Stat. Cent. Tech. Rep. no. 2*, Prepared for Army, Navy and Air Force under Contract NONR 404(11), (Task NP 042–21) with the Office of Naval Research, February 10, 1960. Ellis R. Ott, Analysis of Means—A Graphical Procedure, *Ind. Qual. Control*, vol. 24, no. 2, pp. 101–109, August, 1967. (Reproduced with permission of the editor of Industrial Quality Control.) Also see Chaps. 11, 12, and 13.

[2] The material in this section is very important; however, it can be omitted without seriously affecting the understanding of subsequent sections.

Then, corresponding to the value of Pr found from this equation, Z_α is determined from Table A-1. Values of Z_α found via Eq. (5-2) are shown in Table 5-1 for $\alpha = .10, .05, .01$, and selected values of k.

TABLE 5-1 Nonrandom Variability

Standard given; df $= \infty$; See also Table A-7

k	$Z_{.10}$	$Z_{.05}$	$Z_{.01}$
1	1.64	1.96	2.58
2	1.96	2.24	2.81
3	2.11	2.39	2.93
4	2.23	2.49	3.02
5	2.31	2.57	3.09
6	2.38	2.63	3.14
7	2.43	2.68	3.19
8	2.48	2.73	3.22
9	2.52	2.77	3.26
10	2.56	2.80	3.29
15	2.70	2.93	3.40
20	2.79	3.02	3.48
24	2.85	3.07	3.53
30	2.92	3.14	3.59
50	3.08	3.28	3.72
120	3.33	3.52	3.93

Numerical Example

Compute $Z_{.05}$ in Table 5-1 for $k = 3$:

$$Pr^3 = 0.95$$
$$\log Pr = (1/3) \log (.95)$$
$$= 9.99257 - 10$$

and
$$Pr = 0.98304$$

From Appendix Table A-1, we find that corresponding decision lines drawn at $\bar{p} \pm Z_{.05} \hat{\sigma}_p$ require that $Z_{.05} = 2.39$.

Note 1: When lines are drawn at $\bar{p} \pm 2\sigma$ about the central line, it is commonly believed that a point outside these limits is an indication of an assignable cause with risk about 5%. The risk on an established control chart of a stable process is indeed about 5% if we apply the criterion to a single point just observed; but if applied, for example, to 10 points simultaneously, the probability of at least 1 point of the 10 falling outside 2-sigma limits by chance is

$$1 - (0.954)^{10} = 1 - 0.624 = 0.376$$

That is, if many sets of 10 points from a stable process are plotted with the usual 2-sigma limits, over one-third of the sets (37.6%) are expected to have one or more points outside those limits.   This is seldom recognized.

Also just for interest, what about 3-sigma limits? If many sets of 30 points from a stable process are plotted with usual 3-sigma limits, then

$$1 - (.9973)^{30} = 1 - 0.922 \text{ or } 7.8\%$$

of the sets are expected to have one or more points outside those limits.

Conversely, in order to provide a 5% risk for a set of 10 points considered as a group, limits must be drawn at

$$\pm Z_{.05}\hat{\sigma} = \pm 2.80\hat{\sigma}$$

as shown in Table 5-1.

Note 2:   Or consider an accumulated set of 20 means ($k = 20$).   About one out of twenty is expected to be outside the lines drawn at $\bar{p} \pm 2\hat{\sigma}_p$. Consequently, decision lines to study 20 groups simultaneously must be at some distance beyond $\bar{p} \pm 2\hat{\sigma}_p$.   Table 5-1 shows that the lines should be drawn at

$$\bar{p} \pm 3.02\hat{\sigma}_p \qquad \text{for } \alpha = .05$$

and at
$$\bar{p} \pm 3.48\hat{\sigma}_p \qquad \text{for } \alpha = .01$$

EXAMPLE 5-1:   Consider the following intriguing problem offered by Siegel[1]: "Does the post position on a circular track have any influence on the winner of a horserace?"

Data on post positions of the winners in 144 eight-horse fields were collected from the daily newspapers.   Position 1 is that nearest the inside rail.

TABLE 5-2   Winners at Different Post Positions

Post position:	1	2	3	4	5	6	7	8	Total
No. of winners:	29	19	18	25	17	10	15	11	144
Percent:	20.1	13.2	12.5	17.3	11.8	7.0	10.4	7.7	$\bar{P} = 12.5\%$

The calculations for an analysis of means (ANOM) with *standard given* and $\bar{p} = 1/8 = .125$ follows

$$\hat{\sigma}_p = \sqrt{\frac{(.125)(.875)}{144}} = .0275$$

[1] S. Siegel, *Nonparametric Statistics for the Behavioral Sciences*, pp. 45–46, McGraw-Hill Book Company, New York, 1956.

For[1] $k = 7$, we have $Z_{.05} = 2.68$ and $Z_{.01} = 3.19$.   The decision limits are:

Risk	LCL	UCL
.05	.051	.199
.01	.037	.213

These have been drawn in Fig. 5-1 following certain conventions:
1.   The sample size, $n = 144$, is written in the upper-left corner of the chart.
2.   The risks, .05 and .01, are shown at the end of the decision lines.
3.   The points corresponding to the eight post positions are connected by a dotted line in order to recognize comparisons better.
4.   The values of the decision lines are written adjacent to them.

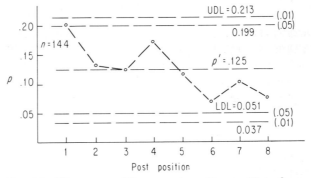

Fig. 5-1 Winners at different post positions. (Data from Table 5-2.)

DISCUSSION: The point corresponding to post position 1 is between the (.05) and (.01) upper lines[2]; this indicates that position 1 has a better than average chance of producing a winner ($\alpha < .05$).   Figure 5-1 supports what might have been predicted: if positions have any effect, the best position would surely be that one nearest the rail, and the worst would be near the outside.   Not only does the graph show position 1 in a favored light, it also indicates a general downward trend in the winners starting from the inside post positions.   (There is not enough evidence to support, conclusively, the possibility that position 4 is superior to positions 2 and 3.   There seems little choice among positions 6, 7, and 8.)

Factors to Use in Making k Comparisons, No Standard Given

Factors for *standard given* were obtained easily in the preceding section. However, situations where they can be used in solving production problems seldom occur.   In the great majority of troubleshooting situations, there is

---

[1] Although there are eight positions, there are only seven *independent* positions.   (When any seven of the p_i are known, the eighth is also known.)   We enter Table 5-1 with $k = 7$. It is evident that the decision is not affected whether $k = 7$ or $k = 8$ is used.   This situation seldom if ever arises in a production application.

[2] The author's chi-square analysis of this data also indicates that there is a significant difference between positions with a risk between .05 and .01.

no standard given; but it is very useful to compare individual performances with the *overall average group performance*.

The comparison procedure used here is called analysis of means, *no standard given*. The procedure is outlined in Table 5-3 and illustrated in several case

---

TABLE 5-3   Analysis of Means, Attribute Data, One Independent Variable

---

STEP 1:   Obtain a sample of n_i items from each of k sources and inspect each sample. (It is preferable to have all n_i equal.)   Let the number of defective or nonconforming units in the k samples be $d_1, d_2, \ldots, d_k$, respectively.

STEP 2:   Compute the fraction or percent defective of each sample.

$$p_i = d_i/n_i \qquad P_i = 100 d_i/n_i$$

STEP 3:   Plot the points corresponding to the k values, p_i or P_i.

STEP 4:   Compute the grand average $\bar{p}$ or $\bar{P}$ and plot it as a line:

$$\bar{p} = \sum d_i / \sum n_i \qquad \bar{P} = 100 \sum d_i / \sum n_i$$

STEP 5:   Compute a standard deviation, using average $\bar{n}$ initially if there is variation in sample size.

$$\hat{\sigma}_p = \sqrt{\frac{\bar{p}(1 - \bar{p})}{\bar{n}}} \qquad \hat{\sigma}_P = \sqrt{\frac{\bar{P}(100 - \bar{P})}{\bar{n}}}$$

STEP 6:   From Table 5-4 or Appendix Table A-8, obtain the value of H_α corresponding to k and α.   Draw decision lines:

$$\text{UDL: } \bar{p} + H_\alpha \hat{\sigma}_p \qquad \bar{P} + H_\alpha \hat{\sigma}_P$$
$$\text{LDL: } \bar{p} - H_\alpha \hat{\sigma}_p \qquad \bar{P} - H_\alpha \hat{\sigma}_P$$

STEP 7:   Accept the presence of statistically significant differences (assignable causes) indicated by points above UDL and/or below LDL with risk α.   Otherwise accept the hypothesis of randomness of the k means (i.e., no statistically significant differences).

STEP 8:   Process improvement: consider ways of identifying the nature of and reasons for significant differences.

---

histories.   Factors, designated by H_α, provide *decision lines* for the important case of *no standard given*

$$\bar{p} \pm H_\alpha \hat{\sigma}_p \qquad \text{or} \qquad \bar{P} \pm H_\alpha \hat{\sigma}_P$$

when analyzing attribute data, or

$$\bar{X} \pm H_\alpha \sigma_{\bar{x}}$$

when analyzing variables data are needed.   The computation of H_α is much more difficult than the earlier computation of Z_α.   References are given to their derivation.[1]   Some factors H_α to use when analyzing attribute data which is reasonably normal are given in Table 5-4.[2]

When n and p do not permit the assumption of normality, a method of computing the exact probability of a percent defective to exceed a specified value is possible.[3]

TABLE 5-4   Analysis of Means: No Standard Given; df $= \infty$

Comparing k Groups with Their Group Average: (Especially for Use with Attribute Data) $\bar{P} \pm H_\alpha \hat{\sigma}_{\bar{P}}$; $\bar{X} \pm H_\alpha \hat{\sigma}_{\bar{x}}$. (See also Table A-8 for df $= \infty$).

$k = $ no. of groups	$H_{.10}$	$H_{.05}$	$H_{.01}$
2	1.16	1.39	1.82
3	1.74	1.93	2.39
4	1.94	2.15	2.61
5	2.08	2.29	2.76
6	2.19	2.40	2.87
7	2.27	2.49	2.95
8	2.34	2.55	3.02
9	2.39	2.61	3.07
10	2.44	2.65	3.12
15	2.62	2.82	3.29
20	2.74	2.94	3.39
30	2.89	3.08	3.53
40	2.99	3.19	3.62
60	3.12	3.31	3.73

[1] Ellis R. Ott, Analysis of Means, *Rutgers Tech. Rep. no. 1*, Aug. 10, 1958.   Prepared for Army, Navy, and Air Force under Contract NONR 404(11) (Task NR 042-021) with the Office of Naval Research.   Ellis R. Ott, Analysis of Means—A Graphical Procedure, *Ind. Qual. Control*, vol. 24, no. 2, pp. 101–109, August, 1967.   The values of H_α in Tables 5-4 and Appendix A-8 are the averages of the upper and lower bounds in the table of M. Halperin, S. W. Greenhouse, J. Cornfield, and J. Zalokar: Tables of Percentage Points for the Studentized Maximum Absolute Deviate in Normal Samples, *J. Amer. Stat. Ass.*, pp. 185–195, vol. 50, 1955.   The authors surmise that the true value is closer to the lower value than to the upper one; the average of the two then seems a logical choice especially in process improvement studies.   Readers interested in the derivation and theory associated with these factors and their applications are referred to parts I and III of the excellent series by Dr. Edward G. Schilling, A Systematic Approach to the Analysis of Means, *J. Qual. Technol.*, pt. I, vol. 5, no. 3, pp. 93–108, July, 1973; and pts. II and III, vol. 5, no. 4, pp. 147–159, October, 1973.   Also Lloyd S. Nelson, Factors for the Analysis of Means, *J. Qual. Technol.*, vol. 6, no. 4, pp. 175–181, October, 1974.

[2] The binomial distribution is reasonably normal for those values of np and nq greater than 5 or 6 and p and q are greater than say 5 %.   See Eq. (3-3).

[3] Sidney S. Lewis, Analysis of Means applied to percent defective data, *Proc. Rutgers All-Day Conf. Qual. Control*, 1958.

The following notes pertain either to the use of ANOM or to an under-standing of the procedures.

Note 1:   The procedures for p_i and P_i can be combined easily as in Fig. 5-2.   Simply compute UDL and LDL using percents, for example, and indicate the percent scale P on one of the vertical scales (the left one in Fig. 5-2). Then mark the fraction scale p on the other vertical scale.

Note 2:   Values of H_α are given in Tables A-8 and 5-4 for three risks. We shall frequently draw both sets of decision lines expecting to bracket some of the points.   (These three levels are to be considered as convenient reference values and not strict bases for decisions.)   A risk of somewhat more than 5 % is often a sensible procedure.

Note 3:   When $k = 2$, and the assumption of normality is reasonable, the comparison of the two values of p is just "Student's t test."[1]   Values of H_α corresponding to $k = 2$ are

$$H_\alpha = \frac{\sqrt{2}\,t_\alpha}{2}$$

where t_α is from a two-tailed t table corresponding to df $= \infty$.   Thus the ANOM, for $k = 2$, is simply a graphical t *test*, with df $= \infty$.

In Case History 5-2, as in the previous Example 5-1, the prior author also used a chi-square analysis.   His conclusion regarding the question of statistical significance of the data agrees with that of ANOM.   It may be helpful to some readers to explain that ANOM is one alternative to a chi-square analysis.   A chi-square analysis is not as sensitive as ANOM to the deviation of one or two sources from average, or to trends and other order character-istics.   A chi-square analysis is more sensitive to overall variation of k responses.   The ANOM is very helpful to the scientist and engineer in identifying specific sources of differences, the magnitude of differences, and is a graphical presentation with all its benefits.

5-4   Introduction to Case Histories

The mechanics of ANOM using attribute data are used in the following case histories.   Whatever analysis is used when analyzing data in a trouble-shooting or process-improvement project is important only as it helps in finding avenues to improvement.   Any analysis is incidental to the overall procedure of approaching a problem in production.   The case histories have been chosen to represent applications to different types of processes and products.   They have been classified below according to the number of inde-pendent variables employed, where independent variables are to be interpreted as discussed in Sec. 4-2.

The planned procedures for obtaining data in Secs. 5-5, 5-6, 5-7, and 5-8

[1] See Sec. 11-4.

are especially useful throughout industry; yet there is little organized information published on the subject.

Many of the ideas presented here are applied also to variables data in Chaps. 11, 12, and 13.

Outline of Case Histories (CH) which follow in this chapter

5-5   One Independent Variable with k Factors

CASE HISTORY 5-1   Spot-welding Electronic Assemblies[1]

Excessive rejections were occurring in the mount assembly of a certain type of electronic tube. Several hundreds of these mounts were being produced daily by operators, each using her own spot-welding machine. The mount assemblies were inspected in a different area of the plant, and it was difficult to identify the source of welding trouble.[2]

The department forelady believed that the trouble was caused by substandard components delivered to her department; an oxide coating was extending too far down on one component. In fact, there was evidence to support her view. The foreman of the preceding operation agreed that the components he was sending her were below standard. Even so, whenever any operation with as many as three or four operator-machine combinations is in trouble, a special short investigation is worthwhile. This is true even when the source of trouble is accepted to be elsewhere.

This example discusses a straightforward approach to the type of problem

[1] Ellis R. Ott, Trouble-Shooting, *Ind. Qual. Control, Practical Aids*, vol. 11, no. 9, June, 1955.

[2] In regular production, each operator was assigned to one specific welding machine. No attempt was made in this first study to separate the effects of the operators from those of the machines.

described above.   It is characterized by (1) the production of a product which can be classified only as "satisfactory" or "unsatisfactory," with (2) several different operators, machines, heads on a machine, or jigs and fixtures all doing the same operation.   The procedure is to select in a carefully planned program small samples of the product for a *special study*, inspecting each one carefully, and recording these sample inspection data for careful analysis.   Experience has shown that these small samples, obtained in a well-planned manner and examined carefully, usually provide more useful information for corrective action than information obtained from 100 percent inspection.

COLLECTING DATA

An inspector was assigned by the forelady to obtain five mounts (randomly) from each operator-welder combination at approximately hourly intervals for two days; then $n = (8)(2)(5) = 80$.   Each weld was inspected immediately, and a record of each type of weld defect was recorded by operator welder on a special record form.   Over the two-day period of the study,

TABLE 5-5   Welding Rejects by Operator Machine (Samples of $n = 80$)

Operator	No.	Percent
A	3	3.75
B	6	7.5
C	8	10.0
D	14	17.5
E	6	7.5
F	1	1.25
G	8	10.0
H	1	1.25
I	8	10.0
J	10	12.5
K	1	1.25

$\Sigma = 66$

$p = 66/880 = .075$

$P = 7.5\%$

$$\hat{\sigma} = \sqrt{\frac{(7.5)(92.5)}{80}} = 2.94\%$$

Decision line: $\alpha = .05$, $k = 11$

$\text{UDL} = 7.5\% + (2.68)(2.94)$

$\quad\quad = 15.4\%$

records were obtained on 11 different operator welders: the percent defective from these eleven combinations, labeled A, B, C, ..., K, have been plotted in Fig. 5-2. The average percent of weld rejects for the entire group for the two-day study was $\bar{p} = \frac{66}{880} = 0.075$ or $P = 7.5\%$; this was just about the rate during recent production.

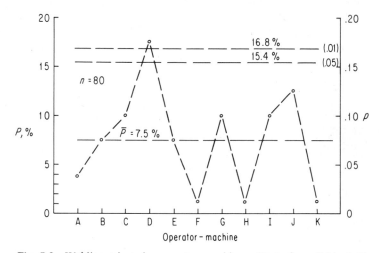

Fig. 5-2 Welding rejects by operator machine. (Data from Table 5-5.)

DISCUSSION

Several different factors could have introduced trouble into this spot-welding operation. One factor was substandard components, as some believed. But were there also differences among spot welders, operators, or such factors as the time of day (fatigue), or the day of the week? Did some operators need training? Did some machines need maintenance? We chose to study a combination of operators each with her own regular machine; the forelady decided to get data from 11 of them.

When we had the data, we plotted it and computed decision lines in Fig. 5-2. Combination D exceeded the upper limit ($\alpha = .01$); three combinations F, H, and K were "low." In discussing these four operators, the forelady assured us without any hesitation that:

- Operator D was both "slow and careless."
- Operator F was very fast and also very careful, and it was her frequent practice to *repeat* a weld.
- Operator H was slow, but careful.
- Operator K was one about whom she knew little because she was not a regular.

CONCLUSION

Pooling the attribute information from small samples (of five per hour over a two-day period) indicated the existence of important differences in operator-welder combinations. These differences were independent of the quality of components being delivered to the department. Efforts to improve the troublesome spraying oxide coating in the preceding department should be continued, of course.

These observed differences in welding suggest also:

1.   Combinations *F, H,* and *K* should be watched for clues to their successful techniques in the hope that they can then be taught to others.

2.   Combination *D* should be watched to check the forelady's unfavorable impression of her.

3.   Also the desirability of studying the effect of repeat welding at subsequent stages in the manufacturing process should be studied. This may be an improvement at the welding stage; but its effect on through the assembly needs assessment.

CASE HISTORY 5-2   A Corrosion Problem with Metal Containers[1]

The effects of copper on the corrosion of metal containers was studied by adding copper in three concentrations. After being stored for a time, the containers were examined for failures of a certain type. The data are summarized in Table 5-6 and plotted in Fig. 5-3. The large increase in defectives

TABLE 5-6   Effect of Copper on Corrosion

Level of copper, ppm	Containers examined, n	failures, d_i	Fraction failing	Percent failing
5	80	14	$p_i = .175$	17.5
10	80	36	$p_2 = .450$	45.0
15	80	47	$p_3 = .588$	58.8
Totals	240	$\bar{p} = 97/240$	$= .404$	$\bar{P} = 40.4\%$

is very suggestive that an increase in parts per million (ppm) of copper produces a large increase in failures. The increase is significant both economically and statistically.

FORMAL ANALYSIS: *ANOM*

$$\hat{\sigma}_P = \sqrt{\frac{\bar{P}(100 - \bar{P})}{n}} = 5.5\% \quad \text{for } \bar{P} = 40.4\%$$
$$n = 80$$

[1] H. C. Batson, Applications of Factorial Chi-Square Analysis to Experiments in Chemistry, *Trans. Amer. Soc. Qual. Control,* pp. 9–23, 1956.

For $k = 3$ and $\alpha = .01$, Table A-8 gives $H_{.01} = 2.39$.   Then

$$\bar{P} \pm H_{.01}\hat{\sigma}_P = 40.4 \pm (2.39)(5.5)$$
$$UDL(.01) = 53.5\%$$
and
$$LDL(.01) = 27.3\%$$

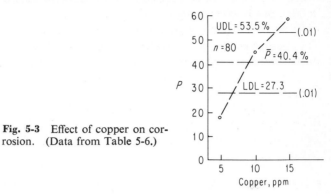

Fig. 5-3   Effect of copper on corrosion.   (Data from Table 5-6.)

One point is below the LDL; one point is above the UDL.   There is no advantage in computing decision lines for $\alpha = .05$.

Whether the suggested trend is actually linear will not be discussed here, but if we assume that it is linear, the increase in rejections per ppm from 5 to 15 ppm is

$$Average\ increase = \frac{58.8\% - 17.5\%}{10} = 4.13\% \text{ per ppm}$$

This was considered a very important change.

CASE HISTORY 5-3   End Breaks in Spinning Cotton Yarn[1]

THE PROBLEM: An excessive number of breaks in spinning cotton yarn was being experienced in a textile mill.   It was decided to make an initial study on a sample of eight frames to determine whether there were any essential differences in their behavior.   Rather than take all the observations at one time, it was decided to use random time intervals of 15 min until data were on hand for ten such intervals on each of the eight frames.

Each frame contained 176 spindles.   As soon as a break occurred on a spindle, the broken ends were connected or "pieced" together and spinning resumed on that spindle.   (The remaining 175 spindles continued to spin during the repair of a spindle.)   Thus the number of end breaks during any 15-min interval is theoretically unlimited, but we know from experience that it is "small" during ordinary production.

[1] Dr. Sundari Vaswani and Ellis R. Ott, Statistical Aids in Locating Machine Differences, *Ind. Qual. Control*, vol. 11, no. 1, July, 1954.

The selection of a 15-min interval was an arbitrary decision for the initial study.   Similarly, it was decided to include eight frames in the initial study.

The number of end breaks observed in 15 min per frame is shown in Table 5-7 and in Fig. 5-4.

CONCLUSIONS: It is apparent that there is an appreciable difference between frames.   Those with averages outside of the (.01) decision lines are:

Excessive breaks: frames 5 and 8

Few breaks: frames 2, 3, and 7

The analysis using circles and triangles in Table 5-7 given in analysis 1 below, provides some insight into the performance of the frames.

ANALYSIS 1:   *a "quick analysis"*

The average number of breaks per time interval is $\bar{c} = \overline{np} = 13.54$.   Then for a Poisson distribution (Sec. 3-4)

$$\hat{\sigma}_{np} = \sqrt{13.54} = 3.68$$

for individual entries in Table 5-7.   Let us consider behavior at $\bar{c} \pm 2\sigma$ level since we are interested in detecting possible sources of trouble:

$$13.54 + 2(3.68) = 20.90 \text{ (figures in circles)}[1]$$
$$13.54 - 2(3.68) = 6.18 \text{ (figures in triangles)}[1]$$

TABLE 5-7   End Breaks during Spinning Cotton Yarn

Sample no.	Frame no. 1	2	3	4	5	6	7	8	Total
1	13	7	(22)	15	20	(23)	15	14	129
2	18	10	7	12	19	17	18	(22)	123
3	8	8	(21)	14	15	16	8	8	98
4	13	12	8	10	(23)	/3\	12	20	101
5	12	/6\	9	(27)	(32)	/4\	9	18	117
6	/6\	/6\	/6\	17	(34)	12	/1\	(24)	106
7	16	20	/5\	9	8	17	7	(21)	103
8	(21)	9	/2\	13	10	14	7	17	93
9	17	14	9	(24)	(21)	8	/6\	(33)	132
10	16	7	7	10	14	10	/6\	11	81
Frame Avg.	14.0	9.9	9.6	15.1	19.6	12.4	8.9	18.8	Grand Avg. = 13.54

[1] In practice, we use two colored pencils.   This analysis is a form of NL gaging; see Chap. 7.

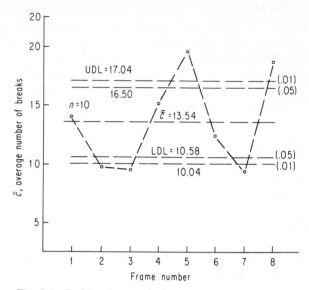

Fig. 5-4   End breaks on spinning frames.

CONCLUSIONS: A visual inspection of the individuals so marked suggests:

1.   Frames 4, 5, and 8 are suspiciously bad since there are circles in each column and no triangles.

2.   Frames 2 and 7 look good; there are at least two triangles in each and no circles.   (Frame 3 shows excellent performance except for the two circled readings early in the study.)

ANALYSIS 2:   *ANOM.   The mechanics to obtain decision lines in Fig.* 5-4

Each frame average is of $n = 10$ individual observations.   In order to compare them to their own group average, we compute

$$\hat{\sigma}_{\bar{c}} = \hat{\sigma}/\sqrt{n} = 3.68/\sqrt{10} = 1.16$$

From Table A-8[1], values of H_{α} for $k = 8$ are: $H_{.05} = 2.55$ and $H_{.01} = 3.02$. *Then for* $\alpha = .05$

$$UDL(.05) = 13.54 + 2.55(1.16) = 16.50$$
$$LDL(.05) = 13.54 - 2.55(1.16) = 10.58$$

and for $\alpha = .01$

$$UDL(.01) = 17.04$$
$$LDL(.01) = 10.04$$

---

[1] The individual observations are considered to be of Poisson type; this is somewhat skewed with a longer tail to the right.   However, averages of as few as four such terms are essentially normally distributed.   Consequently, it is proper to use Table A-8; see Theorem 3, Chap. 1.

A further comment: Other proper methods of analyzing the data of Table 5-7 include chi-square and analysis of variance.   Each of them indicates non-randomness of frame performance; they need to be supplemented to indicate specific presses giving different behavior and the magnitude of that behavior difference.

PROCESS ACTION RESULTING FROM STUDY.   As a result of this initial study, an investigation was conducted on frames 5 and 8 which revealed, among other things, defective roller coverings and settings.   Corrective action resulted in a reduction in their average breaks to 11.8 and 8, respectively; a reduction of about 50%.   A study of reasons for better performance of frames 2, 3, and 7 was continued to find ways to make similar improvements in other frames in the factory.

CASE HISTORY 5-4   An Experience with a Bottle Capper

This capper has eight rotating heads.   Each head has an automatic adjustable chuck designed to apply a designated torque.   Too low a torque may produce a *leaker*; too high a torque may break the plastic cap or even the bottle.

It is always wise to talk to line operators and supervisors: "Any problem with broken caps?"   "Yes," she answered, "quality control has specified a high torque, and this is causing quite a lot of breakage."   After watching

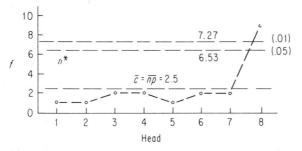

Fig. 5-5 Cap breakage at different heads.   Actual value of n is unknown, but 50 is a guess.

the capper a few minutes, a simple tally of the number of broken caps from each head was made.   (See Table 5-8.)

Head 8 is evidently breaking almost as many caps as all others combined (see formal analysis below).   Too high a torque specification?   Or inadequate adjustment on head 8?   The answer is obviously the latter.   In theory, broken caps may be a consequence of the capper, the caps, or the bottles. It is human nature to attribute the cause to "things beyond my responsibility."

TABLE 5-8   Plastic Caps Breaking at the Capper

Head no.	f(Number broken)
1	1
2	1
3	2
4	2
5	1
6	2
7	2
8	9

DISCUSSION: If there had been no significant differences between heads, what then?

1.   How many cavities are in the bottle mold?   Probably four or eight. Let us hold out (collect) 20 or 30 broken-capped bottles and check the mold numbers of the bottles which are (or should be) printed during molding. Often, the great majority of defectives will be from one or two bottle molds, or

2.   How many cavities are producing caps?   Probably 8 or 16.   Let us take the same 20 or 30 broken-capped bottles and check the cavity numbers of the caps (also printed at molding).   It is not unusual to find a few bottle-cap cavities responsible for a preponderance of broken caps.

FORMAL ANALYSIS: The *number* of breaks on each head is known for the period of observation.   Opportunity for breaks was "large," but the incidence was "small" (see Sec. 3-4); a Poisson distribution is a reasonable assumption.

$$\bar{c} = \overline{np} = 20/8 = 2.5; \hat{\sigma} = \sqrt{2.5} = 1.58$$
$$H_{.05} = 2.55 \text{ for } k = 8$$

Then

$$\text{UDL}(.05) = \overline{np} + H_{.05}\,\hat{\sigma} = 2.5 + 4.03 = 6.53$$

Also, $\text{UDL}(.01) = 7.27$

CONCLUSION: The point corresponding to head 8 is above UDL(.01); this simply supports the intuitive visual analysis that head 8 is out of adjustment.

5-6   Two Independent Variables

Introduction

Our emphasis here and elsewhere will be upon planning and analyzing data from studies to identify *sources* of trouble; engineering and production personnel then use information from them to reduce that trouble.   The ideas presented in Chap. 4 will be illustrated in these discussions. In particular, *block-type* independent variables will be used frequently. Troubleshooting can usually be improved by *data collection plans* which employ more than one independent variable. Such plans speed up the process of finding the sources of trouble with little or no extra effort. This Sec. 5-6 will consider the important and versatile case of *two independent variables*; Sec. 5-7 the case of *three independent* variables.

When using temperatures of 100°, 120°, 140°, for example, it is said that the independent variable (temperature) has been used at three *levels*. Similarly, if a study considers three machines and two shifts, it is said that the study considers machines at three *levels* and shifts at two *levels*.

Consider a study planned to obtain data at a levels of variable A and b levels of variable B. When data from every one of the $(a \cdot b)$ possible combinations is obtained, the plan is called a *factorial design*. When A and B are each at *two* levels, there are $2^2 = 4$ possible combinations; the design is called a 2^2 factorial (two-squared factorial). They are very effective and used frequently.

Two Independent Variables: A 2^2 Factorial Design

This procedure will be illustrated by Case History 5-5; then the analysis will be discussed.

CASE HISTORY 5-5   Comparing Effects of Operators and Jigs in a Glass-beading Jig Assembly (Cathode-ray Guns)

Regular daily inspection records were being kept on twelve different hand-operated glass-beading jigs. The records indicated that there were appreciable differences in the number of rejects from different jigs although parts in use came from a common source. It was not possible to determine whether the differences were attributable to jigs or operators without a special study. There was conflicting evidence, as usual. For example, one jig had just been overhauled and adjusted; yet it was producing more rejects than the departmental average. Consequently, its operator (Harry) was considered to be the problem.

The production foreman, the production engineer, and the quality control engineer arranged an interchange of the operator of the recently overhauled jig with an operator from another jig to get some initial information. From the recent production, prior to interchange, fifty units from each operator were examined for two quality characteristics: (1) *alignment* of parts, and (2) *spacing* of parts. The results for alignment defects in the morning's sample are shown in Fig. 5-6 in combinations 1 and 4.

Then the two operators interchanged jigs. Again, a sample of fifty units of each operator's assembly was inspected; the results of the before and after interchange are shown in Fig. 5-6. The same inspector examined all samples.

ALIGNMENT DEFECTS: Totals for the 100 cathode-ray guns assembled by each operator are shown at the bottom of Fig. 5-6; totals for the 100 guns assembled on each jig are shown at the right; and the numbers of rejects produced on the original and interchanged machines are shown at the two bottom corners.

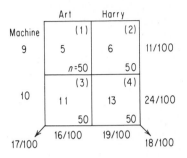

Fig. 5-6 Alignment defects found in samples during an interchange of two operators on two machines. (The number of defects is shown in each square at the center, and the sample size in the lower-right corner. See Case History 5-5.)

Operators	Jigs	Interchange
Art: 16/100 = 16%	9: 11/100 = 11%	Original machines: 18/100 = 18%
Harry: 19/100 = 19%	10: 24/100 = 24%	Interchanged machines: 17/100 = 17%

DISCUSSION: The difference in jig performance suggests a problem with jig 10. This difference is called a *jig main effect*. (Any significant difference between operators would be called an *operator main effect*.) This surprised everyone, but was accepted without any further analysis.

The performance of jig 10 is significantly worse than that of jig 9 (see Fig. 5-7) even though it had just been overhauled. The magnitude of the difference is large:

$$\bar{\Delta} = 24\% - 11\% = 13\%$$

Neither the small difference observed between the performances of Art and Harry nor between the performance of the men *before* and *after* the interchange is statistically significant.

On the basis of the above information, all operators were called together and a program of extending the study in the department was discussed with them. The result of the interchange of Art and Harry was explained; they were much interested and entirely agreeable to having the study extended.

AN EXTENSION OF THE INTERPRETATION FROM THE STUDY. An interpretation of such a difference would be that the two operators performed differently when using their own machine than when using a strange machine. Such preferential behavior is called an *interaction*; more specifically here, it is an operator-machine interaction.

A variation of this procedure and interpretation has useful implications. *If* the operators were not told of the proposed interchange until *after* the sample of production from their own machines had been assembled, then:

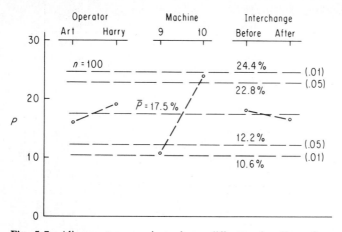

Fig. 5-7 Alignment comparison shows difference in effect of machines, but not in operators or before-and-after effect (ANOM). (Data from Fig. 5-6.)

1.   The number of defectives in combinations 2 and 3 made *after* the interchange (Fig. 5-6), *could well* be a consequence of more careful attention to the operation than was given *before* the interchange.   Since the number of defects *after* the interchange is essentially the same as before, there is no suggestion from the data that "attention to the job" was a factor of any consequence in this study.

2.   It would be possible in other 2^2 production studies that a proper interpretation of an observed difference between the two diagonals of the square (such as in Fig. 5-6) might be a mixture (combination) of "performance on their own machines" and "attention to detail."   Such a mixture is said to represent a *confounding* of the two possible explanations.

SPACING DEFECTS: The same cathode-ray guns were also inspected for *spacing* defects.   The data are shown in Fig. 5-8.

Operators   *Jigs*

Art: $6/100 = 6\%$ 9: $3/100 = 3\%$

Harry: $8/100 = 8\%$ 10: $11/100 = 11\%$

Before–After Interchange

Before: $9/100 = 9\%$

After: $5/100 = 5\%$

In Fig. 5-9, the difference between jigs is seen to be statistically significant for spacing defects, risk less than 5%. Since it seemed possible that the before-after interchange difference might be statistically significant for $\alpha = .10$, a third pair of decision lines have been included; the pair of points for B, A lie inside them, however. There is the possibility that the interaction *might* prove to be statistically significant if a larger sample had been inspected.

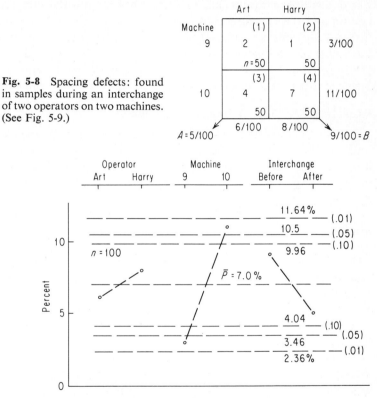

Fig. 5-8 Spacing defects: found in samples during an interchange of two operators on two machines. (See Fig. 5-9.)

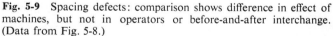

Fig. 5-9 Spacing defects: comparison shows difference in effect of machines, but not in operators or before-and-after interchange. (Data from Fig. 5-8.)

FORMAL ANALYSIS

$\bar{P} = 7.0\%$; $k = 2$ in each of the three comparisons.

$$\hat{\sigma}_P = \sqrt{\frac{7.0(93.0)}{100}} = 2.55$$

DECISION LINES (in Fig. 5-9)

For $\alpha = .05$, $H_{.05} = 1.39$

$$\text{UDL} = 10.54$$
$$\text{LDL} = 3.46$$

For $\alpha = .10$, $H_{.10} = 1.16$

$$\text{UDL} = 9.96\%$$
$$\text{LDL} = 4.04\%$$

Two Independent Variables: A Typical axb Factorial Design

The design of experiments has been described often with examples from agriculture and the chemical industries. It is at least equally important to use many of the same concepts in the electrical, electronic, and mechanical fields, but rather less complicated versions of them are recommended for troubleshooting studies in industry. The following example represents a small factorial experiment which was carried out three times in three days.

CASE HISTORY 5-6   A Multistage Assembly[1]

In many complicated assembly operations, we do not find the problems until the final inspection report made at the end of the assembly. Sometimes it is feasible to carry an identification system through assembly, and establish major sources of trouble on a regular, continuing basis. Many times, however, it is not feasible to maintain an identification system in routine production. In the study considered here, no one could determine who was responsible for a poor quality or inoperative unit found at final inspection. This operator says, "They are good when they leave me"; another says, "It's not my fault." No one accepts the possibility of being responsible.

We discuss an experience just like this in which a routing procedure through assembly was established on a sampling basis. The procedure was conceived in frustration; it is remarkably general and effective in application.

A particular phonograph pickup cartridge was well designed in the sense that those cartridges which passed the final electrical test performed satisfactorily. However, too many acoustical rejects were being found at final testing, and the need of an engineering redesign had been considered and was being recommended.

There are, or course, many engineering ways of improving the design of almost any product; a redesign is often an appropriate approach to the solution of manufacturing quality problems. Perhaps a change in certain components or materials or other redesign is considered essential. But *there is an alternative method*, too frequently overlooked, and this is to determine whether the components, the assembly operators, and the jigs or fixtures—any aspect of the entire production process—are capable of a major improvement.

The following study was planned to compare assembly operators at two of the many stages of a complicated assembly process.

[1] Ellis R. Ott, Achieving Quality Control, *Qual. Prog.*, May, 1969.   (Figures 5–10, 5–12, 5–13, and 5–14 reproduced by permission of the editors.)

The two stages were chosen during a meeting called to discuss ways and means. Present were the production supervisor, the design engineer, and the specialist on planning investigations. During the meeting, different production stages thought to be possible contributors to the acoustical defects were suggested and discussed critically. Two block-type variables were chosen for inclusion in this exploratory study: then at every other stage, each tray in the study was processed at the same machine, by the same operator, throughout in the same way as nearly as possible. No one was at fault; of course not. The purpose of the study was to determine whether substantial improvements might be possible within the engineering design of the cartridge by finding ways to adjust assembly procedures.

■ Four *operators* at stage A, each with her own particular machine, were included; the four operator-machine combinations[1] are designated as A_1, A_2, A_3, and A_4.

■ Also included in the study were *three operators* performing a *hand operation* using only tweezers; these operators are designated as C_1, C_2, and C_3.

Fig. 5-10 Routing card used to obtain data on pickup cartridge assembly.

```
                    Tray 1
                 Routing Card

          Operation      Position

              A          Op. A₁
              B          Mch. B₁*
              C          Op. C₁
              D          Op. D₃*
              E          Insp. S*

      No. units inspected: 40
      No. of rejects found:
         Type a:  0
         Type b:  0
         Type c:  0

      Date:  4/9            S
                          Inspector
```

*Same for all 12 trays

■ *A three-by-four factorial* design with every one of the $3 \cdot 4 = 12$ combinations of A and C was planned. Twelve trays—or perhaps 16—can usually be organized and carried around a production floor without mishap. More than 15 or 16 is asking for trouble. Each standard production tray had spaces for 40 cartridges.

[1] The operators and machines were confounded deliberately. This was an exploratory study, and problems associated with interchanging operators and machines were considered excessive in comparison to possible advantages.

■ A routing ticket as in Fig. 5-10 was put in each of the 12 trays to direct passage through the assembly line.   The 12 trays were numbered 1, 2, 3, ..., 12.   All components were selected at random from a common source.

■ Each cartridge (unit) was inspected for all three listed defects, (a), (b), and (c) and the entries in Fig. 5-11 indicate the number of each type of defects found at inspection.   Since defect type c was found most frequently, Fig. 5-12 is shown for type c only.   A mental statistical analysis, or "look

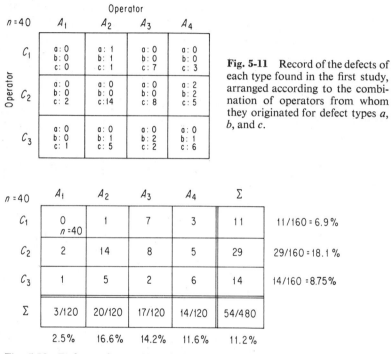

Fig. 5-11   Record of the defects of each type found in the first study, arranged according to the combination of operators from whom they originated for defect types a, b, and c.

$n=40$	A_1	A_2	A_3	A_4	Σ	
C_1	0 ($n=40$)	1	7	3	11	11/160 = 6.9%
C_2	2	14	8	5	29	29/160 = 18.1%
C_3	1	5	2	6	14	14/160 = 8.75%
Σ	3/120	20/120	17/120	14/120	54/480	
	2.5%	16.6%	14.2%	11.6%	11.2%	

Fig. 5-12   Defects of type (c) only.   (Data from Fig. 5-11.)   Total defects of this type shown at right and at bottom by operator.

test" at the data of Fig. 5-12, indicates clearly that C_2 is an operator producing many rejects.   Also A_1 is substantially the best of the four operator-machine combinations.

■ This was surprising and important information.   Since not all results are as self evident, an analysis is given in Fig. 5-13, first for columns A and then for rows C.

■ This analysis shows that the differences were large and of practical significance as well as being statistically significant.   Also, on the basis of differences indicated by this study, certain adjustments were recommended by engineering and manufacturing following a careful study and comparison of the operators at their benches.   The study was repeated two days later.

The very few type c defects found are shown in Fig. 5-14. The greatly improved process average of $\bar{P} = (6)(100)/480 = 1.2\%$ compares strikingly with the earlier $\bar{P} = 11.2\%$ which had led to considering an expensive redesign of components to reduce rejects. The improvement was directed by the same men who had decided that a redesign was the only solution to the problem.

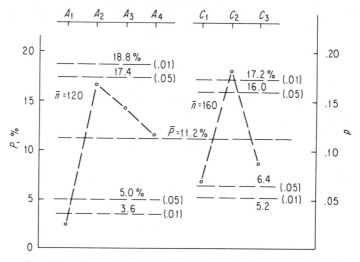

Fig. 5-13 Comparing significant effects of operator-machine combinations A and C (ANOM). (Data from Fig. 5-12.) (Type c defects.)

Fig. 5-14 Number of defects found in second study of pickup cartridge assemblies. (Type c defects.)

$n = 40$	A_1	A_2	A_3	A_4	Σ
C_1	0 / 40	0	0	1	1
C_2	0	0	3	1	4
C_3	0	0	0	1	1
Σ	0	0	3	3	6/480 = 1.2%

■ Formal analysis is shown for Figs. 5-12 and 5-13. The overall percent defective is

$$\bar{P} = 100D/(12)(40) = 5400/480 = 11.2\%$$

Then

$$\hat{\sigma}_P = \sqrt{\frac{(11.2)(88.8)}{N}}$$

where $N = (3)(40) = 120$ when comparing columns: $\hat{\sigma}_P = 2.9\%$

and $N = (4)(40) = 160$ when comparing rows: $\hat{\sigma}_P = 2.5\%$

Decision lines for the analysis of means are as follows:

Columns A: $k = 4$, $\hat{\sigma}_P = 2.9\%$, $H_{.05} = 2.15$, $H_{.01} = 2.61$

$$\begin{array}{ccc} & \alpha = .05 & \alpha = .01 \\ \bar{P} \pm H_\alpha \hat{\sigma}_P: \text{UDL} = & 17.4 & 18.8\% \\ \text{LDL} = & 5.0 & 3.6\% \end{array}$$

Rows C: $k = 3$, $\hat{\sigma}_P = 2.5$, $H_{.05} = 1.93$, $H_{.01} = 2.39$

$$\begin{array}{ccc} & \alpha = .05 & \alpha = .01 \\ \text{UDL} = & 16.0 & 17.2\% \\ \text{LDL} = & 6.4 & 5.2\% \end{array}$$

CASE HISTORY 5-7   Machine Shutdowns (Unequal n_i)

This case history presents a variation in the type of data employed.   It is different also in that the sample sizes are *not all equal*.

It is routine procedure in some plants to designate the source of data by the machine, shift, and/or operator.   The data recorded[1] in Table 5-9 serves to illustrate a procedure of obtaining data for a process-improvement

TABLE 5-9   Talon's Press-shift Performance Record

Press number	Shift	Number of times checked	Number of shutdowns
1	A	50	2
	B	55	7
	C	40	4
2	A	45	3
	B	55	3
	C	55	14
3	A	40	0
	B	35	3
	C	45	0
4	A	50	6
	B	55	9
	C	60	11
5	A	60	4
	B	45	3
	C	60	6

[1] J. Stuart Zahniser and D. Lehman, Quality Control at Talon, Incorporated, *Ind. Qual. Control*, pp. 32–36, March, 1951.   (Reproduced by kind permission of the editor.)

project and of providing an analysis when sample sizes are not all equal. The data relate to the performance of five different presses (machines) over three shifts. Table 5-9 indicates both the number of times each press was checked and the number of times its performance was so unsatisfactory that the press was shut down for repairs. The quality of performance is thus indicated by *frequency of shutdowns*. We quote from the Zahniser-Lehman article:

As the product comes from these presses, there are 57 separate characteristics that require an inspector's audit. It takes two or three minutes to complete the examination of a single piece. Yet the combined production from these presses reaches more than a million a day. To cover this job with a series of charts for variables would require a minimum of 15 inspectors, . . . (We) use a . . . "shut-down" chart. The shut-down chart is a *p*-chart on which each point gives the percentage of checks resulting in shut-downs for a given press on a given shift during a two-week period. On this chart, *n* represents the number of times the press has been checked on this shift during the particular period . . .

The percentage of checks resulting in shut-downs in the department is 10%. The average number of checks per press per shift is 750/15 = 50.

The *speed* of the presses has been increased by 32% since control charts were first applied. Nevertheless, we find that the percentage of audits which result in shut-downs has been cut squarely in half. Obviously the quality of product coming from them is (also) vastly better than it was three years ago, even though our charts measure quality only indirectly.

The enhancement of records by charting a continuing history is demonstrated clearly.

The data of Table 5-9 have been rearranged in Table 5-10 in the form of an obvious three-by-five (3 · 5) factorial design. The numbers in the lower

TABLE 5-10   Table of Shutdowns

Shift	Press 1	Press 2	Press 3	Press 4	Press 5	Total, Percent
A	$d = 2$ $n = 50$	3 45	0 40	6 50	4 60	15/245 = 6.1
B	7 55	3 55	3 35	9 55	3 45	25/245 = 10.2
C	4 40	14 55	0 45	11 60	6 60	35/260 = 13.4
Total	13/145	20/155	3/120	26/165	13/165	$\bar{P} = 75/750$ $= 10\%$
Percent	9.0	12.9	2.5	15.7	7.9	

righthand corner refer to the number of check inspections made. The percent of all shutdowns for each shift (across the five presses) has been indicated in the column at the right. The percent of shutdowns for each press across the three shifts is shown at the bottom.

PRESS PERFORMANCE: The percent of shutdowns on presses 1 through 5 is

$$9.0\%, 12.9\%, 2.5\%, 15.7\%, \text{ and } 7.9\%$$

The excellent performance (2.5%) of press 3 should be of most value for improving the process.

We compute tentative decision lines as shown in Fig. 5-15a for risks (.05) and (.01). These will be adjusted subsequently.

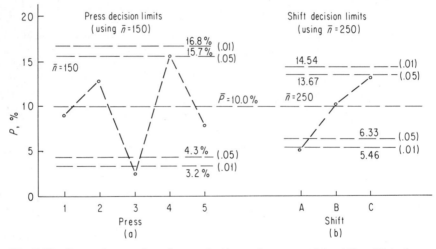

Fig. 5-15 Comparing number of press shutdowns by press and by shift. (Data from Table 5-10.)

PRESS PERFORMANCE: ($k = 5$, $\bar{N} = 750/5 = 150$)

Press 3: This is below the tentative (.01) decision line. A look now at Table 5-10 shows that press 3 was checked only 120 times (compared to the average of $\bar{N} = 150$). A recomputation of decision limits for $N = 120$ shows a slight increase in limits which does not affect materially the conclusion that press 3 performs significantly better than the overall average.

Press 4: This is just on the tentative (.05)-decision line. A check shows that this press was checked $N = 165$ times—more than average. A recomputation of decision lines using $N = 165$ instead of 150 will shrink slightly the limits for press 4; see Fig. 5-16. There is reason to expect that some way can be found to improve its performance.

SHIFT PERFORMANCE: $(k = 3, \overline{N} = 750/3 = 250)$

Shift A: This is at the (.01)-decision limit—and the shutdown rate is just about *one-third* that of shift C. Possible explanations include:

1. More experienced personnel on the shift A.
2. Better supervision on the shift A.
3. Less efficient checking on press performance.
4. Better conditions for press performance (temperature, lighting, humidity, as examples).

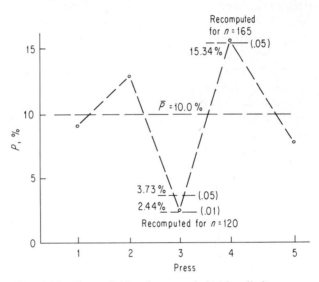

Fig. 5-16 Figure 5-15 redrawn and decision limits recomputed using actual n_i instead of average $\bar{n}$ for two borderline points. (Data from Table 5-10.)

ADJUSTED DECISION LINES are now obtained for the actual values N_i, with $\alpha = .05$ for press 4 and $\alpha = .01$ for press 3. Decision lines in Fig. 5-15a were computed for average $\overline{N} = 150$. Only presses 3 and 4 are near the decision lines and are the only ones for which the decision might be affected when the actual Ns are used to recompute:

Press 3 (LDL): $N = 120$ from Table 5-10

$$\hat{\sigma}_P = \sqrt{\frac{(10)(90)}{120}} = 2.74\%$$

$$\text{LDL}(.01) = 10.0 - (2.76)(2.74) = 2.44\%$$

Press 4 (UDL): $N = 165$

$$\hat{\sigma}_P = \sqrt{\frac{900}{165}} = 2.33\%$$

$$\text{UDL}(.05) = 10.0 + (2.29)(2.33) = 15.34\%$$

These two changes in decision lines are shown in Fig. 5-16 by dotted lines. The slight changes would hardly affect the decisions on whether to investigate. Unless the variation of an individual N from average $\overline{N}$ is as much as 40%, it will probably not warrant recomputation.

5-7 Three Independent Factors

Introduction: Some of you have had actual experience using multifactor experimental designs. Many of you have not, and it is fairly common for new converts to propose initial experiments with four, five, and even more independent variables.

Anyone beginning the use of more than one independent variable (factor) is well-advised to limit the number of variables to two. There are several reasons for the recommendation. Unless someone industrially experienced in the methods is guiding the project, *something* is almost certain to go wrong in the implementation of the plan, or the resulting data will present difficulties of interpretation. These typical difficulties can easily lead to plant-wide rejection of the entire concept of multivariable studies. The advantage of just two independent variables over one is usually substantial; it is enough to warrant a limitation to two until confidence in them has been established. Reluctance to use more than one independent variable is widespread—it is the rule, not the exception. An initial failure can be serious, and the risk is seldom warranted.

After some successful experience with two independent variables—including an acceptance of the idea by key personnel, three variables often offer opportunities for getting even more advantages. The possibilities differ from case to case but they include economy of time, materials, and testing, and a better understanding of the process being studied. Some or all of the three variables should ordinarily be of the block or chunky type, especially in troubleshooting expeditions.

There are two designs (plans) using three independent factors which are especially useful in exploratory projects in a plant. The 2^3 *factorial* design (read "two cubed")—i.e., three independent variables each at two levels—is least likely to lead to mixups in carrying out the program and will result in minimal confusion when interpreting results. Methods of analysis and interpretation are discussed in Case Histories 5-8 and 5-9.

The 2^3 factorial design provides for a comparison of the following effects:
1. *Main effects* of each independent variable (factor).
2. *Two-factor interactions* of the three independent variables.

These different comparisons are obtained with the same number of experimental units as would be required for a comparison of the main effects and at the same level of significance. An added advantage is that the effect of each factor can be observed under differing conditions of the other two factors.

3. *Three-factor interaction* of the three variables. Technically this is a possibility. Experience indicates, however, that this is of lesser importance in troubleshooting projects with attribute data. The *mechanics* of three-factor interaction analysis will be indicated in some of the case histories.

CASE HISTORY 5-8   Strains in Small Glass Components

The production of many industrial items involves combinations of hand operations with machine operations. This discussion will pertain to radio tubes. Excessive failures had arisen on a reliable type of tube at the "boiling-water" test in which samples of the completed tubes were submerged in boiling water for 15 s and then plunged immediately into ice water for 5 s. Too many stem cracks were occurring where the stem was sealed to the wall tubing. A team was organized to study possible ways of reducing the percent of cracks. They decided that the following three questions related to the most probable factors affecting the stem strength.

1. Should air be blown on the glass stem of the tube after sealing? If so, at what pounds per sq. in. (psi)?

2. Should the mount be molded to the stem by hand operation or by using a jig (fixture)?

3. The glass stems can be made to have different strain patterns. Can the trouble be remedied by specifying a particular pattern?

FACTORS SELECTED: It was decided to include two levels of each of these three factors.

$$Air \quad A_1: \quad 2.5 \text{ psi air blown on stem after sealing}$$
$$A_2: \quad \text{No air blown on stem after sealing}$$
$$Jig \quad B_1: \quad \text{Stem assembly using a jig}$$
$$B_2: \quad \text{Stem assembly using only hand operations (no jig)}$$
$$Stem \ Tension \quad C_1: \quad \text{Normal stem (neutral to slight compression)}$$
$$C_2: \quad \text{Tension stem (very heavy)}$$

Approximately 45 stems were prepared under each of the eight combinations of factors, and the number of stem failures on the boiling water test is indicated in the squares of Table 5-11*a* and *b*. These are two common ways of displaying the data. Manufacturing conditions in combination 1, for example, were at levels A_1, B_1, C_1 for $n = 42$ stems; there were two stem cracks. Stems in combination 2 were manufactured under conditions A_2, B_1, C_2, etc.

MAIN EFFECTS: Half the combinations were manufactured under air conditions A_1; those in the four groups (1), (3), (5), and (7). The other half (2), (4), (6), (8) were manufactured under air conditions A_2. Then, in comparing the effect of A_1 versus A_2, data from these two groupings are pooled:

A_1:   (1,3,5,7) had 24 stem cracks out of 173; 24/173 = 0.139

A_2:   (2,4,6,8) had 5 stem cracks out of 179; 5/179 = 0.028

Similarly, combinations for the *B*s and *C*s are displayed in Table 5-12.

TABLE 5-11 **A Study of Stem Cracking: A 2^3 Production Design**

	A_1	A_2		A_1	A_2
B_1	C_1 (1) 2 $n=42$	C_2 (2) 0 44	B_1	C_2 (5) 6 44	C_1 (6) 0 44
B_2	C_2 (3) 7 $n=45$	C_1 (4) 4 44	B_2	C_1 (7) 9 42	C_2 (8) 1 47

$$\bar{p} = 29/352 = 0.082$$

(a)

		A_1		A_2	
		B_1	B_2	B_1	B_2
C_1		(1) 2 $n=42$	(7) 9 42	(6) 0 44	(4) 4 44
C_2		(5) 6 44	(3) 7 45	(2) 0 44	(8) 1 47

(b)

TABLE 5-12 **Computations for Analysis of Means**
Data from Table 5-11

Summary		Interaction
Air	A_1: (1,3,5,7) $24/173 = 0.139$	AC:
	A_2: (2,4,6,8) $5/179 = 0.028$	Like: (1,2,7,8): $12/175 = 0.069$
		Unlike: (3,4,5,6): $17/177 = 0.096$
		AB:
Stem	B_1: (1,2,5,6) $8/174 = 0.046$	Like: (1,4,5,8): $13/177 = 0.073$
Assembly	B_2: (3,4,7,8) $21/178 = 0.118$	Unlike: (2,3,6,7): $16/175 = 0.091$
		BC:
Stem	C_1: (1,4,6,7) $15/172 = 0.087$	Like: (1,3,6,8): $10/178 = 0.056$
Tension	C_2: (2,3,5,8) $14/180 = 0.078$	Unlike: (2,4,5,7): $19/174 = 0.109$
		ABC:
		(1,2,3,4): $13/175 = 0.074$
		(5,6,7,8): $16/177 = 0.090$

Points corresponding to values shown in Table 5-12 have been plotted in Fig. 5-17. The logic and mechanics of computing decision lines are given below, following a discussion on decisions.

DECISIONS FROM FIG. 5-17: The most important single difference is the advantage of A_2 over A_1; 13.9% versus 2.8%. The magnitude of this difference is of tremendous importance and is statistically significant. Fortunately, it was a choice which could easily be made in production.

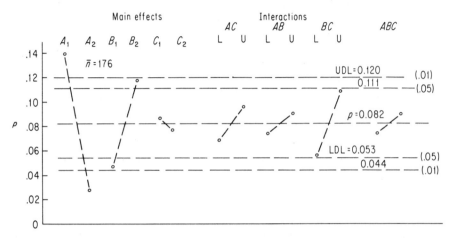

Fig. 5-17 Comparing effects of three factors on glass stem cracking: three main effects and their interactions. (Data from Table 5-12.)

A second result was quite surprising; the preference of B_1 over B_2. The converse had been expected. The approximate level of risk in choosing B_1 over B_2 is about $\alpha = .01$; and the magnitude of the advantage—about 7%—was enough to be of additional economic interest.

No two-factor interaction is statistically significant at the .05 level and the BC interaction "just barely" at the .10 level. This latter decision can be checked by using the factor $H_{.10} = 1.16$ from Table A-14. Then, the recommended operating conditions are A_2B_1; and two possibilities follow:

$$A_2B_1 \text{ and } C_1 \text{ or } A_2B_1 \text{ and } C_2$$

i.e., combinations 2 and 6 with 0 and 0 cracked stems.

Some *slight* support for a choice may be seen from the BC-interaction diagram (Fig. 5-17), which gives "the nod" to those B and C having *like* subscripts, i.e., to combination 6.

MECHANICS OF ANALYSIS—ANOM (FIG. 5-17)

For the initial analysis, we consider all eight samples to be of size $\bar{n} = 44$. Then each comparison for main effects and interactions will be between $k = 2$ groups of four samples each, with $\bar{N} = 4(44) = 176$ stems.

The total defectives in the eight combinations is 29

$$\bar{p} = 29/352 = 0.082 \text{ or } 8.2\%$$

and

$$\hat{\sigma}_P = \sqrt{\frac{(8.2)(91.8)}{176}} = 2.1\% \quad \text{and} \quad \hat{\sigma}_p = 0.021$$

DECISION LINES (FOR FIG. 5-17)

$$\underline{\alpha = .05} \quad \bar{p} \pm H_{.05}\,\hat{\sigma}_p = 0.082 \pm (1.39)(0.021)$$

$$UDL = 0.111$$
$$LDL = 0.053$$

$$\underline{\alpha = .01}$$

$$UDL = 0.120$$
$$LDL = 0.044$$

These decision lines are applicable not only when comparing main effects but also to the three two-factor interactions and to the three-factor interaction.

TWO-FACTOR INTERACTIONS—DISCUSSION

In the study, it is possible that the main effect of a variable A is significantly different under condition B_1 than it is under condition B_2; then, there *is said to be an* "$A \times B$ ('A times B') two-factor interaction."

If the main effect of A is essentially (statistically) the same for B_1 as for B_2, then there is no $A \times B$ interaction. The mechanics of analysis for any one of the three possible two-factor interactions have been given in Table 5-12 without any discussion of the meaning.

In half of the eight combinations, A and B have the same or *like* (L) subscripts; namely (1,4,5,8). In the other half, they have different or *unlike* (U) subscripts; namely (2,3,6,7). The role of the third variable is always disregarded when considering a two-factor interaction:

$$AB: \text{Like} \quad (1,4,5,8) \text{ has } 13/177 = 0.073 \text{ or } 7.3\%$$
$$AB: \text{Unlike} \ (2,3,6,7) \text{ has } 16/175 = 0.91 \text{ or } 9.1\%$$

The difference between 9.1% and 7.3% does not seem large; and it is seen in Fig. 5-17 that the two points corresponding to AB(L) and AB(U) are well within the decision lines. We have said this means there is *no significant $A \times B$ interaction*. This procedure deserves some explanation.

In Fig. 5-18, the decreases in stem failures in changing from A_1 to A_2 are as follows:

Under Condition B_1: drops from $8/86 = 9.3\%$ to $0/88 = 0\%$; a drop of 9.3%.

Under condition B_2: drops from $16/87 = 18.4\%$ to $5/91 = 5.5\%$: a drop of 12.9%

Are these changes significantly different (statistically)? If the answer is "yes," then there is an $A \times B$ interaction.

Consider the differences under conditions B_1 and B_2 and assume that they are not statistically equal.

$$A_1 B_2 - A_1 B_1 \neq A_2 B_2 - A_2 B_1 \qquad (5\text{-}3)$$

i.e., is $9.1\% \neq 5.5\%$?

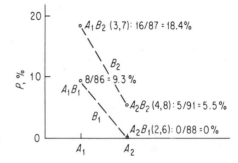

Fig. 5-18 A graphical comparison of effect on stem cracks: the upper line shows the decrease in changing from A_1 to A_2 under condition B_2; the lower line shows the decrease in changing from A_1 to A_2 under condition B_1. Intuitively, the effects seem quite comparable. (Data from Table 5-11.)

This can be rewritten as

$$A_1 B_2 + A_2 B_1 \neq A_1 B_1 + A_2 B_2 \qquad (5\text{-}4)$$

From Table 5-12, corresponding combinations are

Unlike (2,3,6,7) $\neq$ Like (1,4,5,8)

i.e., is $9.1\% \neq 7.3\%$?

That is, the two lines are *not* parallel if the points corresponding to AB: Like *and* AB: Unlike are statistically different, i.e., fall outside the decision lines of Fig. 5-17. Relation (5-4) is a simple mechanical comparison to compute when testing for an AB interaction. The decision lines to be used in Fig. 5-17 are exactly those used in comparing main effects.

Similar combinations to be used when testing for $A \times C$ and $B \times C$ interactions are shown in Table 5-12.

Note: Also, the combinations used to test for a three-factor, $A \times B \times C$, interaction are given in Table 5-12. If an apparent three-factor interaction is observed, it should be recomputed for possible error in arithmetic, choice of combinations, or unauthorized changes in the experimental plan, such as failure to "hold constant" or randomize—all factors not included in the program. With very few exceptions, main effects will provide most opportunities for improvement in a process; but two-factor interactions will sometimes have enough effect to be of interest.

CASE HISTORY 5-9   A Problem in a High-speed Assembly Operation (Broken Caps)

CRACKED AND BROKEN CAPS: (See Fig. 5-19.)   Cracked and broken caps are a constant headache in pharmaceutical firms.   One aspect of the problem was discussed in Case History 5-4.   It was recognized that too many caps were being cracked or broken as the machine screwed them onto the bottles. Besides the obvious costs in production, there is the knowledge that some defective caps will reach the ultimate consumer; no large-scale 100% inspection can be perfect.   When Mr. C., the department head, was asked about it, he said the problem had been investigated; "We need stronger caps." Being curious, we watched the operation awhile.   It seemed that cracked caps were not coming equally from the four lines.

Production was several hundred per minute

The filling-capping machine had four adjacent lines to four capper positions. At each, beginning with an empty bottle,

a soft plastic ring was squeezed on,

a filler nozzle delivered the liquid content,

a hard plastic marble was pressed into the ring, and

a cap was applied and tightened to a designated torque.

Fig. 5-19 Components in a toiletry assembly. (Case History 5-9.) The complete labeled assembly; a soft plastic ring; a hard plastic marble; a hard plastic cap; a glass bottle.

Each of the four lines had a separate mechanical system, including a capper and torque mechanism.   An operator inspector stood at the end of the filling machine; she would remove bottles with cracked caps whenever she saw them.   We talked to Mr. C. about the possibilities of a quick study to record the number of defects from the four capper positions.   There were two possibilities: a bucket for each position where defective caps could be thrown and then counted, or an ordinary sheet of paper where the operator inspector could make tally marks for the four positions. He preferred the second method and gave necessary instructions.

After some 10 or 15 min, the tally showed:

Capper Head	Cracked caps
1	2
2	0
3	17
4	1

We copied the record and showed it to Mr. C. He said, "I told you. We need stronger caps!" Frustrated a bit, we waited another hour or so for more data.

Capper Head	Cracked caps
1	7
2	4
3	88
4	5

We now discussed the matter with Mr. C. for almost 30 min; he was sure the solution was stronger caps. Sometimes he almost convinced me! But then he agreed that capper head 3 could hardly be so *unlucky* as to get the great majority of weak caps. He called the chief equipment engineer, and we had a three-way discussion. Yes, they had made recent adjustments on the individual torque heads. Perhaps the rubber cone in head 3 needed replacement.

Following our discussion and their adjustments on the machine, head 3 was brought into line with the other three. The improved process meant appreciably fewer cracked and broken caps in production *and* fewer shipped to customers. It is rarely possible to attain perfection. I dismissed the problem for other projects.

STRONGER CAPS? Then it occurred to me that we ought to give some thought to Mr. C.'s earlier suggestion: stronger caps. Mr. C. had a lot of experience in this business; he might now possibly be a little chagrined; besides there might be a chance to make further improvement. So we reopened the matter with him. Exclusive of the capper heads, why should a cap break? Perhaps because of any of the following:

1. *Caps:* wall thickness, angle of threads, distances between threads, different cavities at molding; irregularities of many dimensions—the possibilities seemed endless.

2. *Bottles:* the angle or sharpness of threads on some or all molds, diameters, distances. This seemed (to me) more likely than caps.

3. *Rings:* perhaps they exert excessive pressures some way.

4. *Marbles:* these were ruled out as quite unlikely.

SELECTION OF INDEPENDENT VARIABLES TO STUDY. The traditional approach would be to measure angles, thickness, distances, etc; this would require much manpower and time.

TABLE 5-13   Data from a 2^3 Factorial Production Study of Reasons for Cracked Caps
Data from Case History 5-9, Displayed in Two Useful Forms

	B_1	B_2			B_1	B_2
R_1	C_1 (1) 9	C_2 (2) 33			C_2 (5) 51	C_1 (6) 27
R_2	C_2 (3) 20	C_1 (4) 21			C_1 (7) 13	C_2 (8) 28

Table 5-13a

	B_1		B_2	
	R_1	R_2	R_1	R_2
C_1	9 (1)	13 (7)	27 (6)	21 (4)
C_2	51 (5)	20 (3)	33 (2)	28 (8)

Table 5-13b

The number* of assemblies in each combination was 2,000; the number of cracked and broken caps is shown in the center.

$$\bar{c} = 202/8 = 25.25$$
$$\hat{\sigma} = \sqrt{25.25} \quad \text{and} \quad \hat{\sigma}_{\bar{c}} = \hat{\sigma}/\sqrt{4} \text{ when comparing averages of 4 groups}$$

$\Sigma B_1(1,3,5,7) = 93;\ \bar{B}_1 = 23.25 \qquad \Sigma C_1(1,4,6,7) = 70;\ \bar{C}_1 = 17.5$
$\Sigma B_2(2,4,6,8) = 109;\ \bar{B}_2 = 27.25 \qquad \Sigma C_2(2,3,5,8) = 132;\ \bar{C}_2 = 33.0$

$\Sigma R_1(1,2,5,6) = 120;\ \bar{R}_1 = 30.0$
$\Sigma R_2(3,4,7,8) = 82;\ \bar{R}_2 = 20.5$

* We have chosen to analyze the data as being Poisson type.

The question was asked: "How many vendors of caps? Of bottles? Of rings?" The answer was two or three in each case. Then how about choosing vendors as block variables? Since a 2^3 study is a very useful design, we recommended the following vendors: two for caps, two for bottles, and two for rings. This was accepted as a reasonable procedure.

A 2^3 ASSEMBLY EXPERIMENT. Consequently, over the next two or three weeks, some 8,000 glass bottles were acquired from each of two vendors B_1, B_2; also, 8,000 caps from each of two vendors, C_1, C_2; and 8,000 rings from each of two vendors, R_1, R_2.

It took some careful planning by production and quality control to organize the flow of components through the filling and capping operation and to identify cracked caps with the eight combinations. The assembly was completed in one morning. The data are shown in Tables 5-13a, b. From the table alone, it seemed pretty clear that the difference in cracked caps between vendors C_2 and C_1 must be more than just chance; 132 compared to 70. (Also see Fig. 5-20.)

It was a surprise to find that combination 5, $B_1R_1C_2$, which produced 51 rejects, was assembled from components *all from the same vendor*!

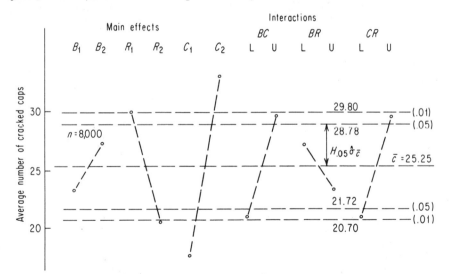

Fig. 5-20 Comparing effects of bottles, rings, and caps from different vendors on cracked caps. (Main effects and two-factor interactions.) Data from Tables 5-13b and 5-15.

SUMMARY—DISCUSSION: (see Fig. 5-20)

Caps: The largest difference is between vendors of caps. The difference is of practical interest as well as being statistically significant ($\alpha < .01$); the overall breakage from C_2 is almost twice that of C_1. Also C_2 caps crack more often than C_1 caps for *each* of the four bottle-ring combinations. This is a likely reason that Mr. C. had believed they needed "stronger caps," since any change from vendor C_1 to C_2 would increase cracking. Thus the reason for excessive cracking was from a joint origin; the adjustment of the capper had effected an improvement, and the selection of cap usage offers some opportunities. There were good reasons why it was not feasible for purchasing to provide manufacturing with only the best combination $B_1 R_1 C_1$. What should be done? The vendor of C_2 can study possible reasons for excessive weakness of his caps: Is the trouble in specific molding cavities? Is it in general design? Is it in plastic or molding temperatures? In certain critical dimensions?

In the meantime, *can purchasing favor* vendor C_1? Production itself should *avoid* using the very objectionable $B_1 R_1 C_2$ combination. (A rerun of the study a few days later showed the same advantage of C_1 over C_2; and that $B_1 R_1 C_2$ gave excessive rejects.)

OTHER MAIN EFFECTS

Rings. The effect of rings is seen to be statistically significant (α about 5%); the magnitude of the effect is less than for caps. It can also be seen that the effect of rings when using C_2 is quite large (combining B_1 and B_2); the effect is negligible when using C_1. This interdependence is also indicated by the *CR* interaction.

TABLE 5-14   Effects of Rings and Bottles Using Only Caps C_1
Data from Table 5-13

	B_1	B_2	
R_1	(1) 9	(7) 27	36
R_2	(6) 13	(4) 21	34
	22	48	$\bar{\bar{c}} = 17.5$
	$\bar{R}_1 = 18$	$\bar{B}_1 = 11$	
	$\bar{R}_2 = 17$	$\bar{B}_2 = 24$	

Bottles. The effect of bottles as a main effect is the least of all three. (Most surprising to me!) However consider *that half* of the data in Table 5-14; these data are from Table 5-13b for only the better cap C_1.

The data for this 2^2 design, using C_1 only, shows a definite advantage of using bottle B_1 in any combination with R. Also in Fig. 5-21, the advantage is seen to be statistically significant, $\alpha = .01$. (Note: this is a *BC* interaction.)

TABLE 5-15   Computations for Two-factor Interactions
Cracked Cap: Data from Table 5-13

Decision lines	*Computation for two-factor interactions*			
$\alpha = .05$	BC:	Like $(1,2,7,8) = 22 + 61 = 83$	Avg. $= 20.75$	
$\overline{\text{UDL}} = \bar{c} + h_{.05}\,\hat{\sigma}_{\bar{c}}$		Unlike $(3,4,5,6) = 48 + 71 = 119$	29.75	
$= 25.25 + (1.39)(2.5)$		$\overline{202}$		
$= 25.25 + 3.53 = 28.78$				
$\text{LDL} = 25.25 - 3.53 = 21.72$	BR:	Like $(1,5,4,8) = 60 + 49 = 109$	27.25	
		Unlike $(2,6,3,7) = 33 + 60 = 93$	23.25	
$\alpha = .01$		$\overline{202}$		
$\overline{\text{UDL}} = 25.25 + (1.82)(2.5)$				
$= 25.25 + 4.55 = 29.80$	CR:	Like $(1,3,6,8) = 36 + 48 = 84$	21.0	
$\text{LDL} = 25.25 - 4.52 = 20.70$		Unlike $(2,4,5,7) = 34 + 84 = 118$	29.5	
		$\overline{202}$		

FORMAL ANALYSIS: (see Fig. 5-20.) The percent of cracked caps is small and n is large; we shall simplify computations by assuming a Poisson distribution: $\bar{c} = 202/8 = 25.25$

$$\hat{\sigma}_c = \sqrt{25.25} = 5.02 \quad \text{for individuals}$$

$$\hat{\sigma}_{\bar{c}} = \hat{\sigma}_c/\sqrt{4} = 2.51 \quad \text{for averages of 4}$$

FORMAL ANALYSIS CAPS C_1 ONLY: (see Fig. 5-21.)

$\bar{c} = 70/4 = 17 \cdot 5$; $\hat{\sigma}_c = \sqrt{17.5} = 4.18$; $\hat{\sigma}_{\bar{c}} = 4.18/\sqrt{2} = 2.96$ for averages of two groups. Then

$$\text{UDL}(.01) = 17.50 + (1.82)(2.96)$$
$$= 17.50 + 5.39$$
$$= 22.89$$
$$\text{LDL}(.01) = 12.11$$

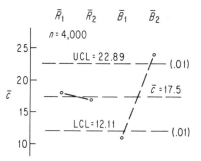

Fig. 5-21 Comparing effects of bottles and rings from different vendors when using caps from the better vendor. (Data from Table 5-14.)

5-8 A Very Important Experimental Design[1]: $\frac{1}{2} \times 2^3$

The 2^2 and 2^3 designs are useful strategies to use initially when investigating problems in many industrial processes. A third equally important strategy, discussed here, is more or less a combination of the 2^2 and 2^3 designs. It

[1] See also Sec. 12-6.

enables the experimenter to study effects of three different factors with only four combinations of them instead of the eight in a 2^3 design. This "half-rep of a two cubed" or 2×2 Latin Square design is especially useful in exploratory studies in which the quality characteristics are attributes.

In Table 5-16a and b, two particular halves of a complete 2^3 factorial design are shown. Some data based on this design are shown in Fig. 5-22.

TABLE 5-16   Two Special Halves of a 2^3 Factorial Design

	P_1		P_2				P_1		P_2	
F_1	T_1	(1)	T_2	(2)		F_1	T_2	(5)	T_1	(6)
F_2	T_2	(3)	T_1	(4)		F_2	T_1	(7)	T_2	(8)
	(a)						(b)			

The reasons for choosing only a special half of a 2^3 factorial design are reductions in time, effort, and confusion. Especially when it is expected that the effects of the three factors are probably independent, one should not hesitate to use a 2×2 Latin Square design. In such a 2×2 Latin Square, the main effect of any variable may possibly be confounded with an inter-action of the other two variables. This possible complication is often a fair price to pay for the advantage of doing only half the experimental combi-nations.

CASE HISTORY 5-10   Winding Grids

This case history presents two practical procedures:
1. A 2×2 Latin Square design using attribute data.
2. A graphical presentation of data allowing simultaneous comparisons of four types of defects instead of the usual single one.

Introduction[1]

Grids are important components of radio tubes. They go through the following manufacturing steps:
1. They are wound on a grid lathe. There are several grid lathes is use and the tension T on the lateral wire can be varied on each. After winding, they are transported to an operator called a hand-puller.

[1] Fred Ennerson, Ralph Fleischmann, and Doris Rosenberg, A Production Experiment Using Attribute Data, *Ind. Qual. Control*, vol. 8, no. 5, pp. 41–44, March, 1952.

2.   The hand-puller P uses a pair of tweezers to remove loose wire from the ends.   The loose wire is inherent in the manufacturing design.   The grids are then transported to a forming machine.

3.   Each forming machine has its forming operator F.   After forming, the grids go to inspection.

Following these operations, inspectors examine the grids for the four characteristics of an attribute nature, go no-go; spaciness, taper, damage, slant.

DESIGN OF THE EXPERIMENT

In a multistage operation of this kind, it is difficult to estimate just how much effect the different steps may be contributing to the total rejections being found at inspection.   Since the percent of rejections was economically serious, it was decided to set up a production experiment to be developed jointly by representatives of production, production engineering, and quality control.   They proposed and discussed the following subjects.

■ *Grid lathes:*   It was decided to remove any effect of different grid lathes by using grids from only one lathe.   The results of this experiment cannot then be transferred automatically to other lathes.

However, it was thought that the tension of the lateral wire during winding on the grid lathe might be important.   Consequently, it was decided to include *loose* tension T_1 and *tighter* tension T_2 in the experiment.   Levels of T_1 and T_2 were established by production engineering.

■ *Pullers:*   The probable effect of these operators was expected to be important.   Two of them were included in the experiment; both considered somewhat near average.   They are designated by P_1 and P_2.   Others could be studied later if initial data indicated an important difference between these two.

■ *Forming Operators:*   It was judged that the machine operators had more effect than the machines.   Two operators F_1 and F_2 were included, but both operated the *same* machine.

■ *Inspection:*   All inspection was done by the *same* inspector to remove any possible difference in standards.

■ *Design of the experiment:*   Actually the design of the experiment was being established during the discussion which led to the selection of three factors and two levels of each factor.

It would now be possible to proceed in either of two ways:

1.   Perform all $2^3 = 8$ possible combinations, or

2.   Perform a special half of the combinations chosen according to a 2×2 Latin Square arrangement such as in Table 5-16a.

Since it was thought that the effects of the different factors were probably *independent*, the Latin Square design was chosen instead of the full 2^3 factorial.

■ *Number of grids* to include in the experiment: The number was selected after the design of the experiment had been chosen.   Since grids were moved by production in trays of 50, it was desirable to select multiples of 50 in each of the four squares.   It was decided to include 100 grids in each for a total of 400 grids in the experiment.   This had two advantages: it allowed the entire experiment to be completed in less than a day and had minimum interference with production, and it was expected that this many grids would detect economically important differences.

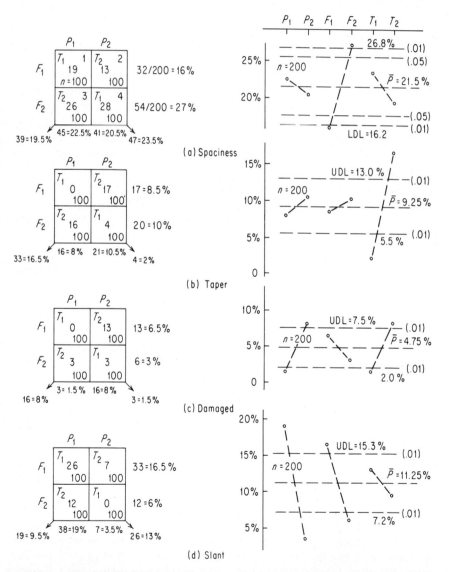

Fig. 5-22 Effects of pullers, formers, and tension on four defect types. (Computations from Table 5-17.)

To obtain the data for this experimental design, 200 grids were wound with loose tension T_1 on the chosen grid lathe and 200 with tighter tension T_2. These 400 grids were then " hand-pulled " and "formed" according to the chosen schedule. The numbers of rejects for each characteristic, found at inspection, are shown in the center of squares in Fig. 5-22. The number of grids in each combination is shown in the lower-right corner.

ANALYSIS OF THE DATA: (ANOM)

Main effects: By combining the data within the indicated pairs of squares we have the percents of rejects for spaciness as follows:

$P_1(1,3)$: $45/200 = 22.5\%$
$P_2(2,4)$: $41/200 = 20.5\%$
$F_1(1,2)$: $32/200 = 16.0\%$
$F_2(3,4)$: $54/200 = 27.0\%$
$T_1(1,4)$: $47/200 = 23.5\%$
$T_2(2,3)$: $39/200 = 19.5\%$

These are shown in Fig. 5-22a.

CONCLUSIONS

By examining the four charts in Fig. 5-22, we see where to place our emphasis for improving the operation.   It should be somewhat as follows:

Tension: A loose tension (T_1) on the grid lathe is preferable to a tight tension T_2 with respect both to taper and damage (Fig. 5-22b,c).

Forming operators: These have an effect on spaciness and slant (Charts a, d). Operator F_2 needs instruction with respect to spaciness; and operator F_1 with respect to slant.   This is very interesting.

Hand pullers: Again, one operator is better on one characteristic and worse on another.   Operator P_1 is a little more careful with respect to damage, but is ruining too many for slant (Fig. 5-22c,d).

It may be that there are other significant effects from these three factors; but if so, larger samples in each block would be needed to detect such significance.   This experiment has provided more than enough information to suggest substantial improvements and extensions in the processing of the grids.

It is interesting and helpful that each operator is better on one quality characteristic and worse on another.   Each operator can be watched for what is done right (or wrong), and whatever is learned can be taught to others. Sometimes it is argued that people are only human, so that while they are congratulated for good performance, they also can be taught how to improve their work.

COMPUTATION OF DECISION LINES: (ANOM): 2×2 Latin Square

The computation in a 2×2 Latin Square design proceeds exactly as in a 2^2 factorial design.   First, the overall percent defective $\bar{P}$, is determined for each defect type.   Then *decision lines are drawn* at: $\bar{P} \pm H_\alpha \hat{\sigma}_P$.   Each comparison is between two totals of $N = 200$.

TABLE 5-17   Computations of Decision Lines (ANOM)
Data of Fig. 5-22

■ *Spaciness:*   Comparing $k = 2$ groups of 200 each, $\bar{P} = 86/400 = 21.5\%$

$$\hat{\sigma}_P = \sqrt{\frac{(21.5)(78.5)}{200}} = 2.90\%$$

For $\alpha = .05$:
  UDL $= \bar{P} + H_\alpha\hat{\sigma}_P$
    $= 21.5 + (1.39)(2.90)$
    $= 25.5\%$
  LDL $= P - H_\alpha\hat{\sigma}_P$
    $= 17.5\%$

For $\alpha = .01$:
  UDL $= 21.5 + (1.82)(2.90)$
    $= 26.8\%$
  LDL $= 16.2\%$

■ *Taper:* $k = 2$ groups of 200 each: $\bar{P} = 37/400 = 9.25\%$

$$\hat{\sigma}_P = \sqrt{\frac{(9.25)(90.75)}{200}} = 2.05\%$$

For $\alpha = .05$:
  (Not needed)

For $\alpha = .01$:
  UDL $= 9.25 + (1.82)(2.05)$
    $= 13.0\%$
  LDL $= 5.5\%$

■ *Damaged:* $k = 2$ groups of 200 each: $\bar{P} = 19/400 = 4.75\%$

$$\hat{\sigma}_P = \sqrt{\frac{(4.75)(95.25)}{200}} = 1.50\%$$

For $\alpha = .05$:
  (Not needed)

For $\alpha = .01$:
  UDL $= 4.75 + (1.82)(1.50)$
    $= 7.50\%$
  LDL $= 2.0\%$

■ *Slant:* $k = 2$, $\bar{P} = 45/400 = 11.25\%$

$$\hat{\sigma}_P = \sqrt{\frac{(11.25)(88.75)}{200}} = 2.23\%$$

For $\alpha = .05$:
  UDL $= 11.25 + (1.39)(2.23)$
    $= 14.35$
  LDL $= 8.15$

For $\alpha = .01$:
  UDL $= 11.25 + (1.82)(2.23)$
    $= 15.3$
  LDL $= 7.2$

5-9   Practice Exercises

Exercise 5-1—Based on a Case History

Defective Glass Bottles: The use of quite small attribute samples taken at regular time intervals during production can provide evidence of important differences in the production system and indicate sources to be investigated for improvements.

Background: A meeting was arranged by telephone with a quality control man from a company whose only product was glass bottles.   This was one of the few times I ever attempted to give specific advice to anyone in a meeting without visiting his plant or having had previous experience in his industry. The plant was a hundred miles away; he seemed intelligent; and we had a sensible discussion when we met.

The following points were established during our discussion:

1.   There were too many rejects: the process was producing about 10% rejects of different kinds.

2.   Knowledge of rejects was obtained from an acceptance sampling operation or a 100% inspection of the bottles.   The inspection station was in a warehouse separate from the production areas; the usual purpose of inspection was to cull out the rejects before shipping the bottles to their customers. The information was not of much value for any process improvement effort; often obtained a week after bottles were made and too late to be considered representative of current production problems.

3.   Large quantities of glass bottles were being produced.   Several machines were operating continuously on three shifts, and for seven days per week.   Each machine had many cavities producing bottles.

My visitor returned to his plant and made the following arrangements:

■ A plant committee was organized representing production, inspection, and industrial engineering, to study causes and solutions to the problem of defects.

■ An initial sampling procedure was planned for some quick information. From the most recent production, samples of 15 per hour were to be chosen at random from: (1) each of three machines (on the hot end), on (2) each of three shifts, and (3) over seven days.

■ The sample bottles were to be placed in slots in an egg-carton type box marked to indicate the time of sampling as well as machine number, shift, and date.

■ After the bottles were collected and inspected, the number and type of various defects were recorded.   The data in Table 5-18 show only the total of all rejects.   (A breakdown by type of defect was provided but is not now available.)

Major Conclusions which you may reach:

1.   There were fundamental differences between the three machines, and differences between shifts.

2.   There was a general deterioration of the machines, or possibly in raw materials, over the seven days.   A comparison of this performance pattern with the scheduled maintenance may suggest changes in the maintenance schedule.

3.   Each machine showed a general uptrend in rejects; one machine is best and another is consistently the worst.

TABLE 5-18 Defective Glass
Bottles from Three Machines—
Three Shifts and Seven Days

Date	Shift	Machine 1	Machine 2	Machine 3
8/12	A	1	4	4
	B	4	0	4
	C	12	6	9
8/13	A	3	6	30
	B	2	8	46
	C	2	7	27
8/14	A	2	1	1
	B	8	11	15
	C	8	7	17
8/15	A	4	11	10
	B	5	7	11
	C	4	6	11
8/16	A	10	8	9
	B	6	12	10
	C	7	15	19
8/17	A	7	11	15
	B	12	9	19
	C	24	8	18
8/18	A	8	6	16
	B	10	12	17
	C	8	19	15

Number of days: 7
Number of machines: 3
Number of shifts: 3
   Total $N = (63)(120) = 7,560$
   $n = (8)(15) = 120$/shift/day/machine

4.   There is an unusual increase in rejects on all shifts on August 13 on one machine only.   Manufacturing records should indicate whether there was any change in the raw material going to that one machine.   If not, then something was temporarily wrong with the machine.   The records should show what adjustment was made.

Suggested Exercises: Discuss possible effects and *type* of reasons which might explain differences suggested below.   Prepare tables and charts to support your discussion.

1. *Effect of days.* All machines and shifts combined. Is there a significant difference observed over the seven days?
2. *Effect of machines.* Each machine with three shifts combined. What is the behavior pattern of *each* machine over the seven days?
3. *Effect of shift.* Each shift with three machines combined. What is the behavior pattern of each shift over the seven days?
4. Use only the data from the last four days as data for an analysis of means (including a discussion of findings and recommendations): (*a*) main effects only, (*b*) shift-machine interaction, (*c*) machine-day interaction.

Exercise 5-2: Wire Treatment

During processing of wire it was decided to investigate the effect of three factors on an electrical property of the wire.

- Three factors were chosen to be investigated:

T: Temperature of firing
D: Diameter of heater wire
P: The pH of a coating

- It was agreed to study these three factors at two levels of each. The experimental design was a 2×2 Latin Square.

- The quality characteristic was first measured as a variable; the shape of the measurement distribution was highly skewed with a long tail to the right. Very low readings (measurements) were desired; values up to 25 units were acceptable but not desirable. (Upper specification was 25.) It was agreed, arbitrarily for this study, to call *very low* readings (<5) *very good*; and high readings (>14) *bad*. Then the analysis was to be made on *each* of these two *attribute* characteristics.

TABLE 5-19   Wire Samples from Spools Tested after Firing under Different Conditions of Temperature, Diameter, and pH
The Design Used in This Production Study Was a 2×2 Latin Square

| | A. *Very Good Quality* | | | B. *Bad Quality* | |
	T_1	T_2		T_1	T_2
	P_1	P_2		P_1	P_2
D_1	A: 8/12 S: 4/12 H: 9/12	10/12 10/12 8/12	D_1	A: 0/12 S: 7/12 H: 1/12	1/12 0/12 4/12
	P_2	P_1		P_2	P_1
D_2	A: 8/12 S: 9/12 H: 7/12	7/12 7/12 5/12	D_2	A: 3/12 S: 1/12 H: 3/12	5/12 1/12 5/12

■ After this initial planning, it was suggested and accepted that the Latin Square design would be carried out under each of three *firing* conditions:

A: fired in air

S: fired by the standard method already in use

H: fired in hydrogen.

The data are shown in Table 5-19.   Whether the *very good* or *bad* qualities are most important in production is a matter for others to decide.

Suggested Exercises:

1. Compare the effectiveness of the three firing conditions, A, S, and H.   Then decide whether or not to pool the information from all three firing conditions when studying the effects of T, D, and P.
2. Assume now that it is sensible to pool the information of A, S, and H; make an analysis of T, D, and P effects.
3. Prepare a one- or two-page report of recommendations.

6

Two Special Strategies
in Troubleshooting

The two special methods of this chapter can be very effective in many situations:

- Disassembly and reassembly
- A special screening program for many treatments

6-1   Disassembly and reassembly

Any assembled product which can be readily disassembled and then reassembled can be studied by the general procedure of this chapter. The method with two components as in the first example below is standard procedure. But it is not standard procedure when three or four components are reassembled; the method has had many applications since the one in Case History 6-1.

> **EXAMPLE 6-1:** While walking through a pharmaceutical plant, we saw some bottles with crooked caps; the caps were crooked on some bottles but straight on others. The foreman said, "Yes, some of the caps are defective." Out of curiosity, we picked up a bottle with a crooked cap and another with a straight cap and interchanged them. But the "crooked" cap was now straight and the "straight" cap was now crooked. Obviously, it was not this cap but the *bottle* which was defective. No additional analysis was needed, but a similar check on a few more crooked assemblies would be prudent.

145

CASE HISTORY 6-1   Noisy Kitchen Mixers[1]

During the production of an electric kitchen mixer, a company was finding rejects for noise at final inspection.   Different production experiments had been run to determine causes of the problem, but little progress had been effected over several months of effort.   It was agreed that new methods of experimentation should be tried.

CHOICE OF FACTORS TO INCLUDE IN THE EXPERIMENT

There were different theories advanced to explain the trouble; each theory had some evidence to support it and some to contradict it.   A small committee representing production, engineering, and quality control met to discuss possible reasons for the trouble.   The usual causative variables had been tested without much success.

One gear component (henceforth called " gears ") was suspected; it connected the top half and bottom half of the mixer.   But there was no assurance that gears were a source of noise or the only source.   A production program to inspect gears for " out of round " was being considered; then it was expected to use only the best in assembly.

Then the question was aked: " If it isn't the gears, is the trouble in the top half or the bottom half of the mixer?"   There was no answer to the question.   "Is it feasible to disassemble several units and reassemble them in different ways?"   The answer: "Yes."   Since each half is a complicated assembly in itself, it was agreed to isolate the trouble in one-half of the mixer rather than look for the specific reason for trouble.   There were now three logical factors to include in the study:

$$
\begin{aligned}
&\text{Tops} \qquad &(T)\\
&\text{Bottoms} \qquad &(B)\\
&\text{Gears} \qquad &(G)
\end{aligned}
$$

The trouble must certainly be caused by one or more of these separate factors (main effect) or perhaps by the interrelation of two (interaction). Further experiments might be required after seeing the results of this preliminary study.

ARRANGEMENT OF FACTORS IN THE EXPERIMENT

The object of this troubleshooting project was to determine why some of the mixers were noisy.   There was no test equipment available to measure the degree of noise of the mixer, but only that it was good G or noisy N

It was agreed to select six mixers which were definitely noisy; and an equal number of good mixers.   Then a program of interchange (reassemblies of tops, bottoms, and gears) was scheduled.   During the interchanges, those mixer reassemblies which included a gear from a noisy mixer should test

---

[1] Ellis R. Ott, A Production Experiment with Mechanical Assemblies, *Ind. Qual. Control*, vol. 9, no. 6, 1953.

noisy *if* the gear was the cause; or if the top or bottom was the cause, then any reassembly which included a top or bottom from a noisy mixer should test noisy.   Thus it might be expected that half of the reassemblies (containing a gear from a noisy mixer) would test noisy, and the other half test good.

The reassembly of components from the three different groups was scheduled according to the design of Table 6-1 which shows also the number of noisy mixers, out of a possible six, in each of the reassembled combinations. After reassembly (with parts selected at random), each mixer reassembly was rated by the original inspector as either noisy or good.   In case of doubt, a

TABLE 6-1   Data on Reassemblies of Mixers

	N Gears		*G* Gears	
n = 6	*N* tops	*G* tops	*N* tops	*G* tops
N-bottoms	(1) $4\frac{1}{2}$	(2) 2	(3) 6	(4) 2
G-bottoms	(5) $4\frac{1}{2}$	(6) 3	(7) 6	(8) $1\frac{1}{2}$

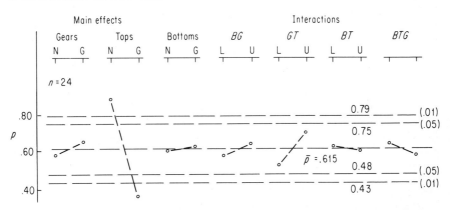

Fig. 6-1 A formal comparison of mixer performance (analysis assumes independence) in reassemblies using subassemblies from six noisy and six good mixers. (Data from Table 6-2.)

rating of $\frac{1}{2}$ was assigned.   For example, group 7 indicates all six mixers from the reassembly of *G* gears, *N* tops, and *G* bottoms were noisy.   No one type of component resulted in all *noisy* mixers nor all *good* mixers.   But tops from noisy mixers were a major source of trouble.   This was a *most unexpected* development and produced various exclamations from those who had been intimately associated with the problem.

Two things are immediately evident from Table 6-1:

1. Noisy gears *do not* reassemble consistently into noisy mixers, and
2. Noisy tops *do* reassemble almost without exception into noisy mixers.

FORMAL ANALYSIS

There were $6 \times 8 = 48$ reassemblies; the fractions of noisy ones are shown in Table 6-2 and graphically in Fig. 6-1.

TABLE 6-2   Computations for Main Effects and Interactions (ANOM)

	Number of noisy reassemblies Main effects;		*Two-factor interactions:*		
Gears:	N: (1,2,5,6):	$14/24 = 0.583$	TB:	(Like) (1,3,6,8):	$15/24 = 0.625$
	G: (3,4,7,8):	$15.5/24 = 0.646$		(Unlike) (2,4,5,7):	$14.5/24 = 0.604$
Tops:	N: (1,3,5,7):	$21/24 = 0.875$	TG:	(Like) (1,4,5,8):	$12.5/24 = 0.520$
	G: (2,4,6,8):	$8.5/24 = 0.354$		(Unlike) (2,3,6,7):	$17/24 = 0.708$
Bottoms:	N: (1,2,3,4):	$14.5/24 = 0.604$	BG:	(Like) (1,2,7,8):	$14/24 = 0.583$
	G: (5,6,7,8):	$15/24 = 0.625$		(Unlike) (3,4,5,6):	$15.5/24 = 0.646$
		$\bar{p} = 0.6145$			

Three-factor interactions:
TBG: $(-)$ (1,4,6,7): $15.5/24 = 0.646$
$(+)$ (2,3,5,8): $14/24 = 0.583$

Formal analysis:

$$\hat{\sigma}_p = \sqrt{\frac{(0.615)(0.385)}{24}} = 0.099$$

DECISION LINES (Fig. 6-1)

$\underline{\alpha = .05}$ $p \pm H_{.05}\sigma_p = 0.615 \pm (1.39)(0.099) = 0.615 \pm 0.138$

$$\text{UDL} = 0.75$$
$$\text{LDL} = 0.48$$

$\underline{\alpha = .01}$

$$\text{UDL} = 0.615 + 0.180 = 0.79$$
$$\text{LDL} = 0.615 - 0.180 = 0.43$$

DISCUSSION

Before this study, gears had been the suspected source of trouble. Can we say, now, that gears have no effect? The interaction analysis in Fig. 6-1 indicates that the only effect which might be suspect is the top-gear relationship. Although no top–gear decision lines have been drawn for $\alpha = .10$, top–gear combinations *may* warrant a continuing suspicion that more extreme out-of-round gears result in noisy mixers with some tops.

But the most important result is that of the tops, and engineering studies can be designed to localize the source of trouble within them.   This was done subsequently, I was told, by dividing tops into three areas and making reassemblies in a manner similar to that used in this study.

The decision to choose six noisy mixers and six good mixers was dictated primarily by expediency.   With this number of mixers, it was estimated that the reassembling and testing could be completed in the remaining 2h of the work day.   This was an important factor because some of the committee members were leaving town the next morning, and it was hoped to have some information on what would happen.   Secondly, it was thought that the cause of the trouble would be immediately apparent with even fewer reassembled mixers than six of each kind.

This type of 2^3 study with mechanical or electrical-mechanical assemblies is an effective and quick means of localizing the source of trouble.   It is quite general, and we have used it many times with many variations since this first experience.

Note: See Case Histories 15-3 and 15-4 on a general strategy in troubleshooting: "Ideas from patterns of data."

6-2   A Special Screening Program for Many Treatments[1]

Introduction

The periodic table contains many trace elements.   Some will increase the light output from the phosphor coating on the face of a radar tube.   This type of light output is called *cathodeluminescence*.   The coating produces luminescence by an electron beam.   How do we determine which trace element to add to a new type of coating?

There are many other examples of problems involving the screening of many possible treatments.   Many chemicals have been suggested as catalysts in certain usages.   Many substances are the possible irritants causing a particular allergy.   Many substances are tested as possible cures for a cancer. How can the testing of many possibilities be expedited?

This chapter considers one general strategy to provide answers to problems of this type where there are many items to be investigated.   How should they all be examined using only a few tests?   The amount of testing can be reduced drastically under certain assumptions.   Testing sequences involving many factors have been developed over the past three decades. These sequences have their origins in the two-level factorial experiment. In Case History 5-10 it was discussed how the 2^3 factorial design can be split into two Latin-Square blocks of four runs each; thus with a change in the assumptions, we can test the three factors with only four of the eight

[1] Ellis R. Ott and Frank W. Wehrfritz, A Special Screening Program for Many Treatments, *Stat. Neerl.*, Special Issue in Honour of Prof. H. C. Hamaker, July, 1973, pp. 165–170.

combinations and not perform the other four. As the number of factors increases, there are many other ways of dividing the 2^n runs into blocks; each strategy involves the extent to which the experimenter decides to relax the assumptions.

On the other hand, the basic 2^n factorial array can be augmented with additional data points, and the assumptions can then support quadratic estimates. Thus it is apparent from the developmental history of applied statistics that the number of tests or data points bear a direct relationship to the assumptions made at the planning stage for gathering data and to the testing of significance of effects seen when the data are finally at hand.

A screening program: In the case of screening many possible factors or treatments, under certain assumptions it is possible to reduce drastically the amount of testing.

Theorem: With n separate tests, it is possible to screen $(2^n - 1)$ treatments at the chosen levels as having a positive or negative effect, and to identify the effective treatment under assumptions given below.

Assumptions

1. It is feasible to combine more than one treatment in a single test. For example, several trace elements can be included in the same mix of coating.

2. No treatment is an inhibitor (depressant) for any other treatment. It is not unusual to observe a synergetic effect from two combined substances; such an effect would favor their joint inclusion. (The combining of two treatments which adversely affect each other would not be desirable.)

3. The effect of any treatment is either positive or negative (effective or not effective). For example, it is possible to determine whether the light output of one mix is brighter than that of another.

4. The effect of a treatment is consistent (not intermittent).

5. No more than one effective treatment is among those being studied. (There may be none.)

These assumptions are the basis of this initial discussion. However in application each assumption can be modified or disregarded as warranted by the conditions of a specific experiment. Modifications of the assumptions would require a reconsideration of the logic. For example, a numerical value of the yield of a process might be available on each run; this measure can then be used instead of considering only whether the run is a success or a failure. Replicates of each run would then provide a measure of the process variability. The following discussion is based on the listed assumptions, however.

Examples of Screening Programs

Screen 7 different treatments with three tests ($n = 3$)
Screen 15 different treatments with four tests ($n = 4$)
Screen 31 different treatments with five tests ($n = 5$)
Each of the n tests will include 2^{n-1} treatments.

EXAMPLE 6-2:   As an example, when the experimenter is planning three tests ($n = 3$), seven treatments or factors ($k = 2^n - 1 = 7$) can be allocated to the three tests.   Each test will include four treatments ($2^{n-1} = 4$).   The treatments or factors are designated as $X_1, X_2, X_3, X_4, X_5, X_6, X_7$ and assigned to these numbers as desired.   Table 1 shows which of the treatments to combine in each test.   The array of plus and minus signs is the *design matrix* indicating the *presence* or *absence* of a treatment (or high and low concentrations of a treatment).   The experimental responses are designated as E_i; each E is simply a ($+$) or a ($-$) when assumption 3 is being accepted.

The identification of the effective treatment is made by matching the pattern of experimental responses, E_1, E_2, E_3, with one of the columns of treatment identification. When the ($+$) and ($-$) results of the three tests match a column of ($+$) and ($-$) in Table 6-3, this *identifies* the single causative treatment.   If, for example, the three treatments yield the vertical sequence ($+ - +$), then X_3 is identified as the cause.

TABLE 6-3   A Screening Design for $2^3 - 1 = 7$ Factors

Treatments* included	Treatment identification							Experimental response
	X_1	X_2	X_3	X_4	X_5	X_6	X_7	
Test 1: X_1, X_2, X_3, X_5	+	+	+	−	+	−	−	E_1
Test 2: X_1, X_2, X_4, X_6	+	+	−	+	−	+	−	E_2
Test 3: X_1, X_3, X_4, X_7	+	−	+	+	−	−	+	E_3

* *Note:* each test combines four of the treatments.

DISCUSSION:

A discussion of possible answer patterns for the three tests involving the seven treatments follows:

No positive result: If none of the three tests yields a positive result, then none of the seven treatments is effective (assumptions 2 and 4).

One positive result: If, for example, T_1 alone yields a positive effect, then treatment X_5 is effective.   The reasoning is as follows: the only possibilities are the four treatments in T_1.   It can't be either X_1 or X_2 because they are both in T_2 which gave a negative result: it can't be X_3 which is also in T_3 which gave a negative result.   Then it must be X_5.

Two positive results: If T_1 and T_2 both yield positive results and T_3 yields negative (E_1 and E_2 are $+$; E_3 is $-$), then X_2 is the effective treatment.   The reasoning is similar to that for one positive experimental result; the decision that it is X_2 can be made easily from Table 6-3.   Simply look for the order ($+ + -$) in a column; it appears uniquely under X_2.

Three positive results: The ($+ + +$) arrangement is found under treatment X_1.   It is easily reasoned that it cannot be X_2 since X_2 does not appear in test 3 which gave a positive response; and similar arguments for each of the other variables other than X_1.

EXAMPLE 6-3:   When $n = 4$, let the $2^4 - 1 = 15$ treatments be

$$X_1, X_2, X_3, \ldots, X_{15}$$

Then a representation of the screening tests and analysis is given in Table 6-4.   Note that each test combines $8 = 2^{n-1}$ treatments.

TABLE 6-4 A Screening Design for $2^4 - 1 = 15$ Factors

	\multicolumn{15}{c}{Treatment identification*}														Experimental Response
	1	2	3	4	5	6	7	8	9	10	11	12	13	14	15	
T_1: $X_1 X_2 X_3 X_4\ X_6\ X_8\ X_{10}\ X_{12}$	+	+	+	+	−	+	−	+	−	+	−	+	−	−	−	E_1
T_2: $X_1 X_2 X_3 X_5\ X_6\ X_9\ X_{11} X_{13}$	+	+	+	−	+	+	+	−	+	−	+	−	+	−	−	E_2
T_3: $X_1 X_2 X_4 X_5\ X_7\ X_8\ X_{11} X_{14}$	+	+	−	+	+	−	+	+	−	−	+	−	−	+	−	E_3
T_4: $X_1 X_3 X_4 X_5\ X_7\ X_9\ X_{10} X_{15}$	+	−	+	+	+	−	+	−	+	+	−	−	−	−	+	E_4

* The treatments may also be designated by the letter $A, B, C, \ldots, O$: (Case History 6-2)

Test 1: A B C D F H J L
Test 2: A B C E F I K M
Test 3: A B D E G H K N
Test 4: A C D E G I J O

There is a unique combination of the plus and minus signs corresponding to each of the 15 variables; this uniqueness identifies the single cause (assumption 5). No variable is effective if there is no positive response.

FEWER THAN $2^n - 1$ TREATMENTS TO BE SCREENED: Frequently, the number of treatments k to be screened is not a number of the form $2^n - 1$. Then designate the k treatments as

$$X_1, X_2, X_3, \ldots, X_k$$

When $n = 3$ and $k = 5$, for example, carry out the three tests T_1, T_2, T_3, disregarding entirely treatments X_6 and X_7.

TABLE 6-5   A Screening Design for Five Factors

	Treatment identification					Experimental response
	X_1	X_2	X_3	X_4	X_5	
$T_1: X_1, X_2, X_3, X_5$	+	+	+	−	+	E_1
$T_2: X_1, X_2, X_4$	+	+	−	+	−	E_2
$T_3: X_1, X_3, X_4$	+	−	+	+	−	E_3

Note: We would not expect either T_2 alone or T_3 alone to give a positive result; that would be a puzzler under the assumptions. (Possible explanations: a gross experimental blunder or an intermittent effect.)

Again, if there are fewer than 15 treatments to be screened (but more than 7, which employs only three tests), assign numbers to as many treatments as there are and ignore the balance of the numbers. The analysis in Table 6-4 is still applicable.

AMBIGUITY IF ASSUMPTION 5 IS NOT APPLICABLE: One seldom can be positive, in advance, whether there *may possibly be two or more effective treatments* in the group to be screened. If during the experiment, some combination of the treatments gives a greatly superior performance, this is an occasion for rejoicing. But economics is a factor which may require or desire the specific identification of causes. Let us consider the case of seven treatments being screened (Table 6-3):

■ ONE POSITIVE TEST RESPONSE: no ambiguity possible; the indicated treatment is the only possibility.

■ TWO POSITIVE TEST RESPONSES: If both T_1 and T_2 give positive responses, then it may be X_2 alone or any two or three of the three treatments X_2, X_5, and X_6.

The possible ambiguity can be resolved in a few tests; an obvious procedure would be to run tests with X_2, X_5, and X_6 individually. However, when there seems to be little possibility of having found more than a single positive treatment, run a single test with X_5 and X_6 combined. If the result is negative, then the single treatment is X_2.

CASE HISTORY 6-2   Screening Some Trace Elements

Some of the earth's trace elements have important effects upon some quality characteristics of cathode-ray tubes. Something is known about these effects, but not enough. Hoping to identify any outstanding effect upon the light-output quality characteristic, a screening study was planned. Fifteen trace elements (designated A, B, C, $\ldots$, O) were mixed in four phosphor slurries in the combinations shown in Table 6-6 (eight different trace elements were included in each slurry run). $A(+)$ indicates those elements which were included in a test and a $(-)$ indicates those which were not included. The measured output responses of the four slurries are shown in the column at the right.

TABLE 6-6 **Variables Data in a Screening Design for 15 Factors (Trace Elements)**

	C_4^4	C_3^4			C_2^4						C_1^4				Experimental response
	A	B	C	D	E	F	G	H	I	J	K	L	M	N	O	
Test 1	+	+	+	+	−	+	−	+	−	+	−	+	−	−	−	46
Test 2	+	+	+	−	+	+	−	−	+	−	+	−	+	−	−	84
Test 3	+	+	−	+	+	−	+	+	−	−	+	−	−	+	−	44
Test 4	+	−	+	+	+	−	+	−	+	+	−	−	−	−	+	51

■ Previous experience with this characteristic had shown that the process variability was small; consequently, the large response from run 2 is "statistically significant."

■ Also, the response from test 2 was a definite improvement over ordinary slurries which had been averaging about 45 to 50. The other three output responses, 46, 44, and 51, were typical of usual production. The four test responses can be considered to be: $(- + - -)$. Under the original assumptions of this study plan, the identity of the responsible trace element must be M.

■ One cannot be sure, of course, that the uniqueness assumption is applicable. Regardless, the eight trace elements of run 2 combine to produce an excellent output response. At this point in experimentation, the original fifteen trace elements have been reduced to the eight of run 2 with strong evidence that the improvement is actually a consequence of M alone. Whether it is actually a consequence of M alone or some combination of two or more of the eight elements of run 2 can now be determined in a sequence of runs. Such a sequence might be as follows:

The first run might be with M as the only one, the second with the seven other than M. If there is still uncertainty, experiments could continue eliminating one trace element at a time.

6-3 Other Screening Strategies

One can find other screening strategies discussed in the technical literature. Anyone who has reason to do many screening tests should consider this preceding strategy and consult the published literature for others.

The foregoing allocation of experimental factors to the tests is based on combinatorial arrays. As such, this strategy serves to reduce the initial large number of factors to more manageable size.

7
Narrow-limit Gaging

7-1 Introduction

Go no-go gaging has *advantages* over measurements which are made on a variables scale; less skill and time are usually required. But also, the tradition of gaging has been established in many shops even when it may be entirely feasible to make measurements.

However, there are real *disadvantages* associated with gaging. Large sample sizes are required to detect important changes in the process. This is expensive when the test is nondestructive; it becomes exorbitant when the test is destructive. The function of inspection is a dual one: (1) it is to separate the sheep from the goats, of course; but (2) it should provide a warning feedback of developing trends. Go no-go gages made to the specifications provide little or no warning of approaching trouble. When the process produces only a small percent of units out of specifications, a sample selected for gaging will seldom contain any out-of-spec units. By the time out-of-spec units are found, a large percentage of the product may already be out of specifications, and we are in real trouble.

Hopefully there is a procedure which retains the important advantages of gaging but improves its efficiency. Narrow-limit gaging is such a method. It is a gaging procedure; it is versatile; it is applicable to chemical as well as to mechanical and electrical applications. Required sample sizes are only nominally larger than equivalent ones when using measurements.

The discussion in this chapter centers about *narrowed* or *compressed* gages used to guide a process. They function to prevent trouble rather than to wait until sometime after manufacture to learn that the process has not been operating satisfactorily. A process can be guided only if information from gaging is made available to production in advance of a substantial increase in defectives.

The variation of some processes over short periods is often less than permitted by the specifications (tolerances). It is then economical to allow some shift in the process, provided a system is operating which detects the *approach* of rejects.

7-2   Outline of an NL-Gaging Plan

At the start, narrowed or compressed gages (NL gages) must be specified and prepared. They may be mechanical ones made in the machine shop; they may simply be limits computed and marked on a dial gage or computed and used with any variables measurements procedure.

NL-gages are narrowed by an amount indicated by $t\sigma$; see Fig. 7-1.

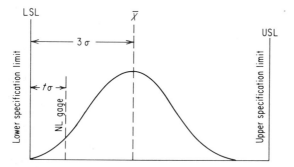

Fig. 7-1   Definition of $t\sigma$ for NL-gage.

Small samples of size n are usually gaged at regular time intervals; n may be as small as 4 or 5 and is not usually greater than 10. (The sample is of the most recent production when being used for process control.)

A specified number c of items in a sample of n will be allowed to fail[1] the NL gages. If there are c or fewer items nonconforming to the NL gages in a sample of n, the process is continued without adjustment. If more than c nonconforming items are found, then the process is to be adjusted.

[1] Any unit which fails an NL gage can be regaged at the actual specifications to determine salability.

Separate records are kept of the number of units which fail the smaller NL gage and of the number failing the larger NL gage.

In the applications discussed here, there are upper and lower specifications, and the distance between them is larger than the process capability. That is, $(USL - LSL) > 6\sigma$.

It is assumed that the process produces a product whose quality characteristic is a reasonably normal distribution (over a short time interval). See "Hazards," Sec. 7-6.

Basic Assumptions for NL Gaging

1.   An estimate of the basic process variability is available or can be made. Perhaps an estimate can be made from a control chart on ranges or perhaps from experience with a similar application.

2.   The difference between the upper and lower specification limits (USL, LSL) is greater than 6σ; i.e., $USL - LSL > 6\sigma$.

This assumption means that some shifting in the process average is acceptable.   It also means that only one tail of the distribution need be considered when computing operating characteristic curves (OC curves).

7-3   Selection of a Simple NL-Gaging Sampling Plan

Those who have used $\overline{X}$, R charts are familiar with the usefulness of small samples of $n = 4$ or 5.   Samples as large as 9 or 10 are not often used; they are too sensitive and indicate many shifts and peculiarities in the process which are not important problems.

Then those of you who are familiar with $\overline{X}$, R charts will approve of an NL-gage plan which gives process guidance comparable to that of an $\overline{X}$, R chart for $n = 4$ or 5.   Three such plans are the following:

A. $n = 5, c = 1, t = 1.0$

D. $n = 4, c = 1, t = 1.2$

F. $n = 10, c = 2, t = 1.2$

Two OC curves are shown in Fig. 7-2, along with that of an $\overline{X}$ control-chart plan, $n = 4$.   A discussion of the construction of operating characteristic curves (OC curves) of some plans is given in Sec. 7-5.

When guiding a process, we may believe that there is need for more information than provided by an $\overline{X}$, R chart using $n = 5$.   If so, we usually take samples of five *more frequently* in preference to increasing the size of n.   The same procedure is recommended for an NL-gage system.

The effectiveness of NL-gaging in helping prevent trouble is improved when we *chart* the information from successive samples.   These charts indicate the approach of trouble in time to take preventive action.

Since an indication of approaching trouble is not possible in a plan with $c = 0$, the smallest recommended value is $c = 1$.   A frequent preference is a plan with $n = 4$ or 5, $c = 1$, and $t = 1$.

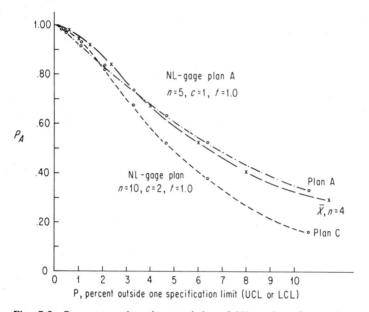

Fig. 7-2 Some operating characteristics of NL-gaging plans and a variables control chart on $\bar{X}$, $n = 4$.   OC curves are shown for plans *A* and *C* (data from Table 7-2).   The OC curves of plans *A* and *D* are very close to that of an $\bar{X}$ chart, $n = 4$.   For that reason, the curve for plan *D* has not been drawn.

CASE HISTORY 7-1   Extruding Plastic Caps and Bottles

The mating fit of a semiflexible cap on a bottle depends on the *inside diameter* (ID) of the cap and the *outside diameter* (OD) of the bottle.

SOME PERTINENT INFORMATION

1.   The molded plastic caps and bottles shrink after leaving the mold and during cooling.   We found it reasonable to immerse them in cold water before NL-gages were used.   Sometimes they are held in a plastic bag during immersion.   Gaging could then be done shortly after extrusion.

2.   The ID and OD dimensions can be adjusted by certain temperature changes in the machine molds and by other machine adjustments.   It requires specific knowledge of the process to effect these machine changes on diameter without introducing visual defects into the product.

3.   The usual production control check on these two diameters is by gaging; a plug gage for ID and a ring gage for OD.   It is traditional to use plug gages made to the maximum and minimum specifications.   Then by the time they find a reject, large numbers of out-of-spec caps or bottles are already in the bin.   Since it is rarely economical to make a 100% inspection of caps or bottles, the partial bin of the product must be scrapped.

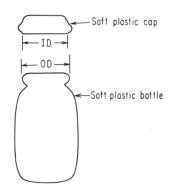

Fig. 7-3 Molded plastic bottle components.

4.   It is possible to purchase dimensional equipment to measure the OD and the ID.   However they are slow to use, not as accurate as one would expect, require more skill than gaging, and the plotting of data is more elaborate.

5.   Each cap/bottle has the cavity of origin molded in it because differences between cavities are common.   However, it requires excessive time to establish the cavity numbers represented in a sample and then to measure and record diameters.

DETERMINING THE VARIABILITY OF CAP ID.   On one type of plastic cap, the specifications were

$$USL = 1.015 \text{ in. and } LSL = 1.00 \text{ in.}$$

Samples of three caps from each of the 20 cavities were gaged with a series of six gages having diameters of 1.000 in., 1.003 in., 1.006 in., 1.009 in., 1.012 in., and 1.015 in.   The department participated in measuring diameters with these plug gages.   It was first determined that the ID of a cap could be determined to within 0.001 in. or 0.002 in. with this set of gages.   Then the ID of samples of three caps were "measured" with them and ranges of $n = 3$ computed.   From these measurements we computed

$$\hat{\sigma} = \bar{R}/d_2 \cong 0.003 \text{ in.}$$

We already had plug gages to measure 1.003 in. and 1.012 in.; these corresponded to NL gages compressed by $t\hat{\sigma} \cong 0.003$ $(t = 1.0)$.   We decided to use the plan: $n = 10$, $t = 1.0$, and $c = 1$; random samples of 10 would allow more representative sampling of the 20 cavities.[1]   Other plans using different values of n and c might have been equally effective, of course.

The NL-gaging plan was used to guide the process, as planned originally. But also, several *special studies* were made under different process adjustments; the NL gages were used to measure and compare the effects of these changes. Data from a typical study were tabulated as in Table 7-1.   The usual study used a 2^2 or a 2^3 design as in Chap. 5.

TABLE 7-1 A Sampling Method of Estimating Process Relation to Specifications (1.000 – 1.015 in.) Using a Sequence of 5 Go, No-Go Gages

($n=10$) Sample no.	Classification steps						
	<1.000	1.000– 1.003	1.003– 1.006	1.006– 1.009	1.009– 1.012	1.012– 1.015	>1.015
1					1	8	1
2					7	3	
3			1	8	1		
4			3	7			
5			5	5			
6			4	6			
7			etc.				
8							

The numbers in the columns suggest a possible sequence of classifications from samples of 10 using gages milled to low and high dimensions as follows:

	Low, in.	High, in.
G_1	1.000	1.003
G_2	1.003	1.006
G_3	1.006	1.009
G_4	1.009	1.012
G_5	1.012	1.015

These five gages permit the seven classifications shown at the top of columns above.

CONSEQUENCES.   Much of the art of adjusting very expensive and complicated equipment was replaced by cause-and-effect relationships which were developed as in Table 7-1.   A production process which had been a source of daily rejects, aggravation, and trouble began gradually to improve.

Then the department was expanded by purchasing equipment for the manufacture of plastic bottles; the critical dimension was now the OD of the

[1] See item 5 above.

neck. The same general approach which had been used for caps was still applicable; ring gages when narrowed by .003 in. from the LSL and the USL proved satisfactory NL gages.

Soft plastic caps/bottles are produced in very large quantities and the cost of a single unit is not great. There are serious reasons why traditional manufacturing controls discussed in (3) and (4) above are not satisfactory.

Industrial experiences with NL gages have shown them to be practical and effective.

CASE HISTORY 7-2   Chemical Titration

INTRODUCTION

Several multiheaded presses were producing very large quantities of a pharmaceutical product in the form of tablets. It was intended to double the number of presses which would require an increase in the amount of titration and the number of chemists; this was at a time when analytical chemists were in short supply. It was decided to explore the possibility of applying gaging methods to the titration procedure. The following NL-gaging plan was a joint effort of persons knowledgeable in titration procedures and applied statistics.

SOME PERTINENT INFORMATION

1.   Data to establish the variability of tablet-making presses were already in the files; they were used to provide the estimate $\hat{\sigma} \cong 0.125$ grains.

2.   Specifications on individual tablets were LSL = 4.5 grains, USL = 5.5 grains.

3.   Then $6\hat{\sigma} = 0.75$ is less than the difference USL-LSL of 1.0 grains. A choice of $t = 1.2$ with $\hat{\sigma} = 0.125$ gives $t\hat{\sigma} \cong 0.15$. The chemists agreed that this was feasible. The lower NL-gage value was then 4.65 grains, and the upper NL-gage value was 5.35 grains.

SAMPLING.   It was proposed that we continue the custom of taking several samples per day from each machine; then an OC curve of our NL-gage plan was desired which would be comparable to an $\overline{X}$, R chart, $n = 4$ or 5.   Some calculations led to the plan; $n = 4$, $t = 1.2$, and $c = 1$. (See Table 7-3 for the computation of the OC curve.)

A semiautomatic charging machine was adjusted to deliver titrant required to detect by color change:

1.   Less than 4.65 grains on the first charge.
2.   More than 5.35 grains on the second charge.

CONSEQUENCES.   With minor adjustments, the procedure was successful from the beginning. The accuracy of the gaging method was checked regularly by titration to endpoint.

Shifts on individual presses were detected by the presence of tablets outside

the NL gages, but usually within specifications.   The presses could be adjusted to make tablets to specifications.   The required number of chemists was
not doubled when the increased number of tablet presses began operation—in
fact the number was reduced by almost half.

7-4   Sequential NL-Gaging Plans

Introduction

Almost everyone accepts the premise that visual records should be kept of
process performance.   Almost everyone is a bit careless in the matter, too.
Consider a process with samples taken frequently and a visual record being
kept.   Then it may be satisfactory to permit a shift in process to go undetected
on a single sample *provided* it is detected on a second or third sample.   A
double-phased plan has proved to be practical to use on a production floor;
the second phase is based on the *accumulated evidence from the last three
samples*.   Since a visual chart is being kept, the accumulated total can be
done mentally.

For example, the double plan ($n = 5$, $c = 1$; $n = 15$, $c = 2$) with $t = 1.0$
provides joint criteria for machine adjustment on a nonconforming characteristic.   This is referred to as Plan E.

Adjustment of Process

Check with the NL gage a sample of five pieces of the most recent production
at regular time intervals (quarter-hourly, half-hourly, hourly, or as experience
indicates a need).

■ Record the number of pieces which are high and the number low on the
chart (see Fig. 7-4).

■ The machine shall be adjusted on the nonconforming characteristic (to
NL gage) when and only when either

1.   Two or more pieces fail the NL gages in the last *single* sample ($n = 5$,
$c = 1$ criterion), or

2.   Three or more pieces fail the NL gages in the *accumulation* of the last
three samples ($n = 15$, $c = 2$ criterion).

■ Continue otherwise to operate the machine without adjustment.

■ When a rejection occurs on a single sample (and the process is then
adjusted), only the single-sample criterion is applied until two successive conforming samples have been obtained.   Then the criterion, $n = 15$, $c = 2$, also
is operative.

Note: The probability that Plan A, for example, will detect a process producing $P = 2.1\%$ defective is $P_D = (1 - 0.835) = .165$ (see Table 7-4).   The
probability that the same plan A will approve 2.1% defective on all of three
successive samplings is

$$(.835)^3 = .58$$

and that it will detect it at least once is $(1 - .58) = .42$.   The probability of detecting a 2.1% defective process can be increased by including the pooled information from the last three samples with the $n = 15$, $c = 2$ criterion. Some probabilities are given in Table 7-4, and OC curves are shown in Fig. 7-7.

CASE HISTORY 7-3   Thickness of Oxide-coated Metal

Trays holding 25 nickel cathodes were sprayed with an oxide coating.   A critical characteristic was the thickness of the coating being applied by several passes across each tray.

SOME PERTINENT INFORMATION

1.   The process was too variable.   It was not possible to use 100% inspection to select the good ones; the softness of the coating made any gaging or measurement a destructive process.

2.   Not only was it destructive to measure; it was difficult because the oxide-coated surface was very rough and uneven.   Gaging was easier.

3.   The cost of rejecting a tray of sprayed cathodes and reworking them was not much, but it reduced the output and there was no assurance that reworked trays would be any better.   Good cathodes required that the process itself be good.

4.   Sprayed cathodes were assembled into electronic tubes, then tested for electronic characteristics which were dependent upon the thickness of the cathode coating.   A rejected tube was not reworkable and meant a major loss.

PROCEDURE

It was decided to replace the existing process control procedure by NL gaging.   The gages were compressed by 1.0σ $(t = 1.0)$.   The double NL-gaging plan was: $n = 5$, $c = 1$ and $n = 15$, $c = 2$.

The OC curves of this plan corresponding to the single sample and the three accumulated samples $(n = 15)$ are shown in Fig. 7-7.

From each tray of cathodes which had been sprayed, five were selected and checked with the NL gages.   The number of oversize (high) and undersize (low) cathodes were marked on the chart as in Fig. 7-4.

By studying the behavior of the spraying, it was soon learned when and how the process should be adjusted: by cleaning the spray guns, by increasing or decreasing the number of passes, by instructing the operator as to the speed of passes.

The improvements in this process were of different kinds:

1.   It was possible to use NL gaging as an acceptance sampling plan on trays of sprayed cathodes and thus eliminate a holdup on the production line.

2.   Because of rapid determination of the state of control available by go no-go gaging, the spray operator had current information to use in adjusting

the process.   This plan quickly reduced the number of trays sent back for additional spray passes (cathodes undersized), and simultaneously reduced the number of cathodes which were scrapped for being oversize from an average of 20 % to less than 1 %.   With less rework flowing through the production line, it was possible to reduce the inspection personnel while increasing the yield of good cathodes.

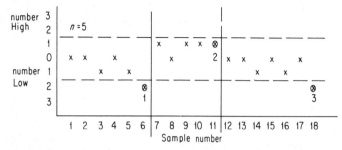

Fig. 7-4   An NL-gage chart for spraying cathodes.   (Plan: $n = 5$, $c = 1$ and $n = 15$, $c = 2$ with gage compressed one standard deviation, i.e., $t = 1.0$.)   *Notes*: (1) Sprayer cleaned after failing $n = 5$, $c = 1$ criterion; (2) Number of spray-passes reduced after a conference with foreman (process failed the three combined sample criterion, $n = 15$, $c = 2$); (3) Number of spray-passes increased after conference with foreman (process failed $n = 5$, $c = 1$ criterion).

3.   Even more important, however, was the uniformity of cathode thickness.   It was possible to reduce the overall spread of the sprayed cathodes by a factor of 50 % using NL gaging.   This improvement was so radical and so important in subsequent operations that the completed product of which the cathodes were a subassembly was improved from being mediocre to being a successful product on the market.

CASE HISTORY 7-4   Machine-shop Dimensions

Some aircraft navigational instruments use parts machined with great precision.   It was customary in this shop to measure critical dimensions to the nearest ten-thousandth.   The specifications on one part were 0.2377 to 0.2383 in. (a spread of 0.0006 in.).   Data on hand indicated a machine capability of ± 0.0002, i.e., an estimated $\hat{\sigma} = (0.0004)/6$.   The realities of measurement would not permit using limits compressed less than 0.0001 in.; this corresponded to $t \cong 1.5$.   The double plan was: $n = 5$, $c = 1$ and $n = 15$, $c = 2$.

The toolmaker would measure a machined piece with a toolmaker's micrometer and indicate by a check the reading which he observed as in Fig. 7-5. This chart is a combination between a variables chart ($n = 1$) and NL-gage chart.   It is a form which was accepted and maintained by "old-line" machine operators.

The machine operators were willing to make checkmarks above and below the NL-gage lines. Previously, their practice had been to flinch and make a sequence of three or four consecutive checkmarks at UCL = 0.2383. Then rechecks later of production at these times would show oversized parts. The psychology of making checks outside NL gages but within specifications resulted in resetting the tool before rejects were machined.

Although no physical NL gages were made for this particular machine shop application, the entire concept of adjusting the process was exactly that of NL gaging.

	Nov. 2										Nov. 4			
				1						2				
.2383			✓	Ⓥ	NL gage			✓	✓	Ⓥ				
.2382	✓✓	✓✓	✓✓	✓✓✓		✓	✓✓✓	✓✓	✓✓	✓✓✓				
.2381	✓✓	✓✓✓	✓✓		✓	✓✓✓	✓✓	✓✓	✓✓	✓✓	✓	✓	✓✓	
.2380	✓				✓✓	✓✓	✓✓				✓✓	✓✓		
.2379					✓✓						✓✓	✓		
.2378					NL gage									
.2377														
Time:	8	9	10	11	12	1	2	3	4	5	8	9	10	

Fig. 7-5 Adjustment chart on a screw machine operation using NL-gaging principles. (Plan: $n = 5$, $c = 1$ and $n = 15$, $c = 2$.) *Notes:* (1) Sample failed $n = 5$, $c = 1$ criterion. Tool was reset. (2) Sample failed $n = 15$, $c = 2$ criterion. Tool was reset.

7-5   OC curves of NL-Gage Plans[1]

It is not easy at first to accept the apparent effectiveness of NL gaging with small samples. True, the OC curves in Fig. 7-2 do indicate that some NL-gaging plans are very comparable to ordinary $\overline{X}$, R control charts. But actual experience is also helpful in developing a confidence in them.

We used samples of $n = 4$, 5, 10, and 15 in preceding examples. It will be seen that OC curves comparable to $\overline{X}$, R charts, $n = 4$, can be obtained from NL-gaging plans using

$$n = 4 \text{ or } 5 \qquad t = 1.0 \text{ to } 1.2 \qquad \text{and } c = 1$$

We show the method of deriving OC curves for $n = 5$ and 10 in Table 7-2. Curves for many other plans can be derived similarly.

Two different types of percents will be used in this discussion:

1. P will represent the percent outside the *actual specification*. It appears as the abscissa in Fig. 7-7. It is important in assessing the suitability of a particular sampling plan. It appears as column 4 in Table 7-2.

2. P' will represent the percent outside the NL gage corresponding to each value of P. It appears as column 1 in Table 7-2. It is an auxiliary percent used in Table A-5 to determine probabilities P_A.

[1] May be omitted by reader.

TABLE 7-2   Deriving Operating Characteristic Curves (OC curves) for Some NL-Gage Plans with Gage Compressed by 1.0σ ($t = 1.0$)

(1) $P' = \%$ to left of NL gage	(2) $BC =$ $3 - t - z$ $= 2 - z$ for $t = 1.0$	(3) $AC =$ $3 - z =$ $t + (2) =$ $1 + (2)$	(4) $P = 100p$ $= \%$ to left of LSL	P_A PLAN A $n = 5,$ $c = 1$	P_A PLAN B $n = 5,$ $c = 2$	P_A PLAN C $n = 10$ $c = 2$
2%	2.055	3.055	0.1%	.996	1.0	.999
4	1.75	2.75	0.3	.985	.999	.994
6	1.55	2.55	0.5	.968	.998	.981
10	1.28	2.28	1.1	.919	.991	.930
15	1.036	2.036	2.1	.835	.973	.820
20	0.84	1.84	3.3	.737	.942	.678
25	0.675	1.675	4.7	.633	.896	.526
30	0.524	1.524	6.4	.528	.837	.383
40	0.252	1.252	10.6	.337	.683	.167
50	0	1.0	15.9	.188	.500	.055

Derivation of OC Curves

On the vertical scale in Fig. 7-7 we show the *probability of acceptance*, P_A; it represents the probabilities that the process will be *approved* or *accepted without adjustment* under the NL-gaging plan for different values of P. To obtain P_A, we use the binomial tables A-5.

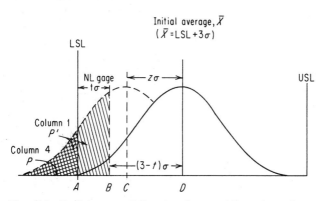

Fig. 7-6 Deriving an OC curve for an NL-gaging plan (general procedure). Details are given in Tables 7-2 and 7-3 (where $z\sigma$ is the distance $\bar{X}$ is assumed to have shifted).

■ Since Table A-5 is easiest to use with integral percents, we first assign selected integral values for percents P' to the left of the NL gage; these are shown in column 1 of Table 7-2.   Then P_A can be obtained immediately from the Table A-5 for *any pair* of values of n and c.   They are shown for three different plans A, B, and C.

■ We now have *ordinates* P_A for the OC curve and need to determine their corresponding abscissas P; they are shown in column 4. This column is derived from column 1 in four steps:

1. We first designate by $z\sigma$ the distance that $\overline{X}$ shifts (see Fig.7-6). Then for any pair of n and c

$$BC = (3 - t - z)\sigma$$

When $t = 1$, this gives $(2 - z)$; this is the heading of column 2. Values in column 2 are determined from Table A-1, areas under the normal curve, corresponding to selected values of P' in column 1.

2. From Fig. 7-6, we see that

$$AC = BC + t\sigma = (3 - z)\sigma$$

Compute values in column 3 by adding $t = 1.0$ to values in column 2.

3. Obtain percent values P in column 4 from Table A-1, areas under the normal curve. These correspond to entries in column 3.

4. Plot points corresponding to column 4 on the horizontal axis and column 5 on the vertical axis (Fig. 7-7).

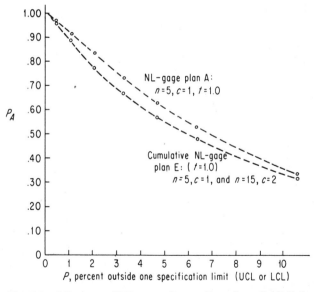

Fig. 7-7 OC curves of NL-gage plans. (Data from Table 7-4).

7-6 Hazards

There is a potential error in values of P_A if our estimate of σ is in substantial error. In practice, our estimate of σ might be in error by 25%, for example. Then instead of operating on a curve corresponding to $t = 1.0$, we either operate on the curve corresponding to $t = 1.25$ when our estimate is too large, or we operate on the curve corresponding to $t = 0.75$ when our estimate is too small. In either case, a difference of this small magnitude does not appear to be an important factor.

Suppose that the portion of the distribution nearest the specification is not normally distributed. In most instances this is more of a statistical question than a practical one, although there are notable exceptions in certain electronic characteristics, for example. In machining operations, we have never found enough departure from a normal distribution to be important except when units produced from different sources (heads, spindles) are being combined. Even then, that portion of the basic curve nearest the specification limit (and from which we draw our sample) is typically normal.

TABLE 7-3   Deriving an OC Curve for NL-Gage Plan $n = 4$, $t = 1.2$, $c = 1$

The OC curve of this plan is very similar to that of an $\bar{X}$ chart, $n = 4$. See Fig. 7-2.

$P' = \%$ to left of NL gage, (1)	BC $= 3 - t - z$ $= 1.8 - z$ for $t = 1.2$ (2)	AC $= 3 - z =$ $t + (1.8 - z) =$ $t + (2) =$ $1.2 + (2)$ (3)	$P = 100p=$ $\%$ to left of LSL (4)	NL-gage plan D $n = 4$, $t = 1.2$ $c = 1$ P_A
1	2.33	3.53	0.00	.999
5	1.645	2.845	0.23	.986
10	1.285	2.485	0.65	.948
15	1.037	2.237	1.3	.89
20	0.84	2.04	2.1	.82
25	0.675	1.875	3.0	.74
30	0.52	1.72	4.3	.65
40	0.25	1.45	7.3	.47
50	0.00	1.20	11.5	.31
60	−0.25	0.95	17.1	.18

If the distribution is *violently* nonnormal, or if an error is made in estimating σ, the NL-gaging system still provides control of the process but not necessarily at the predicted level.

In discussing a similar situation, Tippett[1] remarks that there need not be too much concern about whether there was an "accurate and precise statistical result, because in the complete problem there were so many other elements which could not be accurately measured."

[1] L. H. C. Tippett, *Technological Applications of Statistics*, John Wiley & Sons, Inc., New York, 1950.

TABLE 7-4 Some Probabilities for OC Curves of NL Gages

(1) $P' = \%$ to left of NL gage	(2) $P = 100p =$ % to left of LSL	Plan A* $n = 5,$ $c = 1,$ $t = 1.0$	Sequential Plan E† (Plan A *and* $n = 15, c = 2$)
2%	0.1%	.996	.995
4	0.3	.985	.980
6	0.5	.968	.955
10	1.1	.919	.884
15	2.1	.835	.775
20	3.3	.737	.668
25	4.7	.633	.571
30	6.4	.528	.481
40	10.6	.337	.320
50	15.9	.188	.184

* From Table 7-2.

† *Note:* Plan E: $P_A = 1 - P_R$
where $P_R = \Pr(x \geq 2) + \Pr^3(x = 1)$, and each P_R is for Plan A. (See Fig. 7-7.)

Discussion

We have used NL gages in a variety of process-control applications over the last several years. Both from experience and the underlying theory, we find that NL gages offer a major contribution to a study of industrial processes even when it is possible to use $\overline{X}$, R charts. There are different reasons which recommend NL gages:

1. Only gaging is required—no measurements.

2. Even for samples as small as *five*, the *sensitivity* is comparable to control charts with samples of *four* and *five*.

3. *Record keeping* is simple and effective. Charting the results at the machine is simpler and faster than with $\overline{X}$, R charts. The number of pieces which fail to pass the NL gages can be charted by the operator himself. Trends in the process and shifts in level are often detected by the operator before trouble is serious. Operator comprehension is often better than with $\overline{X}$, R charts.

4. NL-gage plans may be applied in many operations where $\overline{X}$, R charts are not feasible, thereby bringing the sensitivity of $\overline{X}$, R charts to many difficult problems.

7-7 Selection of an NL-Gage Plan

The selection of an NL-gage plan is similar to the selection of an $\overline{X}$, R plan. The same principles are applicable. A sample size of five in either is usually adequate. A sample of ten will sometimes be preferred with NL gaging; it provides more assurance that the sample is representative of the process. We recommend the following plans, or slight modifications of them, since their sensitivity corresponds closely to an $\overline{X}$, R chart with $n = 5$:

Plan A	Plan F	Plan D
$n = 5$	$n = 10$	$n = 4$
$t = 1.0$	$t = 1.2$	$t = 1.2$
$c = 1$	$c = 2$	$c = 1$

Various charts and ideas presented in this chapter are reproduced from an article by Ellis R. Ott, and August B. Mundel, Narrow-limit Gaging, *Ind. Qual. Control*, vol. 10, no. 5, March, 1954. They are used with the permission of the editor.

8

On Sampling to Provide a Feedback of Information

8-1   Introduction

Incoming inspection departments traditionally decide whether to accept an entire lot of a product submitted by a vendor.   Factors such as the reputation of the vendor, the urgency of the need for the purchased material, and the availability of test equipment influence this vital decision—sometimes to the extent of eliminating all inspection of a purchase.

In contrast, some companies even perform 100% inspection for non-destructive characteristics and accept only those individual units which conform to specifications.   However, 100% screening inspection of large lots does not ensure 100% accuracy. The inspection may fail to reject some non-conforming units and/or reject some conforming units.   Fatigue, boredom, distraction, inadequate lighting, test-equipment variation and many other factors introduce substantial errors into a screening inspection.

Sampling offers a compromise in time and expense between the extremes of 100% inspection and no inspection.   It can be carried out in several ways.   First, a few items, often called a "grab sample," may be taken from the lot indiscriminately and examined visually or measured for a quality characteristic or group of characteristics.   The entire lot may then be accepted or rejected on the findings from the sample.   Another procedure is to take some fixed percentage of the lot as the sample.   This was once a fairly standard procedure.   However, this practice results in large differences in protection for different sized lots.   Also, the vendor can "play games" by his choice of lot size, submitting small lots when his percent defective is large, and thus increasing the probability of their acceptance.

This chapter presents and discusses the advantages and applications of scientific acceptance sampling plans.[1]   These plans designate sample sizes for different lot sizes.   If the number of defective units found in a sample exceeds the number specified in the plan for that lot and sample size, the entire lot is rejected.   A rejected lot may be returned to the vendor for reworking and improvement before being returned for resampling, it may be inspected 100 percent by the vendor or vendee as agreed, or it may be scrapped.   Otherwise the entire lot is accepted except for any defectives found in the sample.

In the early 1940s, the United States Government adopted the policy of requiring acceptance sampling plans as a basis for acceptance or rejection of submitted lots of electronic tubes.   Thirty years later acceptance of virtually all mass-produced product is based on such plans.   The most frequently used governmental plans are the Military Standards Acceptance Plans by Attributes (MIL-STD-105D).

Historically, the primary function of acceptance sampling plans was, naturally enough, acceptance-rejection of lots.   The United States Armed Forces served almost exclusively as the customer.   Application of acceptance sampling plans was a police function; they were designed as protection against accepting lots of unsatisfactory quality.   However, the vendor and customer nomenclature can also be applied to a shipping and receiving department within a single manufacturing plant or to any point within the plant where material or product is received for further processing.   Variations in the use of scientific sampling plans are, for instance:

1.   At incoming inspection in a production organization.

2.   As a check on a product moving from one department or process of a plant to another.

3.   As a basis for approving the startup of a machine.

4.   As a basis for adjusting an operating process or machine before approving its continued operation.

5.   As a check on the outgoing quality of product ready for shipment to a customer.

8-2   Other Scientific Sampling Plans

The control chart for attributes discussed in Chap. 3 is one possible system of surveillance in any of these situations.   Another method, similar to the Military Standards Acceptance Plans by Attributes, is a single or double

---

[1] Various sampling plans in usage are referenced in the bibliography.   The emphasis of this discussion is on some basic ideas related to acceptance sampling plans.

sampling plan or set of plans for nondestructive testing of attributes, such as the Dodge Romig[1] sampling inspection tables.

Consider the following single sampling plan applied to a process.

Plan: n = 45, c = 2.

This notation indicates that:

■ A random sample of $n = 45$ units is obtained—perhaps taken during the last half-hour or some other chosen period, possibly from the last 1,000 items produced, or even the last 45 units if interest on the present status of the process is primary.   The quantity from which the sample is taken is called a lot.

■ The 45 units are inspected for quality characteristic A which may be a single quality characteristic or a group of them.   If it is a group of them, the characteristics should usually be of about equal importance and be determined at the same inspection station.

■ If not more than two ($c = 2$) defective units are found in the sample, the entire lot (or process) except for defectives is accepted for characteristic A; i.e., the entire lot is accepted if 0, 1, or 2 defectives are found.   When more than 2 defectives are found in the sample, the *lot* is *not* acceptable.

In addition to this decision to accept or reject, a second important use of a plan is a *feedback system*, providing information to help production itself (or the vendor) improve the quality of subsequent lots as produced.   In any case such plans often exercise a healthy influence on the control of a process. This will be discussed in Secs. 8-11, 8-12, and 8-13.

8-3   A Simple Probability

What may we expect to happen (on the average) if many successive samples from the process are examined under the above plan, $n = 45$, $c = 2$?   What fraction of samplings will approve the process for continuance?   To provide an answer, additional information is required.   Let us assume first, for example, that the actual process is stable and producing 5% defective, i.e., the probability that any single item is defective is $p = .05$ or $P = 5\%$.

Discussion

From Table A-5 of binomial probabilities, the probability[2] P_A of no more than $c = 2$ defectives in a sample of 45, with $p = .05$ is

$$P(x \leq 2) = .608 \text{ or } 60.8\% \tag{8-1}$$

[1] Harold F. Dodge and Harry G. Romig, *Sampling Inspection Tables, Single and Double Sampling*, 2nd ed., John Wiley and Sons, Inc., New York, 1959.

[2] The symbol P_A (read "P sub A") represents the "probability of acceptance." When the acceptance plan relates to an entire lot of a product, the P_A is the probability that any particular lot will be accepted by the plan when it is indeed the stated percent defective. Thus we shall talk about *accepting or rejecting a process* as well as accepting or rejecting a lot.

8-4   Operating-characteristic Curves of a Single Sampling Plan

There are two areas of special interest in practice.

1.   What happens when lots with a very small percentage of defective units are submitted for acceptance? A *good* plan would usually accept such lots on the basis of the sample.

2.   What happens when lots with a "large" percentage of defective units are submitted? A *good* plan ought to, and usually will, reject such lots on the basis of the sample.

As in Sec. 8-3, values of P_A have been obtained for selected values of P and have been tabulated in Table 8-1 and graphed in Fig. 8-1. The resulting curve is called the *operating-characteristic* curve (OC curve) of the sampling plan, $n = 45$, $c = 2$.

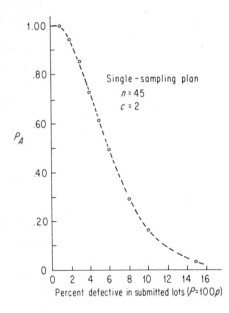

Single-sampling plan

$n = 45$

$c = 2$

Fig. 8-1   Operating-characteristic curve of a single sampling plan for attributes $(n = 45, \quad c = 2)$. The probability of a submitted lot being accepted, P_A, is shown on the vertical axis while different percent defective in submitted lots is shown on the horizontal axis. (Data from Table 8-1.)

Discussion: Regarding (Fig. 8-1)

■ When lots with less than 1% defective are submitted to the plan, only occasionally will they be rejected; $P_A = 1.0$.

■ When lots with more than 10% defective are submitted, the probability of acceptance is small; $P_A \cong .10$.

■ Lots with P between 2% and 10% defective have a probability of acceptance which drops sharply.

■ Whether the plan $n = 45$, $c = 2$ is a reasonable plan to use in a particular application has to be given consideration.

TABLE 8-1   Probabilities P_A
of Finding $x \leqq 2$ **in a Sample**
of $n = 45$ **for Different Values**
of p
Values from Table of bino-
mials, A-5

p, in percent	$P_A = P(x \leqq 2)$
0	1.00
1	.99
2	.94
3	.85
4	.73
5	.61
6	.49
8	.29
10	.16
15	.03

8-5   But Is It a Good Plan?

Whether the plan $n = 45$, $c = 2$ is a sensible, economical plan for a specific application involves the following points:

1.   Sampling plans for process control and improvement should provide signals of economically important changes in production quality, a deterioration or improvement in the process, or other evidence of fluctuations.   Are signals important in this application during ordinary production or in a process improvement project?   Should a set of plans be devised to detect important differences between operators, shifts, machines, vendors?   Improvements of industrial processes are often relatively inexpensive.

2.   What are the costs of using this plan versus not using any?

   a. What is the cost to the company if a defective item is allowed to proceed to the next department or assembly?   If it is simple and inexpensive to eliminate defectives in subsequent assembly, perhaps no sampling plan is necessary.   If it is virtually impossible to prevent a defective from being included in the next assembly, and if this assembly is expensive and is ruined thereby, failure to detect and eliminate an inexpensive component cannot be tolerated.

   b. What is the cost of removing a defective unit by inspection?   What is the cost of improving it by reworking it?   What is the possibility of improving the process by reducing or eliminating defective components?   When the total cost of permitting $P\%$ defective items to proceed to the next assembly is equal to the cost of removing the defectives or improving the process, there is an economic standoff.

When the costs of sampling and the possible consequent 100% screening are less than the alternative costs of forwarding $P\%$ defectives, *some* sampling plan should be instituted.

3. Does this sampling plan minimize total amount of inspection? The Dodge-Romig tables provide plans for different lot sizes and AOQLs and LTPDs (see Secs. 8-6, 8-7, and 8-8). These plans were designed to minimize the total inspection resulting from the inspection of the sample(s) and whatever 100% screening inspection is required on lots which fail sampling.

Note: In process control we often use smaller sample sizes than required by a plan when our dependence on quality is only the acceptance-rejection aspect of the plan. Convenience sometimes stipulates the use of smaller sample sizes, referred to as *convenience samples*. *Any sampling plan* which detects a deterioration of quality and sends rejected lots or records of them back to the producing department can have a most salutary influence on production practices.

Many companies use one type of acceptance procedure on purchases and another on work in process, or outgoing product. In contracting the purchase of materials, it is common practice to specify the sampling procedure for determining acceptability of lots. Agreement to the acceptance procedures may be as critical to the contract as price or date of delivery.

8-6 Average Outgoing Quality (AOQ) and Its Maximum Limit (AOQL)

These two concepts will be discussed here with reference to a single-sampling rectification inspection plan for attributes (nondestructive test) which includes the following steps:

1. A lot rejected by the plan is given a 100% screening inspection. All defectives are removed and replaced by nondefectives; i.e., the lot is rectified. It is then resubmitted for sampling before acceptance.

2. Defectives are always removed when found and replaced by nondefectives even in the samples.

As a consequence of (1) and (2), the *average outgoing quality* of lots (AOQ) passing through the sampling station will be improved. Since very good lots will usually be accepted by the sampling plan, their AOQ will be improved only slightly (see Fig. 8-2). Lots with a larger percent of defectives will be rejected more often and their defectives removed in screening. Their AOQ will be improved substantially (Fig. 8-2).

The *worst possible* average situation is represented by the height of the *peak* of the AOQ curve. This maximum value is called the *average outgoing quality limit* (AOQL). In Fig. 8-2, AOQL $\cong 3\%$. This very useful AOQL concept forms the basis for a system of sampling plans. Several plans are available in Dodge-Romig for each AOQL from 0.1% to 10%.

Any sampling plan will provide information on the quality of a lot as it is submitted—certainly more information[1] than if no inspection is done. But some plans require much too large a sample for the need; some specify ridiculously small samples. The AOQL concept is helpful in assessing the adequacy of the plan under consideration and/or indicating how it could be improved. When a 3% AOQL system is used, the worst possible long-term average accepted will be 3%. But this could occur only if the producer always fed 5% defective to the sampling station. Except in this unlikely event, the average outgoing quality[2] will be less than 3%.

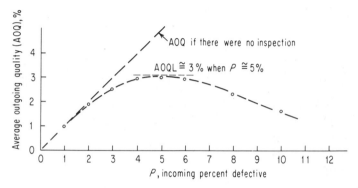

Fig. 8-2 Average outgoing quality (AOQ) compared to incoming percent defective P. (AOQ is after any lots which fail the inspection plan have been 100% inspected; see Table 8-2, cols. 1 and 3.)

8-7 Computing the Average Outgoing Quality (AOQ) of Lots from a Process Producing $P\%$ Defective

When a sequence of lots is submitted to an acceptance plan $n = 45$, $c = 2$, what is the AOQ for different values of p?

Consider first the case for $p = .05$; the number of defectives in an average lot of size $N = 2,000$, for example, is $Np = 100$. The average number of

---

[1] Other valuable information on its quality could be provided by a production control chart(s). These charts are usually available to us only when the vendor is a department of our own organization; but this is not necessarily so. A basis for control-chart information on incoming material can often be established with outside vendors.

[2] There is a hint of a spurious suggestion from Fig. 8-2; namely, that one way to get excellent product quality is to find a supplier who provides a large percent of defectives! This is not really a paradox. The only way to ensure good quality product is to provide *good* manufacturing practices; dependence upon 100% inspection is sometimes a short-term " necessary evil."

A friend told me about taking two friends to his company's country club for dinner. All three ordered clams on the half-shell. After an exceptionally long wait, the waiter brought three plates of clams. He apologized for the delay: "Am very sorry, sir, but we had to open and throw out an awful lot of clams to find these good ones!" Would you eat the clams he served?

defectives *removed* from the lot as a consequence of the sampling plan come from two sources:

1. From the *sample*. Average number removed is

$$np = (.05)(45) = 2.25$$

2. From *lots* which are rejected by the plan. We designate the probability of a lot being rejected by

$$P_R = 1 - P_A = 1 - .61 = .39 \tag{8-2}$$

Then the additional average number of defectives removed from these rejected lots is

$$p(N - n)P_R = (.05)(1955)(.39) = 38.12 \tag{8-3}$$

Then the total average number of defectives *removed* from a lot is the sum of these two:

$$np + p(N - n)P_R = 2.25 + 38.12 = 40.37 \tag{8-4}$$

The average number of defectives remaining in a lot divided by N is the AOQ: $100 - 40.37 = 59.63$ and

$$AOQ = 59.63/2,000 = 0.0298 = 2.98\%$$

Consider now the general case. The average number of defectives in a lot is Np. From Eq. (8-4), the number removed is

$$np + p(N - n)P_R$$

TABLE 8-2   Average Outgoing Quality (AOQ) of Lots Proceeding Past an Acceptance Sampling Station Using the Plan $n = 45$, $c = 2$

Lots which fail to pass sampling are submitted to 100% screening with replacement of defectives. See Eq. (8-5) for method of approximating AOQ.

P	P_A	$AOQ = P \cdot P_A$
0	1.00	0
1	.99	.99
2	.94	1.88
3	.85	2.55
4	.73	2.92
5	.61	3.05
6	.49	2.94
8	.29	2.32
10	.16	1.60
15	.03	0.45

Then

$$\text{AOQ} = \frac{Np - [np + p(N - n)P_R]}{N} = pP_A\left(1 - \frac{n}{N}\right)$$

Since the value of n/N is very small,

$$\text{AOQ} \cong pP_A \tag{8-5}$$

Equation (8-5) was used[1] to compute values of AOQ in Table 8-2.

Also, the operating-characteristic curves of two commonly used systems of sampling plans have been computed and appear along with the sampling tables.   For those who have an interest in mathematical consideration of probabilities, the following is presented.

The probability P_A of a lot of size N being accepted on the basis of a random sample of 45 drawn from 2,000 units of a lot is the sum of the probabilities of there being 0, 1, or 2 defectives in the sample:

$$P_A = P(x = 0) + P(x = 1) + P(x = 2) \tag{8-6}$$

Each of these three probabilities can be expressed in terms of the number of possible combinations.   In a lot of $N = 2,000$ units having 5% defective, the number of defective units is 100, and the number of nondefective units is 1,900.   The Eq. (8-6) can be written explicitly

$$P_A = [C(100, 0) \cdot C(1,900, 45) + C(100, 1) \cdot C(1,900, 44)$$

$$+ C(100, 2) \cdot C(1,900, 43)] \div C(2000, 45)$$

$$= \left(\frac{1900!}{45!\,1855!} + (100)\frac{1900!}{44!\,1856!} + \frac{(50)(99)1900!}{43!\,1857!}\right) \div \frac{2000!}{45!\,1955!} \tag{8-7}$$

The representation of this as decimal fraction requires a programmed computer, or a table of logarithms of factorials.

[1] Anyone intending to become expert in devising sampling plans should become familiar with the mechanics of computing probabilities such as the following, based on sampling from lots of size N and with changing probabilities as each item is drawn from the lot.

When an item is drawn from a lot with Np defectives, the probability that the *next* item will be defective is *not quite* equal to p:

■ If the first item drawn is defective, then $(Np - 1)$ defectives remain, and the probability that the second item will be defective is

$$\frac{Np - 1}{N - 1} = \frac{(N - 1)p - (1 - p)}{N - 1} = p - \frac{1 - p}{N - 1}$$

This is evidently only slightly *less* than p.

■ However, if the first item withdrawn is *not* defective, then the probability that the second item will be defective is

$$\frac{Np}{N - 1} = \frac{(N - 1)p + p}{N - 1} = p + \frac{p}{N - 1}$$

This is only slightly *more* than p.

For ordinary practical purposes, it is adequate to regard the characteristics of sampling plans as sampling from a production process with fixed fraction defective p.   An expert in the field will want to learn how computers can be used to calculate probabilities.

8-8   Other Important Concepts Associated with Sampling Plans

Average Minimal Total Inspection: including inspection of the samples and the 100% screening of those lots which are rejected by the plan. Both Dodge-Romig systems, AOQL and LTPD, include this principle.

Acceptable-quality Level (AQL): a notion of the largest average percent defective which is still considered acceptable. The MIL-STD-105 series emphasize this concept. Sometimes an attempt is made to formalize the concept as " that quality in percent defective which the consumer is willing to accept about 95% of the time such lots are submitted." This definition has been the basis for some heated arguments.

Point of Indifference.[1]   That level of percent defective in lots which will be accepted *half the time* when submitted ($P_A = 50\%$).

Good Quality Is a Consequence of Good Manufacturing. Good quality is not the result of inspection; inspection is often considered a "necessary complement." Most important is the role that acceptance sampling plans can play in providing useful information to help manufacturing improve its processes (see Sec. 8-11).

Lot Tolerance Percent Defective Plans. To many consumers, it seems that the quality of *each* lot is so critical that the average outgoing quality concept does not offer adequate protection. The customer often feels a need for a lot-by-lot system of protection. Such systems have been devised and are called *lot tolerance percent defective plans* (LTPD). These are provided in Dodge-Romig for values of *P* from 0.5% to 10%.

8-9   Risks

The vendor/producer wants reasonable assurance (a small producer's risk) that he faces only a small risk of rejection when he submits lots having a small percent defective. In Fig. 8-1, the *producer's risk* is about 5% for lots with 2% defective and less than 5% for better lots. This may be reasonable and acceptable to the producer on some product items and not on others; negotiation is normally required.

The vendee/consumer wants reasonable assurance (a small consumer's risk) that lots with a large percent defective will usually be rejected. In Fig. 8-1, the consumer's risk is seen to be about 16% for lots submitted with 10% defective; less than 16% for larger percents defective.

Compromises between the consumer and producer are necessary. Two systems in wide use provide a range of possibilities between these two risks; the Dodge-Romig plans and the MIL-STD-105 series.

[1] Hugo C. Hamaker, Some Basic Principles of Sampling Inspection by Attributes, *Appl. Stat.*, vol. 7, pp. 149–59, 1958.

8-10   Military Standards 105D

Tightened and Reduced Inspection MIL-STD-105D is used extensively in acceptance sampling for government contracts and for many nongovernmental applications as well. The plans are based on an *acceptable quality level* concept (AQL). Purchase specifications often include AQLs; sample sizes are established by the lot sizes. The *producer's risk* is emphasized when AQL plans are chosen. Plans are intended to protect the producer when he is producing at or better than the AQL level, unless there is a previous history or other basis for questioning the quality of his product. When he submits product from a process at the AQL level, it will be accepted "almost always." Since OC curves drop only gradually for percent defectives slightly larger than the AQL value, such product will have a fairly high probability of acceptance. The producer's interest is protected under criteria designated as *normal inspection*.

How then is the consumer protected? Whenever there is reason to doubt the quality level of the producer, MIL-STD-105D plans provide stricter criteria for acceptance. These plans are called *tightened inspection*. Criteria are provided in the plans to *govern switching from normal to tightened* inspection. Proper use of MIL-STD-105D demands that the rules for shifting from normal to tightened inspection be observed.

When the producer has an excellent record of quality on a particular item, the MIL-STD-105D plans permit a reduction in sample sizes by switching to *reduced inspection*. This shift to *reduced inspection* is not designed to maintain the AQL protection, but to allow a saving in inspection effort by the consumer.

For use with individual lots, specific plans can be selected by referring to OC curves printed in the standard. For more details on MIL-STD-105D, see Quality and Reliability Handbook (*H*53), available from the Superintendent of Documents, Washington, D.C.

8-11   Feedback of Information

Problems, Problems, Everywhere

Problems always abound when manufacturing any product; they may be found both during processing and in the finished product. Problems may result from product design, vendor quality, testing inadequacies, and on and on. It is tempting to blame the problem on factors outside our own immediate sphere of responsibility. As a matter of fact, there are occasions when a vendor is known to be supplying low-quality items; there are also occasions when we have examined our process very carefully without finding how to improve it. There are two standard procedures that, though often good in themselves, can serve to postpone careful analysis of the production process:

1. On-line inspection stations (100% screening). These can become a way of life.

2.   On-line acceptance sampling plans which prevent excessively defective lots from proceeding on down the production line, but have no feedback procedure included.

These procedures become bad when they allow or encourage carelessness in production.   It gets easy for production to shrug off responsibility for quality and criticize inspection for letting bad quality proceed.

More Than a Police Function

No screening inspection should simply separate the good from the bad, the conforming from the nonconforming, the sheep from the goats.   No on-line acceptance sampling system should serve merely a police function by just keeping unsatisfactory lots from continuing on down the production line. Incorporated in any sampling system should be procedures for the recording of important detailed information on the number and types of production defects.   It is a great loss when these data are not sent back to help production improve itself.   A form for use in reporting such information is vital although preparing an effective one is not always a simple task.

Any systematic reporting of defects which can trigger corrective action is a step forward.   Contentions that the start of a system should be postponed— "we aren't ready yet"—should be disregarded.   Get started.   Any new information will be useful in itself and will suggest adjustments and improvements.

Defect Classification

Any inspection station has some concepts of " good " and " bad."   This may be enough to get started.   But corrective action on the process cannot begin until it is known what needs correction.   At a station for the visual inspection of enamel bowls, items for a sampling sheet (Table 15-2) were discussed with the regular inspector, a foreman, and the chief inspector.   Table 15-6 was similarly devised for weaving defects in cloth.   Some general principles can be inferred from them.   Table 8-3 and the discussion below offer some ideas for record sheets associated with single-sampling acceptance plans.

■ Give some consideration to the *seriousness* of defects.   Table 15-3 uses two categories, *serious* and *very serious*.   Categories can be defined more carefully after some experience with the plan.   (More sophisticated plans may use three or four categories.)

■ Characterize defects into *groups* with some regard for their *manufacturing source*.   This requires advice from those familiar with the production process. In Table 15-2, for example, *black spots* are listed both as A-4 and A-5, and B8 and B9.   They were the result of different production causes.   Corrective action is better indicated when they are reported separately.

Also note Metal Exposed, A-6, A-7, and A-8, and B-5, B-6, and B-7.

■ Do not list too many different defect types; limit the list to those which

TABLE 8-3   Lot by Lot Record Acceptance Sampling (Single Sampling)

Department: *Mounting*
Tube Type: *6AK5*
Item: *Grid*
Test: *Visual*

Sampling Plan: $n = 45$, $c = 2$

Date	Time	n	Inspector	Spacy	Taper	Damage	Slant	Other	Total	Action	Comments
2/5/73	10⁰⁰	45	mB	2	1	0	1		4	R	
	12⁰⁰	45	mB	3	0	1	2		6	R	
	2⁰⁰	45	aR	1	0	0	1		2	A	
	4⁰⁰	45	aR	2	0	0	1		3	R	
Daily Total		180		8	1	1	5		15		

Circulation:
gma   WCF
FFR   RMA

occur most often; then list "Others." When some other defect appears important, it can be added to the list.

■ Eventually, information relating to the natural sources of defects may be appropriate; individual machines, operators, shifts. Even heads on a machine or cavities in a mold may perform differently.

Sampling Versus 100% Inspection

Information from samples is usually more helpful than from 100% inspection because:

1. In 100% screening, inspection is often terminated as soon as *any* defect is found in the unit. This can result in undercounting important defects. In a sample, however, inspection of a unit can usually be continued until *all* quality characteristics have been checked and counted.

2. Much 100% inspection is routine and uninspiring by its very nature. Records from such inspection are often full of inaccuracies and offer little useful information for improvement. Small samples give some release from the boredom and allow more careful attention to listed defect items. They also permit recognition and attention to peculiarities which occur.

3.   With the use of small, convenient, fixed-size samples information can be fed back as illustrated in two case histories in Chap. 15.   The resulting improvements in those situations had been thought impossible.   Also see Case History 3-2.

Teeth and Incentives

Firmness and tact are important when persuading anyone that he is at fault and that he can correct it.   There are various possibilities.

1.   Some major companies physically return defectives back to the erring department.   Others have them repaired by a repair department, but charge the repair back to the erring department.   A department can often improve itself if suitable information is fed back.

2.   The physical holdup of product proceeding down the line has a most salutary effect.   When no complaints or records on bad quality are made, but instead bad product continues on down the line, it is almost certain to induce carelessness.   It says, loud and clear, "Who cares?"

3.   Even a control chart on percent defective (a p chart) posted in the manufacturing department *can* provide encouragement.   Used carefully, this can have as much interest and value as a golf score to an individual or a department.

8-12   Where Should a Feedback Begin?

There is no *one* answer, but there are some guidelines.

1.   An acceptance plan may already be operating but serving only as a police function.   Attach a feedback aspect, organized so as to suggest important manufacturing problems.

2.   *Sore thumb.*   Sometimes a large amount of scrap or a failure to assemble will indicate an obvious problem.   Often no objective information is available to indicate its severity, the apparent sources, or whether it is regular or intermittent.   Start a small-scale sampling with a feedback.   This may be a formal acceptance sampling plan or a *convenience* sample large enough to provide some useful information.   (A sample of $n = 5$ will not usually be large enough[1] when using attribute data, but frequently, a sample of 25 or 50 taken at reasonable time intervals will be very useful.)

3.   *Begin at the beginning?*   It is often proposed that any project to improve should start at the beginning of the process, making any necessary adjustments at each successive step.   Then at the end of the process, it is argued, there will be no problems.   This approach appeals especially to those in charge of the manufacturing processes.   Sadly, it is often not good practice.

First, there is rarely an opportunity to complete such a well-intentioned project.   A "bigger fire" develops elsewhere, and this one is postponed, often indefinitely.

[1] For an exception, see Case History 5-1 (spot welding).

Second, most of the steps in a process are usually right.   In the process of following operations step by step, and in checking each successive operation, much time is lost unnecessarily.   Usually it proves better to start at the *back* end; find the major problems occurring in the final product.   Some will have arisen in one department, some in another.   The method of the following section, 8-13, was designed to pinpoint areas in manufacturing which warrant attention, whether from raw materials or components, process adjustment, engineering design, inspection, or other reason.

8-13   Outgoing Product Quality Rating (OPQR)

Introduction

This is a program which gets to the source of difficulties in a hurry.   Further, it enlists the cooperation of various departments.   The method starts by *rating* small samples of the outgoing product.   This outgoing product quality rating program[1] was suggested by a plan[2] developed in connection with complicated electronic and electrical equipment.   A well-known pharmaceutical house utilized this system for a major drive on package quality. It is equally applicable in many other industries.

In the OPQR program, each product is sampled daily just before being placed in shipping cases.   The sample items are then inspected visually and a demerit rating assigned according to the type and magnitude of defects observed.   The rating is done by a department which is independent of manufacturing.   The procedure is primarily for *information* and feedback purposes and is *not* a police function:

1.   *It is an information service* to top management, providing an objective evaluation of outgoing product.   In many companies, careful information is provided to assure management that the organization is geared to produce high quality at a reasonable cost.   But how many such managements can claim accurate information on the actual product quality as it goes to the customer?   Many *assume* good quality because the product has "had 100% inspection."   But how many really know, for example, how many inoperative radios leave their plant; how many refrigerators leave with scratched doors; how many phonograph records have audio imperfections; how many of their solder joints or welds are defective?   Reliable answers would usually provide important and surprising information.

2.   Another important function of an OPQR rating program is to *pinpoint areas in manufacturing* which warrant attention.   These may include

[1] William C. Frey, A Plan for Outgoing Quality, *Mod. Packag.*, October, 1962.   Besides special details in our Table 8-4, Fig. 8-3, and the classification of defects, other ideas and phrases from the article are included here.   Permission for these inclusions from the author and publisher are gratefully acknowledged.

[2] Harold F. Dodge and Mary N. Torrey, A Check Inspection and Demerit Rating Plan, *Ind. Qual. Control*, vol. 13, no. 1, July, 1956.

raw materials (or components), process adjustment, engineering design, inspection, etc. It provides a much faster and surer method of getting to trouble areas than does the alternative method of following production step by step from the beginning on through successive stages.

Outline of the Program

1. Members of this study committee were named from top management, sales, manufacturing, and quality control.

2. Two standard products were selected for study.

3. For this initial study 50 sample bottles of each product were collected at stated intervals each day for a period of one week from each manufacturing line and product. The usual sample should be smaller, perhaps 20, and never more than 40 per line per day.

4. These samples were examined carefully by an independent checker. Each bottle with any deviation from perfection was tagged, the defects recorded as in the attached OPQR weekly summary from Table 8-4, and saved for the committee.

5. The study committee examined the visual defects found and added others which it was felt might occur.

6. Defects were classified into four categories.[1] A demerit rating was attached to each of the four.

7. Regular meetings were held to discuss findings and plan future progress.

Defect Classification

What is a defect? What is a nonconforming unit? Invariably, these are difficult questions to answer especially with visual defects. An upside down label is clearly a defect; dirty bottles and wrinkled labels are not desirable, but there are all degrees of dirty bottles and wrinkles. A discussion of the types of defects which might possibly be found in one's product is rather academic until actual facts are obtained. Thus, one of the first steps agreed upon by the planning committee, appointed to activate the program, was to obtain such information.

The four defect categories accepted were the following:

1. Minor: These are items which are not perfect; they are objectionable, but so slightly objectionable that management would agree that these items should not be removed from the production line, if observed. However, it is desired that corrective efforts be made to reduce the number of subsequent defects of this category. (Slightly crooked labels are typical.)

2. Moderately Serious: These are nonfunctional package defects of a somewhat more serious nature. They would probably be noticed by the customer, although they would probably not incur a loss of good will. They are sufficiently objectionable, however, to require line inspectors to cull them out

[1] Harold F. Dodge and Mary N. Torrey, A Check Inspection and Demerit Weighting Plan, *Ind. Qual. Control*, vol. 13, no. 1, pp. 5–12, July, 1956.

of production since they should not reach the customer (e.g., an upside-down, dirty, or wrinkled label).

3. Serious: These are appearance defects or functional defects which would certainly result in loss of good will and possibly result in loss of a customer. (A broken plastic cap or a short fill are examples.)

4. Very Serious: This category is reserved for those rare defects which could conceivably result in bodily injury.

In this program the demerit rating values assigned to each category in accordance with its estimated importance were; minor $= 2$ demerits; moderately serious $= 10$; serious $= 25$ and very serious $= 50$. Control charts for the overall demerit rating were established (per hundred units of each product).

In an initial discussion, it often proves difficult to get agreement on levels of defects which are tolerable. Every company official, whether he represents manufacturing, sales, or management, is reluctant to accept quality standards which are short of perfection or to agree that even a single serious defective can be tolerated. To refute this concept, consider this question: "What percent of airplane accidents are tolerable in commercial flights in the U.S. ?" The immediate answer, of course is "none"; however, we recognize that to guarantee this standard, all flights would have to be grounded. This approach helped make it possible to establish initial working standards of quality for the pharmaceutical program.

Within each defect category were grouped defects which were related to each machine within the plant. As shown in an attached OPQR weekly summary, Table 8-4, many defects came from the labeler. This relationship to a

TABLE 8-4 OPQR: Outgoing Product Quality Rating—Weekly Summary*

Group headers: 50 Demerits D Very Serious | 25 Demerits C Serious | B (10 Demerits) Moderately serious — Labeller | A Minor (2 Demerits) — Labeller — Materials

Week	N	Chipped Thread	Total Demerits	Brcken cap	Total Demerits	Loose Label	Very Crooked Label	Serious Wrinkle	Very Dirty Label	Free Fluid	Cracked Cap	Scorched Cello.	Miscellaneous	Total Demerits	Illegal Code	Crooked Label	Wrinkled Label	Sl. Loose Label	Scuffed Label	Ripped Label	Dirty Label	Print Imperfection	Cap Imperfection	Holiday in Cap	Slight Fr. Fl.	Dirty Cap	Torn Cello.	Damaged carton	Miscellaneous	Total Demerits	Total Demerits per 100 Units
9/15	120												1	10	10	3	3					2				2				42	$52 \times .83 = 43$
9/22	200								1	1	1			30	2	17	3		3						4	3		3	5	82	$112 \times .5 = 56$
9/29	200					2				1				30		2	17	2	3	3							1	1		64	$94 \times .5 = 47$
10/6	200					1				2	1			40	3	1	4	4	2	4		4				2	2			54	$94 \times .5 = 47$
10/13	180							1	2	1	1	1	2	80	4	8	1	1	1	8		4				2		2		70	$150 \times .56 = 84$
10/20	160								1	9			1	110		17	2	1	1	3	1	1	3			2	3	3		74	$184 \times .625 = 115$
10/27	195									2				20	1	9	4	9	2	2	2	3	2	2		5	4			96	$116 \times .51 = 59$

a: Materials   b: Labeller   c: Filler   d: Cartoner

* Note to reader: This form and the accompanying chart are on "Ditto-Master." A new line (point) is added each week to the master; copies are then run and sent to each name on the circulation list. Alternatively, copies can be run off weekly and distributed.

machine is helpful in providing an effective information feedback procedure. In this plant, outgoing product quality rating reports are published weekly. The report consists of a dittoed rating control chart (with a new point plotted each week) plus a detailed listing of the defectives which led to the overall rating value.   Occasionally, when the weekly reports stimulate interest in certain production areas, daily reports are furnished on critical items in that area so that the interested department has an independent detailed analysis of difficulties being found.

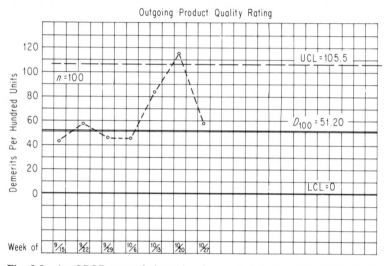

Fig. 8-3 An OPQR control chart showing control limits.   (See Table 8-4.)

Additional Applications

One important function of this program is in comparing the production quality with previous production.   Is the quality from line 1 similar to line 2? If there is a marked difference, where is the major departure?   The OPQR program provides answers to these and other similar questions.

Occasionally a defect is found on the shelf of a drugstore.   It is important to know whether this was something which might represent a sporadic occurrence or an epidemic at the time the product left the plant, or whether it is a characteristic which developed subsequently.   The production man, who was sometimes skeptical of the program initially, found it very useful to quote the OPQR records which provide objective testimony about defects which developed after the product left the plant.   It is also important to know systematically and regularly about how many off-standard items are being shipped; when, for example, a field complaint is received, you can tell the vice president that not all the toothpaste tubes went out empty.   (He actually bought some empty ones in a drug store.)

Summary: OPQR

We have found the outgoing product quality rating procedure adaptable to cosmetic and pharmaceutical products and an appropriate means to initiate and extend a quality control program.   It very quickly pinpoints areas where quality improvement is warranted and is both an insurance policy and an information service to the production management.   This approach to an extension of a total quality program merits your consideration.

TABLE 8-5   Computation of Standard Quality Demerit Level and Control Limits ($\overline{QD}_n$ and σ_n) per n Units

---

Assigned Class Demerit Weights in this project:
  Class D defect: $50 = w_D$
  Class C defect: $25 = w_C$
  Class B defect: $10 = w_B$
  Class A defect: $2 = w_A$
Now

$$\overline{QD} = \frac{(w_A)d_A + (w_B)d_B + (w_C)d_C + (w_D)d_D}{N}$$

where d_A, d_B, d_C, and d_D represent the number of each class of defect found in the N items inspected.   In this example, $N = 2{,}400$, $d_A = 302$, $d_B = 60$, $d_C = 1$, and $d_D = 0$.   Then

$$\overline{QD} = 0.512 \quad \text{and} \quad \overline{QD}_{100} = 51.2$$

This value is the central line in Fig. 8-3.   Now when we assume a Poisson distribution of demerits we obtain:

$$\hat{\sigma}_{100} = \sqrt{\frac{100[(50)^2(0) + (25)^2(1) + (10)^2(60) + 2^2(302)]}{N = 2{,}400}}$$

$$= \sqrt{\frac{783{,}300}{2{,}400}} = 18.1 \text{ demerits per } n = 100 \text{ units}$$

In Fig. 8-3: $\text{UCL} = \overline{QD}_{100} + 3\hat{\sigma}_{100}$
            $= 51.2 + 54.3 = 105.5$
       $\text{LCL} = 51.2 - 54.3 \cong \text{zero}$

9
Ideas from Outliers–
Variables Data

9-1   Introduction

Preceding Chaps. 3 through 8 have emphasized methods of investigating defects, either in the product or the process.   Every plant has serious and important problems related to defects.   Problems and opportunities for improvement may also be analyzed from *measurement data*.   The discussion of troubleshooting with variables data shall not be separated from that of attribute data.   Every plant has both, and a professional will need to be knowledgeable in both.   Some small part of the discussions in Chap. 9 and subsequent chapters will repeat or overlap those of earlier chapters.

This overlap has been planned to make the consideration of variables data relatively independent of the earlier chapters for those readers who feel a greater need to emphasize variables data first.   The reader is reminded that the ideas and methods of Chaps. 1 and 2 are basic to the following considerations.

9-2   Ideas from Outliers[1]

Since data with questionable pedigrees are commonplace in every science, it is important to have objective signals or clues to identify them.   Strong feelings exist among scientists on the proper uses to be made of those which

---

[1] Other terms besides *outlier* in common usage include *maverick* and *wild-shot*.

are suspected: one school of thought is to "leave them in"; other schools have different ideas.   If the outlier represents very good or very bad quality, perhaps it represents evidence that some important, but unrecognized, effect in process or measurement was operative.   Is this a signal which warrants a planned investigation?   Is it a typical blunder warranting corrective action?   Some excellent articles have been written on the implications of outliers and methods of testing for them.[1]

There are important reasons why the troubleshooter may want to detect the reasons for an outlier:

1.   It may be an important signal of unsuspected important factor(s) affecting the stability of the process or testing procedure.

2.   A maverick occurring in a small sample of four or five may have enough effect to cause $\bar{X}$ to fall outside[2] one of the control limits on $\bar{X}$.

We would not want to make an adjustment on the process average which has been signaled by a maverick.

3.   A maverick (outlier) left in a relatively small collection of data may have a major effect when making comparisons with other samples.

CASE HISTORY 9-1   A Chemical Analysis—An R Chart As Evidence of Outliers

The percent by chemical analysis of a specific component A in successive batches of a plastic monomer became important evidence in a patent-infringement dispute.   The numbers in column 1 of Table 9-1 represent the chemical analysis of individual, consecutively produced, several-ton batches of monomer.   A crucial question was whether the chemical analyses on certain batches were reliable.   Many more analyses than those shown in Table 9-1 were in evidence.

The recommended sequence of steps taken in any statistical analysis of data begins with plotting; in this set by plotting $\bar{X}$ and R charts where subsets were formed from five consecutive batches.[3]   Table 9-1 lists only subsets 11 through 18.   This analysis will assume there is no other evidence.   In Fig. 9-1, we see that the control limits on the $\bar{X}$ chart include all the $\bar{X}$ points; the $\bar{R}$ chart has an outage in subset 14 and another in 17.   What are some possible reasons for these two outages?   Is it a general increase in variability, or is it the presence of mavericks?

---

[1] Frank E. Grubbs, Procedures for Detecting Outlying Observations in Samples, *Technometrics*, vol. 11, no. 1, pp. 1–21, February, 1969.   Also, Frank Proschan, Testing Suspected Observations, *Ind. Qual. Control*, pp. 14–19, January, 1957.

[2] Any point falling outside control limits will be called an "outage."

[3] It is important to use a control-chart analysis, but it is not important here whether to choose subsets of five or of four.   It is my opinion that the maintenance of $\bar{X}$ and R charts as a part of the production system would have prevented the difficulties which arose, provided the evidence from the chart had been utilized.

TABLE 9-1   Record of Chemical Analyses (column 1) Made on Consecutive Batches of a Chemical Compound

Column 2 Shows a "Material Balance" Content Calculated for the Same Batches As Column 1.

Subset no.	(1) Chemical analysis, %	$\bar{X}$ $n = 5$	Range $n = 5$	(2) Material balance, %
11	2.76			4.12
	3.66			3.69
	3.47			3.92
	3.02			4.14
	3.55	3.29	0.90	3.70
12	3.55			3.74
	3.10			3.74
	3.28			3.65
	3.13			3.63
	3.21	3.25	0.45	3.92
13	3.66			3.95
	3.40			3.96
	3.25			3.95
	3.36			3.95
	3.59	3.45	0.41	3.76
14	1.32			4.10
	3.32			3.71
	2.91			4.12
	3.81			3.77
	3.47	2.97	2.49	4.15
15	3.70			3.79
	3.59			3.75
	3.85			3.72
	3.51			3.83
	4.12	3.75	0.61	3.77
16	4.08			3.65
	3.66			3.76
	3.66			3.65
	3.47			5.39
	4.49	3.87	1.02	3.96
17	3.85			3.78
	3.47			3.58
	3.32			5.35
	2.94			4.52
	1.43	3.00	2.42	5.46
18	3.51			4.15
	3.74			3.89
	3.51			3.96
	3.63			3.63
	3.36	3.55	0.38	5.27

We decide to retain the two subgroups with outages when computing $\bar{R}$, although we then obtain an estimate of σ which is probably large; this procedure is conservative and will be followed at least for now.

$$\hat{\sigma} = \bar{R}/d_2 = 1.085/2.33 = 0.47$$

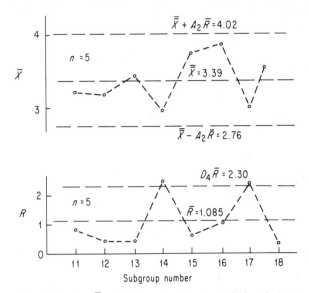

Fig. 9-1 An $\bar{X}$ and R control-chart analysis of data. Table 9-1, col. 1. Subsets of $n = 5$, $\hat{\sigma} = \bar{R}/d_2 = 0.47$.

DISCUSSION:

■ The 3-sigma control limits on *individual batches* have been drawn, using this conservatively large estimate (see Fig. 9-2). We see that one batch analysis in subset 14 is below the lower 3-sigma limit; also, one low batch analysis is seen in subset 17. We must conclude that the analyses on these two batches are significantly different from those of their neighbors. There are two possible explanations for the two outages (based on logic alone):

1. The chemical content of these two batches is indeed significantly lower than others (and dangerously close to a critical specification).

2. There was an error (blunder) either in the chemical analysis or in the recording of it.

It is not possible to determine, now, which of the two possibilities is completely responsible. The preceding analysis does present evidence of important errors.

■ At the time that these batches were produced and analyzed, chemical procedures were available which might have established conclusively which was the actual source of error. Such methods would include: reruns of the chemical analysis, visual and physical tests on other batch properties, checks on the manufacturing log sheets in the material balance calculation, discussions with plant personnel.

■ The column 2 figures were obtained on the basis of batch entries in the process log book. The materials balance, column 2, is computed for each batch on the assumption that the amounts of ingredients shown in the log

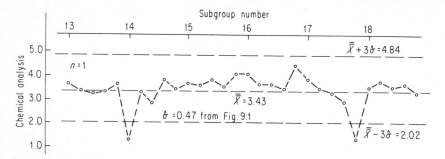

Fig. 9-2 Individual batch analyses showing two outages.

book are actually correct. This assumption is very critical. Whenever there is a substantial discrepancy between columns 1 and 2 on a batch, it is advisable to make *immediate* and careful checks on the reasons for the discrepancy.

9-3 Other Objective Tests for Outliers

In Case History 9-1, eight different subgroups, $n = 5$, were analyzed. The R chart of Fig. 9-1 showed two outages; individual batches responsible for the outages were easily identified. This R chart identification of outliers is applicable when the amount of data is " large."

When we have only a few observations, other criteria to test for possible outliers can be helpful. Two such criteria are the following:

1. An R Chart of Moving Ranges As a Test for Outliers

In studying a process, observations should usually be recorded in the order of production. Data from Table 9-2 have been plotted in Fig. 9-3a—these are individual observations. There seems to be no obvious grouping at different levels, no obvious shift in average, nothing unusual when the number of runs is counted, no cycle; but the second observation is "somewhat" apart from the others. Possibly an outlier?

A *moving range*, MR, $n = 2$, is the *positive difference between two consecutive observations*. Moving ranges, $|X_{i+1} - X_i|$, $n = 2$, behave like ordinary ranges, $n = 2$. In Table 9-2, the moving ranges have been written

TABLE 9-2   Estimating σ from a Moving Range

X_i	MR
1. 0.110	
2. 0.070	0.040
3. 0.110	0.040
4. 0.105	0.005
5. 0.100	0.005
6. 0.115	0.015
7. 0.100	0.015
8. 0.105	0.005
9. 0.105	0.000
10. 0.098	0.007
	$0.012 = X_1 - X_{10}$

$$\overline{MR} = 0.0144$$
$$D_4(\overline{MR}) = (3.27)(0.0144)$$
$$= 0.047$$
$$\hat{\sigma} = \overline{MR}/d_2$$
$$= 0.0144/1.13$$
$$= 0.0127$$

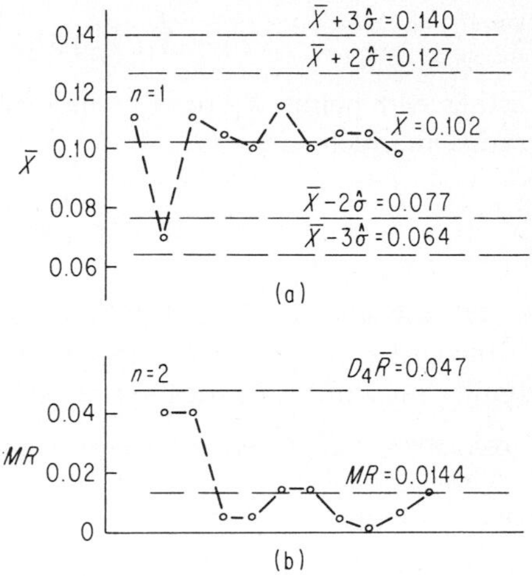

Fig. 9-3 A chart check for an outlier. (Data of Table 9-2.)

in the column adjacent to the original x_1 observations; except that the tenth entry is $|(x_1 - x_{10})|$. Then

$$\overline{MR} = \frac{\sum (MR_i)}{10} = 0.0144$$

The upper control limit on the moving-range chart, Fig. 9-3b, is

$$\text{UCL} = D_4(\overline{MR}) = (3.27)(0.0144) = 0.047$$

where D_4 is the ordinary factor for ranges, Table 2-3 or Table A-4.

The second observation in Table 9-2 is responsible for the first two points being near the UCL in Fig. 9-3b; thus $X_2 = 0.070$ is suspected of being an outlier.

Also, control limits have been drawn in Fig. 9-3a for $n = 1$ at

$$\overline{X} \pm 3\hat{\sigma} \quad \text{and at} \quad \overline{X} \pm 2\hat{\sigma}$$

where $\hat{\sigma} = 0.013$. The point corresponding to $X_2 = 0.070$ is between the $2\hat{\sigma}$ and $3\hat{\sigma}$ lines. This is additional evidence, consistent with that of Fig. 9-3b, indicating this one observation to be an outlier with risk between $\alpha = .05$ and .01. Consequently, an investigation for the reason is recommended.

2. Dixon's Test for a Single Outlier in a Sample of n

Consider the *ordered* set of n random observations from a population presumed to be normal:

$$X_1, X_2, X_3, \ldots, X_{n-1}, X_n$$

Either end point, X_1 or X_n, may be an outlier. Dixon studied[1] various ratios and recommends

$$\mathbf{r}_{10} = \frac{X_2 - X_1}{X_n - X_1}$$

to test the smallest X_1 of being an outlier in a sample of $n = 3, 4, 5, 6,$ or 7. If the largest X_n is suspect, replace $(X_2 - X_1)$ by $(X_n - X_{n-1})$. When $n > 7$, similar but different ratios are recommended in Table A-9.

EXAMPLE 9-1: Consider the previous data of Table 9-2, $n = 10$. From Table A-9 we are to compute:

$$\mathbf{r}_{11} = \frac{X_2 - X_1}{X_{n-1} - X_1} = \frac{0.098 - 0.070}{0.110 - 0.070} = 0.70$$

This computed value of $\mathbf{r}_{11} = 0.70$ exceeds the tabular entry 0.597 in Table A-9, corresponding to a very small risk of .01. We decide that the 0.070 observation does not belong to the same universe as the other nine observations. This conclusion is consistent with the evidence from Figs. 9-3a and b.

    Whether the process warrants a study to identify the reason for this outlier and the expected frequency of future similar low mavericks is a matter for discussion with the engineer.

9-4   Two Suspected Outliers on the Same End of a Sample of n[2]

Besides the control chart, the following two procedures are suggested as tests for a pair of outliers:

    1. *Dixon's test after excluding the more extreme of two observations:* proceed in the usual way by testing the one suspect in the $(n - 1)$ remaining observations. If there are three extreme observations, exclude the two most extreme and proceed by testing, Appendix Table A-9, the one suspect in the $(n - 2)$ remaining observations.

    Consider the 10 measurements of Grubbs in the example below, where the two smallest suggest the possibility of having a different source than the other eight; see Fig. 9-4.

Analysis with Dixon's Criterion: Exclude the lowest observation. Then in the remaining nine: $x_1 = 2.22$, $x_2 = 3.04$, $x_8 = 4.11$, and $x_9 = 4.13$.

---

[1] W. J. Dixon, Processing Data for Outliers, *Biom.*, vol. 9, pp. 74–89, 1953.
[2] This section is not vital to subsequent discussions and may be omitted.

Form the ratio

$$r_{11} = \frac{x_2 - x_1}{x_8 - x_1} = \frac{0.82}{1.89} = .43$$

Analysis: This ratio is larger than the critical value of 0.352, for $\alpha = .20$ and smaller than 0.441 for $\alpha = .10$.

Fig. 9-4   Data with two suggested outliers on the same end. (See Example 9-2.)

Decision: Then we consider both of the suspected observations to be from a different source if we are willing to accept a risk between .10 and .20.

2.   A test for *two outliers on the same end provided by Grubbs*[1] is based on the ratio of the sample sum of squares when the doubtful values are excluded to the sum when included.

EXAMPLE 9-2:   Following are ten measurements of percent elongation at break test on a certain material: 3.73, 3.59, 3.94, 4.13, 3.04, 2.22, 3.23, 4.05, 4.11, and 2.02.   Arranged in ascending order of magnitude[2] these measurements are: 2.02, 2.22, 3.04, 3.23, 3.59, 3.73, 3.94, 4.05, 4.11, 4.13.   We can test the two lowest readings simultaneously by using the criterion $S_{1,2}^2/S^2$ of Table A-10.   For the above measurements

$$S^2 = \sum_{i=1}^{n} (x_i - \bar{x})^2 = \frac{n \sum x_i^2 - (\sum x_i)^2}{n} = \frac{10(121.3594) - (34.06)^2}{10}$$

$$S^2 = 5.351$$

and

$$S_{1,2}^2 = \sum_{i=3}^{n} (x_i - \bar{x}_{1,2})^2 = \frac{(n-2) \sum_{i=3}^{n} x_i^2 - (\sum_{i=3}^{n} x_i)^2}{(n-2)}$$

where $\bar{x}_{1,2} = \sum_{i=3}^{n} x_i/(n-2)$

$$= \frac{8(112.3506) - (29.82)^2}{8} = 1.197$$

Then,

$$S_{1,2}^2/S^2 = 1.197/5.351 = 0.224$$

From Table A-10, the critical value of $S_{1,2}^2/S^2$ at the 5% level is 0.2305.   Since the calculated value is *less* than this, we conclude that *both* 2.02 and 2.22 are outliers, risk 5%.   This compares with a risk between 10% and 20% by the previous analysis.

[1] Frank E. Grubbs, *loc. cit.*
[2] Also see Fig. 9-4.

10

Variability—
Estimating and Comparing

10-1 Introduction

The ideas and methods of Chaps. 1, 2, and 4 will be extended in Chaps. 10 to
13. To many, the use of variables is most natural; it is a standard and
effective way of studying the behavior of many production processes and
scientific relations. Under many conditions, decisions can be made with
much smaller samples than when using attribute data.

The variability of a stable process may be different on one machine than
another, or under one set of conditions than under another. Such variabilities in a process can introduce difficulties in the comparison of averages or
other measures of central tendency. Some methods of comparison are given
in Chap. 11.

Comparisons of variability and of averages will depend upon estimates of
variation. Statistical tables will be used in making some of these comparisons. The computation of some of these tables has depended upon the
number of *degrees of freedom*, df, associated with estimates of the *variance* σ^2
and standard deviation σ. The number of degrees of freedom may be
different when computing estimates in different ways. The number of df
associated with different methods of computation will be indicated.

Section 10-2 has been included for those who enjoy looking at extensions
and ramifications of statistical procedures. It may be omitted without
seriously affecting the understanding of subsequent sections.

198

10-2   Statistical Efficiency and Bias in Variability Estimates

Two terms used by statisticians have technical meanings suggested by the terms themselves. They are *unbiased* and *statistically efficient*. As the sample size is increased, a consistent statistic approaches a fixed value with errors that tend to be normally distributed. If the expected value of the statistic is equal to the population parameter, the estimate is called *unbiased*. A statistic which is the least variable for a given sample size is said to be the most *efficient statistically*.

In the definition of variance, Eq. (10-1), the denominator $(n - 1)$ is used; this provides an unbiased estimate of the unknown population statistic σ^2. We might also expect the square root of s^2 to be an unbiased estimate of σ; actually this is "not quite" the case. However, it is unusual for anyone to make an adjustment for the slight bias.

An unbiased estimate[1] is

$$\hat{\sigma} = \frac{1}{c_4} \sqrt{\frac{\Sigma(X_i - \bar{X})^2}{n - 1}}$$

where some values of c_4 are given in Table 10-1 but seldom used.

TABLE 10-1   Factors c_4 to Give an Unbiased Estimate:

$$\hat{\sigma} = \frac{s}{c_4} = \frac{1}{c_4} \sqrt{\frac{\Sigma(X_i - \bar{X})^2}{n - 1}}$$

n	c_4
4	0.92
6	0.95
10	0.97
25	0.99
∞	1.00

The concept of statistical efficiency is discussed in texts on theoretical statistics. It permits some comparisons of statistical procedures especially under the assumptions of normality and stability. For example, the definition of the variance s^2 in Eq. (10-1) would be the most efficient of all possible estimates *if* the assumptions were satisfied. However, the statistical efficiency of $\hat{\sigma}$ based on the *range*, $\hat{\sigma} = \bar{R}/d_2$, is only slightly less than that obtained in

[1]ASQC Standard A1 (proposed), *Ind. Qual. Control*, p. 217, October, 1967.

TABLE 10-2 Statistical Efficiency of $\hat{\sigma} = \bar{R}/d_2$ in Estimating the Population Parameter from k Small Samples

n	Statistical efficiency
2	1.00
3	0.992
4	0.975
5	0.955
6	0.93
10	0.85

relation (10-1) even when the assumptions are satisfied.   When they are not satisfied, the advantages often favor $\hat{\sigma} = \bar{R}/d_2$.

Statistical methods can be important in analyzing production and scientific data, and it is advisable that such methods be as statistically efficient as possible.   But cooperation between engineering and statistical personnel is essential; both groups should be ready to compromise on methods so that the highest overall simplicity, feasibility, and efficiency are obtained in each phase of the study.

10-3   Estimating σ and σ^2 from Data; One Sample of Size n

In Chap. 1, Table 1-3, the mechanics of computing $\bar{X}$ and $\hat{\sigma}$ from *grouped data* with large n were presented:

$$\hat{\sigma} = m\sqrt{E_2 - E_1^2}$$

where
$$E_1 = \frac{\Sigma f_i d_i}{n},$$

$$E_2 = \frac{\Sigma f_i d_i^2}{n} \tag{1-4b}$$

The histogram procedure serves a dual purpose: (1) it presents the data in a graphical form which is almost invariably useful, and (2) it provides a simple form of numerical computation which can be carried through without a desk calculator or other computer.

In some process-improvement studies, we shall have only *one set of data* which is too small to warrant grouping.   Let the n independent, random observations from a stable process be: $X_1, X_2, X_3, \ldots, X_n$. Then the variance σ^2 of the process can be estimated[1] by

$$s^2 = \hat{\sigma}^2 = \frac{\Sigma(X_i - \overline{X})^2}{n - 1} \qquad df = n - 1 \qquad (10\text{-}1a)$$

$$= \frac{n\Sigma X_i^2 - (\Sigma X_i)^2}{n(n - 1)} \qquad (10\text{-}1b)$$

The following sections show that the comparison of two process variabilities is based on variances rather than standard deviations.

10-4   Data Consisting of k Subsets of r (or n)[2] Two Procedures

Introduction

Important procedures are presented in this section which will be applied continually throughout the remaining chapters of this book.   They are summarized in Sec. 10-6 and Table 10-6.   It is recommended that you refer to them as you read through this chapter.

■ The *mechanics* of computing $\hat{\sigma}$ from a series of small rational subgroups of size n was discussed in Sec. 1-12.   We usually considered k to be as large as 25 or 30.   Then

$$\hat{\sigma} = \overline{R}/d_2 \qquad (10\text{-}2)$$

where d_2 is a constant (see Table A-4) with values depending only on n (or r).   An important advantage of this control-chart method is its use in checking the stability of process variation from the R chart.

This estimate $\hat{\sigma}$ in Eq. (10-2) is *unbiased*.   However, squaring to obtain $\hat{\sigma}^2 = (\overline{R}/d_2)^2$ has the seemingly peculiar effect of producing a bias in $\hat{\sigma}^2$.   The bias can be removed by the device of replacing d_2 by a slightly modified factor d_2^* (read " d-two star ") depending on both the number of samples k and the number of replicates, r.   See Table A-11.   That is, the variance

$$\hat{\sigma}^2 = (\overline{R}/d_2^*)^2 \qquad (10\text{-}3a)$$

is unbiased.   Also

$$\hat{\sigma} = \overline{R}/d_2^* \qquad (10\text{-}3b)$$

is slightly biased much as s in Eq. (10-1) is biased.   We shall sometimes use this biased estimate $\overline{R}/d_2^*$ especially when k is less than say 4 or 5 in

[1] Equations (1-4b) and (10-1) differ slightly in having denominators of n and $(n - 1)$, respectively.   This is inconsequential when n is as large as 20 or 25.

[2] In our industrial experiences, we often obtain repeated (replicated) observations from the same or similar sets of conditions.   The small letter r will be used to represent the number of observations in each combination of conditions.   There will usually be k sets of conditions each with r replicates.   The letter n will usually be reserved to use when two or more samples of size r are pooled.

connection with certain statistical tables based on the bias of s in estimating σ. (This is somewhat confusing; the differentiation *is not critical*, as can be seen by comparing values of d_2 and d_2^*.)   The degrees of freedom df associated with the estimate Eq. (10-3a or b) are also given in Table A-11 for each value of k and r.   However, a simple comparison indicates that there is a loss of essentially 10% when using this range estimate, i.e.,

$$\mathrm{df} \cong (0.9)k(r - 1), \qquad k > 2 \tag{10-4}$$

■ There is an alternate method of computing $\hat{\sigma}^2$ from a series of rational subgroups of varying sizes $r_1, r_2, r_3, \ldots, r_k$.   Begin by computing a variance s_i^2 for each sample from Eq. (10-1) to obtain: $s_1^2, s_2^2, s_3^2, \ldots, s_k^2$.   Then

$$s_p^2 = \hat{\sigma}^2 = \frac{(r_1 - 1)s_1^2 + (r_2 - 1)s_2^2 + \cdots + (r_k - 1)s_k^2}{r_1 + r_2 + \cdots + r_k - k} \tag{10-5a}$$

Each sample contributes $(r_i - 1)$ degrees of freedom for the total shown in the denominator of Eq. (10-5a).   This estimate $\hat{\sigma}^2$ in Eq. (10-5a) is unbiased.

When $r_1 = r_2 = r_3 = \cdots = r_k = r$, the denominator becomes simply

$$\mathrm{df} = k(r - 1)$$

Equation (10-5a) is applicable for either large or small sample sizes r_i.

Note: When $k = 2$ and $r_1 = r_2 = r$, Eq. (10-5a) becomes simply the average

$$s_p^2 = \hat{\sigma}^2 = \frac{s_1^2 + s_2^2}{2} \qquad \mathrm{df} = 2(r - 1) \tag{10-5b}$$

10-5   Comparing Variabilities of Two Populations

Consider two machines, for example, producing items to the same specifications.   The product may differ with respect to some measured quality characteristic either because of differences in variability or because of unstable average performance.

Two random samples from the same machine (or population) will also vary.   We would not expect the variability of the two samples to be exactly equal.   Now if many random samples are drawn from the same machine (population, process), how much variation is expected in the variability of these samples?   When is there enough of a difference between computed variances of two samples to indicate that they are *not* from the same machine or not from machines performing with the same basic variability?

This question can be answered by two statistical methods: the *variance ratio test* (F test) and the *range-square-ratio test* (F_R test).

Variance Ratio Test (F test)

This method originated with Professor George W. Snedecor who designated it the "F test" in honor of the pioneer agricultural researcher and statistician, Sir Ronald A. Fisher.   The method is simple in mechanical application.

Method: Given two samples of sizes n_1 and n_2, respectively, *considered to be from the same population;* compute s_1^2 and s_2^2 and *designate the larger value by s_1^2.* What is the expected "largest ratio," with risk α, of the *F ratio*

$$F = s_1^2/s_2^2 \tag{10-6}$$

To answer, we will need *degrees of freedom* (df) for
Numerator (s_1^2): $\mathrm{df}_1 = n_1 - 1$, and
Denominator (s_2^2): $\mathrm{df}_2 = n_2 - 1$
The two degrees of freedom will be written as

$$F(\mathrm{df}_1, \mathrm{df}_2) = F(n_1 - 1, n_2 - 1)$$

Critical values, F_α, are given in Tables A-12, corresponding to selected values of α and $F(n_1 - 1, n_2 - 1)$. The tables are constructed so that the df across the top of the tables applies to df_1 of the numerator (s_1^2); the df along the left side applies to df_2 of the denominator (s_2^2).

EXAMPLE 10-1: The 25 tests on single-fiber yarn strength from two different machines are shown in Table 10-3; they are plotted in Fig. 10-1. The graph suggests the possibility that machine 56 is basically more variable than machine 49. A formal comparison can be made by the *F* test, Eq. (10-6), using

$$\hat{\sigma}^2 = \frac{n(\Sigma x^2) - (\Sigma x)^2}{n(n-1)}$$

Fig. 10-1 Breaking strength of single fiber yarn from two machines. (Data from Table 10-3.)

COMPUTATIONS: *Machine 56*
$$n(\Sigma x^2) = 25(496.1481) = 12,403.7025$$
$$(\Sigma x)^2 = (110.71)^2 \quad = 12,256.7041$$
$$\overline{\hspace{3.5cm} 146.9984}$$

$$n(n-1) = 600$$

$s_1^2 = 146.9984/600 = 0.245 \qquad \mathrm{df} = 24$

Machine 49
$$n(\Sigma x^2) = 25(456.1810) = 11,404.525$$
$$(\Sigma x)^2 = (106.56)^2 \quad = 11,355.034$$
$$\overline{\hspace{3.5cm} 49.491}$$

$$n(n-1) = 600$$

$s_2^2 = 49.491/600 = 0.082 \qquad \mathrm{df} = 24$

TABLE 10-3   Data: Breaking
Strength   of   Single-fiber   Yarn
Spun on Two Machines

Machine 49	Machine 56
3.99	5.34
4.44	4.27
3.91	4.10
3.98	4.29
4.20	5.27
4.42	4.24
5.08	5.12
4.20	3.79
4.55	3.84
3.85	5.34
4.34	4.94
4.49	4.56
4.44	4.28
4.06	4.96
4.05	4.85
4.34	4.17
4.00	4.60
4.72	4.30
4.00	4.21
4.25	4.16
4.10	3.70
4.35	3.81
4.56	4.22
4.23	4.25
4.01	4.10

We now compare the two variabilities by the F ratio, Eq. (10-6).

$$F = s_1^2/s_2^2 = 0.245/0.082 = 2.99 \qquad df = F(24,24)$$

CRITICAL VALUE of F:

$$\text{for } \alpha = .01, \; F_{.01} = 2.66$$

Since our test ratio 2.99 is larger than 2.66, we declare that the variability of machine 56 is greater than machine 49, with very small risk, $\alpha < .01$.

EXAMPLE 10-2:   Using cathode sleeves made from one batch of nickel (melt A), a group of 10 electronic tubes was processed and an electrical characteristic (*transconductance*, G_m) was measured.   Using nickel cathode sleeves from a new batch (melt B), a second test group of 10 tubes was processed and G_m was read.   Is there evidence that "the population variability" represented by tubes from melt B will be significantly different from melt A?

TABLE 10-4 Data: Measure-
ments of Transconductance of
Two Groups of Tubes Made from
Two Batches (melts) of Nickel

Melt A	Melt B
4,760	6,050
5,330	4,950
2,640	3,770
5,380	5,290
5,380	6,050
2,760	5,120
4,140	1,420
3,120	5,630
3,210	5,370
5,120	4,960
$\bar{A} = 4,184.0$	$\bar{B} = 4,861.0$
$(n = 10)$	$(n = 10)$
	$\bar{B}' = 5,243.3$
	$(n = 9)$

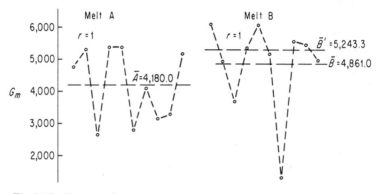

Fig. 10-2 Transconductance readings on electronic tubes from two batches
of nickel. (Data from Table 10-4.)

The first step, as usual, is to plot the data (Fig. 10-2).

The data are typical; neither set has an entirely convincing appearance of randomness. One obvious possibility is that the 1,420 reading in melt B is an outlier. The
Dixon test for an outlier, $n = 10$, is

$$r_{11} = \frac{x_2 - x_1}{x_{k-1} - x_1} = \frac{3,770 - 1,420}{6,050 - 1,420} = 0.508$$

This computed value, 0.508, exceeds the critical value of 0.477, for $\alpha = 0.05$ and $n = 10$,
Table A-9. This is "reasonably" convincing evidence that something peculiar occurred
with the seventh tube in melt B either during production or testing to obtain the 1,420
reading.

Much of the variability of melt B is contributed by the suspected outlier observation. What happens if we remove the 1,420 observation and compute F? (Note: B' is used to indicate the nine observations with 1,420 deleted.)

$$s_1^2 = s_A^2 = 1,319,604 \qquad n = 10$$
$$s_2^2 = s_{B'}^2 = 477,675 \qquad n = 9$$

Then

$$F = s_1^2/s_2^2 = (1,319,604)/(477,675) = 2.77 \qquad df = F(9,8)$$

Now this F exceeds $F_{.10} = 2.56$ but not $F_{.05} = 3.39$. This "suggests" that product from melt A may be more variable than product from melt B' (one maverick removed), but is not entirely convincing.

There are important engineering considerations which must be the basis for deciding whether to consider melt B to be basically less variable than melt A, and whether to investigate reoccurrences of possible mavericks in either group.

On the other hand, what are the consequences, statistically, if the 1,420 observation is *not* considered to be a maverick? When the variance of melt B is recomputed with all 10 observations,

$$s_B^2 = 1,886,388$$

The F ratio becomes

$$F = s_1^2/s_2^2 = (1,886,388)/(1,319,604) = 1.43 \qquad df = F(9,9)$$

Even if the engineer were willing to assume a risk of $\alpha = .25$, he still would not be justified in considering the variability of the two samples to be different when the 1,420 (suspected maverick) is left in the analysis, since $F = 1.43$ is less than either $F_{.10} = 2.44$ or even $F_{.25} = 1.59$.

REMARKS: The change in decision which results from removing the 1,420 observation is not entirely unexpected when we observe the patterns of melt A and melt B; melt A gives an appearance of being more variable than melt B. These above statistical computations tend to support two suppositions:

1. That the observation 1,420 is an outlier.
2. That melt A is not a single population but a bimodal pattern having two sources, one averaging about 5,000 and the other about 3,000. This suspicion may justify an investigation either into the processing of the radio tubes or the uniformity of melt A in an effort to identify two sources "someplace in the system" and make appropriate adjustments.

(See Case History 11-4 for more discussion of this set of data.)

Range-square-Ratio Test, F_R

In this chapter, we have considered two methods of computing unbiased estimates of the variance, $\hat{\sigma}^2$: the mean-square, $\hat{\sigma}^2 = s^2$, and the range-square estimate, $\hat{\sigma}^2 = (\bar{R}/d_2^*)^2$. In the preceding section, two process variabilities were compared by forming an F ratio and comparing the computed F with tabulated critical values F_α. When data sets are available from two processes, or from one process at two different times, in the form of k_1 sets of r_1 from one and as k_2 sets of r_2 from a second, then we may use the *range-square-ratio*[1] to compare variabilities.

$$F_R = \frac{(\bar{R}_1/d_2^*)^2}{(\bar{R}_2/d_2^*)^2} \tag{10-7}$$

[1] A. J. Duncan, *loc. cit.* Values of r_1 and r_2 usually should be no larger than 6 or 7.

with

$$df_1 \cong (0.9)k_1(r_1 - 1) \qquad df_2 \cong (0.9)k_2(r_2 - 1) \qquad (10\text{-}8)$$

The statistical significance of F_R is then compared to critical values in the F table A-12 for degrees of freedom in relation (10-8). Details of the procedure are given below in Examples 10-3 and 10-4.

EXAMPLE 10-3: This example concerns Case History 2-2 on chemical concentration. A visual inspection of Fig. 10-3 shows 11 range points representing a period from May 14 into May 18 to be above the median. This long run is suggestive of a shift in the variability of the process during this period. Does the range-square-ratio test offer any evidence on variability?

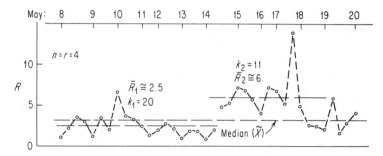

Fig. 10-3 Evidence of increased process variability (Example 10-3).

We see an estimated average of $\bar{R}_1 = 2.5$ for the $k_1 = 20$ points during the period from May 8 into May 14, then a jump to an estimated $\bar{R}_2 = 6$ for the next 11 points, and possibly a drop back to the initial average during the period of the last 7 points. This is a conjecture, i.e., a tentative hypothesis.

RANGE-SQUARE-RATIO TEST: (Data of Fig. 10-3)
$\bar{R}_1 = 2.5$, $k_1 = 20$, $r_1 = 4$, with $df_1 \cong (0.9)(20)(3) = 54$
$\bar{R}_2 = 6.0$, $k_2 = 11$, $r_2 = 4$, with $df_2 \cong (0.9)(11)(3) = 30$

Then

$$F_R = \frac{(\bar{R}_2/d_2^*)^2}{(\bar{R}_1/d_2^*)^2} \cong 36/6.25 = 5.76 \qquad df \cong F(30,54)$$

In Table A-12, no critical value of F is shown for 30 and 54 df, but one is shown for 30 and 60 df; it is $F_{.01} = 2.03$. Since our test ratio, 5.76, is much larger than any value in the vicinity of $F_{.01} = 2.03$, there is no need or advantage in interpolating.

The range-square-ratio test supports the evidence from the long run that a shift in variability did occur about May 14. The process variability was not stable; an investigation at the time would have been expected to lead to physical explanations.

Control charts, $\bar{X}$, R, are helpful in process-improvement studies: these often indicate shifts in $\bar{R}$ (as well as in $\bar{X}$). Then the range-square-ratio test can be applied easily as a check, and investigations made into possible causes.

EXAMPLE 10-4: Another use of the range-square-ratio test is in comparing variabilities of two analytical chemical procedures. The data of Table 10-5 pertain to the ranges of three determinations of a chemical characteristic by each of four analysts on (blind)

TABLE 10-5 Variability (As Measured by Ranges, $r = 3$) of Two Methods of Chemical Analysis Using Four Analysts

Method	Barrels	Analysts				
		I	II	III	IV	
A	1	2.0	3.1	0	1.5	
	2	0.5	2.0	2.5	0.3	
	3	1.5	1.9	1.5	0.8	
	4	2.5	0.5	1.0	0.3	$\bar{R}_A = 1.37$
B	1	0.5	1.3	1.0	1.0	
	2	0.5	1.4	0	0.9	
	3	1.0	0.8	0.5	0.3	
	4	1.0	0.7	1.0	0.3	$\bar{R}_B = 0.75$

samples from each of four barrels.   In the first set, determinations are made by method A and in the second by method B.   The question is whether the experimental variability of the second method is an improvement (reduction) over the first.   It is assumed that the experimental variability is independent of analyst and sample so that the 16 ranges can be averaged for each set.   Here we have:

$$\bar{R}_1 = 1.37 \qquad \bar{R}_2 = 0.75$$
$$r_1 = 3 \qquad r_2 = 3$$
$$k_1 = 16 \qquad k_2 = 16$$

and from Table A-11, $df_1 = 29.3$ and $df_2 = 29.3$, or $df \cong (0.9)k(r-1) = 29$ from Eq. (10-4).

Then
$$F_R = \frac{(1.37)^2}{(0.75)^2} = 3.3 \qquad df \cong F(29, 29)$$

From F table A-12, we find $F_{.05} = 1.87$.   Since our computed $F_R = 3.3$ is in excess of the critical (.05) value, we conclude that the variability of the second method is an improvement over the variability of method A.

10-6   Summary

This chapter has presented different methods of computing estimates of σ and σ^2 from data.   These estimates are used in comparing process variabilities under operating conditions.   Frequent references will be made to the following estimates:

- $\hat{\sigma} = \bar{R}/d_2$: used when the number of subgroups k is as large as 25 or 30, and even smaller (see Note below).   See Eq. (1-13).   Gives unbiased estimate for all k.
- $\hat{\sigma} = \bar{R}/d_2^*$: used when the number of subgroups k is quite small and in association especially with other tables designed for use with the slightly biased estimate s.

We frequently use this estimate in association with factors from Table A-15 which was designed for use with the similarly biased estimate s.

Note: In Table A-11, it may be seen that $d_2 < d_2^*$ in each column; thus, the two estimates above will differ slightly, and

$$\bar{R}/d_2 > \bar{R}/d_2^*$$

Consequently, the use of d_2 with a *small number* of subgroups will simply produce a slightly more conservative estimate of σ in making comparisons of k means. We shall usually use d_2^* in the case histories of the following chapters.

Two methods of comparing process variability have been discussed in Sec. 10-5: the F test and the range-square-ratio test (F_R).

An outline of some computational forms is given in Table 10-6. The different procedures for computing $\hat{\sigma}$ are quite confusing unless used frequently. Those forms which will be most useful in the following chapters are marked.

TABLE 10-6   Summary: Estimating Variability

Different procedures for computing $\hat{\sigma}$ are quite confusing unless used frequently. Forms which will be used most often in the following chapters are marked with the superscript [*].

Computing Measures of Variation from k Sets of r Each

[#]1. $\hat{\sigma} = \bar{R}/d_2$ $\left.\begin{array}{l} \end{array}\right\}$ df $\cong (0.9)k(r-1)$ unbiased   Eq. (1-13)

[#]2. $\hat{\sigma} = \bar{R}/d_2^*$ Also Table A-11   slightly biased   Eq. (10-3)

3. $\hat{\sigma}^2 = (\bar{R}/d_2^*)^2$ unbiased   Eq. (10-3)

4. $\hat{\sigma}^2 = \dfrac{(r_1 - 1)s_1^2 + (r_2 - 1)s_2^2 + \cdots + (r_k - 1)s_k^2}{r_1 + r_2 + \cdots + r_k - k}$ unbiased   Eq. (10-5)

$$df = r_1 + r_2 + \cdots + r_k - k$$

[#]5. $\hat{\sigma}_{\bar{x}} = \hat{\sigma}/\sqrt{r}$ Eq. (1-7)

Computing Measures of Variation from One Set of n

[#]6. $\hat{\sigma} = m\sqrt{E_2 - E_1^2}$ $df = n - 1$ Eq. (1-4b)

where $E_1 = \dfrac{\Sigma f_i d_i}{n}$ $E_2 = \dfrac{\Sigma f_i d_i^2}{n}$

7. $s^2 = \hat{\sigma}^2 = \dfrac{\Sigma (X_i - \bar{X})^2}{n - 1}$ $df = n - 1$ unbiased   Eq. (10-1a)

8. $s^2 = \hat{\sigma}^2 = \dfrac{n\Sigma X_i^2 - (\Sigma X_i)^2}{n(n - 1)}$ unbiased   Eq. (10-1b)

9. $s = \hat{\sigma} = \sqrt{\dfrac{\Sigma (X_i - \bar{X})^2}{n - 1}}$ slightly biased   Eq. (10.1)

11

Comparing Two Process Averages

11-1 Introduction

The introduction of Chap. 5 discusses several important ideas.   Although it is an introduction to troubleshooting using attribute data, the ideas are equally pertinent to studies using variable data.   It is suggested that you reread the ideas in the introductory section.

This discussion begins with a comparison at two levels of just one independent variable.   When data from two experimental conditions are compared, how can we judge objectively whether they justify our initial expectations of a difference between the two conditions?   Three statistical methods are presented to judge whether there is objective evidence of a difference greater than expected only from chance.   This is a typical decision to be made, with *no standard given.*

11-2 Tukey's Two-sample Test to Duckworth's Specifications[1]

There are important reasons for becoming familiar with the Tukey procedure: no desk calculator is needed; such a procedure may well be used more often and "compensate for (any) loss of mathematical power.   Its use is to indicate

[1] John W. Tukey, A quick, compact, two-sample test to Duckworth's specifications, *Technometrics*, vol. 1, no. 1, pp. 31–48, February, 1959.

the weight of the evidence roughly.   If a delicate and critical decision is to be made, we may expect to replace it or augment it with some other procedure."

Tukey Procedure

Given two groups of r_1 and r_2 measurements taken under two conditions. The requirement for comparing the experimental conditions by this criteria is that

The largest observations of the two be in one sample (A_2) and the smallest in the other (A_1).   Let the number of observations in A_2 which are larger than the largest in A_1 be a, and let the number in A_1 smaller than the smallest in A_2 be b where neither a nor b is zero.   (Count a tie between A_1 and A_2 as 0.5.)   Critical values of the sum of the two counts, $a + b$, for a two-sided test are given in Table 11-1.   The test is essentially independent of sample sizes if they are not too unequal, i.e., the ratio of the larger to the smaller is less than 4/3.

TABLE 11-1   Critical Values of the Tukey-Duckworth Sum
Also See Table A-13

Approximate risk	Critical values of the sum $a + b$
.09	6
.05	7
.01	10
.001	13

CASE HISTORY 11-1   Nickel-Cadmium Batteries

In the development of a nickel-cadmium battery, a project was organized to find[1] some important factors affecting capacitance.

The data in Table 11-2 were obtained at stations C_1 and C_2 (other known independent variables believed to have been held constant).   Is the difference in process averages from the two stations statistically significant?

Some form of graphical representation is always recommended and the credibility of the data considered.   The individual observations have been plotted in Fig. 11-1.   There is no obvious indication of an outlier or other lack of stability in either set.   Also, the criteria for the Tukey-Duckworth procedure are satisfied, and the sum of the two counts is

$$a + b = 6 + 6 = 12$$

This exceeds the critical sum of 10 required for risk $\alpha \cong .01$ (Table 11-1).

[1] See Case History 12-2 for additional discussion.

TABLE 11-2   Data: Capacitance of Nickel-Cadmium Batteries Measured under Two Conditions

C_1	C_2
0.6	1.8
1.0	2.1
0.8	2.2
1.5	1.9
1.3	2.6
1.1	2.8
$\bar{C}_1 = 1.05$	$\bar{C}_2 = 2.23$
$R_1 = 0.9$	$R_2 = 1.0$

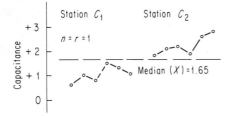

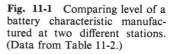

Fig. 11-1   Comparing level of a battery characteristic manufactured at two different stations. (Data from Table 11-2.)

11-3   Analysis of Means, $k = 2$, $r_1 = r_2 = r$

There is hardly need of any additional evidence than the Tukey two-sample analysis to decide that changing from C_1 to C_2 (Table 11-2) will increase capacitance.   However, Analysis of Means (ANOM) for variables data, discussed previously in Chap. 5 for attribute data, will be presented here and used later with many sets of variables data.

ANOM will be used first to compare two processes represented by samples, then applied in this chapter to 2^2 and 2^3 experimental designs.   The importance of 2^2 and 2^3 designs in troubleshooting, pilot-plant studies, and initial studies warrants discussion separate from the more general approach in Chap. 12 where the number of variables and levels of each is not restricted to two.

Just as with attribute data it is often good strategy to identify possible problem sources quickly and leave a definitive study till later.   The choice of some independent variables to be block-type variables is usually an important short cut in that direction.

Formal Analysis

■ From Table 11-2 ($k = 2$, $r = 6$), values of the two averages and ranges are known.   They are shown in Fig. 11-2.   The two range points are inside the control limits.

■ From Table A-11,

$$\hat{\sigma} = \bar{R}/d_2^* = 0.95/2.60 = 0.365$$

and

$$\hat{\sigma}_{\bar{x}} = \hat{\sigma}/\sqrt{r} = (0.365)/\sqrt{6} = 0.149$$

$$\text{df} \cong (0.9)2(6 - 1) = 9$$

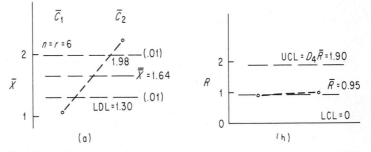

Fig. 11-2 Comparing two process averages by analysis of means (variables). (Data from Table 11-2.)

■ From Table A-14 for $k = 2$ and df $= 9$; $H_{.05} = 1.60$, $H_{.01} = 2.30$.
■ *Decision lines*

$$\bar{C} \pm H_{.01}\hat{\sigma}_{\bar{x}} = 1.64 \pm (2.30)(0.149)$$

For $\alpha = .01$

$$\text{UDL} = 1.64 + 0.34 = 1.98$$
$$\text{LDL} = 1.64 - 0.34 = 1.30$$

TABLE 11-3   Summary: Mechanics of Analysis of Means, ANOM, for Two Small Samples with $r_1 = r_2 = r$

STEP 1. Obtain and plot the two sample ranges. Find $\bar{R}$ and $D_4\bar{R}$. If both points fall below $D_4\bar{R}$, compute[†]

$$\hat{\sigma} = \bar{R}/d_2^* \quad \text{and} \quad \hat{\sigma}_{\bar{x}} = \hat{\sigma}/\sqrt{r}$$

Also df $\cong (0.9)k(r - 1) = 1.80(r - 1)$ for $k = 2$. (Or see Table A-11.)

STEP 2. Plot points corresponding to $\bar{A}$, $\bar{B}$, and their average $\bar{X}$.

STEP 3. Compute $H_\alpha\hat{\sigma}_{\bar{x}}$, and draw decision lines

$$\text{UDL} = \bar{X} + H_\alpha\hat{\sigma}_{\bar{x}}$$
$$\text{LDL} = \bar{X} - H_\alpha\hat{\sigma}_{\bar{x}}$$

usually choosing values of $\alpha = .10$, .05, and .01 to bracket the two sample averages.

STEP 4. When the pair of points falls outside a pair of decision lines, their difference is statistically significant, risk α.

Note: Points $\bar{A}$ and $\bar{B}$ will be symmetrical with $\bar{X}$ when $r_1 = r_2$.

[†] Find d_2^* in Table A-11 for $k = 2$ and r.

■ These two decision lines are shown in Fig. 11-2a; the two C points are outside them. We conclude that there is a statistically significant difference in capacitance resulting in a change from station C_1 to C_2. This is in agreement with the Tukey procedure above.

11-4   Student's t test to Compare Averages of Two Stable Processes

Note: This section may be omitted without affecting understanding of subsequent sections.

EXAMPLE 11-1: (Again use data of Table 11-2; $k = 2$, $r_1 = r_2 = r = 6$.)

The t *statistic* to compute is:

$$t = \frac{\bar{C}_2 - \bar{C}_1}{s_p \sqrt{\dfrac{1}{r_1} + \dfrac{1}{r_2}}} \tag{11-1}$$

STEP 1:   Compute

$$s_1^2 = \hat{\sigma}_1^2 = \frac{r \Sigma x^2 - (\Sigma x)^2}{r(r-1)}$$

$$= \frac{6(7.15) - (6.3)^2}{30} = 0.107$$

$$s_2^2 = \hat{\sigma}_2^2 = \frac{6(30.70) - (13.4)^2}{30} = 0.155$$

STEP 2:   Check for evidence of possible inequality of variances with the F test, Eq. (10-6),

$$F = \frac{0.155}{0.107} = 1.45 \qquad \text{with df} = F(5,5)$$

In Table A-12, we find critical values: $F_{.05} = 5.05$ and $F_{.10} = 3.45$.

STEP 3:   Since $F = 1.45$ is less than even the critical value $F_{.10}$, we accept equality of variances of the two processes and proceed to estimate their common pooled[1] variance. From Eq. (10-5b)

$$s_p^2 = \frac{s_1^2 + s_2^2}{2} = \frac{(0.107) + (0.155)}{2} = 0.131$$

and $$s_p = \sqrt{0.131} = 0.362$$

Since $r_1 = r_2$ in Eq. (11-1), the denominator becomes

$$\hat{\sigma}_{\bar{A}} = \frac{\sqrt{2} s_p}{\sqrt{r}} = \sqrt{2}\, s_{\bar{x}} = 0.209 \tag{11-3}$$

[1] When $r_1 \neq r_2$, then

$$s_p^2 = \frac{(r_1 - 1)s_1^2 + (r_2 - 1)s_2^2}{r_1 + r_2 - 2} \tag{11-2}$$

See Eq. (10-5a).

STEP 4:   Then finally compute from Eq. (11-1)

$$t = \frac{\bar{C}_2 - \bar{C}_1}{0.209} = \frac{1.18}{0.209} = 5.64 \qquad df = 10$$

The critical value found in Table A-15 for $df = 10$ is: $t_{.01} = 2.76$.

STEP 5:   *Decision*:   Since our $t = 5.64$ is larger than $t_{.01} = 2.76$, we decide that the process represented by the sample C_2 is operating at a higher average than the process represented by the sample C_1 with a high degree of confidence (with risk less than $\alpha = .01$).

SOME COMPARISONS OF t TEST AND ANOM IN ANALYZING DATA OF TABLE 11-2

In Fig. 11-2*b*, both range points fall below UCL(R), and we accept homogeneity of variability in the two processes.   This agrees with the results of the F test above.

Then $\hat{\sigma} = \bar{R}/d_2^* = 0.95/2.60 = 0.365$.   This estimate $\hat{\sigma}$ agrees closely with the pooled estimate $s_p = 0.362$ in step 3.

The decision lines in Fig. 11-2*a* are drawn about $\bar{\bar{C}}$ at a distance $\pm H_\alpha \hat{\sigma}_{\bar{x}}$.   It can be shown that

$$\pm H_\alpha \hat{\sigma}_{\bar{x}} = \pm \frac{1}{2} t_\alpha \frac{s_p \sqrt{2}}{\sqrt{r}} \qquad \text{i.e.} \qquad H_\alpha = \frac{t_\alpha}{\sqrt{2}}$$

Thus the decision between the two process averages is made from looking at Fig. 11-2*a* instead of looking in the t table.   The ANOM is just a graphical t test *when $k = 2$*.   It is an extension of the t test when $k > 2$.

When $r_1 \neq r_2$ or when r *is not small*, we use Eq. (10-5a) in estimating $\hat{\sigma}$ for ANOM. When $r_1 = r_2 = r$ *is small*—say less than 6 or 7, the efficiency of the range in estimating $\hat{\sigma}$ is very high (see Table 10-2); the loss in degrees of freedom (df) is only about 10% as we have seen.

11-5   Magnitude of the Difference between Two Means

At least as important as the question of statistical significance is the question of *practical or economic significance*.   The observed *sample difference* in capacitance in Table 11-2 is

$$\bar{\Delta} = \bar{C}_2 - \bar{C}_1 = 2.23 - 1.05 = 1.18$$

this was found to be statistically significant.   It is now the scientist engineer who must decide whether the observed difference is large enough to be of practical interest.   If the data were not coded, it would be possible to represent the change as a percent of the average, $\bar{C} = 1.640$.   In many applications, a difference of 1% or 2% is not of practical significance; a difference of 10% or so would often be of great interest.   The decision must be made for each case, usually by design or quality engineers.

If the study in Table 11-2 were repeated with another pair of samples for stations C_1 and C_2, we would not expect to observe exactly the same average difference $\bar{\Delta}$ as observed this first time.   (However, we *would* expect the average difference for $r = 6$ to be statistically significant, risk $\alpha \cong .01$.)   The confidence limits on the difference are given (for any risk α) by the two extremes

$$\bar{\Delta}_1 = (\bar{C}_2 - \bar{C}_1) + 2H_\alpha \hat{\sigma}_{\bar{x}}$$
$$\bar{\Delta}_2 = (\bar{C}_2 - \bar{C}_1) - 2H_\alpha \hat{\sigma}_{\bar{x}} \qquad \text{risk } \alpha \qquad (11\text{-}4)$$

We have, with risk $\alpha = .01$ for example:

$$\bar{\Delta}_1 = 1.18 + 2(0.343) = 1.87$$

and $\qquad\qquad \bar{\Delta}_2 = 1.18 - 2(0.343) = 0.49$

Or, we found the effects of C_1 and C_2 to differ by 1.18 units; the two processes which $\bar{C}_1$ and $\bar{C}_2$ represent may actually differ by as much as 1.87 units or as little as 0.49 units.   Thus, in Eq. (11-4), the experimenter has a measure of the extreme differences which can actually be found in a process as a result of shifting between levels C_1 and C_2, risk α.

Note: If the points corresponding to C_1 and C_2 should fall exactly on the decision lines, then the population averages may not differ at all; *or*, they may differ by twice the width of the decision lines.

Sometimes, the observed difference may not be of practical interest in itself but may suggest the *possibility* that a larger change in the independent variable might produce a larger effect which *would* then be of interest.   These are matters to discuss with the engineer scientist.

CASE HISTORY 11-2   Height of Easter Lilies on Date of First Bloom[1]

Botanists have learned that many characteristics of plants can be modified by man.   For example, "Easter lilies" grown normally in the garden, in many states, bloom in July or August—not at Easter time.   You would probably not give a second thought to such characteristics as the range of heights you would favor when buying an Easter lily or the number of buds and blooms you would prefer, but they are important factors to the horticulturist.   The referenced study employed a more complex design than either the one presented here or the 2^2 design in Table 12-2.   Botanists and agriculturalists usually have to wait through one or more growing seasons to acquire data.   Their experimental designs often need to be quite complicated to get useful information in a reasonable time.   Industrial troubleshooting and process improvement can often move much faster; additional information can often be obtained within a few hours or days.   Several less-complicated experiments are usually the best strategy here.   This is one reason for our emphasis on three designs: the 2^2, the 2^3, and the 2×2 Latin Square.   A study was made of the height of Easter lilies (on the date of first bloom).   Under two different storage conditions, T_1 and T_2, of Easter lily

[1] Richard H. Merritt, Vegetative and Floral Development of Plants Resulting from Differential Precooling of Planted Croft Lily Bulbs, *Proc. Amer. Soc. Hortic. Sci.*, vol. 82, pp. 517–525, 1963.

bulbs (all other factors believed to have been held constant), the measured heights of plants were

Condition:	T_1	T_2
	28	31
	26	35
	30	31
	$\overline{T}_1 = 28.0$	$32.3 = \overline{T}_2$
	$R_1 = 4$	$4 = R_2$

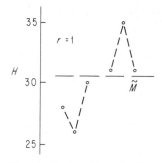

Fig. 11-3 Heights of lilies under two different storage conditions.

ANALYSIS:

■ The *Tukey-Duckworth count* is $a + b = 6$, which is significant at $\alpha \cong .10$ and "almost" significant at $\alpha \cong .05$.

■ A *second analysis (ANOM)*. In Fig. 11-4, points corresponding to $\overline{T}_1$ and $\overline{T}_2$ fall outside the $\alpha = .10$ lines and inside the .05 lines.

CONCLUSION: From this analysis, there is some evidence (risk less than .10 and greater than .05) that a change from condition T_1 to T_2 may produce an increase in the height. The amount of increase is discussed in the following section. The choice of conditions to use in raising Easter lilies and/or

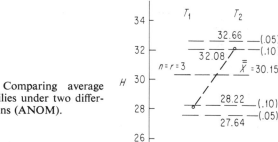

Fig. 11-4 Comparing average heights of lilies under two different conditions (ANOM).

whether to study greater differences in levels of T must be made by the scientist. (Also see Case History 12-1.)

MECHANICS OF COMPUTING DECISION LINES (Fig. 11-4)

$$\hat{\sigma} = \overline{R}/d_2^* = 4.0/1.81 = 2.21$$
$$\hat{\sigma}_{\bar{x}} = \hat{\sigma}/\sqrt{r} = 2.21/1.73 = 1.28$$
$$\text{df} \cong (0.9)k(r - 1) = (0.9)(2)(2) = 3.6$$

Or from Table A-11, df = 3.8 $\cong$ 4

Decision lines at $\overline{\overline{X}} \pm H_\alpha \hat{\sigma}_{\bar{x}}$

$\alpha = .05$

$$UDL = 30.15 + 2.51 = 32.66$$
$$LDL = 30.15 - 2.51 = 27.64$$

$\alpha = .10$

$$UDL = 30.15 + 1.93 = 32.08$$
$$LDL = 30.15 - 1.93 = 28.22$$

■ *Magnitude of difference*

For $\alpha = .10$

$$\bar{\Delta}_1 = (\overline{T}_2 - \overline{T}_1) + 2H_{10}\,\hat{\sigma}_{\bar{x}} = 4.30 + 2(1.93)$$
$$= 4.30 + 3.86 = 8.16 \text{ in.}$$
$$\bar{\Delta}_2 = (\overline{T}_2 - \overline{T}_1) - 2H_{10}\,\hat{\sigma}_{\bar{x}} = 4.30 - 3.86 = +0.44 \text{ in.}$$

Thus the expected average difference may actually be as small as 0.44 in. or as large as 8.16 in., risk $\alpha = .10$.

For $\alpha = .05$

$$\bar{\Delta}_1 = 4.30 + 2H_{.05}\,\hat{\sigma}_{\bar{x}} = 4.30 + 2(2.51) = +9.32$$
$$\bar{\Delta}_2 = 4.30 - 2(2.51) = -0.72$$

A negative sign on $\bar{\Delta}_2$ means that there is actually a small chance that condition T_1 might produce taller plants than T_2; it is a small chance but a possibility when considering confidence limits of $\alpha = .05$.

CASE HISTORY 11-3   Vials from Two Manufacturing Firms

The weights in grams of a sample of 15 vials manufactured by firm A and 12 vials by firm B are given below.   Are vials manufactured by firm A expected to weigh significantly more than those manufactured by firm B? We shall discuss the problems from different aspects.

TABLE 11-4   Data: Vials from Two Manufacturing Firms

Firm	Weight, grams
A:	7.6, 8.3, 13.6, 14.9, 12.7, 15.6, 9.1, 9.3, 11.7, 9.6, 10.7, 8.0, 9.4, 11.2, 12.8 ($r_1 = 15$)
B:	7.1, 7.6, 10.1, 10.1, 8.7, 7.2, 9.5, 10.2, 9.5, 9.0, 7.3, 7.4 ($r_2 = 12$)

INFORMAL ANALYSIS 1:   We begin by plotting the data in a single graph (Fig. 11-5).   We note that all observations from firm B lie below the average

$\bar{A}$ of firm A.   Little additional formal analysis is necessary to establish that the process average from firm A exceeds the process average of firm B.

ANALYSIS 2:   The required conditions for the Tukey-Duckworth test are satisfied, and the counts are: $a + b = 8 + 4.5* = 12$.   This count exceeds the critical count of 10 for risk $\alpha \cong .01$ and almost equals the critical count of 13 for risk $\alpha \cong .001$.   This is in agreement with Analysis 1.

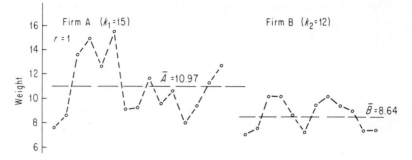

Fig. 11-5   Weights of individual vials from two manufacturing firms.

ANALYSIS 3: STUDENT'S t TEST: $t = \dfrac{\bar{A} - \bar{B}}{s_p\sqrt{\dfrac{1}{r_1} + \dfrac{1}{r_2}}}$

$$\bar{A} = 10.97 \qquad \bar{B} = 8.64$$
$$s_A^2 = 6.34 \qquad s_B^2 = 1.55$$
$$r_1 = 15 \qquad r_2 = 12$$
$$\bar{A} - \bar{B} = 2.33$$

$$s_p = \sqrt{\frac{14(6.34) + 11(1.55)}{25}} = \sqrt{4.23} \qquad \text{from Eq. (11-2)}$$

and

$$\sqrt{\frac{1}{r_1} + \frac{1}{r_2}} = \sqrt{\frac{1}{15} + \frac{1}{12}} = \sqrt{0.150} = 0.39$$

Then

$$t = \frac{2.33}{(\sqrt{4.23})(0.39)}$$
$$= \frac{2.33}{0.80}$$
$$= 2.91$$

* The first and smallest observation in A is a tie with the second one in B.

with $df = r_1 + r_2 - 2 = 25$. The critical value $t_{.01} = 2.79$ for $df = 25$ is clearly exceeded.

DISCUSSION: Thus the three analyses are in agreement that the average product expected from A should exceed that of B, *provided* the basic assumptions are satisfied.

However, consider the patterns of the data in Fig. 11-5. There are four *consecutive* vials from firm A which are appreciably higher than the others. There is enough evidence to raise certain important questions:

1. Is the product from firm A of only one kind, or is it of two or more kinds?

2. Do the four high values from firm A represent higher weights, or is the test equipment unstable (in view of the consecutive peculiarities)?

3. Summary: Is it possible to predict future weights?

COMMENTS: Two basic assumptions in comparing samples from two populations are that *two stable and normally distributed populations are being sampled.* In this example, these assumptions are surely not justified. Of course, if a decision must now be made to choose the firm producing "larger" vials, then firm A would be the choice. But it will then be prudent to sample succeeding lots of product to ensure that the noncontrolled process of firm A does not begin producing vials of a low weight.

We seldom find two sets of data where it is adequate to be satisfied with a single routine test (such as a t test or a Tukey test). Additional worthwhile information comes from "looking at" the data in two or more different ways. Many patterns of nonrandomness occur. Some statistical tests are robust in detecting one pattern, some in detecting others.

CASE HISTORY 11-4   Electronic Tubes

It is the *usual* experience to find one set of data (or both) originating from a nonstable source instead of just one stable source, as often assumed. Let us consider the data of Table 11-5 pertaining to two batches of nickel cathode sleeves (see Example 10-2). Using cathode sleeves made from one batch of nickel (melt A), a group of 10 electronic tubes was processed; then an electrical characteristic (transconductance, G_m) was read on a bridge. Using nickel cathode sleeves from a new batch of nickel (melt B), a second group of 10 tubes was processed and G_m read. Is there evidence that tubes processed from melt B will average a higher G_m than tubes from melt A, as is hoped? (See Fig. 10-2.)

ANALYSIS: A ROUTINE PROCEDURE (NOT RECOMMENDED): If we were to proceed directly with a formal t test, we would first average each group and compute each variance

$$\bar{A} = 4,184.0 \qquad \bar{B} = 4,861.0$$
$$s_A^2 = 1,319,604.4 \qquad s_B^2 = 1,886,387.8$$

TABLE 11-5   Data: Measurements on Electronic Tubes Made from Two Batches of Nickel Cathode Sleeves

Melt A	Melt B
4,760	6,050
5,330	4,950
2,640	3,770
5,380	5,290
5,380	6,050
2,760	5,120
4,140	1,420
3,120	5,630
3,210	5,370
5,120	4,960
$\bar{A} = 4,184.0$	$\bar{B} = 4,861.0$
$(n = 10)$	$(n = 10)$
	$\bar{B}' = 5,243.3$
	$(n = 9)$

Since $r_1 = r_2$, we use the simplified form of the t test from Sec. 11-3, step 3,

$$s_p^2 = \tfrac{1}{2}(s_A^2 + s_B^2) = 1,602,996.1$$

Then $s_p = 1266.1$ and $\sqrt{2}\,s_{\bar{x}} = \dfrac{\sqrt{2}\,(1,266.1)}{\sqrt{10}} = 566.2$

and $t = \dfrac{677}{566.2} = 1.20$ $df = n_1 + n_2 - 2 = 18$

Critical values of t corresponding to 18 df are

$$t_{.20} = 1.330$$

and $$t_{.10} = 1.734$$

Thus, we do *not* have evidence of statistical significance even with risk $\alpha \cong .20$ (or 80% confidence).

This routine application of the t test is not recommended. The suspected outlier in melt B has major effects on the result of a t test, as well as on the average of the process using melt B.

FURTHER ANALYSIS

Consider again the data in Table 11-5 (Fig. 10-2). After excluding 1,420 (the seventh point) in melt B as a suspected maverick, the Tukey counts are easily seen from Fig. 10-2 to be

$a = 3$ (number in melt B larger than any in melt A),

$b = 4$ (number in melt A smaller than any in melt B), and

$(a + b) = 7$

This test on the modified data indicates that the G_m of radio tubes made from nickel cathode sleeves from melt A will average lower than those made from melt B (with risk of about $\alpha = .05$).

ANALYSIS: STUDENT'S t TEST APPLIED TO THE MODIFIED DATA

We may now recompute the t test after excluding the 1,420 observation.

$$\bar{A} = 4184.0 \quad (r_1 = 10) \qquad \bar{B}' = 5243.3 \quad (r_2 = 9)$$
$$\hat{\sigma}_A^2 = 1,319,604 \qquad\qquad \hat{\sigma}_{B'}^2 = 487,675$$

Then from Eq. (11-2)

$$s_p = \sqrt{\frac{9(1,319,604) + 8(487,675)}{17}} = \sqrt{928,108} = 963.4$$

From Eq. (11-1)

$$s_p\sqrt{\frac{1}{10} + \frac{1}{9}} = (963.4)\sqrt{\frac{19}{90}} = 442.2$$

Then $\qquad\qquad t = \dfrac{\bar{B}' - \bar{A}}{442.0} = \dfrac{1,059.3}{442.0} = 2.40 \qquad df = 17$

From Appendix Table A-15, critical values of t, for 17 df are

$$t_{.02} = 2.567$$
$$t_{.05} = 2.110$$

Consequently, this t test (on the modified data) indicates a significant difference between population means with risk about $\alpha \cong .03$ or .04. This result is consistent with analysis 2 but not with analysis 1.

CONCLUSION: Clearly, the one suspected observation in melt B has a critical influence on conclusions about the two process averages. Now it is time to discuss the situation with the engineer. The following points are pertinent:

■ The melt B average is an increase of about 25% over the melt A average. Is the increase enough to be of practical interest? If not, whether 1,420 is left in or deleted is of no concern.

■ There is a strong suspicion that the data of melt A comes from two sources (see Fig. 10-2 and the discussion of Example 10-2). Are there two possible sources (in the process) which may be contributing two-level values to G_m from nickel of melt A?

■ It appears that a serious study should be made of the stability of the tube manufacturing process when using any single melt. The question of "statistical significance" between the two melt sample averages may be less important than the question of process stability.

11-6   Practice Exercises

1. Use moving ranges ($n = 2$) on:
   a. the data of melt A, $n = 10$, to obtain $\hat{\sigma}_A$, and compare this with $s_A = 1{,}149$,
   b. the data for melt B', $n = 9$, to obtain $\hat{\sigma}_B$, and compare with $s_{B'} = 691.1$.

2. Plot moving average and range charts, $n = 2$, for the data of firm A in Case History 11-3. What evidence does this present, if any, regarding the randomness of the data from firm A?

3. Consider all $15 + 12 = 27$ points from the two firms, Case History 11-3, and repeat the procedure of Exercise 2. Does the number and/or length of runs provide evidence of interest?

4. What do we conclude by applying the Tukey test to the two average ranges of Fig. 10-3? Are the conclusions using the range-square-ratio test F_r and Tukey's test in reasonable agreement?

5. Compare the process averages represented by the samples from two machines, Table 10-3. Possibilities include:
   a. Dividing each group into subgroups ($n = 5$, for example)
   b. Using a t test on all 25 observations in each group; or perhaps the first (or last, or both) five or ten of each.

12

Troubleshooting with Variables Data

12-1 Introduction

The ideas on troubleshooting with attribute data, discussed in Chap. 5, are equally applicable when using variables data. Identifying economically important problems, enlisting the cooperation of plant and technical personnel, deciding what independent variables and factors to include—these are usually more important than the analysis of resulting data. These remarks are repeated here to emphasize the importance of reasonable planning prior to the collection of data. The reader may want to review the ideas of Chaps. 4 and 5 before continuing.

This chapter will discuss three very important designs: two factorial designs[1], 2^2 and 2^3, and the "half-replicate" or "two-by-two Latin-Square" design, $\frac{1}{2} \times 2^3$. These are very effective designs, especially when making exploratory studies and in troubleshooting. In Chap. 13, some case histories employing more than two levels of some independent variables are discussed.

Results from a study involving the simultaneous adjustment of two or more independent variables are often not readily accepted by those outside the planning group. For many years, engineers and production supervisors were taught to make studies with just one independent variable at a time. Many

[1] Chap. 5, Secs. 5-6, 5-7, and 5-8.

are skeptical of the propriety of experiments which vary even two independent variables simultaneously.   Yet they are the ones who must accept the analysis and conclusions if the findings in a study are to be implemented.   If they are not implemented, the experiment is usually wasted effort.   It is critical that an analysis of the data be presented in a form which is familiar to engineers and which suggests answers to important questions.   For these reasons the graphical analysis of means is recommended and emphasized here.

12-2   Suggestions in Planning Investigations— Primarily Reminders

The two "levels" of the independent variable may be of a continuous variable which is recognized as a possible causative variable.   Then we may use a common notation: A_- to represent the *lower* level of the variable and A_+ to represent the *higher* level.   Frequently, however, the two "levels" should be block-type variables as discussed in Chap. 4: two machine-operator combinations, two shifts, two test sets, two vendors.   Then we use a more representative notation such as A_1 and A_2 to represent the two levels.

Some amount of replication is recommended, that is, $r > 1$ and perhaps as large as 5 or 6. In many investigations, there is little difficulty in getting replicates at each combination of the independent variables.   A single replicate may possibly represent the process adequately *if* the process is actually stable during the investigation, which is an assumption seldom satisfied.   It should certainly be checked beforehand.   Outliers and other evidences of an unstable process are common even when all known variables are held constant (Chap. 9).   It is even more likely that a single observation would be inadequate when two or three variables are being studied at different levels in a designed experiment.

There may be exceptional occasions where it is practical and feasible to use a design with four or five variables, each at two levels (a 2^4 or a 2^5 design or a fraction thereof).   But leave such complexities to those experienced in such matters.

Any study that requires more than 15 or 20 trays of components to be carried about manually in the plant will require extreme caution in planning and handling to prevent errors and confusion in identification.   It is very difficult to maintain reasonable surveillance when only 8 or 10 trays must be routed and identified through production stages.

Scientists often use appreciably more data than a statistician might recommend for the following reasons:

1.   It has been traditional in many sciences to use very large sample sizes and to have little confidence in results from smaller samples.

2.   Any analysis assumes that the sample chosen for the study is *representative* of a larger population; a larger sample may be required to satisfy this important condition.   Usually, however, replicates of 3, 4, or 5 are adequate.

Evolutionary Operation[1] : The 2^2 design with its center point is the basis of the well-known evolutionary operation (EVOP).   It has appealed especially to the chemical industry in efforts to increase process yields.   During planning of an EVOP program, two independent process variables, A and B, are selected to study.   They may be temperature, throughput rate, percent catalyst, and so on.   Two levels of each variable are chosen within manufacturing specifications, one toward USL and one toward LSL.   Since the difference in levels is usually not large, several replicates may be needed to establish significant differences.

12-3   Analysis of Means, a 2^2 Factorial Design

The method of Chap. 11 is now extended to this very important case of two independent variables (two levels of each).

Main Effects and Two-factor Interaction

In Fig. 12-1, the $\bar{X}_{ij}$ represent the average quality characteristic or response under the indicated conditions.   If the average response $\bar{A}_1$ under conditions B_1 and B_2 is statistically different from the average response $\bar{A}_2$ under the same two conditions, then *factor A is said to be a significant main effect*.[2]

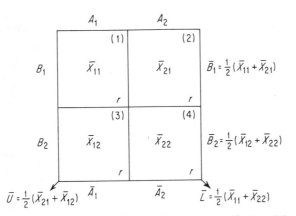

Fig. 12-1 A general display of data in a 2^2 factorial design, r replicates in each average, $\bar{X}_{ij}$.

---

[1] G. E. P. Box, Evolutionary Operation: A Method for Increasing Industrial Productivity, *Appl. Stat.*, vol. 6, pp. 81–101, 1957.

[2] Consider the $\bar{X}_{ij}$ in Fig. 12-1 to be averages of r replicates.   For simplicity we shall abbreviate the notation by writing, for example,

$$\bar{A}_1 = \tfrac{1}{2}(1,3) \text{ for } \tfrac{1}{2}[(1) + (3)] = \tfrac{1}{2}(\bar{X}_{11} + \bar{X}_{12})$$

$$\bar{A}_1 = \tfrac{1}{2}(1,3) \qquad \bar{B}_1 = \tfrac{1}{2}(1,2) \qquad L = \tfrac{1}{2}(1,4)$$

$$\bar{A}_2 = \tfrac{1}{2}(2,4) \qquad \bar{B}_2 = \tfrac{1}{2}(3,4) \qquad U = \tfrac{1}{2}(2,3)$$

where L again represents the average of the two combinations 1 and 4 of A and B having *like* subscripts; U is the average of the two *unlike* combinations.

As before, the mechanics of testing for a main effect with the Analysis of Means is to compare $\bar{A}_1$ with $\bar{A}_2$ and $\bar{B}_1$ with $\bar{B}_2$ using *decision lines*

$$\bar{X} \pm H_\alpha \hat{\sigma}_{\bar{x}} \qquad (12\text{-}1)$$

Actually, there are three comparisons which can be tested against the decision lines in Eq. (12-1). The mechanics of testing for main effects with ANOM can be extended as follows to test for the interaction of A and B:

$\bar{A}_1 = \frac{1}{2}(1,3)$ versus $\bar{A}_2 = \frac{1}{2}(2,4)$ to test for an A main effect

$\bar{B}_1 = \frac{1}{2}(1,2)$ versus $\bar{B}_2 = \frac{1}{2}(3,4)$ to test for a B main effect

$\bar{L} = \frac{1}{2}(1,4)$ versus $U = \frac{1}{2}(2,3)$ to test for an AB interaction

Discussion

I. Change in response to A under condition B_1 $(A_1$ to $A_2) = (2) - (1) = \bar{X}_{21} - \bar{X}_{11}$

II. Change in response to A under condition B_2 $(A_1$ to $A_2) = (4) - (3) = \bar{X}_{22} - \bar{X}_{12}$

Total change in A $= [(2 + 4) - (1 + 3)]$

Average change in A $= 0.5[(2 + 4) - (1 + 3)]$

This average change is called the *main effect of A* and is represented most simply by the symbol

$$\bar{\Delta}_A = \frac{1}{2}[(2,4) - (1,3)]$$

Similarly

$$\bar{\Delta}_B = \frac{1}{2}[(3,4) - (1,2)]$$

Definition: If the A effect I is different under B_1 than II under B_2 then there is said to be a *two-factor* or *AB interaction:*

When the changes I and II are unequal,

$$(2) - (1) \neq (4) - (3)$$

then

$$(2) + (3) \neq (4) + (1)$$

But $[(2) + (3)]$ is the sum of the two cross combinations of A and B with *unlike* U subscripts while $[(1) + (4)]$ is the sum of *like* L subscripts in Fig. 12-1. Briefly, when there is an AB interaction, the sum (and average) of the *unlike* combinations are not equal to the sum (and average) of the *like* combinations.

Conversely, if the sum (and average) of the two terms with *like* subscripts equals statistically[1] the sum (and average) of the two with *unlike* subscripts

$$[(2) + (3)] = [(4) + (1)]$$

then

$$[(2) - (1)] = [(4) - (3)]$$

that is,

$$I = II$$

THEOREM 12-1:   *To test for a two-factor interaction AB, obtain the cross-sums, like (1,4) and unlike (2,3). There is an AB interaction if, and only if, the like sum is not equal to the unlike sum, i.e., their averages are not equal, statistically.*

TABLE 12-1   Analysis of Means in a 2^2 Factorial Design, r Replicates

---

STEP 1.   Obtain and plot the four ranges.   Find $\bar{R}$ and $D_4 \bar{R}$ and use the range chart as a check on possible outliers.   Obtain d_2^* from Table A-11; compute $\hat{\sigma} = \bar{R}/d_2^*$ and $\hat{\sigma}_{\bar{x}} = \hat{\sigma}/\sqrt{2r}$.

$$df \cong (0.9)k(r - 1) = 3.6(r - 1) \qquad \text{for } k = 4$$

(Or see Table A-11)

STEP 2.   Plot points corresponding to the two main effects and interaction:

$$\bar{A}_1 = \tfrac{1}{2}(1,3) \qquad \bar{B}_1 = \tfrac{1}{2}(1,2) \qquad \bar{L} = \tfrac{1}{2}(1,4)$$
$$\bar{A}_2 = \tfrac{1}{2}(2,4) \qquad \bar{B}_2 = \tfrac{1}{2}(3,4) \qquad \bar{U} = \tfrac{1}{2}(2,3) \qquad \bar{\bar{X}} = \tfrac{1}{4}(1,2,3,4)$$

STEP 3.   Obtain H_α from Table A-8 for $k = 2$ and $n = 2r$.   Compute and draw lines at

$$UDL = \bar{\bar{X}} + H_\alpha \hat{\sigma}_{\bar{x}}$$
$$LDL = \bar{\bar{X}} - H_\alpha \hat{\sigma}_{\bar{x}}$$

usually choosing $\alpha = .05$ and then .10 or .01 to bracket the extreme sample averages.

STEP 4.   When a pair of points falls outside decision lines, their difference is statistically significant, risk α.   If points corresponding to $\bar{L}$ and $\bar{U}$ fall outside (or near) the decision lines, proceed as in Fig. 12-2.

Note: In (1), the value $\hat{\sigma} = \bar{R}/d_2^*$ is a measure of the *within-group* variation, i.e., an estimate of inherent variability even when all factors are thought to be held constant.   This *within-group* variation is used as a yardstick to compare *between-factor* variation by the decision lines of (3).

The well-known analysis of variance (ANOVA) measures *within* group variation by a *residual sum of squares*, $\hat{\sigma}_E^2$, whose square root $\hat{\sigma}_E$ will be found to approximate $\hat{\sigma} = \bar{R}/d_2^*$ quite closely in most sets of data.   ANOVA compares *between-group* variation by a series of variance ratio tests (F tests) instead of decision lines.

[1] Being *equal statistically* means that their *difference* is *not* statistically significant, risk α.

It is both interesting and instructive to plot the four combination averages as shown in Fig. 12-2. It always helps in understanding and interpreting the meaning of the interaction. When $[(2) + (3)] = [(1) + (4)]$, the two lines are essentially *parallel*, and there is *no* interaction. Also, when they are *not* essentially parallel, there *is* an $A \times B$ interaction.

This procedure will be illustrated first in Case History 12-1.

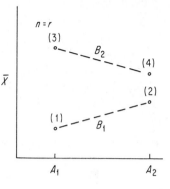

Fig. 12-2 A picture to interpret a two-factor interaction.

CASE HISTORY 12-1 Height of Easter Lilies[1]

INTRODUCTION: Consider data from *two independent variables* in a study of Easter lilies raised in the Rutgers University Greenhouse. The two independent factors considered in this analysis are:

Storage Period (SP): The length of time bulbs were stored in a controlled dormant state, $(SP_1$ and $SP_2)$.

Time (T): The length of time the bulbs were conditioned after the storage period, $(T_1$ and $T_2)$.

TABLE 12-2 Height of Easter Lilies (in.)

	SP_1	SP_2	
T_1	28 (1) 26 30 $\bar{X}_1 = 28.0$ $R_1 = 4$	49 (2) 37 38 $\bar{X}_2 = 41.3$ $R_2 = 12$	$\bar{T}_1 = 34.65$
T_2	31 (3) 35 31 $\bar{X}_3 = 32.3$ $R_3 = 4$	37 (4) 37 29 $\bar{X}_4 = 34.3$ $R_4 = 8$	$\bar{T}_2 = 33.3$
$\bar{U} = 36.8$	$\overline{SP}_1 = 30.15$	$\overline{SP}_2 = 37.8$	$\bar{L} = 31.15$

[1] Other important independent variables and quality characteristics were reported in the research publication. See Richard H. Merritt, *loc. cit.*

The researchers specified levels of *SP* and of *T* from their background of experience. The quality characteristic (dependent variable) considered here is a continuous variable, the height *H* in inches of a plant on the date of first bloom.

Table 12-2 represents data from the four combinations of *T* and *SP*, with $r = 3$ replicate plants in each.

FORMAL ANALYSIS (Fig. 12-3)

   Main effects

$$\overline{SP}_1(1,3) = 30.15 \qquad \overline{T}_1(1,2) = 34.65$$
$$\overline{SP}_2(2,4) = 37.8 \qquad \overline{T}_2(3,4) = 33.3$$

   Interaction

$$\overline{L}(1,4) = 31.15$$
$$\overline{U}(2,3) = 36.8 \qquad \overline{X} = 33.98$$

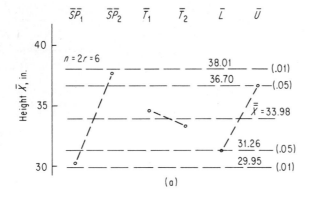

(a)

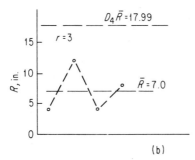

(b)

Fig. 12-3   ANOM data from Table 12-2.   (*a*) Height of Easter lilies; (*b*) ranges of heights.

All four *R* points fall below $D_4\overline{R} = 17.99$ in Fig. 12-3*b*.   Then

$$\hat{\sigma} = \overline{R}/d_2^* = 7.0/1.75 = 4.0$$
$$\hat{\sigma}_{\overline{X}} = 4.0/\sqrt{6} = 1.63$$
$$\text{df} \cong (0.9)k(r - 1) \cong 7$$

DECISION LINES   Fig. 12-3a

$\bar{X} \pm H_\alpha \hat{\sigma}_X$: $\alpha = .05$

$$UDL = 33.98 + (1.67)(1.63) = 36.70$$
$$LDL = 33.98 - (1.67)(1.63) = 31.26$$

$\alpha = .01$

$$UDL = 33.98 + (2.47)(1.63) = 38.01$$
$$LDL = 33.98 - (2.47)(1.63) = 29.95$$

The risks have been drawn in parentheses at the right end of the decision lines.

■ We decide that the major effect is storage period, with a risk between .05 and .01.   There is also a two-factor interaction, risk slightly less than .05.

■ If customers prefer heights averaging about 28 in., then the combination $T_1 SP_1$ is indicated.   If the preference is for heights of about 38 in., additional evidence is needed since the 49-in. plant in (2) and the 29-in. plant in (4) represent possible outliers.

But the effect of storage period is certainly substantial and the effect of time probably negligible.

MAGNITUDE OF THE DIFFERENCE.   From Sec. 11-5, Eq. (11-4), the magnitude of a difference may vary by $\pm 2H_\alpha \hat{\sigma}_{\bar{x}}$ from the observed difference.   Then the expected magnitude of the SP main effect in a large production of Easter lily bulbs is

$$(\overline{SP_2} - \overline{SP_1}) \pm 2H_\alpha \hat{\sigma}_{\bar{x}} =$$
$$7.65 \pm 2(2.72) = 7.65 \pm 5.44 \qquad (\alpha \cong .05)$$

that is by as much as 13.09 in. and as little as 2.21 in.

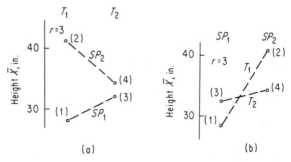

Fig. 12-4 An auxiliary chart to understand the interaction of SP with time.   (Data of Table 12.2.)

DISCUSSION OF THE TIME-BY-STORAGE INTERACTION.   Since the $T \times SP$ was shown to be statistically significant, risk about 5%, there is a preferential pairing of the two variables.   The change in H corresponding to a change from T_1 to T_2 is different when using SP_1 than when using SP_2.   To interpret the interaction, we plot the averages of the four subgroups from Table 12-2 as shown in Fig. 12-4a and b.   Height *increases* when changing from condition T_1 to T_2 at level SP_1 but *decreases* when changing at level SP_2.   The pair of lines (1,3) and (2,4) in Fig. 12-4a and lines (1,2) and (3,4) in Fig. 12-4b are *not essentially parallel*; there is a $T \times SP$ interaction.   It was shown in Fig. 12-3a that the interaction effect is statistically significant, $\alpha \cong .05$.

PEDIGREE OF SOME DATA.   The three heights in combination 2 warrant checking for presence of an outlier.   From Table A-9,

$$r_{10} = \frac{49 - 38}{49 - 37} = 0.915$$

Critical values of r_{10} are

$$0.941 \text{ for } \alpha = .05$$
$$0.925 \text{ for } \alpha = .10$$

The observed ratio is roughly equal to the critical value for $\alpha = .10$. The record books of the scientist should be checked to see whether an error has been made in transcribing the 49-in. observation or whether there are (were) possible experimental clues to explain such a tall plant.   In the formal analysis above, we have included the suspected observation but should now keep a suspicious mind about the analysis and interpretation.

The 29-in. height in combination 4 is also suspect.

If no blunder in recording is found, some other important and possibly unknown factor in the experiment is not being maintained at a constant level.

12-4   Three Independent Variables: A 2^3 Factorial Design

This discussion is about quality characteristics measured on a continuous scale; it parallels that of Sec. 5-7 which considers quality characteristics of an attribute nature.   The mechanics of analysis are slight variations of those in Sec. 12-3 and will be presented here in connection with actual data in the following Case History 12-2.

CASE HISTORY 12-2[1]   Assembly of Nickel-Cadmium Batteries

A great deal of difficulty had developed during production of a nickel-cadmium battery.   As a consequence, a unified team project was organized to find methods of improving certain quality problems.

In an exploratory experiment, three block-type variables were included:
A_1:   Processing on production line 1—using one concentration of nitrate
A_2:   Processing on production line 2—a different nitrate concentration

---

[1] From a term paper prepared for a graduate course at Rutgers University by Alexander Sternberg.   The data have been coded by subtracting a constant from each of the observations; this does not affect the relative comparison of effects.

TABLE 12-3   General Analysis of a 2^3 Factorial Design, $r > 1$

STEP 1.   Plot an R chart (Fig. 12-5b).   Check on possible outliers; when all range points fall below $D_4 \bar{R}$, compute

$$\hat{\sigma}' = \bar{R}/d_2^*$$
$$\hat{\sigma}_{\bar{x}} = \hat{\sigma}'/\sqrt{4r}$$
$$df \cong (0.9)k(r-1)$$

STEP 2.   Obtain averages as shown in Table 12-6 ($n = 4r$)
   a.   Main effects as in Table 12-6.
   b.   Two-factor interactions as in Tables 12-6 and 12-7.
   Plot averages as in Fig. 12-5a.

STEP 3.   Compute decision lines for $k = 2$, $n = 4r$, and $\alpha = .05$ and then for .10 or .01 as appropriate:

$$UDL = \bar{\bar{X}} + H_\alpha \hat{\sigma}_{\bar{x}}$$
$$LDL = \bar{\bar{X}} - H_\alpha \hat{\sigma}_{\bar{x}}$$

   Draw the decision lines as in Fig. 12-5a.

STEP 4.   Any pair of points outside (or near) decision lines indicates a statistically significant difference, risk about α.   Differences which are of practical significance indicate areas to investigate or action to be taken.

STEP 5.   It is sometimes helpful to compute confidence limits on the magnitude of the observed differences, whether a main effect or a two-factor interaction:

$$(\bar{X}_1 - \bar{X}_2) \pm 2H_\alpha \hat{\sigma}_{\bar{x}}$$

(A difference between A_1 and A_2 might be a consequence of lines or concentrations.)

B_1:   Assembly line B-1—using a shim in the battery cells
B_2:   Assembly line B-2—not using a shim

(A difference between B_1 and B_2 might be a consequence of lines or shims.)

C_1:   Processing on Station C-1—using fresh hydroxide
C_2:   Processing on Station C-2—using reused hydroxide

(A difference between C_1 and C_2 might be a consequence of stations or hydroxide.)

All batteries ($r = 6$) were assembled from a *common supply* of components in each of the eight combinations.   The 48 batteries were processed according to a randomized plan, and capacitance was measured at a single test station. The measurements are shown in Table 12-4 and the combination averages in Table 12-5.   (Large capacitances are desired.)

The variation within any subgroup of 6 batteries can be attributed to three possible sources in some initially unknown way:

   1.   Variation attributable to components, materials.
   2.   Variation attributable to manufacturing assembly and processing.
   3.   Variation of testings.

TABLE 12-4   Capacitances of Individual Nickel-Cadmium Batteries in a 2^3 Factorial Design (data coded)
The numbering of the eight columns is consistent with that in Table 12-5.

	A_1				A_2			
	B_1		B_2		B_1		B_2	
	C_1	C_2	C_1	C_2	C_1	C_2	C_1	C_2
	(1)	(5)	(7)	(3)	(6)	(2)	(4)	(8)
	−0.1	1.1	0.6	0.7	0.6	1.9	1.8	2.1
	1.0	0.5	1.0	−0.1	0.8	0.7	2.1	2.3
	0.6	0.1	0.8	1.7	0.7	2.3	2.2	1.9
	−0.1	0.7	1.5	1.2	2.0	1.9	1.9	2.2
	−1.4	1.3	1.3	1.1	0.7	1.0	2.6	1.8
	0.5	1.0	1.1	−0.7	0.7	2.1	2.8	2.5
$\bar{X}$	0.08	0.78	1.05	0.65	0.91	1.65	2.23	2.13
R	2.4	1.2	0.9	2.4	1.4	1.6	1.0	0.7

TABLE 12-5   Averages of Battery Capacitances ($r = 6$) in a 2^3 Factorial Design; Displayed As Two Latin Squares (Data from Table 12-4)

	A_1	A_2
B_1	C_1 (1) $\bar{X}=0.08$ $r=6$	C_2 (2) 1.65
B_2	C_2 (3) 0.65	C_1 (4) 2.23

	A_1	A_2
B_1	C_2 (5) 0.78	C_1 (6) 0.91
B_2	C_1 (7) 1.05	C_2 (8) 2.13

A measure of *within subgroup* variability is

$$\hat{\sigma} = \bar{R}/d_2^* = 1.45/2.55 = 0.57$$

If none of the independent variables is found to be statistically significant or scientifically important, the variation from components and materials is more important than the effect of changes of processing and assembly which have been included in the study.

The following analysis is a direct extension of the analysis of means for a

2^2 investigation, Table 12-1 and Sec. 5-7.   Of the eight combinations in Table 12-4, half were produced at level A_1—those in columns 1, 3, 5, and 7.   We shall designate the *average* of these four column averages as

$$\bar{A}_1(1,3,5,7) = 0.64 \quad \text{with } n = 4r = 24$$

Also $$\bar{A}_2(2,4,6,8) = 1.73$$

An outline of the mechanics of computation for main effects and two-factor interactions is given in Table 12-3; further details follow:

■ $\bar{R} = 1.45$ and $D_4\bar{R} = (2.00)(1.45) = 2.90$

All range points fall below $D_4\bar{R}$ (Fig. 12.5b], and we accept homogeneity of ranges, and compute

$$\hat{\sigma} = \bar{R}/d_2^* = 0.57$$

$$\hat{\sigma}_{\bar{x}} = \frac{\hat{\sigma}}{\sqrt{24}} = \frac{0.57}{4.90} = 0.116 \quad \text{for } n = 4r = 24$$

$$\text{df} \cong 36$$

■ Averages of the 3 *main* effect and 3 two-factor interaction effects are shown in Table 12-6.   Each average is of $n = 4r = 24$ observations.

TABLE 12-6   Averages to Test for Main Effects and Two-Factor Interactions (data of Table 12-4); $n = 4r = 24$

Main effects	Two-factor interactions
$\bar{A}_1(1,3,5,7) = 0.64$	AB: $\bar{L}(1,4,5,8) = 1.305$
$\bar{A}_2(2,4,6,8) = 1.73$	$\bar{U}(2,3,6,7) = 1.065$
$\bar{B}_1(1,2,5,6) = 0.855$	AC: $\bar{L}(1,2,7,8) = 1.23$
$\bar{B}_2(3,4,7,8) = 1.515$	$\bar{U}(3,4,5,6) = 1.14$
$\bar{C}_1(1,4,6,7) = 1.07$	BC: $\bar{L}(1,3,6,8) = 0.94$
$\bar{C}_2(2,3,5,8) = 1.30$	$\bar{U}(2,4,5,7) = 1.43$

■ The decision lines for each comparison are: ($k = 2$, df $\cong 36$)

$$\bar{\bar{X}} \pm H_\alpha \hat{\sigma}_{\bar{x}}$$

For $\alpha = .05$: $H_\alpha = 1.43$

$$\text{UDL}(.05) = 1.185 + (1.43)(0.12)$$
$$= 1.185 + 0.17 = 1.35$$
$$\text{LDL}(.05) = 1.185 - 0.17 = 1.02$$

Since two sets of points are outside these decision lines, we compute another pair.

For $\alpha = .01$, $H_\alpha = 1.92$

$$UDL(01) = 1.185 + 0.223 = 1.41$$
$$LDL(01) = 1.185 - 0.223 = 0.96$$

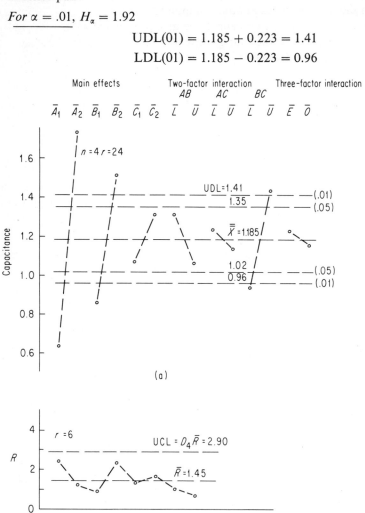

(a)

(b)

Fig. 12-5 (*a*) Electrical capacitance of nickel-cadmium batteries: the ANOM comparisons; (*b*) range chart, nickel-cadmium batteries. (Data from Table 12-4.)

■ Figure 12-5*a* indicates large A and B main effects, and a BC interaction all with risk $\alpha < .01$. The large A main effect was produced by using one specific concentration of nitrate which resulted in a much higher quality battery. Combinations 4 and 8 with A_2 and B_2 evidently are the best. Besides the demonstrated advantages of A_2 over A_1, and of B_2 over B_1, a bonus benefit resulted from no significant difference due to C. This result indicated that a certain expensive compound could be reused in manufacturing and permitted a very substantial reduction in cost.

The presence of a BC interaction caused the group to investigate. It was puzzling at first to realize that the four groups of batteries assembled on line B_1 and processed at station C_2 and those assembled on line B_2 and processed at station C_1 average significantly better than combinations B_1C_1 and B_2C_2. This resulted in the detection of specific differences in the processing and assembling of the batteries. The evaluation lead to improved and standardized process procedures to be followed and a resulting improvement in battery quality.

When all parties concerned were brought together to review the results of the production study, they decided to manufacture a pilot run to check the results. This retest agreed with the first production study; changes were subsequently made in the manufacturing process which were instrumental in improving the performance of the battery and in reducing manufacturing costs.

■ From Eq. (11-4), limits on the *magnitude of the main effects* (for $\alpha = .01$) are

$$\bar{\Delta}_A = (\bar{A}_2 - \bar{A}_1) \pm 2H_\alpha \hat{\sigma}_{\bar{x}}$$
$$= (1.73 - 0.64) \pm 2(0.223)$$
$$= 1.09 \pm 0.45$$
$$\bar{\Delta}_B = (\bar{B}_2 - \bar{B}_1) \pm 2H_\alpha \hat{\sigma}_{\bar{x}}$$
$$= (1.515 - 0.855) \pm 2(0.223), \alpha = .01$$
$$= 0.66 \pm 0.45$$

12-5 Computational Details for Two-factor Interactions in a 2^3 Factorial Design

There are three possible two-factor interactions: AB, AC, and BC. As discussed previously, Theorem 12-1, a test for a two-factor interaction compares those combinations having like subscripts with those having unlike subscripts ignoring the third variable (see Table 12-7).

The four AB combinations having *like subscripts* in Table 12-5 are:

Like: A_1B_1:   (1), (5)
　　　　　A_2B_2 :   (4), (8)
Unlike: A_1B_2 :   (7), (3)
　　　　　A_2B_1:   (2), (6)

Then the two factor AB interaction can be tested by ignoring the third variable C and comparing the averages

$$\bar{L}_{AB}(1,4,5,8) = (0.08 + 2.23 + 0.78 + 2{:}13)/4 = 1.305$$
$$\bar{U}_{AB}(2,3,6,7) = (1.65 + 0.65 + 0.91 + 1.05)/4 = 1.065$$

The comparison above is between the two diagonals of Table 12-7.

TABLE 12-7   Diagram to Display a Selection Procedure to Compute L and U in Testing AB Interaction

	A_1	A_2
B_1	(1,5)	(2,6)
B_2	(7,3)	(4,8)

Unlike (2,3,6,7)   Like (1,4,5,8)

Similar comparisons provide tests for the two other two-factor interactions.

These averages are plotted in Fig. 12-5a.   Each of these averages is (again) of $n = 4r = 24$ observations just as in testing main effects; the two-factor interactions can be compared to the same decision lines as for main effects. Since the pair of points for BC is outside the decision lines for $\alpha = .01$, there is a BC interaction.

Three-factor Interaction in a 2^3 Factorial Design

When all three subscripts are added together, half the sums are even E and half are odd O.   A comparison of those whose sums are even with those which are odd provides a test for what is called a *three-factor interaction*.

$$\overline{ABC}_E(5,6,7,8) = (0.78 + 1.05 + 0.91 + 2.13)/4 = 1.22$$

$$\overline{ABC}_O(1,2,3,4) = 1.15$$

The difference between the three-factor (ABC) averages is quite small (Fig. 12-5a), and the effect is not statistically significant; it is quite unusual for it ever to appear significant.

Many remarks could be made about the practical scientific uses obtained from three-factor interactions which "appear to be significant."   The following suggestions are offered to those of you who find an apparently significant three-factor interaction:

1.   Recheck each set of data for outliers.

2.   Recheck for errors in computation and grouping.

3.   Recheck the method by which the experiment was planned.   Is it possible that the execution of the plan was not followed?

4.   Is the average of one subgroup "large" in comparison to all others? Then discuss possible explanations with the scientist.

5.   Discuss the situation with a professional applied statistician.

12-6   A Very Important Experimental Design: $\frac{1}{2} \times 2^3$

In this chapter we have just discussed 2^2 and 2^3 factorial designs.   They were also discussed in Chap. 5 for data of an attribute nature.   We shall conclude this chapter, as we did Chap. 5, with an example of a 2×2 *Latin Square* or, as it is sometimes called, a *half replicate of a* 2^3.   Some reasons why the design is a very important one were listed in Sec. 5-8; the reasons are just

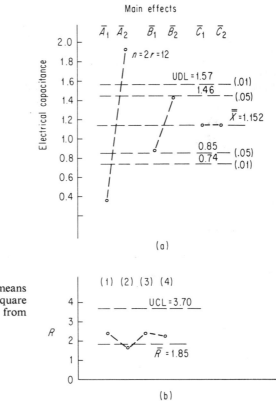

Fig. 12-6 Analysis of means (ANOM) for a Latin Square design $(\frac{1}{2} \cdot 2^3)$. (Data from Table 12-8.)

as applicable when studying response characteristics which are continuous variables.   Either one of the specific halves of a 2^3 design shown previously in Table 12-5 is a Latin Square.

EXAMPLE 12-1: Consider only that portion of the data for a nickel-cadmium battery in Table 12-5 corresponding to the four combinations shown here in Table 12-8. The computations for the analysis are the same as for an ordinary 2^2 factorial design. The averages and ranges are shown in Table 12-8 and plotted in Fig. 12-6.

TABLE 12-8   Battery Capacitances: A Special Half of a 2^3 Design: a Latin Square
Data from Table 12-5

	A_1	A_2	
B_1	C_1 (1) $\bar{X}=0.08$ $R=2.4$	C_2 (2) $\bar{X}=1.65$ $R=1.6$	$\bar{B}_1 = 0.865$
		$r=6$	
B_2	C_2 (3) $\bar{X}=0.65$ $R=2.4$	C_1 (4) $\bar{X}=2.23$ $R=1.0$	$\bar{B}_2=1.44$

$\bar{C}_2 = 1.15$ $\bar{A}_1 = 0.365$ $\bar{A}_2 = 1.94$ $\bar{C}_1 = 1.155$

$\bar{\bar{X}} = 1.152$

MECHANICS OF ANALYSIS:
From Fig. 12-6b the four ranges fall below

$$D_4 \bar{R} = (2.00)(1.85) = 3.70 \qquad \text{for } k=4$$
$$r=6$$

$$\hat{\sigma} = \bar{R}/d_2^* = 1.85/2.60 = 0.71$$
$$\hat{\sigma}_{\bar{x}} = 0.71/\sqrt{12} = 0.205 \qquad n = 2r = 12$$
$$\text{df} \cong (0.9)(4)(5) = 18$$

For $\alpha = .05$:

$$\text{UDL} = 1.152 + (1.49)(0.205)$$
$$= 1.46$$
$$\text{LDL} = 0.85$$

For $\alpha = .01$:

$$\text{UDL} = 1.152 + (2.02)(0.205)$$
$$= 1.57$$
$$\text{LDL} = 0.74$$

For $\alpha = .10$:

Although not computed, the (.10) with the (.05) lines would clearly bracket the B points.

Some comments about the Latin square and full factorial designs.

The two points corresponding to A fall outside the .01-decision lines; the two points corresponding to B are just inside the .05-decision lines.   We note that the magnitude

$$\bar{\Delta}_B = \bar{B}_2 - \bar{B}_1 = 0.575 \text{ in this Latin Square is almost the same as}$$
$$\bar{B}_2 - \bar{B}_1 = 0.660 \text{ in the complete } 2^3 \text{ design (data of Table 12-6).}$$

We see that the principal reason the B effect shows significance more strongly in the 2^3 study than in the Latin Square is the wider decision lines in Fig. 12-6a.   These decision lines are based on only half as many batteries (and df) as those in Fig. 12-5a, namely $n = 2r = 12$ compared to $n = 4r = 24$. This reduction in n results in a larger $\hat{\sigma}_{\bar{x}}$ and requires a slightly larger H_{α}. There is a possible ambiguity as to whether the diagonal averages represent a comparison of a C *main effect, or* an AB interaction.   Similarly each apparent main effect factor may be confounded with an interaction of the other two factors.

When the magnitude of the difference is of technical interest, there are two possible alternatives to consider: (1) Decide on the basis of scientific knowledge—from previous experience or an extra test comparing C_1 with C_2—whether a main effect is more or less plausible than an AxB interaction. (2) It is very unlikely that there is a genuine AxB interaction unless either one or both of A and B is a significant main effect.   Since A and B both have large main effects in this case history, an interaction of some two is not precluded.   The ambiguity can also be resolved by completing the other half of the 2^3 design; this effort will sometimes be justified.   The recommended strategy is to proceed on the basis that main effects are dominant and effect all possible improvements.   The advantages of this design are impressive, especially in troubleshooting projects.

CASE HISTORY 12-3   An Electronic Characteristic

Important manufacturing conditions are frequently difficult to identify in the manufacture of such products as electron tubes.   The factors which control different quality characteristics of a particular tube type often seem incapable of adjustment to meet specifications.   Materials in the cathode coating, for example, are not always critical provided compensating steps can be specified for subsequent processing stages.   Designed production studies with two, three, and sometimes more factors are now indispensable in this and other competitive industries.   It was decided to attempt improvements in contact potential quality by varying three manufacturing conditions considered to affect it in the manufacture of one particular tube type.

The three production conditions (factors) recommended by the production engineer for this experiment were the following:
- plate temperature, designated as P
- filament lighting schedule F
- electrical aging schedule A

On the basis of his experience, the production engineer specified two levels of each of the three factors; levels which he thought should produce substantial differences yet which were expected to produce usable tubes. At the time of this production study, these three factors were being held at levels designated by P_1, F_1, and A_1.   It was agreed that these levels would be continued in the production study; second levels are designated by P_2,

F_2, and A_2.   A 2×2 Latin Square design was chosen for this production study in preference to a 2^3 factorial.

Twelve tubes were sent through production in each of the four combinations of P, F, and A shown in Table 12-9.   All tubes in the study were made from the same lot of components, assembled by the same production line,

TABLE 12-9   Contact Potential Readings in a 2×2 Latin Square

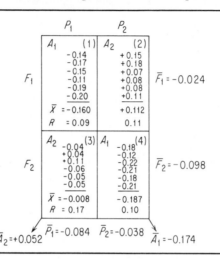

SOURCE: Doris Rosenberg and Fred Ennerson, Production Research in the Manufacture of Hearing Aid Tubes, *Ind. Qual. Control*, vol. 8, no. 6, May, 1952, *Practical Aids*, pp. 94–97. Data reproduced by permission.

and processed randomly through the same exhaust machines at approximately the same time.   After the tubes were sealed and exhausted, each group was processed according to the plan shown in Table 12-9.   Then, electronic readings on contact potential were recorded on a sample of six of each combination.   (All 12 readings are shown in Table 12-10.)

SOME CONCLUSIONS ABOUT CASE HISTORY 12-3

1.   From Fig. 12-7*a* the *change in aging* to A_2 produced a very large improvement.   Also the change from F_1 to F_2 had the undesirable significant effect of lowering contact potential; the change from P_1 to P_2 had a statistically significant improvement (at the .05 level) but of lesser magnitude than the A effect.

The production engineer considered combination 2 to be such a welcome improvement that he immediately instituted a change to it in production $(A_2, P_2, \text{and } F_1)$.   The reduction in rejected tubes was immediately evident.

2.   A *control chart* on different characteristics, including contact potential,

had been kept before the change was made from combination 1 to 2.   Figure 12-8 shows the sustained improvement in $\bar{X}$ after the change.

3.   *Further studies* were carried out to determine whether there were two-factor interaction effects and how additional changes in A and P (in the same direction) and in F (in the opposite direction) could increase contact

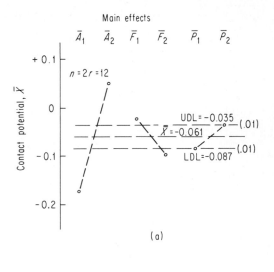

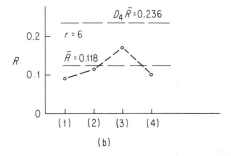

Fig. 12-7 Analysis of three factors in their effects on contact potential. (*a*) ANOM in a 2×2 Latin Square; (*b*) ranges. (Data from Table 12-9.)

potential still further.   Some of these designs were full factorial; some were 2 × 2 Latin Squares.

FORMAL ANALYSIS: (Fig. 12-7)

For $k = 4$, $r = 6$; $\hat{\sigma} = \bar{R}/d_2^* = 0.118/2.57 = 0.046$:

$$\hat{\sigma}_{\bar{x}} = 0.046/\sqrt{12} = 0.0133 \qquad \text{for } n = 2r = 12$$

DECISION LINES: $k = 2$, df $\cong (0.9)(4)(5) = 18$.

$\alpha = .05$

$$\text{UDL} = -0.061 + (1.49)(0.0133) = -0.04$$
$$\text{LDL} = -0.061 - 0.020 = -0.08$$

$\alpha = .01$

$$\text{UDL} = -0.061 + (2.02)(.0133) = -0.03$$
$$\text{LDL} = -0.061 - 0.027 = -0.09$$

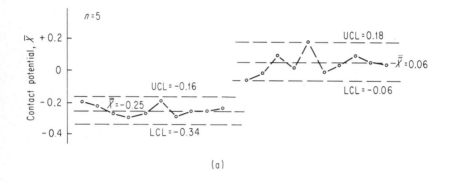

(a)

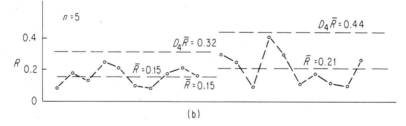

(b)

Fig. 12-8 $\bar{X}$, R control charts from production of hearing-aid tubes before and after changes made as a consequence of the 2×2 Latin Square study discussed in Case History 12-3.

12-7   Practice Exercises

Possible (useful) things to do with the data of Table 12-10:

1. Check each group for outliers and other types of nonhomogeneity by whatever methods you choose. Does the manufacturing process within each group appear reasonably stable (excepting the effects of P, F, A)?
2. Form subgroups, vertically in each column, of 3 or 4 each.
   a. Obtain ranges, $r = 3$ or 4 and make an R chart, for all groups combined.
   b. If the chart shows control, compute $\hat{\sigma} = \bar{R}/d_2^*$ or $\hat{\sigma} = \bar{R}/d_2$

3. Complete an ANOM.
4. Select at random 5 (or 6) of each group; do a formal analysis.
5. How well do the conclusions from the data of Table 12-10 agree with the data, $r = 6$, of Table 12-9?

TABLE 12-10   Contact Potential of Radio Tubes in a 2×2 Latin Square Design, $r = 12$
See Case History 12-3

(1) $P_1F_1A_1$	(2) $P_2F_1A_2$	(3) $P_1F_2A_2$	(4) $P_2F_2A_1$
−0.20	+0.28	−0.08	−0.22
−0.17	+0.07	+0.11	−0.15
−0.18	+0.17	−0.05	−0.10
−0.20	+0.15	−0.01	−0.20
−0.17	+0.16	−0.07	−0.17
−0.25	+0.05	−0.15	−0.14
−0.14	+0.15	+0.04	−0.12
−0.17	+0.18	+0.11	−0.22
−0.15	+0.07	−0.06	−0.21
−0.11	+0.08	−0.04	−0.18
−0.19	+0.11	−0.05	−0.21
−0.20	+0.08	−0.05	−0.18
$\bar{X} = -0.1775$	+0.129	−0.025	−0.175

13
More Than Two Levels of an Independent Variable

13-1 Introduction

Let me reemphasize a vital point, introduced in Chap. 5, that is seldom appreciated even by the most experienced plant personnel: *Within a group of no more than four or five units*—molds, machines, operators, inspectors, shifts, production lines, etc.—*there will be at least one that performs in a significantly different manner.*   The performance may be better or worse, but the difference will be there.   Because even experienced production or management personnel do not expect such differences, demonstrating their existence is an important hurdle to overcome on starting a process improvement study. However, it does not require much investigation to convince the skeptics that there actually are many sources of potential improvement.   The case histories in this book were not rare events; they are typical of those in our experience.

Some simple design strategies aid immeasurably in finding such differences. This too is contrary to the notion that an experienced factory hand can perceive differences of any consequence.   Once production personnel learn to expect differences, they can begin to use effectively the various strategies that help identify the specific units that show exceptional behavior.   Some very effective strategies for this purpose were discussed in Chapter 5.

The importance of designs using two and three variables at two levels of each (2^2 and 2^3 designs) was discussed in Chap. 12. They are especially effective when looking for clues to the sources of problems. Some industrial problems warrant the use of more than two levels of an independent variable (factor), even in troubleshooting. This chapter extends the graphical methods of analysis to three and more levels. Just as in Chap. 5, there are two basic procedures to consider: (1) a *standard given* and (2) *no standard given*.

13-2   An Analysis of k Independent Samples; Standard Given; One Independent Variable

Given a stable process (i.e., one in statistical control) with known average μ and standard deviation σ, we obtain k independent random samples of r each from the given process, and consider all k means simultaneously. Within what interval

$$\mu \pm Z_\alpha \sigma_{\bar{x}}$$

will all k means lie with probability $(1 - \alpha)$?

Under the generally applicable assumption that averages from the process or population are normally distributed, values of Z_α corresponding to $\alpha = .10, .05,$ and $.01$ were derived in Sec. 5-3 for attribute data and are given in Table A-7. They are equally applicable for variables data.[1]

One example, standard given, was discussed in Sec. 5-3; I have had no similar example in troubleshooting. The very important area of no standard given with variables data follows.

13-3   An Analysis of k Independent Samples; No Standard Given; One Independent Variable

This analysis is a generalization of the analysis of means in Sec. 12-3. It compares $k > 2$ means (averages) with respect to their own grand mean $\bar{X}$ instead of being restricted to $k = 2$. More formally, the procedure is the following:

Given k sets of r observations each, but no known process average or standard deviation, the k means will be analyzed simultaneously for evidence of nonrandomness (significant differences). Decision lines, UDL and LDL, will be drawn at

$$\bar{X} \pm H_\alpha \hat{\sigma}_{\bar{x}}$$

Thus the k means are compared to their own group mean $\bar{X}$. If any mean lies outside the decision lines, this is evidence of nonrandomness, risk α.

---

[1] When r is as large as 4, this assumption of normality of means is adequate even if the population of individuals is rectangular, right-triangular, or "almost" any other shape. See Theorem 3, Sec. 1-8.

The factors H_α are functions of both k and the degrees of freedom[1] df in estimating σ. The computation of H_α, no standard given, is much more complicated than the computation of Z_α for the case of standard given, Sec. 5-3. We give the values in Table A-8 for $\alpha = .10, .05,$ and $.01$, without indicating the method of computation.

Table A-8 gives "average percentage points" of the Studentized extreme deviate.[2]

$$\text{UDL} = (\bar{X}_n - \bar{X})/\hat{\sigma}_{\bar{x}}$$
$$\text{LDL} = (\bar{X} - \bar{X}_1)/\hat{\sigma}_{\bar{x}}$$

for selected values of k from $k = 2$ to $k = 60$ and selected degrees of freedom.

CASE HISTORY 13-1   Possible Advantage of Using a Selection Procedure for Ceramic Sheets

During the assembly of electronic units, a certain electrical characteristic was too variable. In an effort to improve the uniformity, attention was directed toward an important ceramic component of the assembly. Ceramic sheets were purchased from an outside vendor. In production these ceramic sheets were cut into many individual component strips. How does the overall variability of assemblies using strips cut from many different sheets compare with variability corresponding to strips within single sheets? Could we decrease the overall variability by rejecting some sheets on the basis of different averages of small samples from them?

There was no record of the order of manufacture of the sheets, but it was decided to cut seven strips from each of six different ceramic sheets. The six sets were assembled into electronic units through the regular production process. The electrical characteristics of the final 42 electronic units are shown in Table 13-1 (also see Table 1-8).

The troubleshooter should ask the question: "Is there evidence from the sample data that some of the ceramic sheets are significantly different from their own group average?" If the answer is "no, the data simply represent random or chance variation about their own average," then there is no reason to expect improvement by using selected ceramic sheets.

ANALYSIS OF MEANS   (ANOM) applied to the data of Table 13-1. (One independent variable at k levels.)

STEP 1:   Plot a range chart (Fig. 13-1b). All points are between $D_3 \bar{R}$ and $D_4 \bar{R}$. Then we compute

$$\hat{\sigma} = \bar{R}/d_2^* = 2.15/2.73 = 0.788$$

and
$$\hat{\sigma}_{\bar{x}} = 0.788/\sqrt{7} = 0.30$$

with df $\cong (0.9)k(r-1) \cong 32$

---

[1] See Table A-11 for df corresponding to the number of samples k of r each; or as in Eq. (10-4)

$$\text{df} \cong (0.9)k(r-1)$$

[2] The symbols $\bar{X}_n$ and $\bar{X}_1$ represent the largest and smallest, respectively, of the k means.

TABLE 13-1   Measurements on an Electronic Assembly

Ceramic sheet	1	2	3	4	5	6
	16.5	15.7	17.3	16.9	15.5	13.5
	17.2	17.6	15.8	15.8	16.6	14.5
	16.6	16.3	16.8	16.9	15.9	16.0
	15.0	14.6	17.2	16.8	16.5	15.9
	14.4	14.9	16.2	16.6	16.1	13.7
	16.5	15.2	16.9	16.0	16.2	15.2
	15.5	16.1	14.9	16.6	15.7	15.9
$\bar{X}$	16.0	15.8	16.4	16.5	16.1	15.0
R	2.8	3.0	2.4	1.1	1.1	2.5

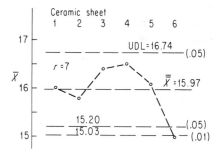

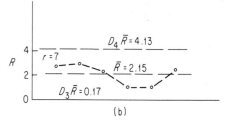

Fig. 13-1 Analysis of mean charts (averages and ranges). (Ceramic sheet data from Table 13-1.)

STEP 2: Obtain the six averages from Table 13-1 and the grand average, $\bar{\bar{X}} = 15.97$. Plot the averages as in (Fig. 13-1a).

STEP 3: Compute decision lines $\bar{\bar{X}} \pm H_\alpha \hat{\sigma}_{\bar{x}}$ for $k = 6$, df $= 32$.

$\alpha = .05$

$$UDL = 15.97 + (2.55)(0.30)$$
$$= 16.74$$
$$LDL = 15.20$$

$$\alpha = .01$$

$$UDL = 15.97 + (3.13)(0.30)$$
$$= 16.91$$
$$LDL = 15.03$$

The decision lines are drawn in Fig. 13-1a; the risk α is indicated in parentheses at the end of each decision line.

STEP 4:   The point corresponding to sample 6, $\overline{X} = 15.0$, is below LDL(.05) and very near LDL(.01) $= 15.03$.   Whether such a point is *just outside* or *just inside* the decision lines will not impress many troubleshooters as representing different bases for action.   If they would reject or accept one, they would similarly reject or accept the other.

STEP 5:   *Interpretation.*   Sample 6 represents a ceramic sheet whose average is significantly different (statistically) from the grand average (risk $\alpha \cong .01$). This evidence supports the proposal to reject ceramic sheets such as 6.

DISCUSSION: After removing sample 6, consider the grand average of the remaining five samples.   Has the removal improved the average of the remaining ceramic sheets enough that they now represent a process average at the given specification of 16.5?   To answer, we shall compare their average to decision lines (standard given) drawn around $\overline{X}' = 16.5$.   The average of the combined 35 observations from the remaining five samples is $\overline{X} = 16.16$; this is shown as a circled point in Fig. 13-2.

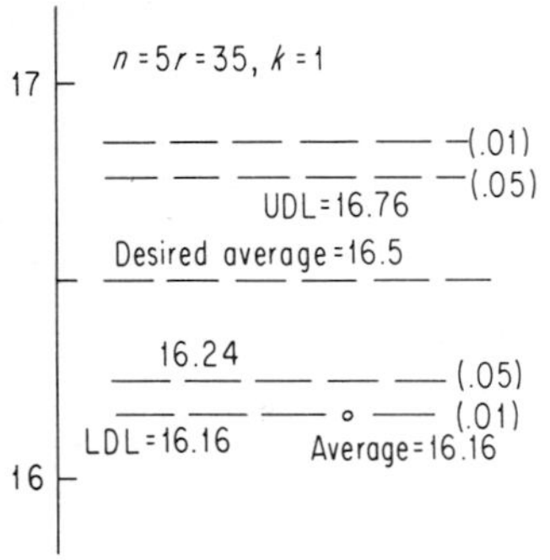

Fig. **13-2** Comparing a group average with a given specification or a desired average (average of first five ceramic sheets compared to desired average).

Decision lines (standard given), using our previous $\hat{\sigma} = 0.788$ are $\mu \pm Z_\alpha \hat{\sigma}_{\overline{x}}$. Using Table A-7: $k = 1$, $n = 5r = 35$, df $\cong 32$

for $\alpha = .05$

$$LDL = 16.5 - (1.96)(0.133) = 16.24$$

for $\alpha = .01$

$$LDL \doteq 16.5 - (2.58)(0.133) = 16.16$$

DECISION: The grand average of the 35 electronic units made from the 35 pieces of ceramic is below the LDL for $\alpha = .05$ and is therefore significantly lower (statistically) than $\overline{X}' = 16.5$, risk $\alpha \cong .05$.   Thus, no plan of rejecting individual ceramic sheets by sampling can be expected to raise the grand average of the remaining to 16.5, risk $< .05$ and about .01.

Technical personnel need to consider three matters based on the previous analyses:

1.   What can be done in processing ceramic sheets by the vendor to increase the average electrical characteristic to about 16.5?   It may take much technical time and effort to get an answer.

2.   Will it be temporarily satisfactory to assemble samples $(r = 7)$ from each ceramic sheet, and either reject or rework any ceramic sheet averaging below 15.20 or 15.03?   (See Fig. 13-1a.)   This would be expected to improve the average somewhat.

3.   Perhaps there are important factors other than ceramic sheets which offer opportunities.   What can be done in the assembly or processing of the electronic assemblies to increase the electrical characteristic?

CASE HISTORY 13-2   Adjustments on a Lathe

A certain grid (for electronic tubes) was wound under five different grid-lathe tensions to study the possible effect on diameter.

Do the dimensions in Table 13-2 give evidence that tension (of the magnitude included in this experiment) affects the diameter?   It was the opinion in the department that increased tension would reduce the diameter.

TABLE 13-2   Grid   Diameters   under Tensions (See Fig. 13-3.)

T_{20}	T_{40}	T_{60}	T_{80}	T_{120}
42	48	46	48	50
46	48	42	46	45
46	46	42	42	49
44	47	46	45	46
45	48	48	46	48
$\overline{X}_i$: 44.6	47.4	44.8	45.4	47.6
R_i: 4	2	6	6	5

INTERPRETATION: All of the points lie within the decision lines; also there is no suggestion of a downward trend in the five averages, as had been predicted.   We *do not* have evidence that the changes in grid-lathe tension affect the grid diameter.

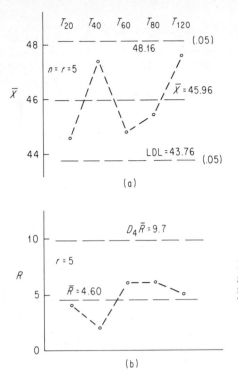

(a)

(b)

Fig. 13-3   Comparing $k = 5$ subgroup means with their own grand mean.   (Grid-lathe data from Table 13-2.)

13-4   Analysis of Means; No Standard Given; More Than One Independent Variable, with r Replicates $(r > 1)$; Main Effects[1]

In Chap. 12, the industrially important cases of two levels each of two and three independent variables were considered.   The extension to more than two levels is outlined in Table 13-3.

[1] Ellis R. Ott and Ronald D. Snee, Identifying Useful Differences in a Multiple-Head Machine, *J. Qual. Technol.*, vol. 5, no. 2, pp. 47–57, April, 1973.   This presents an example of ANOM with $r = 1$.

TABLE 13-3   Summary of Steps in Analysis of Means (Factorial Design)
More than one independent variable, more than two levels of at least one of them, with r replicates in each combination.   No standard given

---

STEP 1.   Plot a range chart.   Accept hypothesis of homogeneity if all k range points lie above $D_3 \bar{R}$ and below $D_4 \bar{R}$.   Compute:
a. $\hat{\sigma} = \bar{R}/d_2^*$ (d_2^* is from Table A-11.)
b. df $\cong (0.9)k(r - 1)$ or obtain df from Table A-11.   (k is the number of subgroups of r each in the data.)
STEP 2.   Let the independent variables be:

X and let its levels be $X_1, X_2, \ldots, X_g$ and

Y and let its levels be $Y_1, Y_2, \ldots, Y_h$, etc.

Compute an $\bar{X}_1, \bar{X}_2, \ldots, \bar{X}_g$ where each $\bar{X}_i$ is the average of all observations performed under experimental condition X_i (at all different levels of Y and any other independent variables). The number of individual observations in $\bar{X}_i$ will be $n/g = k_x$ where n is the total number of individual observations. Similarly, $\bar{Y}_i$ will be the average of $k_y = n/h$ individual observations, etc.

STEP 3. Plot the averages $\bar{X}_i$ on one chart and the $\bar{Y}_i$ averages on the same chart extended.

STEP 4. Compute and draw decision lines (main effects):

for $\bar{X}_i$ using $\hat{\sigma}_{\bar{x}} = \hat{\sigma}/\sqrt{n/g}$, and for $\bar{Y}_i$ using $\hat{\sigma}_{\bar{y}} = \hat{\sigma}/\sqrt{n/h}$. Find $H_{.05}$ from Table A-8 corresponding to df $\cong (0.9)k(r-1)$ and $k = k_x$ for the $\bar{X}_i$ and $k = k_y$ for the $\bar{Y}_i$.

STEP 5. Compute and draw decision lines at:

$$\bar{\bar{X}} \pm H_\alpha \hat{\sigma}_{\bar{x}} \quad \text{and} \quad \bar{\bar{Y}} \pm H_\alpha \hat{\sigma}_{\bar{y}} \quad \text{where } \bar{\bar{X}} = \bar{\bar{Y}} = \bar{G}$$

Any point outside decision lines indicates a statistically significant difference from the group average, risk α.

STEP 6. Interpretation, discussion, decisions.

STEP 7. Interaction analysis (see Sec. 13-5).

It will be more meaningful to compare steps in the analysis of Case History 13-3 with this general outline. A quick rereading of Chap. 12 will also be helpful. Once the basic ideas are understood the procedures are easy without referral to this outline.

CASE HISTORY 13-3 A $2 \times 3 \times 4$ Factorial Experiment; Lengths of Steel Bars

Steel bars were made from two heat treatments and cut on four screw machines at three times (at 8:00 A.M., 11:00 A.M., and 3:00 P.M. all on the same day). The time element involved the possibility of fatigue on the part of the operator which may have included improper machine adjustment.

TABLE 13-4 Data: Lengths of Steel Bars*
A $2 \times 3 \times 4$ Factorial Experiment (Data coded)

| | Heat Treatment W | | | | | Heat Treatment L | | | | |
| | Machine | | | | | Machine | | | | |
	A	B	C	D	Avg.	A	B	C	D	Avg.
	6	7	1	6		4	6	−1	4	
Time	9	9	2	6		6	5	0	5	
1	1	5	0	7		0	3	0	5	
	3	5	4	3		1	4	1	4	
Avg.	4.8	6.5	1.8	5.5	4.6	2.8	4.5	0.0	4.5	2.9
										$\bar{T}_1 = 3.75$
R	8	4	4	4		6	3	2	1	

(Continued overleaf)

	6	8	3	7		3	6	2	9
Time	3	7	2	9		1	4	0	4
2	1	4	1	11		1	1	−1	6
	−1	8	0	6		−2	3	1	3

Avg.	2.3	6.8	1.5	8.3	4.7		0.8	3.5	0.5	5.5	2.6
											$\bar{T}_2 = 3.65$
R	7	4	3	5			5	5	3	6	

	5	10	−1	10		6	8	0	4
Time	4	11	2	5		0	7	−2	3
3	9	6	6	4		3	10	4	7
	6	4	1	8		7	0	−4	0

Avg.	6.0	7.8	2.0	6.8	5.6		4.0	6.3	−0.5	3.5	3.3
											$\bar{T}_3 = 4.45$
R	5	7	7	6			7	10	8	7	

Column Avg.	4.3	7.0	1.7	6.8		2.4	4.7	0.0	4.5
				$\bar{W} = 4.97$				$\bar{G} = 3.95$	$\bar{L} = 2.93$
									$\bar{R} = 5.3$

* Baten, Prof. W. D.: An Analysis of Variance Applied to Screw Machines, *Ind. Qual. Control*, vol. 7, no. 10, April, 1956.

SUMMARY OF AVERAGES (MAIN EFFECTS)

Time	Machine	Heat
$\bar{T}_1 = 3.75$	$\bar{A} = 3.35$	$\bar{W} = 5.0$
$\bar{T}_2 = 3.65$	$\bar{B} = 5.85$	$\bar{L} = 2.9$
$\bar{T}_3 = 4.45$	$\bar{C} = 0.85$	
	$\bar{D} = 5.65$	
$(n_t = 96/3 = 32)$	$(n_m = 96/4 = 24)$	$(n_h) = 96/2 = 48$

STEP 1: Prepare a range chart (Fig. 13-4), with $\bar{R} = 5.3$ and

$$D_4 \bar{R} = (2.28)(5.3) = 12.1$$
$$\hat{\sigma} = \bar{R}/d_2^*$$
$$= 5.3/2.07 = 2.56$$

All the points lie below the control line, and this is now[1] accepted as evidence of homogeneity of ranges.

[1] However, it may be noted that seven of the eight points for time 3 are above the average $\bar{R}$ and this suggests increased variability at time 3. See Sec. 13-6.

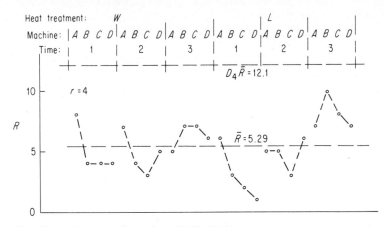

Fig. 13-4 R chart. (Data from Table 13-4.)

STEP 2: The averages have been computed and are shown in Fig. 13-5. It is immediately evident that the largest differences are between machines, and the least with time.

STEP 3: (df $\cong$ 65 in each comparison)

Time	Heat	Machine
$\hat{\sigma}_t = \dfrac{\hat{\sigma}}{\sqrt{32}} = 0.454$	$\hat{\sigma}_h = \dfrac{\hat{\sigma}}{\sqrt{48}} = 0.371$	$\hat{\sigma}_{\bar{m}} = \dfrac{\hat{\sigma}}{\sqrt{24}} = 0.524$
$k_t = 3$	$k_h = 2$	$k_m = 4$
$H_{.05} = 1.98$	$H_{.01} = 1.87$	$H_{.01} = 2.72$
UDL: 4.85	UDL: 4.64	UDL: 5.38
LDL: 3.05	LDL: 3.26	LDL: 2.52

STEP 4: The decision lines have been drawn in Fig. 13-5.

STEP 5: *Interpretation.*

The differences in *machine* settings contribute most to the variability in the length of the steel bars; this can probably be reduced substantially by the appropriate factory personnel. Just which machines should be adjusted, and to what levels, can be determined by reference to the specifications.

The effect of *heat treatments* is also significant (at the 0.01 level). Perhaps the machines can be adjusted to compensate for differences in the effect of heat treatment; perhaps the variability of heat treatment can be reduced in that area of processing. The magnitude of the machine differences is greater than the magnitude of the heat treatment differences.

Time did not show a statistically significant effect at either the 0.01 or 0.05 level. However, it may be worthwhile to consider the behavior of the individual machines with respect to time; this is discussed under *Interactions* (Sec. 13-5).

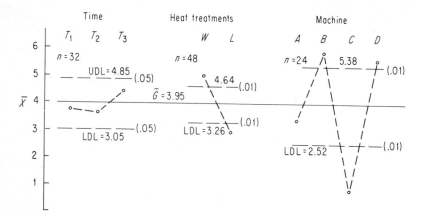

Fig. 13-5 Comparing main effects by ANOM. Length of steel bars. (Data from Table 13-4.)

Whether the magnitudes of the various effects found in this study are enough to explain differences which were responsible for the study must be discussed with the responsible factory personnel: statistical significance has been found. If they are not of practical significance, then additional possible causative factors need to be considered.

13-5   Analysis of Means; No Standard Given; Two-Factor Interactions

Certain combinations of these three factors (heat, machines, and time) may produce an effect not explained by the factors considered separately; such effects are called *interactions*. An answer to the general question of whether a two-factor interaction exists—and whether it is of such a magnitude to be of actual importance—can be presented graphically.[1] Averages are found by ignoring all factors except the two being considered when there are more than two factors. See Table 13.5.

In troubleshooting projects, main effects will usually provide larger opportunities for improvement than interactions—but not always.

[1] See Case Histories 5-5 and 12-1.

Two-factor Interaction Analysis: Machine-
Heat Treatment: Exactly 2 Levels of One
Factor and $k_m \geq 2$ of the Other

The data of Table 13-5 are graphed in Fig. 13-6. It is obvious that the main effect pattern using bars from heat treatment W is similar to the pattern using bars from heat treatment L.

If the average differences $\bar{\Delta}_i$ (Table 13-5 and Fig. 13-7) represent random variation about their own average $\bar{\bar{\Delta}} = 2.05$, there is said to be no interaction ($M \times H$). Otherwise, *there is* an $M \times H$ interaction. (See Definition in Chap. 12.)

The two patterns in Fig. 13-6 will be statistically equivalent if none of the four differences, $\bar{\Delta}_i = \bar{W}_i - \bar{L}_i$, is significantly different from their grand

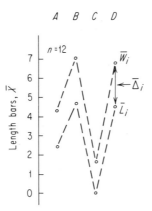

Fig. 13-6 Interaction comparison of patterns, $\bar{W}$ and $\bar{L}$. (Data from Table 13-5.)

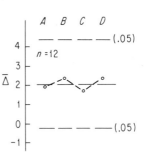

Fig. 13-7 Interaction analysis, $W \times L$: ANOM. (Differences $\bar{\Delta}$ from Fig. 13-6 and Table 13-5.)

TABLE 13-5 Data for M $\times$ H Interaction
Averages of Data from Table 13-4 ($\bar{\bar{\Delta}} = 2.05$)

Heat treatment	Machine			
	A	B	C	D
$\bar{W}$	4.3	7.0	1.7	6.8
$\bar{L}$	2.4	4.7	0.0	4.5
$\bar{W}_i - \bar{L}_i = \bar{\Delta}_i$	1.9	2.3	1.7	2.3

average, $\bar{\bar{\Delta}} = 2.05$.   This can be tested directly[1] by the analysis of means $k = 4$, df $\cong 65$,

$$\hat{\sigma}_{\bar{\Delta}} = \sqrt{2}\,\hat{\sigma}_{\bar{x}} = \sqrt{2}\,\frac{(2.56)}{\sqrt{12}} = 1.04$$

and $H_{.05} \cong 2.21$

$$UDL = \bar{\bar{\Delta}} + H_{.05}\,\hat{\sigma}_{\bar{\Delta}}$$
$$= 2.05 + 2.30 = 4.35$$
$$LDL = -0.25$$

All four points, Fig. 13-7, fall well within the two decision lines, $\alpha = .05$. We conclude that there is no (statistically) significant interaction M × H.

   This method of analysis is a general interaction analysis when either of the two variables is at exactly 2 levels.

Two-factor Interaction Analysis: Each Variable at More Than Two Levels; Time by Machine

Ignoring heat treatment, the averages of the four machines at times T_i are shown in Table 13-6.   They have been graphed in Fig. 13-8.   There is little change in machine C with respect to time, but there are changes in the other three.   The behavior patterns of machines A and B are somewhat similar: these apparent differences in patterns are not easily explained.   There *must have been* machine adjustments during the day.

TABLE 13-6   Data for M × T Interaction.

(Average of Data from Table 13-4)

Machine	Time		
	T_1	T_2	T_3
A	3.8	1.6	5.0
B	5.5	5.1	7.0
C	0.9	1.0	0.75
D	5.0	6.9	5.1

   [1] Given: two independent variables X and Y (in the same units) with averages $\bar{X}$, $\bar{Y}$, and standard deviations, σ_x, σ_y.   Let the differences $Z_i = X_i - Y_i$ be formed by random selections of X_i and Y_i.   Then

$$\sigma_z = \sqrt{\sigma_x^2 + \sigma_y^2}$$

When $\sigma_x = \sigma_y = \sigma$,

$$\sigma_{x-y} = \sigma_\Delta = \sqrt{2\sigma^2} = \sqrt{2}\,\sigma$$

   Note: Also, under the conditions just described, when X_i and Y_i are added to obtain

$$S_i = X_i + Y_i$$

then

$$\bar{S} = \bar{X} + \bar{Y}$$

and

$$\sigma_s = \sqrt{\sigma_x^2 + \sigma_y^2}$$

Are the apparent differences in machine behavior significantly different (statistically)? To analyze the entire set of data for interaction is complicated, and not very meaningful until sources of interaction are pinpointed. But we can compare *any pair* of machines by the preceding method.

The patterns of B and C are probably most similar (see Fig. 13-8); and of A and D least similar. We shall now compare each pair.

1.   The average differences, $\bar{\Delta} = \bar{B} - \bar{C}$ are shown in Fig. 13-9 with decision lines.[1]   The three points are all within the decision lines, and we decide that the patterns of machines B and C are *not* different, $\alpha \cong .05$.

TABLE 13-7   Partial Data for M × T Interaction

(Data from Table 13-6)

Machine	Time		
	T_1	T_2	T_3
$\bar{B}$	5.5	5.1	7.0
$\bar{C}$	0.9	1.0	0.75
$\bar{\Delta}$	4.6	4.1	6.25
		$\bar{\bar{\Delta}} = 4.98$	

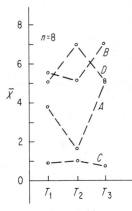

Fig. 13-8   Machine averages over time. (Data from Table 13-6.)

TABLE 13-8   Partial Data for M × T Interaction

(Data from Table 13-6)

Machine	Time		
	T_1	T_2	T_3
$\bar{D}$	5.0	6.9	5.1
$\bar{A}$	3.8	1.6	5.0
$\bar{\Delta}$	1.2	5.3	0.1
		$\bar{\bar{\Delta}} = 2.2$	

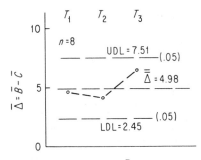

Fig. 13-9   Differences ($\bar{\Delta}$) to test for a machine x time interaction. (Data from Table 13-7.)

[1] Decision lines: $k = 3$, $n = 8$, df $= 65$, $\hat{\sigma} = 2.56$, $\hat{\sigma}_{\bar{\Delta}} = \dfrac{\sqrt{2}\,\hat{\sigma}}{\sqrt{8}}$ are

$$\bar{\bar{\Delta}} \pm H_{.05}\left(\frac{\hat{\sigma}_{\Delta}}{\sqrt{8}}\right) = 4.98 \pm (1.98)(1.28)$$

$$\text{UDL} = 4.98 + 2.53 = 7.51$$
$$\text{LDL} = 2.45$$

2. The patterns of the pair AD appear to be the least similar (see Fig. 13-8). The average differences, $\bar{\Delta} = \bar{D} - \bar{A}$ from Table 13-8 are shown in Fig. 13-10 with decision lines. The point corresponding to T_2 is above the decision line ($\alpha = .05$). We decide that there is a statistically significant difference, $\alpha \cong .01$. An investigation into any adjustments which may have been made on machines or of other time effects may provide an explanation. Knowing that there is a statistically significant difference due either to a main effect or to an interaction can be important information *provided the reasons can be identified.*

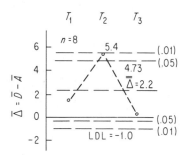

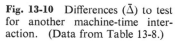

Fig. 13-10 Differences ($\bar{\Delta}$) to test for another machine-time interaction. (Data from Table 13-8.)

13-6 Comparing Variabilities

Introduction

The steel-rod lengths from the four machines, three times, and two heat treatments were being studied because of excessive variability in the finished rods. The comparison of average lengths (Fig. 13-5) shows two major reasons for variability; differences between machines and between heat treatments.

Besides these reasons, some machine(s) may be innately more *variable* than others, independent of their average settings. We can compare variabilities from exactly two processes by using either a range-square-ratio test (F_R) or an F test.[1]

We can apply the method here to compare variabilities from the two heats W and L. There are 12 subgroup ranges in W and another 12 in L; in each subgroup, $r = 4$. Their averages are

$$\bar{R}_W = \tfrac{64}{12} = 5.33 \qquad \bar{R}_L = \tfrac{63}{12} = 5.25$$

These two values are surprisingly close; no further statistical comparison is necessary. A procedure, if needed, would be to compute $(\bar{R}_W/d_2^*)^2$ and $(\bar{R}_L/d_2^*)^2$ and form their ratio

$$F_R = (5.33/5.25)^2 \qquad \text{with df} \cong F(32,32)$$

and compare with values in Table A-12.

---

[1] See Chap. 10.

The range-square-ratio test is applicable only to two levels of a factor. The following procedure *is applicable* to the four machines and the three times.

Analysis of Means to Analyze Variability

1. Internal or Within Machine Variability. Figure 13-11 is a rearrangement of the R chart, Fig. 13-4; it allows a ready, visual comparison of *machine* variabilities. A casual study of Fig. 13-11 suggests the possibility

TABLE 13-9 Subgroup Ranges
Data from Table 13-4; $n = r = 4$

		Heat Treatment					
	W				L		
	Machines						
Time	A	B	C	D	A	B	C	D
1	8	4	4	4	6	3	2	1
2	7	4	3	5	5	5	3	6
3	5	7	7	6	7	10	8	7

$\bar{R}_1 = 32/8 = 4.00$
$\bar{R}_2 = 38/8 = 4.75$
$\bar{R}_3 = 57/8 = 7.12$

$\bar{R}_A = 38/6 = 6.33$
$\bar{R}_B = 33/6 = 5.50$ $\bar{R}_W = 5.33$
$\bar{R}_C = 27/6 = 4.50$ $\bar{R}_L = 5.25$ $\bar{\bar{R}} = 5.3$
$\bar{R}_D = 29/6 = 4.83$

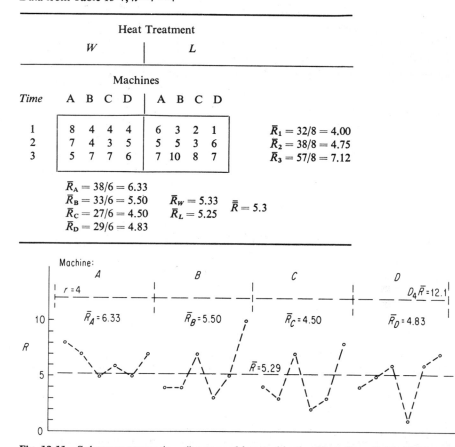

Fig. 13-11 Subgroup ranges ($r = 4$) arranged by machines. (Data from Table 13-9.)

that machine A may be most variable and machines C or D the least; but the evidence is not very persuasive. An objective comparison of their variabilities is the following. The average machine ranges from Table 13-4 have been plotted in Fig. 13-12.

The computation of decision lines requires a measure $\hat{\sigma}_R$ of expected variation of the range R. Although ranges of individual subgroups are not normally distributed, *average* ranges of four (or more) subgroups are essentially normal (Chap. 1, Theorem 3). The standard deviation of ranges can be estimated as follows:

From Table A-4, the upper 3-sigma limit on R is $D_4\bar{R}$, where D_4 has been computed to give an upper control limit at $\bar{R} + 3\hat{\sigma}_R$

$$D_4\bar{R} = \bar{R} + 3\hat{\sigma}_R$$

Then
$$\hat{\sigma}_R = \bar{R}(D_4 - 1)/3 = D_R\bar{R}$$

TABLE 13-10 Values of D_R
Where $\hat{\sigma}_R = D_R\bar{R}$ and
$D_R = (D_4 - 1)/3$

r	D_R	D_4
2	0.76	3.27
3	0.52	2.57
4	0.43	2.28
5	0.37	2.11
6	0.33	2.00
7	0.31	1.92

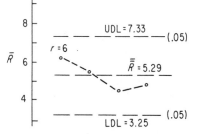

Fig. 13-12 Comparing average machine variabilities. (Data from Fig. 13-11; each point is an average of $r = 6$ ranges.)

Values of the factor D_R are given in Table 13-10 to simplify computation. When comparing any average of these ranges,

$$\hat{\sigma}_R = D_R\bar{R} = (0.43)(5.29) = 2.27$$

When comparing machine averages ($n = 6$) of Fig. 13-12,

$$\hat{\sigma}_R = 2.27/\sqrt{6} = 0.92$$

Decision lines to compare averages of machine ranges are determined with: $df \cong (0.9)k(r - 1) = 65$, $k = 4$, $H_{.05} = 2.21$.

$$UDL(.05) = \bar{R} + H_{.05}\hat{\sigma}_R$$
$$= 5.29 + (2.21)(0.92) = 7.33$$
$$LDL(.05) = 3.25$$

All four points fall within the decision lines ($\alpha = .05$), and there does not appear to be a difference in variabilities of the four machines.

2. **Variability at Different Times.** The range data, Table 13-4, has been rearranged by time in Fig. 13-13.

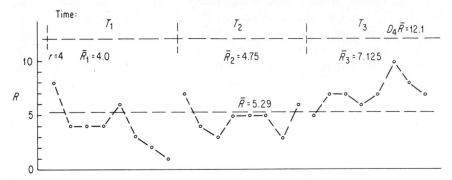

Fig. 13-13 Subgroup ranges ($r = 4$) arranged by time periods. (Data from Table 13-9.)

Analysis 1:   Data for the third period T_3 appears to be significantly large. A comparison[1] of T_3 with a pooling of groups T_1 and T_2 shows an $(a + b)$ count of $(1 + 9) = 10$ which shows significance, $\alpha \cong .01$.

Analysis 2:   analysis of means (Fig. 13-14):

$$\bar{\bar{R}} = 5.29; \ k = 3, \ \text{df} \cong 65; \ n = 8$$
$$\hat{\sigma}_R = D_R \bar{\bar{R}} = 2.27 \ (\text{each } R \text{ is of } r = 4);$$
$$\hat{\sigma}_{\bar{R}} = 2.27/\sqrt{8} = 0.80;$$

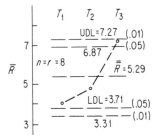

Fig. 13-14 Comparing average time variabilities. (Data from Fig. 13-13; each point is an average of $r = 8$ ranges.)

$\underline{\alpha = .05}$

$$\text{UDL} = 5.29 + (1.98)(0.80)$$
$$= 6.87$$
$$\text{LDL} = 3.71$$

$\underline{\alpha = .01}$

$$\text{UDL} = 5.29 + (2.48)(0.80)$$
$$= 7.27$$
$$\text{LDL} = 3.31$$

[1] See Sec. 11-2.

Interpretation: There is supporting evidence of a time effect on variability, risk $\alpha \cong .05$; with a definite suggestion that it became progressively more variable.   The average at time T_1 is close to the lower (.05) limit and at T_3 is outside the (.05) and close to the (.01) limit.   Then we can consider the behavior of the different individual machines with respect to time.   The data are shown in Fig. 13-15.   Surprisingly, this indicates that machine A is

TABLE 13-11   A Two-way Table (Machine by Time) Ignoring Heat Treatment

Data from Table 13-9; Each Entry Below Is the Average of Two Ranges

	T_1	T_2	T_3
A	7.0	6.0	6.0
B	3.5	4.5	8.5
C	3.0	3.0	7.5
D	2.5	5.5	6.5

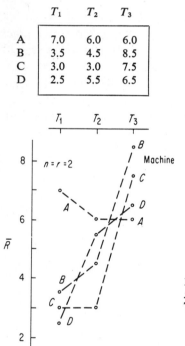

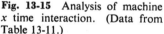

Fig. 13-15 Analysis of machine x time interaction. (Data from Table 13-11.)

affected altogether differently than the other three machines.   This may be a consequence of operator fatigue or of machine maintenance, but it requires technical attention.   The biggest factor in variability is machine effect—proper adjustments on individual machines should quickly minimize this. Secondly, the difference in heat treatment may possibly warrant adjustments for each new batch of rods, at least until the heat treatment process is stabilized.   Probably third in importance is to establish reasons for the effect of time; in fact, this may be of more importance than heat treatment.

13-7   Nonrandom Uniformity

Suppose we were to measure n consecutive steel bars all made on machine A from the same treatment. We would expect variation, not too much and *not too little*. If the n measurements were made and recorded in the order of manufacture, we could count the number of runs above and below the median, and compare them with the expected number (Table A-2). Note that there is a *minimum* number of runs expected (risk α) just as there is a maximum. Either *too few* or *too many* runs is evidence of an *assignable cause* in the process.

A variables control chart ($\overline{X},R$) can signal an assignable cause by *too little* variation; we call this *nonrandom uniformity*.

Many articles have been written about evidence indicating the presence of assignable causes of nonrandomness and some about the identification[1] of the indicated assignable causes. These discussions have usually been concerned with the concept of nonrandom "excessive" variability. The literature has not emphasized that it is sometimes of scientific importance to discuss statistical evidence of *nonrandom uniformity* and to identify types of process behavior which may produce such patterns. Sources of data displaying nonrandom uniformity include: differences in precision between analytical laboratories and sampling from a bimodal population or other sources of nonrational subgroups which produce exaggerated estimates of σ.

Nonrandom Uniformity—Standard Given

As in Sec. 13-2, consider k samples of n each from a process in statistical control with average μ and standard deviation σ. If *all k sample means lie within narrow decision lines* drawn at

$$\overline{X} \pm z_\alpha \hat{\sigma}_{\bar{x}}$$

this shall be considered evidence (with risk α) of *nonrandom uniformity*. Let Pr be the probability that a single point falls by chance between these lines. What must be the value of z_α in order that the probability of all k points falling within such a narrow band shall be only $\mathrm{Pr}^k = \alpha$?

Values of z_α are obtained from $\mathrm{Pr}^k = \alpha$ in the same manner as Z_α was obtained in Sec. 5-3. When $k = 3$, this becomes

$$\mathrm{Pr}^3 = 0.05$$

and $\mathrm{Pr} = 0.368$

Then the corresponding $z_{.05} = 0.48$ is found from a table of areas under the normal curve (Table A-1). Other selected values of z_α have been computed and are shown in Table 13-12.

---

[1] Paul S. Olmstead, How to Detect the Type of an Assignable Cause, pt. 1, Clues for Particular Types of Trouble; pt. 2, Procedure When Probable Cause is Unknown, *Ind. Qual. Control*, vol. 9, no. 3, p. 32; vol. 9, no. 4, p. 22.

TABLE 13-12   Factors to Judge Presence of Nonrandom Uniformity, Standard Given

k	$z_{.05}(k)$	$z_{.01}(k)$
2	.28	.13
3	.48	.27
4	.63	.41
5	.75	.52
6	.85	.62
7	.94	.70
8	1.01	.78
9	1.07	.84
10	1.13	.90
15	1.34	1.12
20	1.48	1.27
24	1.57	1.36
30	1.67	1.47
50	1.89	1.71
120	2.25	2.08

Nonrandom Uniformity—No Standard Given

Some very interesting techniques of analysis are possible in this category. The critical values of N_α have been computed[1], and selected values are given in Table A-18.   It happens rather frequently that points on a control chart all lie very near the process average, and the erroneous conclusion is frequently made that the process is "in excellent control."   The technique of this section provides an objective test of nonrandom uniformity.   The computation of these entries in Table A-18 is much more complicated than for those in Table 13-12; the method is not given here.   Decision lines to use in deciding whether our data indicate nonrandom uniformity are drawn at

$$\overline{X} \pm N_\alpha \hat{\sigma}_{\bar{x}}$$

[1] K. R. Nair, The Distribution of the Extreme Deviate from the Sample Mean and its Studentized Form, *Biom.*, vol. 35, pp. 118–144, 1948.

14

Relationship of
One Variable to Another

14-1   Introduction

Engineers often use scatter diagrams to study possible relationships of one variable to another.   They are equally useful in studying the relationship of data from two sources—two sources which are presumed to produce sets of data where either set should predict the other.   Scatter diagrams are helpful in studying an expected relationship between two sets of data by displaying the actual relationship which does exist under these specific conditions. They often show surprising behavior patterns which give an insight into the process which produced them.   In other words, certain relationships which are expected by scientific knowledge may be found to exist for the majority of the data but not for all.   Every type of nonrandomness (lack of control) of a single variable mentioned in Chap. 2—outliers, gradual and abrupt shifts, bimodal patterns—is a possibility in a scatter diagram which displays the relationship of one set of data to another.   These evidences of nonrandomness may lead an engineer to investigate these unexplained behavior patterns and discover important facts about his process.

For example, one step in many physical or chemical processes is the physical treatment of a product for the purpose of producing a certain effect.   How well does the treatment actually accomplish its expected function on the items?   Does it perform adequately on the bulk of them but differently enough on some items to be economically important? Any study of a quality-characteristic relationship between *before* and *after* a treatment of importance can begin with a display in the form of a scatter diagram. This is especially important when problems of unknown nature and sources exist. The method is illustrated below.

CASE HISTORY 14-1   Radio Tubes

Changes in the internal geometry in certain types of a radio tube during manufacture can be estimated indirectly by measuring changes in the *electrical capacitance*. This capacitance can be measured on a tube while it is still a "mount," i.e., before the mount structure has been sealed into a glass bulb (at high temperature).

During successive stages of a tube assembly, the internal geometry of many (or all) was being deformed at some unknown stage of the process. It was decided to investigate the behavior of a mount before being sealed into a bulb and then the tube after sealing—a *before-and-after* study. Also, it was decided to seal some tubes into bulbs at 800° and some at 900° and to observe the effect of sealing upon these few tubes.

Data are shown in Table 14-1 for 12 tubes sealed at 900° and another 12 sealed at 800°; two of the latter were damaged and readings after sealing were not obtainable. In preparing the scatter diagram, we use principles

TABLE 14-1   12 Tubes at 900° and 12 Tubes at 800°

	At 900°			At 800°	
Tube no.	R-1 before stage A	R-2 after stage A and before stage B	Tube no.	R-1 before stage A	R-2 after stage A and before stage B
1.	0.66	0.60	13.	0.75	0.68
2.	0.72	0.57	14.	0.56	0.49
3.	0.68	0.55	15.	0.72	0.59
4.	0.70	0.60	16.	0.66	0.56
5.	0.64	0.64	17.	0.62	0.52
6.	0.70	0.58	18.	0.56	—
7.	0.72	0.56	19.	0.65	—
8.	0.73	0.62	20.	0.88	0.87
9.	0.82	0.62	21.	0.56	0.46
10.	0.66	0.60	22.	0.76	0.77
11.	0.72	0.62	23.	0.72	0.69
12.	0.84	0.87	24.	0.74	0.70

SOURCE: Ellis R. Ott, A Scatterdiagram Used to Compare "Before" and "After" Measurements, *Ind. Qual. Control*, vol. 8, no. 12, June, 1957. (Reproduced by permission of the editor.)

of grouping for histograms, Sec. 1-4, Chap. 1.   The range of the R-1 readings is from a low of 0.56 to a high of 0.88, a difference of 0.32.   Consequently, a cell width of 0.02 gives us 16 cells, and this conforms with the suggested number of cells (Sec. 1-4).   Similarly, a cell width of 0.02 has been used for the R-2 data.   In practice, tally marks are made with two different colored pencils; in Fig. 14-1, an x has been used for tubes processed at 900° and an o for tubes processed at 800°.   Tube No. 1, at 900°, for example, is represented by an x at the intersection of column 66-67 and row 60-61.

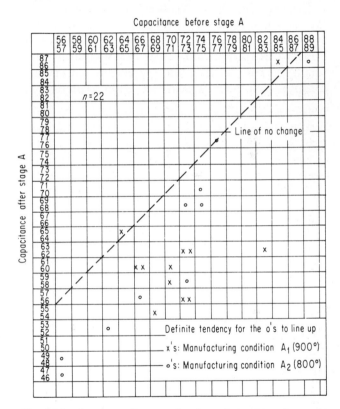

Capacitance before stage A

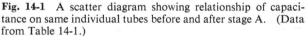

Fig. 14-1 A scatter diagram showing relationship of capacitance on same individual tubes before and after stage A.   (Data from Table 14-1.)

ANALYSIS AND INTERPRETATION: STAGE A

There is an obvious difference in the patterns corresponding to the 12 tubes sealed at 900° and the 10 sealed at 800°; all 22 tubes had had the same manufacturing assembly and treatment in all other respects.   The 900° sealing temperature is deforming the internal geometry in an unpredictable manner; tubes processed at 800° in stage A show a definite tendency to line up.   If the quality characteristics of the tubes can be attained at the 800°, well and good.   If not, then perhaps the mount structure can be strengthened to withstand the 900°, or perhaps a 850° sealing temperature.

In any case, the stage in the process which was deforming the geometry has been identified, and the problem can be tackled.

DISCUSSION: A small number of tubes was sufficient to show a difference in behavior between the two groups.   No analytical measure[1] of the relationship would give additional insight into the problem.

The *line of no change* has been drawn in Fig. 14-1 by joining the point at the maximum corner of the (86-87) cell on both R-1 and R-2 with the similar corner point of the (56-57) cell. R-1 $= R$-2 at each point of the line.   It is evident that the electrical capacitance was unchanged on only three or four tubes.   For all others, it was appreciably reduced during stage A, especially for tubes with lower capacitances.   This represents an unsolved problem.

ANALYSIS AND INTERPRETATION: STAGE B

A scattergram showing the relationship between capacitance *before* and *after* a subsequent stage B in this radio-tube assembly is shown in Fig. 14-2; data are given in Table 14-2.   Capacitance readings appear to be increased quite uniformly by 5% to 10% by stage B of the process.   There are two

TABLE 14-2   Capacitance before and after Stage B

	At 900°			At 800°	
Tube no.	R-2 after stage A and before stage B	R-3 after stage B	Tube no.	R-2 after stage A and before stage B	R-3 after stage B
1.	0.60	0.62	13.	0.68	0.71
2.	0.57	0.63	14.	0.49	0.54
3.	0.55	0.57	15.	0.59	0.63
4.	0.60	0.64	16.	0.56	0.62
5.	0.64	0.70	17.	0.52	0.55
6.	0.58	0.62	18.	0.87	0.88
7.	0.56	0.59	19.	0.46	0.50
8.	0.62	0.66	20.	0.77	0.79
9.	0.62	0.67	21.	0.69	0.76
10.	0.60	0.66	22.	0.70	0.70
11.	0.62	0.65			
12.	0.87	0.88			

[1] *Note:*   There will be occasions when an explicit measure of the before and after relationship is useful to the troubleshooter, but not in this case.   However, we have computed the correlation coefficient r in Sec. 14-4.

possibilities to explain the increase: an actual change in the geometry of the tubes, and/or an adjustment in the test set.[1]

SUMMARY: SCATTER DIAGRAM, BEFORE AND AFTER. In Chap. 2, we discussed certain patterns of data involving one *independent* variable which indicate assignable causes which are of interest to an engineer. We also

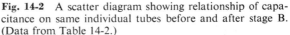
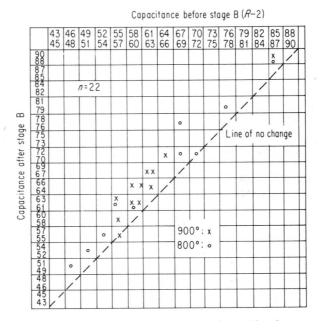

Fig. 14-2 A scatter diagram showing relationship of capacitance on same individual tubes before and after stage **B**. (Data from Table 14-2.)

discussed certain tests available to detect different data patterns. When we study possible relationships between two variables, we have an interest in the pattern of points with respect to a diagonal line (such as a line of no change). The data may show variations of the same or different types as in Chap. 2: gross errors, mavericks, trends, abrupt shifts, short cycles, and long cycles. The tests suggested for the existence of these patterns with respect to a horizontal line *can be extended or adjusted to diagonal lines*. A simple scattergram gives valuable clues which are often entirely adequate[2] for engineering improvements.

---

[1] The reader is referred to Case History 2-4.

[2] They often provide more information of value than the more traditional computation of the correlation coefficient *r*. The computation of *r* from data containing assignable causes may give a deceptive measure of the underlying relationship between the two variables—sometimes too large and sometimes too small. Any computation of *r* should be postponed at least until the scattergram has been examined.

14-2   Graphical Approaches to a Study of Relationships

Figure 14-3 shows a sketch of a half ring that was part of an assembly used in connection with the mounting of an airplane engine.[1]   This half ring contained four contact pads.   All four pads were machined at the same time and were supposed to have the same thickness.   The thickness of each pad was measured with a micrometer to the nearest ten-thousandth of an inch (one tenth of a mil).[2]

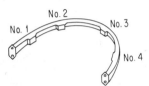

Fig. 14-3   Half-ring engine mount.

Methods of Analysis

There are at least three reasonable approaches to a visual analysis of the data in Table 14-3.

1.   *Control charts*, $\overline{X}$, R, with subgroups chosen in either (or both) of the following ways:

$n = 4$; subgroups of the 4 pads from the same half ring,

$n = 4$ or 5; vertical subgroups (all the same pad) from consecutive half rings.

2.   A *plot of individual dimensions* for each pad displayed so that comparisons between pads are possible.   Such comparisons are, however, often difficult and not very revealing.

3.   *Scatter diagrams* comparing the individual dimensions of one pad with those of another.

Which is most likely to find important differences?   It is hardly possible to predict which procedure is most apt to be meaningful unless one has had experience with this particular machining operation.

---

[1] E. L. Grant and Richard S. Leavenworth, *Statistical Quality Control*, 4th ed., pp. 164–166, McGraw-Hill Book Company, New York, 1972.   Table 14-3 and Fig. 14-3 are reproduced with the kind permission of the authors and publisher.

[2] A simple count shows that 65% of the pad measurements end in a 5 or a 0; we would expect only about 20% if the readings were actually being read to the nearest tenth of a mil. The readings were actually being read to about half a mil.

TABLE 14-3   Thickness of Four Pads on Machined Half Rings

Half-ring number	Pad 1	Pad 2	Pad 3	Pad 4	$\overline{X}$	R
1	933	937	938	935	936	5
2	897	898	915	913	905	18
3	840	900	900	930	892	90
4	900	905	902	900	901	5
5	879	852	873	871	869	27
6	903	890	892	908	898	18
7	930	940	930	920	930	20
8	890	895	897	895	894	7
9	890	900	850	900	885	50
10	900	915	900	905	905	15
11	901	916	901	900	904	16
12	920	890	905	895	902	30
13	920	890	910	880	900	40
14	929	921	924	928	925	8
15	927	914	925	931	924	17
16	907	896	895	908	901	13
17	902	900	903	905	902	5
18	903	900	914	900	904	14
19	870	930	920	920	910	60
20	925	930	920	930	926	10
21	880	895	910	885	890	30
22	890	900	895	895	895	10
23	940	935	930	940	936	10
24	930	935	938	930	933	8
25	915	921	918	927	920	12
26	895	930	925	925	918	35
27	910	907	905	913	908	8
28	905	916	902	928	913	26
29	925	930	910	925	922	20
30	924	928	882	927	915	46
31	925	931	924	930	927	7
32	900	905	925	925	913	25
33	910	910	915	910	911	5
34	900	905	900	910	903	10
35	900	950	920	900	916	50
36	940	938	940	938	939	2
Totals..	..	..	..	..	.. ..	32,772	774

Scatter Diagram

The report does not specify whether the four pads on a half ring were milled on a single- or multiple-head machine. Even if there were only one machine head, it might grind differently at the different pad positions.

Each pad might now be compared with any of the other three on the same half ring; let us compare pads 1 and 4. A scattergram comparing pad 1 with pad 4 is shown in Fig. 14-4. The cell width was chosen to be $m = 5$ for each pad; this gives about 20 cells and makes tallying simple.

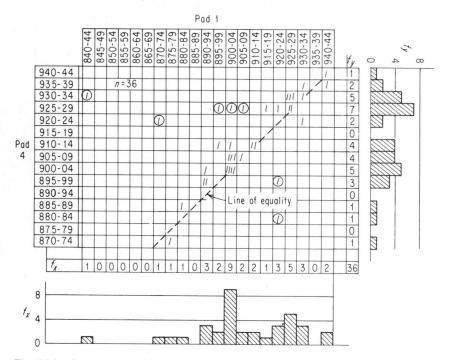

Fig. 14-4   Comparing pad 1 with pad 4 from the same half-ring. (Data from Table 14-3.)

The *line of equality* is shown as a dotted diagonal line. If the two pads are essentially the same, the tally marks should line up along the line of equality. Those tally marks which show least agreement have been circled. There are seven half rings which fail "appreciably" to have the same dimension on these pads even though they were machined at the same time. Five of the 7 half rings are above the line of equality; on them, pad 4 is larger than pad 1. There are two below the line; on them, pad 4 is smaller than pad 1. We might consider the following questions:

1. There must be different machine chucks which hold a half ring during machining. Are there differences in the chucks or in their adjustment by operators?

2.   Is the dimension of an individual pad dependent to some extent upon its dimension as it leaves a premachining stage?

Tentative answers may be possible by holding discussions with persons having a technical knowledge of the process.

The scatter diagram serves a second function; it displays frequency data for a histogram for pad 1 and pad 4.   The histogram for pad 4 is shown on the right in Fig. 14-4.   It suggests strongly that this pad has a bimodal distribution (with peaks at about 900 and 930) with low stragglers.   This can be checked by drawing cumulative histograms on normal probability paper as in Sec. 1-7.

Control-chart Analysis

The control charts in Fig. 14-5 are based on subgroups of four pads from the same half ring.

Run Counts Evidencing Nonrandomness: In Fig. 14-5, $\bar{X} = 910$.   Now two run counts indicate nonrandomness on the $\bar{X}$ chart:

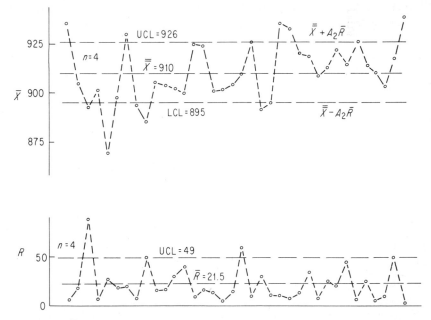

Fig. 14-5 $\bar{X}$ and R charts for thickness of pads on half ring engine mount.   (Data from Table 14-3.)

Of the first 13 points, 11 are below the average; of the last 14, there are 12 above the average.   Clearly, the process average increased from about 905 to about 920.   The increase appears to have come abruptly at about the twenty-third point.   The reason should not be too difficult to establish, if production records have been kept.

The total number of runs about the average is 13.   The expected number is 19; the chance of 13 or fewer runs by chance alone is about .05.   Again, this establishes nonrandomness.

Three-sigma Limits As Evidence of Nonrandomness: *R chart;*   There are four outages on this chart above UCL(R) and another one is close; at least two have suspected mavericks.   The estimate $\hat{\sigma} = \bar{R}/d_2$ may be excessively large because of them.

$\bar{X}$ *chart:*   If we accept $\bar{R} = 0.00215$ in order to compute UCL($\bar{X}$) and LCL($\bar{X}$) in Fig. 14-5, we still find at least 9 $\bar{X}$ points (25%) outside the control limits.   The process average is not stable.

Since there is an abrupt increase in $\bar{X}$ at about the twenty-third point, it would be meaningful to compute an UCL($\bar{X}$) and LCL($\bar{X}$) about the average of the last 14 points.   The process would seem to be more stable over the period following the twenty-third point.

Summary

Figure 14-4 shows frequent and definite lack of agreement between pads 1 and 4 even though machined together.   The scatter diagram provides a simple and effective check on whether two pads on the same half ring are being machined in the same way.   It shows that the *majority* of half rings from pads 1 and 4 agreed closely; it also shows that there is a substantial lack of agreement on 20% to 25% of the half rings.

The control chart for ranges shows four outages, and the control chart for averages and run analysis shows a definite shift in $\bar{X}$.

Thus there are two major types of variability in the process: within rings shown by the scatter diagram and between rings as shown by run analysis and the control chart.   Whether either or both are important types to investigate are matters for engineering to decide.

14-3   Practice Exercises

1. *a.* Prepare 4 simple graphs of the data, $n = 1$, of pads 1, 2, 3, and 4, Table 14-3.   Plot them directly above each other so that the patterns of the four pads of each ring can be compared.
   b. What lacks of randomness suggest possible investigations?
2. *a.* Make a scatter diagram of pad 1 versus pad 3.   Is the relationship of pads 1 and 3 similar to that of pads 1 and 4?
   b. Do you think it worthwhile to make other scatter diagrams?
3. *a.* Would you expect a scatter diagram to be of help in presenting the comparison of the chemical analysis and the materials balance computations of the data in Table 9-1?
   b. Prepare a scatter diagram of the data.
4. *a.* Would you expect a scatter diagram of machine 49 versus 50, for example, in Table 10-3 to be helpful?
   b. Prepare a scatter diagram.
5. Prepare $\bar{X}$, R charts with vertical groupings of data for each column in Table 14-3.   Are there obvious differences on either chart?

6. Make a histogram for each pad, one under the other, data of Table 14-3. Then plot data from pad 1 on normal probability paper as in Chap. 1, Sec. 7; then repeat the procedure if desired from the $\bar{X}$ column of Table 14-3.

7. Using any or all of the methods of analysis (Table 14-3) which seem sensible, do you think:

  a. That all pads are being machined the same?

  b. That the process is stable over the time the data were taken?

  c. That there is a reasonable expectation that the process capability could be improved? If the answer is "yes," do you have suggestions on how you would proceed to attain those improvements?

14-4 The Olmstead-Tukey Quadrant Sum: A Corner Test for Association[1]

Many times it is expected that a continuous variable Y is linearly related to X. From the nature of the machining process of the engine mounts, for example, it had been expected that the dimensions of all four pads would be essentially the same. We chose to plot the actual relationship between pad 1 and pad 4 as indicated by the 36 pairs of measurements in Table 14-3. From our visual scanning of the relationship, as shown in Fig. 14-4, it was evident that a large majority of points were quite near the line $Y = X$. But several of the points were not as close to the line as expected. We often need an objective criterion to support our visual analysis; one is illustrated below.

EXAMPLE 14-1: A nonparametric test for the existence of a relationship is easily applied once the points have been plotted. Figure 14-6 offers the same information as Fig. 14-4 except that it uses a continuous scale. The quadrant sum analysis begins (Fig. 14-6) with finding the horizontal and vertical medians. When there are an even number of pairs (X,Y) and no ties, the median lines will pass between points.[2] The median of pad 1 measurements is between the points at 903 and 905, and the vertical line has been drawn at $X = 904$. The median of pad 4 is through the two points for which $Y = 913$; the horizontal median has been drawn through them. The two medians divide the graph into four quadrants; they have been labeled $+$, $-$, $+$, $-$ with the upper-right and lower-left quadrants being positive (as in trigonometry or analytical geometry).

Beginning at the right side of the diagram, count the number of observations scanning toward the left until forced to cross the horizontal median; our count in Fig. 14-6 is 10, and we attach a $+$ sign to it since the points lie in the $+$ quadrant. Repeat this process scanning from the *top*, then from the *left*, and from the *bottom*. The quadrant sum is

[1] Paul S. Olmstead and John W. Tukey, A Corner Test for Association, *Ann. Math. Stat.*, vol. 18, pp. 495–513, December, 1947; and *Bell Teleph. Syst. Tech. Publ., monogr. B-1515.*

[2] "When the sample size is odd, then we still usually follow the process outlined above. There is a problem only when the counting process meets a point, one of whose coordinates is a median. In this case the authors suggest a simple device, namely: Given $(2n + 1)$ sample pairs (X,Y), let $\bar{X}$ and $\bar{Y}$ be the medians of the X values and the Y values, respectively. Let the pairs in which they occur be $(\bar{X},Y_k)$ and $(X_m,\bar{Y})$ respectively. Replace these two pairs by the single artificial pair (X_m,Y_k). There are now $2n$ pairs and the regular method can be applied," *ibid.*

the algebraic sum of the four terms just counted. This process yields the following counts for Fig. 14-6 where the black solid dots represent contributions to the sum, and the dotted lines indicate the crossings:

From right:	$+10$
From top:	$+\ 4.5$
From left:	$-\ 2$
From bottom:	$+\ 1$
Quadrant sum:	$+13.5$

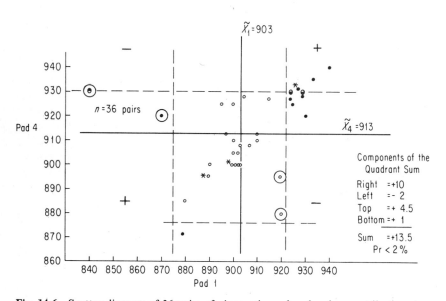

Fig. 14-6   Scatter diagram of 36 pairs of observations also showing contributions to the quadrant sum.   (Data from pads 1, 4 of Table 14-3.)

The sum 13.5 is greater than the 2% critical sum in Table A-15, and we conclude that there is an association between the two pads ($\alpha < .02$).   This agreement is not unexpected since the majority of points in Fig. 14-6 give an appearance of lying close to a 45° line as some had predicted.   The four circled points are quite far removed from such a line. These four points are a consequence of assignable causes of variation, presumably unknown.

The probabilities associated with this test are almost independent of the number of sample pairs.   Four critical quadrant sums and their levels of significance, shown in Table A-16, can be memorized easily.

The set of data which prompted the development of the quadrant sum test is shown in Fig. 14-7.   The accompanying report described it as follows: "The various points appear to be scattered almost completely at random and give little indication of correlation."   Actually, the quadrant sum is 16.5

which is significant, risk less than 1%. The experimenters can be advised that Y is related to X, although the experimental "noise" tends to obscure the relationship. A computation of the ordinary correlation coefficient r, as in Sec. 14-4, would not detect the dependence.

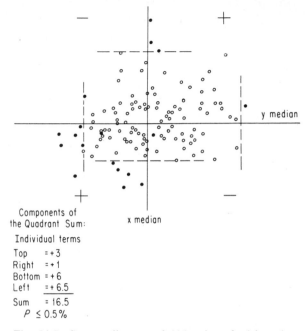

Components of
the Quadrant Sum:

Individual terms

Top   = +3
Right   = +1
Bottom = +6
Left   = +6.5

Sum   = 16.5
$P \leq 0.5\%$

Fig. 14-7 Scatter diagram of 116 pairs of observations (*Paul S. Olmstead and John W. Tukey: A Corner Test for Association, Annals Math. Stat., vol. 18, pp. 495–513, December, 1947. Reproduced with the kind permission of the authors and the editor*).

When a moderate number, say 25 to 200, of paired observations on two quantities are plotted as a scatterdiagram, visual examination frequently detects what seems to be definite evidence of association between the variables. Often in such cases, the usual methods for measuring association do not find statistical significance of association. Visual judgement, particularly by engineers or scientists who may wish to take action on the basis of their findings, gives greater weight to observations near the periphery of the scatterdiagram. This is not always desirable—but often it is very desirable. A quantitative test of association with such concentration of the periphery has been lacking. The Quadrant Sum was developed to fill the gap. Its features of speed and non-parametricity are useful, but secondary from this point of view.[1]

[1] From Olmstead-Tukey, *loc. cit.* Reproduced with permission of the authors and editor.

14-5 Mechanics of Measuring the Degree of Relationship and of Deriving the Regression Equation

Introduction

We have just discussed two procedures pertaining to a study of relationships between two variables:

1. Scatter diagrams
2. Corner association tests (quadrant sum)

The corner association test provides a simple count of peripheral data points which is often important in establishing whether or not there is probably some relationship between two variables, though not easily discernible.

The following sections present a well-known computational procedure; one which may at times give some insight into the sources or natures of process misbehavior. The two general divisions in this presentation are:

1. Computing the *equation of a line of best fit*[1]
2. Computing a *correlation coefficient*

With the advent of computers and computer programs, the practice of computing a value of r from Eq. (14-8) below has become an almost irresistible temptation. Serious decision errors[2] are a frequent consequence of this practice *unless* accompanied by a printout of a scatter diagram. It is important to start *every* analysis of a set of relationship data with a scatter diagram—even though a rough one. Sometimes it is even satisfactory to use ordinary ruled paper.

The line of best fit can be computed and applied without much danger of serious misuse.

Line of Best Fit

A *linear* relationship is assumed between an independent variable X and a dependent variable Y. How can we establish, objectively, a line to predict Y from X when we have n pairs of experimental data, (X_i, Y_i)?

Mathematical Procedure. Consider that a scatter diagram has been drawn, as in Fig. 14-8. We propose to compute the unknown parameters a and b in the equation

$$Y_c = a + b(X_i - \bar{X}) \tag{14-1}$$

where $Y_{c,i}$ denotes the predicted value corresponding to a given X_i. We usually write Y_c instead of $Y_{c,i}$.

The equations to determine a and b (derived below) are

$$a = \Sigma Y_i/n = \bar{Y} \tag{14-2}$$

$$b = \frac{\Sigma(X_i - \bar{X})(Y_i - \bar{Y})}{\Sigma(X_i - \bar{X})^2} = \frac{n\Sigma X_i Y_i - (\Sigma X_i)(\Sigma Y_i)}{n\Sigma X_i^2 - (\Sigma X_i)^2} \tag{14-3}$$

---

[1] In the sense of least squares. This line is usually called a *regression line*.
[2] See Fig. 14-11.

These two parameters are easily computed using a programmed computer or a desk calculator. The equations are derived[1] on the basis of finding a and b such as to *minimize the sum of squares of differences* between *computed* Y_c's and corresponding *observed* Y_i's.

We designate this sum of squares by the functional notation

$$F(a,b) = \Sigma(Y_i - Y_{c_i})^2 = \Sigma[Y_i - a - b(X_i - \bar{X})]^2 \qquad (14\text{-}4)$$

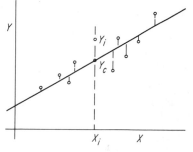

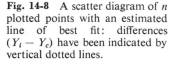

Fig. 14-8 A scatter diagram of n plotted points with an estimated line of best fit: differences $(Y_i - Y_c)$ have been indicated by vertical dotted lines.

$F(a,b)$ is a function of the two unknown parameters a and b; the procedure to minimize $F(a,b)$ is to find the two partial derivatives, set them equal to zero, and solve for a and b.

$$\frac{\partial F}{\partial a} = 2\Sigma[Y_i - a - b(X_i - \bar{X})](-1) \qquad (14\text{-}5)$$

$$\frac{\partial F}{\partial b} = -2\Sigma\{[Y_i - a - b(X_i - \bar{X})](X_i - \bar{X})\} \qquad (14\text{-}6)$$

The sum of the deviations of the X_i about their average $\bar{X}$ is zero
In Eq. (14-5)

$$\Sigma(X_i - \bar{X}) = 0;$$

Then
$$\Sigma(Y_i - a) = 0,$$
$$\Sigma Y_i - na = 0,$$

and
$$a = \Sigma Y_i/n = \bar{Y}$$

as in Eq. (14-2).

To obtain b, we also set the expression in Eq. (14-6) equal to zero to minimize $F(a,b)$. After some algebraic manipulation, we obtain

$$b = \frac{\Sigma(X_i - \bar{X})(Y_i - \bar{Y})}{\Sigma(X_i - \bar{X})^2} \qquad (14\text{-}3)$$

---

[1] This derivation involves some differential calculus. It can be omitted without serious effect on the understanding or the interpretation.

This form, can be simplified for desk calculator computations, and we may write

$$b = \frac{\left[\Sigma X_i\, Y_i - \dfrac{(\Sigma X_i)(\Sigma Y_i)}{n}\right]}{\left[\Sigma X_i^2 - \dfrac{(\Sigma X_i)^2}{n}\right]} \qquad (14\text{-}7a)$$

or

$$b = \frac{[n\Sigma X_i\, Y_i - (\Sigma X_i)(\Sigma Y_i)]}{[n\Sigma X_i^2 - (\Sigma X_i)^2]} \qquad (14\text{-}7b)$$

This gives us the equation of the line of best fit[1] in the sense of least squares

$$Y_c = a + b(X_i - \overline{X}) \qquad (14\text{-}1)$$

It can be noted that the line passes through the average point $(\overline{X}, \overline{Y})$.

A proper interpretation of the line of best fit does *not* require that X be a random variable. With Eq. (14-1), the values of X can be set deliberately at different values to obtain data pairs (X_i, Y_i). This is *entirely different from the important requirements* for the correlation coefficient whose mechanical computation is given later in this section.

Computational Example: What is the regression equation corresponding to the 22 pairs of points in Table 14-1 and Fig. 14-1?

Answer: The following preliminary computations are made, with $n = 22$.

$$\Sigma X_i = 15.56 \qquad \overline{X} = 0.707 \qquad \Sigma X_i^2 = 11.1354$$
$$\Sigma Y_i = 13.76 \qquad \overline{Y} = 0.625 \qquad \Sigma X_i\, Y_i = 9.8778$$

Then from Eq. (14-7b)

$$b = \frac{22(9.8778) - (15.56)(13.76)}{22(11.1354) - (15.56)^2}$$

$$= \frac{3.2060}{2.8652} = 1.119$$

and
$$Y_c = 0.625 + 1.119(X - 0.707)$$

---

[1] Enoch Ferrell suggests the following ingenious procedure. After the scatter diagram has been drawn, stretch a black thread across the figure in what seems to fit the pattern of data dots "best by eye." Then count the number of points on each side of the line and adjust it slightly to have $n/2$ points on each side of the resulting line. Turn the scatter diagram so that the line is horizontal; count the number of runs above and below the line (the median line). Then adjust the line to different positions, always with some $n/2$ points on each side, until a line with *maximum* number of runs is obtained. With a little practice, this is easy if the number of points is not too large.

This procedure gives a line with computation limited to counting; it can be found quickly; and it dilutes the effect of wild observations (mavericks).

Any two points will determine the line:

$$C: \quad \text{When } X = 0.595 \qquad Y_c = 0.500$$
$$D: \quad \text{When } X = 0.855 \qquad Y_c = 0.791$$

The regression line has been drawn through these two points in Fig. 14-10.

It seems doubtful that the equation of the line contributes appreciably in a study of the effect of heat on the capacitance of radio tubes in this trouble-shooting study. But there are occasions where it is a help to have it.

Linear Correlation Coefficient—a Measure of Degree of Relationship between X and Y

Application of the following discussion is critically dependent upon certain assumptions, and these assumptions *are seldom satisfied adequately* in troubleshooting and process-improvement projects.

Procedure: Consider X to be an *independent random, continuous variable*, which is normally distributed and assume also that the dependent variable Y is normally distributed. Let the assumed linear relationship be

$$Y = a + b(X - \overline{X})$$

In a physical problem, we obtain pairs of experimental values (X_i, Y_i), as in Table 14-1, for example. They will not all lie along *any* straight line. For example, we see that they are closer to being on a line in Fig. 14-2 than in Fig. 14-1, especially under 800° conditions.

Then a *measure r of the linear relationship*, under the assumptions below, can be computed from n pairs of values (X_i, Y_i) as follows

$$r = \frac{\Sigma(X_i - \overline{X})(Y_i - \overline{Y})}{\sqrt{\Sigma(X_i - \overline{X})^2} \ \sqrt{\Sigma(Y_i - \overline{Y})^2}} \qquad (14\text{-}8a)$$

$$= \left[\frac{\Sigma(X_i - \overline{X})(Y_i - \overline{Y})}{\Sigma(X_i - \overline{X})^2}\right]\left[\frac{\sqrt{\Sigma(X_i - \overline{X})^2}}{\sqrt{\Sigma(Y_i - \overline{Y})^2}}\right] = \frac{b\hat{\sigma}_x}{\hat{\sigma}_y} \qquad (14\text{-}8b)$$

It makes little sense to compute an r as in Eq. (14-8) unless the following prerequisites have been established (usually by a scatter diagram):

1. X and Y are *linearly* related.
2. X is a random variable, continuous, and normally distributed. (It must *not* be a set of discrete, fixed values; it must *not* be a bimodal set of values; it must be essentially a normal distribution.)
3. The dependent variable Y must also be random and normally distributed. (It must not be an obviously nonnormal set of values.)

A scatter diagram is helpful in detecting evident nonlinearity and bimodal patterns, mavericks, and other nonrandom patterns. The pattern of experimental data should be that of an "error ellipse": one extreme, representing no correlation, would be a circle; the other extreme, representing perfect correlation, would be a straight line.

One Procedure for Computing r for These Data. Before computing r, we refer to Fig. 14-1 and the data of Table 14-1. Values of X are shown in Table 14-4 below, and as a bar chart in Fig. 14-9. Whether the data shown in Fig. 14-9 are not normally distributed is not entirely answered from the histogram alone; some further evidence on the question can be had by plotting the accumulated frequencies Σf_i from Table 14-4 on normal-probability paper, Sec. 1-7, and checking for mavericks (Chap. 9).

TABLE 14-4 Cumulative Frequencies, Capacitance before Stage A
Data from Table 14-1

X	f	Σf
88–89	1	1
86–87	0	1
84–85	1	2
82–83	1	3
80–81	0	3
78–79	0	3
76–77	1	4
74–75	2	6
72–73	6	12
70–71	2	14
68–69	1	15
66–67	3	18
64–65	1	19
62–63	1	20
60–61	0	20
58–59	0	20
56–57	2	22

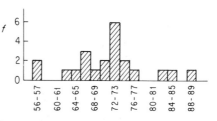

Fig. 14-9 A histogram of $R-1$ capacitance values (before stage A). (Data from Tables 14-1 and 14-4.)

In order to illustrate the computational procedure, we shall proceed now to obtain r from Eq. (14-8b). It must be remembered that any interpretations about r^2 are of questionable validity, here, because we have doubts that the critical assumptions are satisfied.

The basic computations necessary to obtain r have already been made in the example above except for $\Sigma Y^2 = 8.8392$. Previous information needed: $\Sigma X = 15.56$, $\Sigma Y = 13.76$, $b = 1.119$, $\Sigma X^2 = 11.1354$. Then

$$r = \frac{b\hat{\sigma}_x}{\hat{\sigma}_y} = \frac{1.119\sqrt{11.1354 - \dfrac{(15.56)^2}{22}}}{\sqrt{8.8392 - \dfrac{(13.76)^2}{22}}}$$

$$= 0.84$$

We are not sure whether the necessary assumptions are satisfied; nor is it important in this case to be sure.   In fact, we know that the 22 observations came from using both 900° and 800° sealing temperature, *and* that temperature appears to be important whether or not the internal geometry is deformed.

Some Interpretations of r, under the Assumptions

It can be proved that the maximum attainable absolute value of r from Eq. (14-8) is $+1$; this corresponds to a straight line with positive slope.   (Its minimum attainable value of -1 corresponds to a straight line with negative slope.)   Its minimum attainable absolute value is zero; this corresponds to a circle of random points.

Very good predictability of Y from X in the region of data is indicated by a value of r near $+1$ or -1.

Very poor predictability of Y from X is indicated by values of r close to *zero*.

The *percent of relationship* between Y and X explained by the linear Eq. (14-1) is $100r^2$.

Thus $r = 0$ and $r = \pm 1$ represent the extremes of *no* predictability and perfect predictability.

Values of r greater than 0.8 or 0.9 computed from production data are uncommon.

Confidence Intervals on r.   Although we seldom compute r in trouble-shooting projects, the following discussion may occasionally be helpful.

Any n random pairs of data (X_i, Y_i) from a population (process) constitute a sample.   Suppose we were to obtain samples from the population and compute an r for each; we would expect these r's to be different just as we expect different values of $\overline{X}$ and $\overline{Y}$ from those same samples.   What is the true degree of linear relationship, represented by the Greek[1] letter ρ?   The r we compute from a specific sample is an estimate of the true but unknown relationship between the two variables.   Confidence limits on ρ can be obtained from Table A-17 for risks $\alpha = .05$.

In the preceding computations, we found $r = 0.84$ with $n = 22$.   Locate $r = 0.84$ on the abscissa of Table A-17, and determine the intersections of the vertical line for $r = 0.84$ with upper curves for $n = 20$ and 25.   Then inter-polate visually between the curves to obtain the upper 5 % limit for $n = 22$. This is seen to be about 0.92.   Similarly, the intersection of the vertical line for $r = 0.84$ and a lower curve for $n = 22$ gives about 0.63.   Then $0.63 < \rho < 0.92$ with about 95 % confidence.   It can be seen that the limits are quite nonsymmetrical about 0.84.

A Second Computational Procedure for r.   *One important reason* for showing this second procedure is that it automatically begins by plotting a scatter

---

[1] The letter ρ is spelled *rho* in English.

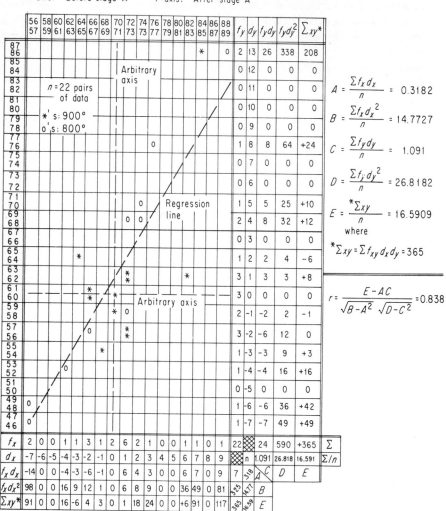

Fig. 14-10 Computation of a correlation coefficient r from a scatter diagram. (Data from Table 14-1, cols. 1 and 2.)

diagram; in fact it is an extension of the scatter diagram of Fig. 14-1 using grouped data.   The procedure is illustrated in Fig. 14-10.   A comparison of the result from Fig. 14-10, $r = 0.838$, agrees with the previous result from using Eq. (14-8b).   The agreement between the two computed values will not usually be as close as this; the grouping effect will usually make a small difference.

The advantage of having a scatter diagram is important in the technical sense of finding causes of trouble.   There are different patterns of data which will indicate immediately the inadvisability of computing an r until the data have been selectively revised to provide reasonable agreement with the required assumptions.

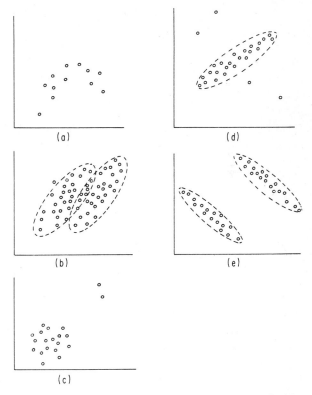

Fig. 14-11 Some frequently occurring patterns of data which lead to seriously misleading values of r and are not recognized as a consequence.

Note: If it is decided to draw a regression line after completing the computation of r, then its equation is

$$Y_c = \bar{Y} + b(X_i - \bar{X})$$

where $b = \dfrac{m_y(E - AC)}{m_x(B - A^2)}$

m_y and m_x = cell widths previously chosen for Y and X.

Misleading Values of *r*.   *Some patterns producing seriously misleading* values of *r* when scatter diagram is *not* considered:

  ■ Figure 14-11*a*; a curvilinear relationship will give a low value of *r*;

  ■ Figure 14-11*b*; two populations each with a relatively high value of *r*. When a single *r* is computed from Eq. (14-8*b*), a low value of *r* results.   It is important to recognize the existence of two sources in such a set of data.

  ■ Figure 14-11*c*; a few mavericks, such as shown, give a spuriously high value of *r*.

  ■ Figure 14-11*d*; a few mavericks, such as shown, give a spuriously low value of *r*.

  ■ Figure 14-11*e*; two populations distinctly separated can give a spuriously high value of *r*.

  All the patterns in Fig. 14-11 are *typical* of sets of production and experimental data.

15

Some Workshops
and Case Histories

15-1 Quality Workshops

An unusual arrangement made it possible to demonstrate methods of trouble-shooting in four quite different types of industry. Two of these experiences are discussed here. The principal reason for these workshops, as they became known, was to develop a national resource of young quality control men to be effective in using and teaching methods of troubleshooting investigations. A dozen young men were formed into four teams, one team on each of the four concurrent projects. Each man had had some rather discouraging previous experiences in industrial process projects. A major obstacle had been in getting anyone to do anything about improving conditions which they found. It was hoped that these projects would give them experience and confidence in organizing feedback systems of information, provide them with an ability to develop effective methods of investigation, and help them get some concrete ideas on how to get cooperative action in using data to guide process improvements. Two weeks were available for the two workshops discussed below.

CASE HISTORY 15-1 Workshop 1: Metal Stamping and Enamelling

Many different enamelled items were made in the plant—such as basins, trays, cups. The manufacture of each product began with punching blanks from large sheets of steel and cold forming them to shape. The enamel was then applied by dipping the item into a vat of enamel slurry and by firing in an oven.   (This enamelling process consisted of two or three coating applications.)   See Table 15-1 for steps in producing an enamelled basin.

As we made our initial tour of the plant, we saw two main visual inspection (sorting) stations: (1) after metal forming (before enamelling) and (2) after

TABLE 15-1   Steps in Producing an Enamelled Basin

STEP 1. *Metal Fabrication:*
    a. Metal punching (one machine with one punching head); Produced circular blanks from a large sheet of steel.
    b. Stampings (three-stage forming): one machine with its dies at each stage to produce rough-edged form.
    c. Trimming; a hand operation using large metal shears.
    d. Cold spinning (a hand operation on a lathe to roll the edge into a band).
    e. Sorting inspection (100%) (no records).
STEP 2. *Acid Bath*
STEP 3. *Enamelling* (Blue and white coats):
    a. Mixing enamel.
    b. Apply blue enamel coating (by dipping).
    c. Fire coating (in ovens).
    d. Apply white enamel coating (by dipping).
    c. Paint border (hand operation).
    f. Final firing.
STEP 4. *Final Inspection:*
    Product classified but no record kept of defects found.

final enamelling (before shipment to the customer).   Either station would be a logical place to collect data.

It is never enough just to collect data.   The sensitivities of various production and inspection groups must be recognized and their participation and support enlisted.   Many projects produce important, meaningful data, which are useless until their interpretations are implemented.   The sequence of steps shown below was important to success in enlisting support of the production study.

TO BEGIN: We arrived at the factory about 8 A.M. and our meeting with the plant manager and workshop team ended about 12:30 P.M.   When asked "When can you begin?" the answer was "Now."

Since we had agreed to begin with visual defects on bowls (Fig. 15-1), the chief inspector and our young quality control men sketched out an inspection sheet which allowed a start of *sampling* at final inspection.   Regular final inspection continued to classify items as:

Fig. 15-1   An enamelled basin.

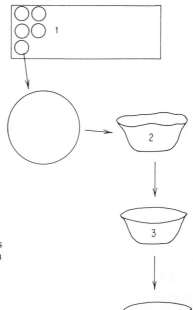

Fig. 15-2   Representation of steps in metal fabrication to form an enamelled basin.

■ First quality—approved for export.

■ Second quality—with minor defects; these sold at a slightly reduced price.

■ Third quality—with some serious defects; these sold at a substantial reduction in price.

The daily inspection sheet (Table 15-2) was used.

TABLE 15-2   Daily Inspection Sheet (Sampling)

Date_____ Sample Size_____	Product: Basin size: 16 cm or 40 cm Stage: Final inspection (after firing)								
Defects	Number inspected	Classification			Number inspected	Summary			Notes
		First	Second	Third		First	Second	Third	
A. Serious									
1. Jig mark									
2. Lump									
3. Nonuniform border									
4. Black spot inside									
5. Black spot outside									
6. Metal exp. (rim)									
7. Metal exp. (border)									
8. Metal exp. (body)									
9. Bad coating									
10. Others									
B. Very serious									
1. Very nonuniform border									
2. Chip									
3. Sheet blister									
4. Dented									
5. Metal exp. border									
6. Metal exp. rim									
7. Metal exp. body									
8. Black spot inside									
9. Black spot outside									
10. Lumps									
11. Very bad coating									
12. Dust particles									
13. Others									

Inspector Signature

Random samples of 30 units from each day's production were inspected for the 16- and 40-cm basins and the numbers of defects of each type recorded. A single basin might have more than one type of defect; an inspection record was kept of all defects found on it. The same inspector was used throughout the workshop to reduce differences in standards of inspection.

PROGRESS: Daily meetings of the workshop team were held to look at the data on the daily sampling inspection sheets. They led to discussions on ways to reduce high-defect items.   Beginning with the first day, information was given to production via the production supervisor and was a major factor in several early corrections.   Then after four days, a summary of the causes of defects was prepared and discussed at a meeting of the workshop team (Table 15-3).

TABLE 15-3   Enamel Basins—Defect Analysis, after Four Days

	Defects observed Number inspected = 4 × 30 = 120											
	40-cm basins						16-cm basins					
Classification of defects	Serious		Very serious		Total		Serious		Very serious		Total	
	no.	%	no.	%	no.	%	no.	%	no.	%	no.	%
Nonuniform border	19	16	—	—	19	16	34	28	12	10	46	38
Blue, black spot	51	42	24	20	75	62	45	37	11	9	56	46
Metal exposed	5	4	3	2	8	6	10	8	32	27	42	35
Sheet blister	—	—	28	23	28	23	—	—	7	6	7	6
Jig mark	1	1	—	—	1	1	9	8	—	—	9	8
Lump	14	12	5	4	19	16	2	2	—	—	2	2
Bad coating	15	13	5	4	20	17	—	—	—	—	—	—
Chips	—	—	3	2	3	2	—	—	—	—	—	—
Dented	—	—	2	2	2	2	—	—	1	1	1	1
Dust particles	—	—	12	10	12	10	—	—	—	—	—	—
Others	—	—	—	—	—	—	—	—	—	—	—	—
Total defects	105 + 82 = 187						100 + 63 = 163					

SEQUENCE OF STEPS IN THE WORKSHOP INVESTIGATION

1.   A workshop team was formed; it included the chief inspector, the production supervisor, two young experienced quality control men, and this author.

2.   A 2-h tour of the plant was made with the workshop team to identify potential stations to gather information.

3.   A meeting with members of the workshop force and the works manager was held following the tour.   The discussion included:

   a. Types of problems being experienced in the plant.

   b. Important cooperative aspects of the project.

   c. Various projects which might be used as the center of this workshop. Management suggested that we emphasize the reduction of visual defects, especially in their large volume 16-cm enamelled bowl (see Fig. 15-1).   The suggestion was accepted.

4. Two locations were approved to begin the workshop:
   a. At final visual inspection: stage 4 in Table 15-1.
   b. At the point of 100% sorting after metal fabrication and forming
   (stage 1*e*) and just before an acid bath which preceded enamelling.
   No records were being kept of the number of actual defects found.
   5. A final oral summary with the works manager, which included an
outline presentation of findings and ideas for improvements suggested by the
workshop data.

SOME FINDINGS: A quick check of Table 15-3 shows that four types of
defects accounted for about 80% of all defects found during the first four
days (a typical experience):

Defect	40 cm	16 cm
1. Blue and black spots	62%	46%
2. Nonuniform border	16%	38%
3. Metal exposed	6%	35%
4. Sheet blister	23%	6%

Many good ideas came from a discussion of this four-day summary sheet.   It
was noticed, for example, that the smaller 16-cm basin had a record of 35%
defects for "metal exposed" while the 40-cm basin—over 6 times as much
area—had only 6%!   "What would explain this peculiar result?"   The
foreman said, "Wait a minute," and left us abruptly; he returned with a
metal tripod used to support both the 16- and 40-cm basins during the firing

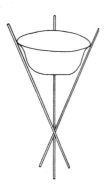

Fig. 15-3   Tripod supporting
16-cm enamelled basin during
firing.

of the enamel coating.   He had suddenly realized what might be happening.
On the small basin, the exposed metal was on the basin rim.   The small
basin nestled down inside the tripod, letting the edges touch the supporting
tripod during firing, and the glaze (Fig. 15-3) often adhered to the tripod as
well as to the basin; when the basin was removed from the tripod, the enamel

pulled off the edge and left metal exposed (a serious defect).   The large basin sat on top of the tripod, and any exposed metal was on the bottom in an area where it was classified as minor.

In this case, the solution was simple to recognize and effect, once the comparison between the two basins was noted, because the foreman was an active member of the workshop team.

SOME SUBSEQUENT SUMMARIES: Four summaries at 3 to 5 days interval were prepared during the two weeks.   The one in Table 15-4 compares the progress on the four major defects which had been found.

TABLE 15-4   Summary Showing Percentage of Major Defects over Four Time Periods

	40-cm basins			16-cm basins			
	Period*			Period			
Major defects	1	2	3	1	2	3	4
Blue and black spots	62.5%	52.3%	58.8%	56.7%	37.2%	27.3%	30.0%
Nonuniform border	15.8%	13.3%	3.3%	38.3%	38.3%	14.6%	23.0%
Metal exposed	6.7%	8.4%	3.3%	35.0%	11.6%	7.3%	2.0%
Sheet blister	23.3%	12.4%	18.9%	5.8%	8.4%	6.7%	2.0%

* Note: No production of 40-cm basin in period 4.

The defects in periods 3 and 4 have decreased considerably except for blue and black spots (40 cm) and sheet blister.   The summary of inspection results was discussed each period with the production people who took various actions, including the following, to reduce defects:

1. Pickling process—degreasing time was increased.
2. Change in enamel solution.
3. Better supervision on firing temperature.

These and other changes were effective in reducing defects.

The record (for 16-cm basins, from Table 15-5) is shown graphically in Fig. 15-4.   A sharp decrease is evident in the critical third-grade quality and an increase in the percent of first quality items.

At the end of the two-week workshop study, the team met again with top management.   Types of accomplishments and problems were discussed (in nonstatistical terms).   Everyone was pleased with the progress attained during the workshop and in favor of extending the methods to other product items.

A summary of some proposed plans for extensions was prepared by the team and presented orally and in writing to management.   It is outlined below.

TABLE 15-5   Changes in Quality Classification over Four Periods
Probably most important was the decrease in third quality

| | 40-cm basins | | | 16-cm basins | | | |
| | Period* | | | Period | | | |
Quality classification	1	2	3	1	2	3	4
First	18.3%	14.2%	23.3%	20.0%	27.5%	48.0%	44.0%
Second	37.5%	58.3%	58.9%	45.0%	49.2%	46.0%	53.3%
Third	44.2%	27.5%	17.8%	35.0%	23.3%	6.0%	2.7%
Total	100.0%	100.0%	100.0%	100.0%	100.0%	100.0%	100.0%

* Note: No production of 40-cm basin in period 4.

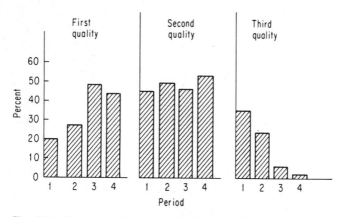

Fig. 15-4 Summary of percent classification of 16-cm enamelled basins over four sampling periods.   (Data from Table 15-5.)

A PLAN FOR THE DEVELOPMENT AND EXTENSION OF A QUALITY CONTROL SYSTEM
AT AN ENAMEL WORKS

1. *Official quality control committee:*   Although quality is the concern of everybody in the organization, it is usually found to be the responsibility of none. It is always important to have a small committee to plan and review progress; and this committee should have as secretary the person who will be charged with the responsibility of implementing the program at the factory level. The committee should meet at least once a week to study the results achieved and plan future action.

The committee should be composed of a management representative, production personnel in charge of the manufacturing and of the enamelling sections, and the chief inspector (chairman), assisted by the quality control person.

2. *Control of visual defects in production:*   Initially, systematic sampling on a routine basis should be done on all items produced every day and at least once a week after conditions have been stabilized.   Inspect for visual defects after machining and after enamelling.   These data should be kept in a suitable file in an easily distinguishable way, product by product.

All data collected should be maintained on a control chart to be kept in the departments concerned, and quality control should bring to the notice of the appropriate personnel any abnormalities that need to be investigated or corrected.

Weekly summaries would be discussed by the quality control committee.

3. *Control of outgoing quality (quality assurance):*   Starting with exported products, a regular check of about 20 items per day should be made on firsts, seconds, and thirds (quality).   Based on appropriate demerit scores for the type and intensity of defects, a demerit chart can be kept in each case for groups of similar products (see Chap. 8).

4. *Control of inspector differences:*   Establish "just acceptable" and "just not acceptable" standards for each defect.   Make it available to all inspectors.   Keep the data of quality assurance for each inspector (sorter).   Summarize the information on a monthly basis to study the extent of misclassification per inspector and take corrective measures to improve poor inspectors (sorters).

5. *Control of nonvisual defects:*   In addition to the visual defects some important quality characteristics that require control are:

    a. Weight of the product
    b. Weight of the enamel on the product
    c. Uniformity of enamelling
    d. Chipping strength of enamelling

The processes have to be studied with regard to the performance on these characteristics and, where required, simple experimentation should be planned for effecting improvements and thereafter routine control with the help of control charts.

6. *Specifications:*   In due course the committee should concern itself with laying down realistic specifications.   The data of paragraphs 2 to 5 would be of immense help.

7. *Incoming material: Acceptance sampling.*   The quality of the materials accepted have a vital bearing on the quality of manufacture.   Acceptance sampling plans may be started on a few vital items and based on experience can be gradually extended.   In each case, it is necessary to *devise suitable forms* so that it will be possible to analyze each product and vendor without too much trouble.

8. *Training:*   There should be a 1-h talk every week with the help of data and charts collected above to a group of workers and supervisors on different

product types; the group will be different for different weeks. The talk should pertain to the data in which the group itself would be interested so as to ensure responsive cooperation.

9. *Regular reports:* On all quality-control data, daily reports should be available to the concerned person in charge of production as well as the works manager and technical adviser.

In each case reports will be short and should pinpoint the achievements as well as points needing attention.

CASE HISTORY 15-2   Workshop 2   An Investigation of Cloth Defects in a Cotton Mill (Loom Shed)

There were special reasons why these workshops were arranged. In this one, as in the preceding one, its principal purpose was to effect a major advance in upgrading the effectiveness of talented young quality-control consultants. Secondly, it was evident that methods found genuinely useful in this particular cotton loom shed could give major benefits to 500 similar cotton loom sheds throughout the region.

SOME BACKGROUND INFORMATION

The advanced age and condition of the looms and loom shed had led the management of the factory to schedule a complete replacement of looms.

The factory had had some previous helpful experience using quality-control methods to increase machine utilization in the spinning department. Consequently, there was a climate of cooperation and hopefulness in this new venture.

There were two shifts, A and B; the same looms were studied on the two shifts.

The 500 looms were arranged in 10 lines of 50 looms each. There were 10 supervisors per shift, one supervising each line of 50 looms. There were 25 loom operators per line (per shift), each operator servicing two looms (in the same line).

The regular inspection practice was to 100% inspect each piece of cloth (which was 18 ft long and 45 in. wide), rating it as good, second, or poor. No record had been kept of the number, type, or origin of defects. Thus inspection provided no feedback of information to guide improvement of the production process. This is quite typical of 100% inspection procedures, unfortunately.

The principles of exploratory investigation used in this inplant workshop study are general ones, applicable in studying defects in many types of technical operations.

SUMMARY OF WORKSHOP

1. *Planning.* The essential sequence of steps used in the workshop study of Case History 15-1 were followed here also.

a. A workshop team was formed representing supervision, technology, and quality control.

b. A tour of the plant was made for obtaining background information to formulate methods of sampling and to prepare sampling inspection records.

c. An initial meeting was held by members of the workshop team with plant management to select the projects for study and outline a general plan of procedure.

d. Frequent meetings of the workshop team with appropriate supervisory and technical personnel were held as the study progressed.

TABLE 15-6   Record of Weaving Defects—Major and Minor—Found in Cloth Pieces over Two Days (from Five Looms on Two Shifts)

All Five Looms in Line 2

Major Defects columns: No Head, Imperfect Head, Crack, Float Wft., Wrong Wft., Others Wft., Float Wp., Long End (6"–18", >18"), Smash, Oily, Rusty, Thick, Others, Border (Selvedge, Flange Cut, Others), Total Major. Minor Defects columns: Float Wft., Wrong Wft., Crack Wft., Others, Float Wp., Long End (3 ends >18 in., 6 in., 6–18 in.), Fluft, Others, Oily, Thin, Thick, Other Spots, Total Minor.

Loom Number	No. Pieces Inspected	No Head	Imperfect Head	Crack	Float Wft.	Wrong Wft.	Others Wft.	Float Wp.	Long End 6"–18"	Long End >18"	Smash	Oily	Rusty	Thick	Others	Selvedge	Flange Cut	Others (Border)	Total Major	Float Wft.	Wrong Wft.	Crack Wft.	Others	Float Wp.	3 ends >18 in.	6 in.	6–18 in.	Fluft	Others	Oily	Thin	Thick	Other Spots	Total Minor
SHIFT A																																		
210	13		1						2	1				1	1				6		4	1	1	8	2								2	18
211	15	1	1	1									2						5	1	3				2						3	1	1	11
223	13								2	1		1	1						5		5			7	4									16
251	15		2										1			1			4		4		1	3	2					1	1		6	18
260	7	2	1									1							4		4		1	5						1			5	16
Σ	63	(3)	(5)	1					(4)	2		(4)	2	1	1	1			24	1	(20)	1	3	(23)	(10)					2	4	1	(14)	79
SHIFT B																																		
210	14								4	1									5		3			5	2	3	1							14
211	14			1					2	1	2	1							7			1		4									2	7
223	12																				2			3	1					1			1	8
251	14												1						1		1			1						1			1	4
260	8																				1			7									1	9
Σ	62			1					(6)	2	2	1	1						13		(7)	1		(20)	3	3	1			1				(6)	42
A & B SHIFTS COMBINED																																		
Σ		3	6	1					(10)	2	2	2	1	4	3	1	1	1	37	1	(27)	1	4	(43)	3	13	1	3	4	1			(20)	121

2. *Data form.* A standard form was prepared in advance; it listed the types of major and minor defects which might be expected (Table 15-6). This form was used by the inspector to record the defects found in the initial investigation and in subsequent special studies.

The factory representatives on the workshop team suggested that certain types of defects were operator-induced (and could be reduced by good, well-trained supervision) and that other types were machine-induced (some of which should be reduced by machine adjustments, when recognized).

3. *Sampling vs.* 100% *in study.* It was not feasible to examine cloth from each of the 500 loom-operator combinations; but even if it had been technically feasible, we would prefer to use a *sampling of looms* for an initial study. Information from a sample of looms can indicate the general types of existing differences, acquaint supervision with actual records of defect occurrences, and permit attacks on major problems more effectively and quickly than by waiting for the collection and analysis of data from all 500 looms.

What specific method of sampling? Any plan to sample from those groupings which might be operating differently is preferred to a random sampling from the entire loom shed. Differences among the 10 line supervisors is an obvious possibility for differences. Within each line, there may be reasons why the sampling should be stratified:

a. Proximity to humidifiers, or sunny and shady walls.

b. Different types of looms, if any.

c. Different types of cloth being woven, if any.

4. *The proposed scheme of sampling looms.* Management was able to provide one inspector for this workshop study. This made it possible to inspect and record defects on the production of about 15 looms on each shift. (One inspector could inspect about 200 pieces of cloth daily.) Each loom produced 6 or 7 pieces of cloth per shift or 12 to 14 pieces in the two shifts. Then an estimate of the number n of looms to include in the workshop study is: $n \cong 200/12 \cong 16$. After discussion with the workshop team, it was decided to select five looms from each of lines 1, 2, 3 on the first day of the study and repeat on the second day; then five looms from lines 4, 5, 6 on the third day and repeat on the fourth day; then lines 7, 8, 9 on two successive days.

This sampling scheme would permit the following comparisons to be made:

a. Between the 10 line supervisors on each shift, by comparing differences in numbers of defects between lines.

b. Between the two shifts, by comparing differences in numbers of defects of the same looms on the two shifts. (Shift differences would probably be attributed either to supervision or operator differences; temperature and humidity were other possibilities.)

c. Between the looms within lines included in the study.

Each piece of cloth was inspected completely, and every defect observed was recorded on the inspection form (see Table 15-6). The technical purpose of this sampling-study workshop was to determine major sources and types of defects in order to indicate corrective action and reduce defects in subsequent production. After an initial determination of major types of differences, it was expected that a sampling system would be extended by management to other looms and operators on a routine basis.

5. *A final oral summary-outline presentation* of findings and indicated differences was held between the workshop team and management. Findings were presented graphically to indicate major effects; specific methods of improving the manufacturing and supervisory processes were discussed. Also, suggestions were made on how to extend the methods to other looms, operators, supervision, and possible sources of differences.

6. *Some findings.* Many different types of useful information were obtained from the two-week study, but improvement began almost immediately. Table 15-6, for example, includes the first two-days' record of defects of five rather bad looms (line 2) on shifts A and B.

    a. The vital few. Five types of defects accounted for 70% of all major defects found during the first two days; it is typical that a few types of defects account for the great majority of all defects.

TABLE 15-7 Most Frequent Major Defects

	Line 2
Type of defects	No. of defects (shifts A and B)
Imp. head	3
Crack	6
Float warp	10
Rust	4
Thick	3
Total	26

Total of these five defect types = 26, i.e., about 70% of all *major* defects.

TABLE 15-8 Most Frequent Minor Defects

	Line 2
Type of defects	No. of defects (shifts A and B)
Long end (3 ends 18 in.)	53
Crack weft	27
Thick	20
Long end (6–18 in.)	13
Total of most frequent types	113

The total of these four types of defects is 113/121 = 93% of all *minor* defects. Corrective action should obviously be directed toward the causes of these four types.

    b. Difference between shifts. Management was surprised when shown that almost twice as many defects, major and minor, came from shift A as from shift B. (See Tables 15-6 and 15-10 and Fig. 15-5.) This observed difference was the reason for a serious study to find the reasons; important ones were found by plant personnel.

    c. Differences between loom-operator combinations in line 2.

        1. *Major defects.* The number of major defects per piece have been computed in Table 15-9; they have been plotted in Fig. 15-6 for loom operators.

TABLE 15-9   Summary of Major Cloth Defects by Machine and Shift

First Two-day Sample on Five Loom-Operator Combinations in Line 2

(Line 2) loom no.	Shift A	Shift B	Σ: Avg. major defect per piece
210	6 13	5 14	11/27 = 0.407
211	5 15	7 14	12/29 = 0.413
223	5 13	0 12	5/25 = 0.200
251	4 15	1 14	5/29 = 0.172
260	4 7	0 8	4/15 = 0.266
Totals	$\bar{A} = 24/63$ = 0.382	$\bar{B} = 13/62$ = 0.209	$\bar{c}$ = Avg. = 0.295 = avg. defects/piece

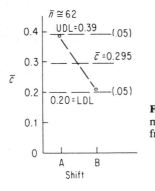

Fig. 15-5 A comparison of major defects by shift. (Data from Table 15-9.)

Analysis for Fig. 15-5.   The number of defects per piece can be considered to follow a Poisson distribution with

$$\hat{\sigma} = \sqrt{\bar{c}}$$

In shifts A and B, the values of n are 63 and 62, respectively. It is a bit more conservative to use the smaller one which gives a slightly larger estimate of $\hat{\sigma}$

$$\bar{c} = 0.295 \qquad \hat{\sigma}_{\bar{c}} = \sqrt{0.295}/\sqrt{62} = 0.0691$$

TABLE 15-10   Summary of Cloth Defects from Shifts A and B on the Same Five Looms
Data from Table 15-6

	Total major	Total minor	No. of pieces
Shift A:	24	79	63
Shift B:	13	42	62
Total:	37	121	

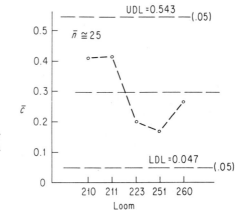

Fig. 15-6 A comparison of major defects by loom-operator. (Data from Table 15-9.)

From Table A-8, the value of $H_{.05} = 1.39$ corresponding to $k = 2$ and df $= \infty$ is used to compute decision lines:

$$\bar{c} \pm (1.39)(0.0691)$$
$$= 0.295 \pm 0.096$$
$$\text{UDL} = 0.39$$
$$\text{LDL} = 0.20$$

Analysis for Fig. 15-6. Except for Loom 260, the $\bar{c}$ values in Table 15-9 are averages of at least $n = 25$ individual observations and the distribution of averages "even for n as small as 4" is essentially normally distributed in most cases. Consequently, factors H_α from Table A-8 (df $= \infty$) are used to compute tentative limits at

$$\bar{c} \pm H_\alpha \hat{\sigma}/\sqrt{n}$$

$$\bar{c} = 0.295$$
$$\hat{\sigma}_{\bar{c}} = \sqrt{0.295} = 0.54 \qquad \hat{\sigma}_{\bar{c}} = 0.54/\sqrt{25} = 0.11$$

Tentative decision lines ($\alpha = 0.05$) for $k = 5$, $n = 25$ and $df = \infty$ are

$$\bar{c} \pm H_{.05} \hat{\sigma}_{\bar{c}} = 0.295 \pm (2.29)(0.11)$$
$$= 0.295 \pm 0.252$$

$$UDL = 0.547$$

$$LDL = 0.043$$

All five points (Fig. 15-6) corresponding to the five loom operators are well within the (.05) tentative decision lines. Although it would be easy to compute adjusted decision lines for $\alpha = 0.05$ corresponding to $n = 27, 29, 25, 29,$ and 15, respectively, no point is close enough to the tentative decision lines to warrant the effort.

Note 1: Because all five points are inside the pair of lines *does not* mean, necessarily, *that there are no differences* in behavior of the five loom-operator combinations. It does mean that we *cannot declare that there is a difference* on the basis of this data where all defects have been lumped together. Experience with many such studies leads us to expect that there will be statistical and practical differences between any five such combinations and they will be indicated when enough additional data are obtained.

There *are* important differences between looms when we consider specific types of major defects in Table 15-6. For instance: we see that loom 210 had 6/27 "float wp" defects (the most common defect) while 251 and 260 each had none. These have been listed in Table 15-11.

TABLE 15-11   Differences between Looms in Line 2 on the Most Common Defect ("float warp")

Loom	No. of pieces	No. of defects
210	27	6
211	29	2
223	25	2
251	29	0
260	15	0

Note 2: All five of these looms are in line 2; they have the same line supervisor but different operators. It was found that more improvements could be expected by improving line supervision than from machine performance.

2. *Minor defects.*   Several comparisons can be made including: shift A has almost twice as many as shift B, and loom 210 has 32 compared to 18 for loom 211.   A formal analysis shows that they differ significantly.

DISCUSSION:

Management maintained a mild skepticism, initially, for this "ivory tower" sampling study but soon became involved.   It interested them, for example, that the number of defects on the *second* day of sampling was substantially lower than on the *first* day!   Supervisors had obtained evidence from the loom records of between loom-operator differences and could give directions on corrective methods.   Improvements came from better operator attention and loom adjustments; operators readily cooperated in making improvements.

The average number of major and minor defects (causing downgrading of cloth) had been 24% prior to the workshop study (i.e., about 0.24 major defects per piece since major defects were the principal cause of downgrading). During this workshop in December, the system of recording and charting the percent of pieces with major defects was begun and continued.

The data from five loom-operators per line immediately showed important differences between lines (supervisors) and loom-operators; the word was passed from supervisor to supervisor of differences being found and suggestions for making substantial improvements.

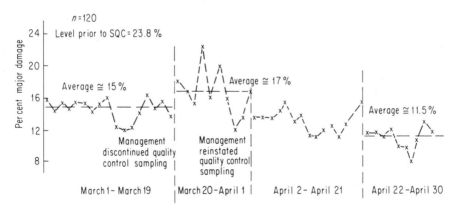

Fig. 15-7   Record of percent major damaged cloth in March and April following start of quality control program.   Average prior to the program was about 24%.

No record is available showing the improvements made by the end of the two-week workshop when a presentation to management outlined the major findings; but management arranged for the sampling procedure to be continued and posted charts of the sampling defects.

Figure 15-7 shows a daily record of the major defects per piece during

March and April; this study began the previous December.   It shows several apparent levels of performance; an explanation of two of them is given in a letter written the following July:

Damages which came down from 24% to 16% a little while after December 19 have now further reduced to 11% as a result of additional sampling checks for quality at the looms.   You will see some periods when the management lifted the controls in the hope that they would not be necessary.   But as soon as things started worsening, they reinstated the procedures laid down earlier.   I consider that progress in this plant is quite satisfactory, and it provides a method immediately applicable to other cotton mills.

15-2   Ideas from Patterns of Data

Introduction

A set of numbers may be representative of one type of causal system when they arise in one pattern, or a different causal system when the same data appear in a different pattern.   A control chart of data which represents a record of a process over a time period almost invariably carries much more meaning than the same data accumulated in a histogram which obscures any time effects.   In similar manner, data on five different looms in one line (as in Table 15-6) offers more creative ideas than the same data if the looms had been randomly chosen from 500 in the loom shed.

There are times, however, when variations in the data appear to be irretrievably lost; sometimes, as discussed below, some semblance of order can be salvaged to advantage.

CASE HISTORY 15-3   Extruding Plastic Components

Hundreds of different plastic products are extruded from plastic pellets. Each product requires a mold which may have one cavity or as many as 16, 20, or 32 cavities producing items purported to be "exactly" alike.   The cavities have been machined from two mating stainless steel blocks; plastic is supplied to all cavities from a common stream of semi-fluid plastic.

It is sometimes recognized that the cavities do *not* perform alike, and it is prudent foresight to require that a cavity number be cut into each cavity; this is then a means of identifying the cavity which has produced an item in the large bin of molded parts.   The importance of these numbers in a feedback system is potentially tremendous.

In assemblies, there are two types of defects.   Those which occur in a random fashion and those which occur in patterns but which are seldom recognized as such.   A pattern, when recognized, can lead to corrective action; an ability to identify these patterns is of real value in troubleshooting.

A bottle for a well-known men's hair toiletry has a soft plastic plug (as in Fig. 15-8).   It is inserted by machine into the neck of a plastic bottle.   It controls excess application of toiletry during use.

Incoming inspection was finding epidemics of "short-shot plugs" in shipments from an out-of-state supplier.   Several discussions were held, by telephone, with the vendor.   The short-shot plugs were incompletely formed, as the term implies.   When they got into production they often jammed the equipment and were also a source of dissatisfaction when they reached the consumer.

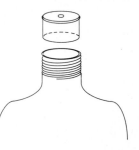

Fig. 15-8   Plastic bottle and plug insert.

A knowledgeable supervisor got involved in the problem and decided that he could get some data at incoming materials inspection.   He knows the importance of determining whether these defects were occurring randomly from the many cavities or in some pattern.   He had several boxes of plugs inspected, and kept the defective short-shot plugs separate.   He got just over 100 of them; by examining them, he identified the cavities which produced them (see Table 15-12).   It is very evident[1] that the defective plugs do not come randomly from the 32 cavities as identified from their mold numbers. He then reasoned (surmised) as follows:

■ Since rejects were found from cavities 1 and 32, it must be a 32-cavity mold, even though some cavities produced no defective plugs.

■ A 32-cavity mold must be constructed as a 4×8 mold rather than a 16×2 mold; and the obvious numbering of molds must be somewhat as in Table 15-13a.   From 15-12, he filled in the number of short-shot plugs corresponding to their cavity of origin (see Table 15-13b).

■ It is evident that almost all defective plugs were produced at the two ends of the mold, and essentially none were produced near the center. Certainly this is not random.   What could produce such a pattern?

■ In any molding process, plastic is introduced into the mold at a source and forced out to individual cavities through small channels in the mating blocks.   Then, the specialist reasoned, the source of plastic must be at the center and not enough was reaching the end cavities.   This was an educated surmise, so he telephoned the vendor.

[1] For those to whom it is not "evident," a formal analysis can be provided.   It is possible and important for a troubleshooter to develop a sense of nonrandomness and resort to formal analysis when the evidence is borderline.   Of course, when the use of data results in a major improvement, any question of "significance" is academic.

TABLE 15-12   Number of Defective Plastic Plugs (Short-shot) from Each of 32 Cavities in a Mold

Cavity no.	No. of defectives	Cavity no	No. of defectives
1	13	17	17
2	1	18	2
3	0	19	0
4	1	20	1
5	0	21	0
6	1	22	0
7	4	23	1
8	10	24	9
9	3	25	8
10	0	26	0
11	0	27	0
12	0	28	0
13	0	29	0
14	0	30	0
15	5	31	1
16	9	32	15

$$N = 101$$

TABLE 15-13a   Numbering of Cavities in the Mold

1	2	3	4	5	6	7	8
9	10	11	12	13	14	15	16
17	18	19	20	21	22	23	24
25	26	27	28	29	30	31	32

TABLE 15-13b   Pattern of Short-Shot Plugs

13	1	0	1	0	1	4	10
3	0	0	0	0	0	5	9
17	2	0	1	0	0	1	9
8	0	0	0	0	0	1	15

The supervisor speaking: "Does your mold have 32 cavities in a 4 × 8 pattern?" "Yes," the vendor answered. "Does it have a center source of plastic?" Again, "Yes, what makes you think so?" Then the supervisor explained the data he had obtained and his reasoning. During the telephone conversation, different ways were suggested as possible improvements for the physical extrusion problem:

1. Clean out or enlarge portions of the channels to the end cavities,
2. Increase the extrusion pressure, and/or
3. Reduce the viscosity of the plastic by increasing certain feed temperatures.

After some production trials, these suggestions resulted in a virtual elimination of short-shot plugs.   Case dismissed.

CASE HISTORY 15-4   Automatic Labellers

Labels are applied to glass and plastic bottles of many kinds: beverage, food, pharmaceuticals.   They may be applied at 400 or 500 a minute or at slower rates.   It is fascinating to watch the intricate mechanism pick up the label, heat the adhesive backing of the label, and affix it to a stream of whirling bottles.   But it can cause headaches from many defect types: crooked labels (see Fig. 15-9), missing labels, greasy labels, wrinkled labels, and others.

Fig. 15-9 Plastic bottle and crooked label.

There are many theories advanced by production supervisors to explain crooked label defects, for example.   Crooked bottles was a common explanation.   Production has even been known to keep one particular crooked bottle in a drawer; whenever a question was raised about crooked labels, the crooked bottle in the drawer was produced.   Now crooked bottles (with nonvertical walls) will surely produce a crooked label.   It takes a bit of courage and tenacity to insist that there may be other more important factors producing crooked labels than just crooked bottles.   Such insistence will mean an effort to collect data in some form.   Is it really justified in the face of that crooked bottle from the drawer?   We thought so.[1]

There were two simple methods of getting data on this problem:

1. Collect some bottles with crooked labels, and measure the (minimum) angle of a wall.   This procedure was not helpful in this case.   In some other problems, defects have been found to come from only certain mold cavities.

2. Collect some 25 (or 50) bottles from each of the six label positions. This requires help from an experienced forelady.   Then inspect and record the extent of crooked labels from each head.   One of our first studies showed crooked labels all coming from *one* particular position—*not* from the six positions randomly.

[1] One must frequently operate on the principle that " My wife is independently wealthy," whether or not it is true.

It is not easy to identify differences in the performance of six heads on a labeller (operating at several hundred per minute) or on any other high-speed multiple-head machine.   And it is easy to attribute the entire source of trouble to crooked bottles, defective labels, or to the responsibility of other departments or vendors.   No one wants to bear the onus: "It's not *my* fault."   But someone in your organization must develop methods of getting sample data from high-speed processes—data which will permit meaningful comparisons of these heads as one phase of a problem-solving project or program.   Then, controls must be established to prevent a relapse following the cure.

CASE HISTORY 15-5   Solder Joints

A solder joint is a simple thing.   In a hearing aid about the size of a pack of cigarettes, there are some 85.   Many of our everyday items, a small transistor radio, a telephone switchboard, a kitchen toaster, all are dependent on solder joints.

When I asked Fritz, the head of a department which assembles hearing-aid chassis, how many defective solder joints he had the reply was, "Well, I don't really know, but not too many."   Having no basis for even a wild guess, I suggested one in a hundred.   "Well, maybe," said Fritz.   So we talked to the quality control supervisor.

How does one proceed to improve soldering?   There are many answers: "better" soldering irons or "better" solder, a quality motivation program or improved instructions to the foreman and operators.   We began a small troubleshooting study by recording the number of defects found on a sample of just ten hearing aids per day.   We recorded the location of defects by making tally marks on a blown-up diagram of the circuitry.   After a few days, it was evident that there were six or seven positions, of the possible 87, responsible for the great majority of defects.

Initial data showed about one defect per 100 solder joints—such as cold solder joints, open joints, shorting contacts.   Spacings were very close (not like a big telephone switchboard or a guided missile, critics argued), and some thought that 1:100 was as good as could be expected.   Besides, solder joints were inspected 100%, so why the concern?

Reductions in defects came quickly.   One wire at a soldering position was given a pretinning.   Another was given a sleeve to eliminate possible shorting.   Specific instructions to individual operators on their soldering techniques also helped.   A control chart on defects was posted and was a surprisingly good motivational factor.

In three months, the continuing samples of 10 units per day showed a reduction of soldering defects to about 1:10,000.   More important (and surprising to many) was the marked improvement in quality of the completed hearing aids.

Once again, quality can only be manufactured into the product—not inspected into it.

Improvements in the hearing-aid assembly required a detailed analysis of individual operator performance (the individual is, indeed, important, and each may require specific help). Group motivation can be helpful, too, in some situations.

Are you investigating the few positions in your operations which account for most of the defects? Are you then establishing continuing control charts, graphical reports and other aspects of a quality feedback system which will help maintain improvements and point to the beginning of later problems which will surely develop? Getting a quality system organized is not easy.

What is the quality problem? What is a good way to attack the problem? Production will have one answer, design may have another, purchasing and testing another, and so on. But you can be sure of one thing: everyone will tell you in some indirect way, "It isn't my fault!" To anticipate this is not cynicism, it is merely a recognition of human nature, shared by all of us.

Almost everyone would like a magic wand, an overall panacea, applying with equal effectiveness to all machines, operators, and situations, thereby eliminating the need for us to give attention to piece-by-piece operation. There are different types of magic wands:

"Give us better soldering irons, or better solder, or better components, or better raw materials and equipment. This will solve the problem!" Of course, one or more such changes may be helpful, but they will not excuse us from the responsibility of working with specific details of processes within our own control to obtain optimum performance.

"Give us operators who care," also known as "if we could only find a way to interest operators on the line in their assignments and get them to pay attention to instructions!" Of course. But in the hearing-aid experience, operators primarily needed to be well-instructed (and reinstructed) in the details of their operations. It was the system of taking samples of 10 units per day that provided clues as to which operators (or machines) needed specific types of instructions.

Each of these improvements can be helpful. Indeed, they were helpful in one way or another in the improvement of hearing-aid defects from a rate of 1:100 units to 1:10,000 units. The critical decision, however, was the one to keep records on individual solder positions in such a way that individual trouble points could be pinpointed and kept under surveillance.

16
Epilogue

Every process and every product is maintained and improved by men who combine some underlying theory with some practical experience. More than that, they call upon an amazing backlog of Yankee ingenuity and know-how to amplify and support that theory. New-product ramrods are real "pioneers"; they also recognize the importance of their initiative and intuition and enjoy the dependence resting on their know-how. However, as scientific theory and background knowledge increase, dependence on native skill and initiative often decreases. An expert can determine just by listening that the points in the distributor of an automobile engine are corroded and need replacement. Similarly, an experienced production man can often recognize a recurring malfunction by characteristic physical manifestations. However, problems become more complicated. Although familiarity with scientific advances will sometimes be all that is needed to solve even complicated problems—whether for maintenance or for improvement, many important changes and problems cannot be recognized by simple observation and initiative no matter how competent the scientist. He should understand that no process is so simple but that data from it will give added insight into its behavior. The typical standard production process has unrecognized complex behaviors which can be thoroughly understood only by studying data from the product it produces. The "pioneer" who accepts and learns methods of scientific investigation to support technical advances in knowledge can be an exceptionally able citizen in the area of his expertise.   Methods in this book can be a boon to him in his old age.

This book has presented different direct procedures for acquiring data to suggest the character of a malfunction or to give evidence of improvement opportunities.   Different types of data and different methods of analysis have been illustrated, which is no more unusual than a medical doctor's use of various skills and techniques in diagnosing the ailments of a patient.   It cannot be stressed too much that the value and importance of the procedure or method are only in its applicability and usefulness to the particular problem at hand.   The situation and the desired end frequently indicate the means.

Discussing the situation with appropriate personnel, both technical and supervisory, at a very early date, before any procedures are planned, will often prevent a waste of time and even avoid possible embarrassment to yourself.   It will also often ensure their subsequent support in implementing the results of the study; but expect them to assure you that any difficulty "isn't my fault."   Often a study should be planned, expecting that it will support a diagnosis made by one or more of them.   Sometimes it does; sometimes it does not.   But the results should pinpoint the area of difficulty, suggest the way toward the solution of a problem, or even sometimes give evidence of unsuspected problems of economic importance.   Properly executed the study will always provide some insight into the process.   A simple remedy for a difficulty may be suggested where the consensus, after careful engineering consideration, had been that only a complete redesign or major change in specifications would effect the desired improvements.

An industrial consultant often has the right and authority to study *any* process or project.   But this is not exactly a divine right.   It is usually no more than a "hunting or fishing" license; you may hunt, but no game is guaranteed.   So find a sympathetic cooperative soul to talk to.   He may be able to clear the path to the best hunting ground.   Some of the most likely areas are:

1.   A spot on the line where rejects are piling up.

2.   On-line or final inspection stations.

3.   A process using selective assembly.   It is fairly common practice in production to separate components A and B each into three categories; low, medium, and high, and then assemble low A with high B, etc.   This process is sometimes a short-term necessary evil, but there are inevitable typical problems which result.

Many things need to be said about the use of data to assist in trouble-shooting.   We may as well begin with the following one, which differs from what we often hear.

Industry is a mass-production operation; it differs radically from most agricultural and biological phenomena which require a generation or more to develop data.   If you do not get enough data from a production study today, more data can be had tomorrow with little or no added expense. Simple studies are usually preferred to elaborate nonreplicated designs which are so common in agriculture, biology, and some industry research and/or development problems.

Throughout this book much use has been made in a great variety of situations of a simple yet effective method of studying and presenting data, the graphical analysis of means.   This method makes use of recent developments in applying control charts to data, and a similar development in designing and analyzing experiments.   Let us look at some of its special advantages:

1.   Computations are simple and easy.   Often no calculator is necessary, but it is possible to program the ANOM for graphical printout on a computer.

2.   Errors in calculation may be shown up, often apparent in a graphical presentation, even to the untrained.

3.   The graphical comparison of effects presents the results in a way which will be accepted by many as the basis for decision and action, encouraging the translation of conclusions into scientific action.

4.   Dealing directly with means (averages) the method provides an immediate study of possible effects of the factors involved.

5.   Not only is nonrandomness of data indicated, but (in contrast to the results from other analyses) the sources of such nonrandomness are immediately pinpointed.

6.   This analysis frequently, as a bonus, suggests the unexpected presence of certain types of nonrandomness which can be included in subsequent studies for checking.

7.   The graphical presentation of data is almost a necessity when interpreting the meaning of any interaction.

Troubleshooters and others involved in process-improvement studies who are familiar with analysis of variance will find the graphical analysis of means a logical interpretative followup procedure.   Others, faced with studying multiple independent variables, will find that the graphical procedure provides a simple immediate and effective analysis and interpretation of data.   I cannot repeat often enough the importance, to the business of troubleshooting, of a well-planned *but simple design.*

Frequently, in setting up or extending a quality control program some sort of organized teaching program is necessary.   Whenever possible, an outside consultant should be the instructor.   But whoever the instructor, he should play a key role in trouble-shooting projects in the plant.   The use of current in-plant data suggested by class members for study will not only provide pertinent and stimulating material as a basis for discussion of the basic techniques of analysis but may actually lead to a discussion of ways of improving some major production problem.   However, not many internal consultants can keep sensitive issues often raised by such discussion in check without serious scars.

Quality control requires consciousness from top management to operator and throughout all departments.   Therefore representatives from purchasing, design, manufacturing, inspection, sales, and related departments should be included in the class for at least selected pertinent aspects of the program.

And what should the course include?   Well, that is what this book is all about.   But to start, keep it simple and basic, encouraging the application of that same "Yankee ingenuity and know-how" to the use of whatever analytical techniques they learn, in the study of data already available.

It is nice at times to have gray hair and appear elderly.   Friends and associates of many years and untold experiences will sometimes come to my rescue.   Not long ago, one responded to my needling when I asked, "Bill, what shall I tell them?"   Slightly paraphrased, here is what he scribbled on a note for me:

- Come right out and tell them to plot the data.
- The important thing is to get moving on the problem quickly; hence, use quick, graphical methods of analysis.   Try to learn something quickly— not everything.   Production is rolling.   Quick, partial help *now* is preferable to somewhat better advice postponed.   Get moving.   Your prompt response will trigger ideas from them too.
- Emphasize techniques of drawing out the choice of variables to be considered, asking "dumb, leading questions."   (How does one play dumb?)
- Develop techniques of making the operator think it was all his idea.
- Make them realize the importance of designing little production experiments and the usefulness of a control chart in pointing up areas where experimentation is needed.   The chart does not solve the problem, but it tells you where and when to look for a solution.
- Say something like "you don't need an $\overline{X}$, R control chart on every machine at first; a p chart may show you the areas where $\overline{X}$, R charts will be helpful."
- Introduce the OPQR philosophy (outgoing product quality rating) of looking at the finished product and noting where the *big* problems are.
- After the data are analyzed you have to tell someone about the solution— like the boss—to get action.   You cannot demand that the foreman follow directions to improve his process, but *his boss* can find a way.   For one thing, the boss' remarks about how the foreman worked his way out of a problem with you can have a salutary effect—on the foreman himself *and* on other foremen.

Now Bill would not consider this little outline a panacea for all ailments, but these were the ideas which popped into his head.   I think they warrant some introspection.

If you have read this far, I have two remaining suggestions:

1.   Skim through the case histories in the book.   If they do not trigger some ideas about your own plant problems, then at least one of us has failed.

2.   If you did get an idea, then get out on the line and get some data! (Not too much, now.)

Appendix

TABLE A-1   Areas under the Normal Curve

Proportion of Total Area under the Curve to the Left of a Vertical Line Drawn at $\bar{X} + Z\sigma$, Where Z Represents Any Desired Value from $Z = 0$ to $Z = \pm 3.9$

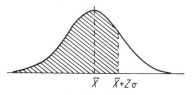

Z	0.09	0.08	0.07	0.06	0.05	0.04	0.03	0.02	0.01	0.00
−3.0	0.00100	0.00104	0.00107	0.00111	0.00114	0.00118	0.00122	0.00126	0.00131	0.00135
−2.9	0.0014	0.0014	0.0015	0.0015	0.0016	0.0016	0.0017	0.0017	0.0018	0.0019
−2.8	0.0019	0.0020	0.0021	0.0021	0.0022	0.0023	0.0023	0.0024	0.0025	0.0026
−2.7	0.0026	0.0027	0.0028	0.0029	0.0030	0.0031	0.0032	0.0033	0.0034	0.0035
−2.6	0.0036	0.0037	0.0038	0.0039	0.0040	0.0041	0.0043	0.0044	0.0045	0.0047
−2.5	0.0048	0.0049	0.0051	0.0052	0.0054	0.0055	0.0057	0.0059	0.0060	0.0062
−2.4	0.0064	0.0066	0.0068	0.0069	0.0071	0.0073	0.0075	0.0078	0.0080	0.0082
−2.3	0.0084	0.0087	0.0089	0.0091	0.0094	0.0096	0.0099	0.0102	0.0104	0.0107
−2.2	0.0110	0.0113	0.0116	0.0119	0.0122	0.0125	0.0129	0.0132	0.0136	0.0139
−2.1	0.0143	0.0146	0.0150	0.0154	0.0158	0.0162	0.0166	0.0170	0.0174	0.0179
−2.0	0.0183	0.0188	0.0192	0.0197	0.0202	0.0207	0.0212	0.0217	0.0222	0.0228
−1.9	0.0233	0.0239	0.0244	0.0250	0.0256	0.0262	0.0268	0.0274	0.0281	0.0287
−1.8	0.0294	0.0301	0.0307	0.0314	0.0322	0.0329	0.0336	0.0344	0.0351	0.0359
−1.7	0.0367	0.0375	0.0384	0.0392	0.0401	0.0409	0.0481	0.0427	0.0436	0.0446
−1.6	0.0455	0.0465	0.0475	0.0485	0.0495	0.0505	0.0516	0.0526	0.0537	0.0548
−1.5	0.0559	0.0571	0.0582	0.0594	0.0606	0.0618	0.0630	0.0643	0.0655	0.0668
−1.4	0.0681	0.0694	0.0708	0.0721	0.0735	0.0749	0.0764	0.0778	0.0793	0.0808
−1.3	0.0823	0.0838	0.0853	0.0869	0.0885	0.0901	0.0918	0.0934	0.0951	0.0968
−1.2	0.0985	0.1003	0.1020	0.1038	0.1057	0.1075	0.1093	0.1112	0.1131	0.1151
−1.1	0.1170	0.1190	0.1210	0.1230	0.1251	0.1271	0.1292	0.1314	0.1335	0.1357
−1.0	0.1379	0.1401	0.1423	0.1446	0.1469	0.1492	0.1515	0.1539	0.1562	0.1587
−0.9	0.1611	0.1635	0.1660	0.1685	0.1711	0.1736	0.1762	0.1788	0.1814	0.1841
−0.8	0.1867	0.1894	0.1922	0.1949	0.1977	0.2005	0.2033	0.2061	0.2090	0.2119
−0.7	0.2148	0.2177	0.2207	0.2236	0.2266	0.2297	0.2327	0.2358	0.2389	0.2420
−0.6	0.2451	0.2483	0.2514	0.2546	0.2578	0.2611	0.2643	0.2676	0.2709	0.2743
−0.5	0.2776	0.2810	0.2843	0.2877	0.2912	0.2946	0.2981	0.3015	0.3050	0.3085
−0.4	0.3121	0.3156	0.3192	0.3228	0.3264	0.3300	0.3336	0.3372	0.3409	0.3446
−0.3	0.3483	0.3520	0.3557	0.3594	0.3632	0.3669	0.3707	0.3745	0.3783	0.3821
−0.2	0.3859	0.3897	0.3936	0.3974	0.4013	0.4052	0.4090	0.4129	0.4168	0.4207
−0.1	0.4247	0.4286	0.4325	0.4364	0.4404	0.4443	0.4483	0.4522	0.4562	0.4602
−0.0	0.4641	0.4681	0.4721	0.4761	0.4801	0.4840	0.4880	0.4920	0.4960	0.5000

Z	0.00	0.01	0.02	0.03	0.04	0.05	0.06	0.07	0.08	0.09
+0.0	0.5000	0.5040	0.5080	0.5120	0.5160	0.5199	0.5239	0.5279	0.5319	0.5359
+0.1	0.5398	0.5438	0.5478	0.5517	0.5557	0.5596	0.5636	0.5675	0.5714	0.5753
+0.2	0.5793	0.5832	0.5871	0.5910	0.5948	0.5987	0.6026	0.6064	0.6103	0.6141
+0.3	0.6179	0.6217	0.6255	0.6293	0.6331	0.6368	0.6406	0.6443	0.6480	0.6517
+0.4	0.6554	0.6591	0.6628	0.6664	0.6700	0.6736	0.6772	0.6808	0.6844	0.6879
+0.5	0.6915	0.6950	0.6985	0.7019	0.7054	0.7088	0.7123	0.7157	0.7190	0.7224
+0.6	0.7257	0.7291	0.7324	0.7357	0.7389	0.7422	0.7454	0.7486	0.7517	0.7549
+0.7	0.7580	0.7611	0.7642	0.7673	0.7704	0.7734	0.7764	0.7794	0.7823	0.7852
+0.8	0.7881	0.7910	0.7939	0.7967	0.7995	0.8023	0.8051	0.8079	0.8106	0.8133
+0.9	0.8159	0.8186	0.8212	0.8238	0.8264	0.8289	0.8315	0.8340	0.8365	0.8389
+1.0	0.8413	0.8438	0.8461	0.8485	0.8508	0.8531	0.8554	0.8577	0.8599	0.8621
+1.1	0.8643	0.8665	0.8686	0.8708	0.8729	0.8749	0.8770	0.8790	0.8810	0.8830
+1.2	0.8849	0.8869	0.8888	0.8907	0.8925	0.8944	0.8962	0.8980	0.8997	0.9015
+1.3	0.9032	0.9049	0.9066	0.9082	0.9099	0.9115	0.9131	0.9147	0.9162	0.9177
+1.4	0.9192	0.9207	0.9222	0.9236	0.9251	0.9265	0.9279	0.9292	0.9306	0.9319
+1.5	0.9332	0.9345	0.9357	0.9370	0.9382	0.9394	0.9406	0.9418	0.9429	0.9441
+1.6	0.9452	0.9463	0.9474	0.9484	0.9495	0.9505	0.9515	0.9525	0.9535	0.9545
+1.7	0.9554	0.9564	0.9573	0.9582	0.9591	0.9599	0.9608	0.9616	0.9625	0.9633
+1.8	0.9641	0.9649	0.9656	0.9664	0.9671	0.9678	0.9686	0.9693	0.9699	0.9706
+1.9	0.9713	0.9719	0.9726	0.9732	0.9738	0.9744	0.9750	0.9756	0.9761	0.9767
+2.0	0.9773	0.9778	0.9783	0.9788	0.9793	0.9798	0.9803	0.9808	0.9812	0.9817
+2.1	0.9821	0.9826	0.9830	0.9834	0.9838	0.9842	0.9846	0.9850	0.9854	0.9857
+2.2	0.9861	0.9864	0.9868	0.9871	0.9875	0.9878	0.9881	0.9884	0.9887	0.9890
+2.3	0.9893	0.9896	0.9898	0.9901	0.9904	0.9906	0.9909	0.9911	0.9913	0.9916
+2.4	0.9918	0.9920	0.9922	0.9925	0.9927	0.9929	0.9931	0.9932	0.9934	0.9936
+2.5	0.9938	0.9940	0.9941	0.9943	0.9945	0.9946	0.9948	0.9949	0.9951	0.9952
+2.6	0.9953	0.9955	0.9956	0.9957	0.9959	0.9960	0.9961	0.9962	0.9963	0.9964
+2.7	0.9965	0.9966	0.9967	0.9968	0.9969	0.9970	0.9971	0.9972	0.9973	0.9974
+2.8	0.9974	0.9975	0.9976	0.9977	0.9977	0.9978	0.9979	0.9979	0.9980	0.9981
+2.9	0.9981	0.9982	0.9983	0.9983	0.9984	0.9984	0.9985	0.9985	0.9986	0.9986
+3.0	0.99865	0.99869	0.99874	0.99878	0.99882	0.99886	0.99889	0.99893	0.99896	0.99900

SOURCE: Grant and Leavenworth, Statistical Quality Control, 4 ed., 1972, pp. 642–43.

TABLE A-2   Critical Values of the Number of Runs N_R above and below the Median in $n = 2$ m Observations

n	m	Significantly small critical values of N_R		Significantly large critical values of N_R	
		$\alpha = .01$	$\alpha = .05$	$\alpha = .05$	$\alpha = .01$
10	5	2	3	8	9
12	6	2	3	10	11
14	7	3	4	11	12
16	8	4	5	12	13
18	9	4	6	13	15
20	10	5	6	15	16
22	11	6	7	16	17
24	12	7	8	17	18
26	13	7	9	18	20
28	14	8	10	19	21
30	15	9	11	20	22
32	16	10	11	22	23
34	17	10	12	23	25
36	18	11	13	24	26
38	19	12	14	25	27
40	20	13	15	26	28
42	21	14	16	27	29
44	22	14	17	28	31
46	23	15	17	30	32
48	24	16	18	31	33
50	25	17	19	32	34
60	30	21	24	37	40
70	35	25	28	43	46
80	40	30	33	48	51
90	45	34	37	54	57
100	50	38	42	59	63
110	55	43	46	65	68
120	60	47	51	70	74

SOURCE: S. Swed and Churchill Eisenhart, Tables for Testing Randomness of Sampling in a Sequence of Alternatives, *Ann. Math. Stat.*, vol. 14, pp. 66–87, 1943. (Reproduced by permission of the editor.)

TABLE A-3 Runs above and below the Median of Length s in $n = 2m$ Observations with n As Large As 16 or 20

s	Expected number of length exactly s	Expected number of length greater than or equal to s
1	$\dfrac{n(n+2)}{2^2(n-1)} \cong n/2^2$	$(n+2)/2 = \text{(total number)}$
2	$\dfrac{n(n+2)}{2^3(n-1)} \cong n/2^3$	$\dfrac{(n+2)(n-2)}{2^2(n-1)} \cong n/2^3$
3	$\dfrac{n(n+2)(n-4)}{2^4(n-1)(n-3)} \cong n/2^4$	$\dfrac{(n-4)(n+2)}{2^3(n-1)} \cong n/2^3$
4	$\dfrac{n(n+2)(n-6)}{2^5(n-1)(n-3)} \cong n/2^5$	$\dfrac{(n+2)(n-4)(n-6)}{2^4(n-1)(n-3)} \cong n/2^4$
5	$\dfrac{n(n+2)(n-6)(n-8)}{2^6(n-1)(n-3)(n-5)} \cong n/2^6$	$\dfrac{(n+2)(n-6)(n-8)}{2^5(n-1)(n-3)} \cong n/2^5$
6	$\dfrac{n(n+2)(n-8)(n-10)}{2^7(n-1)(n-3)(n-6)} \cong n/2^7$	$\dfrac{(n+2)(n-8)(n-10)}{2^6(n-1)(n-3)} \cong n/2^6$

TABLE A-4 Factors to Use with $\bar{X}$, R Control Charts for Variables Choose n to Be Less than Seven When feasible
These Factors Assume Sampling from a Normal Universe

n	D_3	D_4	A_2	d_2
2	0	3.27	1.88	1.13
3	0	2.57	1.02	1.69
4	0	2.28	0.73	2.06
5	0	2.11	0.58	2.33
6	0	2.00	0.48	2.53
7	0.08	1.92	0.42	2.70
8	0.14	1.86	0.37	2.85
9	0.18	1.82	0.34	2.97
10	0.22	1.78	0.31	3.08

1. Estimating: $\hat{\sigma} = \bar{R}/d_2$
   (for $k > 15$)
2. 3σ limits on range:
   $$\text{UCL} = D_4\bar{R}$$
   $$\text{LCL} = D_3\bar{R}$$
3. 3σ limits on $\bar{X}$:
   $$\text{UCL} = \bar{\bar{X}} + A_2\bar{R}$$
   $$\text{LCL} = \bar{\bar{X}} - A_2\bar{R}$$

TABLE A-5 Binomial Probability Tables

The probabilities of exactly x occurrences are given in the columns headed by x; the cumulative probabilities of $c \leqq x$ are given in the column headed by c. Each number is $1,000 \Pr(x)$. (For brevity, where values of $\Pr(x)$ and $\Pr(c)$ are both zero, they are omitted.)

$n = 4$

	$p = .01$			$p = .02$			$p = .03$	
x	$\Pr(x)$	$\Pr(c)$	x	$\Pr(x)$	$\Pr(c)$	x	$\Pr(x)$	$\Pr(c)$
0	961		0	922		0	885	
1	039	999	1	075	998	1	110	995
2	001	1,000	2	002	1,000	2	005	1,000

	$p = .04$			$p = .05$			$p = .06$	
x	$\Pr(x)$	$\Pr(c)$	x	$\Pr(x)$	$\Pr(c)$	x	$\Pr(x)$	$\Pr(c)$
0	849		0	815		0	781	
1	142	991	1	171	986	1	199	980
2	009	1,000	2	014	1,000	2	019	999
						3	001	1,000

	$p = .07$			$p = .08$			$p = .09$	
x	$\Pr(x)$	$\Pr(c)$	x	$\Pr(x)$	$\Pr(c)$	x	$\Pr(x)$	$\Pr(c)$
0	748		0	716		0	686	
1	225	973	1	249	996	1	271	957
2	025	999	2	033	998	2	040	997
3	001	1,000	3	002	1,000	3	003	1,000

	$p = .10$			$p = .15$			$p = .20$	
x	$\Pr(x)$	$\Pr(c)$	x	$\Pr(x)$	$\Pr(c)$	x	$\Pr(x)$	$\Pr(c)$
0	656		0	522		0	410	
1	292	948	1	368	890	1	410	819
2	049	996	2	098	988	2	154	973
3	004	1,000	3	011	999	3	026	998
			4	001	1,000	4	002	1,000

SOURCE: Entries in these tables were obtained by rounding off selected entries in tables from two books: for $n < 50$, from *Tables of the Binomial Probability Distribution*, National Bureau of Standards, Applied Mathematics Series 6, 1950, Superintendent of Documents, Washington, D.C. 20025; for $n = 50$, 75, 100 from 50–100 *Binomial Tables*, Harry G. Romig, John Wiley & Sons, Inc., New York.

$n = 4$

	$p = .25$				$p = .30$				$p = .40$	
x	Pr(x)	Pr(c)		x	Pr(x)	Pr(c)		x	Pr(x)	Pr(c)
0	316			0	240			0	130	
1	422	738		1	412	652		1	346	475
2	211	949		2	265	916		2	346	821
3	047	996		3	076	992		3	154	974
4	004	1,000		4	008	1,000		4	026	1,000

$p = .50$

x	Pr(x)	Pr(c)
0	063	
1	250	313
2	375	688
3	250	938
4	062	1,000

$n = 5$

	$p = .01$				$p = .02$				$p = .03$	
x	Pr(x)	Pr(c)		x	Pr(x)	Pr(c)		x	Pr(x)	Pr(c)
0	951			0	904			0	859	
1	048	999		1	092	996		1	133	992
2	001	1,000		2	004	1,000		2	008	1,000

	$p = .04$				$p = .05$				$p = .06$	
x	Pr(x)	Pr(c)		x	Pr(x)	Pr(c)		x	Pr(x)	Pr(c)
0	815			0	774			0	734	
1	170	985		1	204	977		1	234	968
2	014	999		2	021	999		2	030	998
3	001	1,000		3	001	1,000		3	002	1,000

	$p = .07$				$p = .08$				$p = .09$	
x	Pr(x)	Pr(c)		x	Pr(x)	Pr(c)		x	Pr(x)	Pr(c)
0	696			0	659			0	624	
1	262	958		1	287	946		1	309	933
2	039	997		2	050	995		2	061	994
3	003	1,000		3	004	1,000		3	006	1,000

Table A-5 (Continued)

$n = 5$

	$p = .10$				$p = .15$				$p = .20$	
x	Pr(x)	Pr(c)		x	Pr(x)	Pr(c)		x	Pr(x)	Pr(c)
0	590			0	444			0	328	
1	328	919		1	392	835		1	410	737
2	073	991		2	138	973		2	205	942
3	008	1,000		3	024	998		3	051	993
				4	002	1,000		4	006	1,000

	$p = .25$				$p = .30$				$p = .40$	
x	Pr(x)	Pr(c)		x	Pr(x)	Pr(c)		x	Pr(x)	Pr(c)
0	237			0	168			0	078	
1	396	633		1	360	528		1	259	337
2	264	896		2	309	837		2	346	683
3	088	984		3	132	969		3	230	913
4	015	999		4	028	998		4	077	990
5	001	1,000		5	002	1,000		5	010	1,000

	$p = .50$	
x	Pr(x)	Pr(c)
0	031	
1	156	188
2	313	500
3	313	813
4	156	969
5	031	1,000

$n = 10$

	$p = .01$				$p = .02$				$p = .03$	
x	Pr(x)	Pr(c)		x	Pr(x)	Pr(c)		x	Pr(x)	Pr(c)
0	904			0	817			0	737	
1	091	996		1	167	984		1	228	965
2	004	1,000		2	015	999		2	032	997
				3	001	1,000		3	003	1,000

	$p = .04$				$p = .05$				$p = .06$	
x	Pr(x)	Pr(c)		x	Pr(x)	Pr(c)		x	Pr(x)	Pr(c)
0	665			0	599			0	539	
1	277	942		1	315	914		1	344	882
2	052	994		2	075	988		2	099	981
3	006	1 000		3	010	999		3	017	998
				4	001	1,000		4	002	1,000

$n = 10$

<table>
<tr><td colspan="3">$p = .07$</td><td colspan="3">$p = .08$</td><td colspan="3">$p = .09$</td></tr>
<tr><td>x</td><td>Pr(x)</td><td>Pr(c)</td><td>x</td><td>Pr(x)</td><td>Pr(c)</td><td>x</td><td>Pr(x)</td><td>Pr(c)</td></tr>
<tr><td>0</td><td>484</td><td></td><td>0</td><td>434</td><td></td><td>0</td><td>389</td><td></td></tr>
<tr><td>1</td><td>364</td><td>848</td><td>1</td><td>378</td><td>812</td><td>1</td><td>385</td><td>775</td></tr>
<tr><td>2</td><td>123</td><td>972</td><td>2</td><td>148</td><td>960</td><td>2</td><td>171</td><td>946</td></tr>
<tr><td>3</td><td>025</td><td>996</td><td>3</td><td>034</td><td>994</td><td>3</td><td>045</td><td>991</td></tr>
<tr><td>4</td><td>003</td><td>1,000</td><td>4</td><td>005</td><td>999</td><td>4</td><td>008</td><td>999</td></tr>
<tr><td></td><td></td><td></td><td>5</td><td>001</td><td>1,000</td><td>5</td><td>001</td><td>1,000</td></tr>
</table>

<table>
<tr><td colspan="3">$p = .10$</td><td colspan="3">$p = .15$</td><td colspan="3">$p = .20$</td></tr>
<tr><td>x</td><td>Pr(x)</td><td>Pr(c)</td><td>x</td><td>Pr(x)</td><td>Pr(c)</td><td>x</td><td>Pr(x)</td><td>Pr(c)</td></tr>
<tr><td>0</td><td>349</td><td></td><td>0</td><td>197</td><td></td><td>0</td><td>107</td><td></td></tr>
<tr><td>1</td><td>387</td><td>736</td><td>1</td><td>347</td><td>544</td><td>1</td><td>268</td><td>376</td></tr>
<tr><td>2</td><td>194</td><td>930</td><td>2</td><td>276</td><td>820</td><td>2</td><td>302</td><td>678</td></tr>
<tr><td>3</td><td>057</td><td>987</td><td>3</td><td>130</td><td>950</td><td>3</td><td>201</td><td>879</td></tr>
<tr><td>4</td><td>011</td><td>998</td><td>4</td><td>040</td><td>990</td><td>4</td><td>088</td><td>967</td></tr>
<tr><td>5</td><td>001</td><td>1,000</td><td>5</td><td>008</td><td>999</td><td>5</td><td>026</td><td>994</td></tr>
<tr><td></td><td></td><td></td><td>6</td><td>001</td><td>1,000</td><td>6</td><td>006</td><td>999</td></tr>
<tr><td></td><td></td><td></td><td></td><td></td><td></td><td>7</td><td>001</td><td>1,000</td></tr>
</table>

<table>
<tr><td colspan="3">$p = .25$</td><td colspan="3">$p = .30$</td><td colspan="3">$p = .40$</td></tr>
<tr><td>x</td><td>Pr(x)</td><td>Pr(c)</td><td>x</td><td>Pr(x)</td><td>Pr(c)</td><td>x</td><td>Pr(x)</td><td>Pr(c)</td></tr>
<tr><td>0</td><td>056</td><td></td><td>0</td><td>028</td><td></td><td>0</td><td>006</td><td></td></tr>
<tr><td>1</td><td>188</td><td>244</td><td>1</td><td>121</td><td>149</td><td>1</td><td>040</td><td>046</td></tr>
<tr><td>2</td><td>282</td><td>526</td><td>2</td><td>233</td><td>383</td><td>2</td><td>121</td><td>167</td></tr>
<tr><td>3</td><td>250</td><td>776</td><td>3</td><td>267</td><td>650</td><td>3</td><td>215</td><td>382</td></tr>
<tr><td>4</td><td>146</td><td>922</td><td>4</td><td>200</td><td>850</td><td>4</td><td>251</td><td>633</td></tr>
<tr><td>5</td><td>058</td><td>980</td><td>5</td><td>103</td><td>953</td><td>5</td><td>201</td><td>834</td></tr>
<tr><td>6</td><td>016</td><td>996</td><td>6</td><td>037</td><td>989</td><td>6</td><td>111</td><td>945</td></tr>
<tr><td>7</td><td>003</td><td>1,000</td><td>7</td><td>009</td><td>998</td><td>7</td><td>042</td><td>988</td></tr>
<tr><td></td><td></td><td></td><td>8</td><td>001</td><td>1,000</td><td>8</td><td>011</td><td>998</td></tr>
<tr><td></td><td></td><td></td><td></td><td></td><td></td><td>9</td><td>002</td><td>1,000</td></tr>
</table>

<table>
<tr><td colspan="3">$p = .50$</td></tr>
<tr><td>x</td><td>Pr(x)</td><td>Pr(c)</td></tr>
<tr><td>0</td><td>001</td><td></td></tr>
<tr><td>1</td><td>010</td><td>011</td></tr>
<tr><td>2</td><td>044</td><td>055</td></tr>
<tr><td>3</td><td>117</td><td>172</td></tr>
<tr><td>4</td><td>205</td><td>377</td></tr>
<tr><td>5</td><td>246</td><td>623</td></tr>
<tr><td>6</td><td>205</td><td>828</td></tr>
<tr><td>7</td><td>117</td><td>945</td></tr>
<tr><td>8</td><td>043</td><td>989</td></tr>
<tr><td>9</td><td>010</td><td>999</td></tr>
<tr><td>10</td><td>001</td><td>1,000</td></tr>
</table>

Table A-5 (Continued)

$n = 15$

	$p = .01$			$p = .02$			$p = .03$	
x	$\Pr(x)$	$\Pr(c)$	x	$\Pr(x)$	$\Pr(c)$	x	$\Pr(x)$	$\Pr(c)$
0	860		0	739		0	633	
1	130	990	1	226	965	1	294	927
2	009	1,000	2	032	997	2	064	991
			3	003	1,000	3	009	1,000

	$p = .04$			$p = .05$			$p = .06$	
x	$\Pr(x)$	$\Pr(c)$	x	$\Pr(x)$	$\Pr(c)$	x	$\Pr(x)$	$\Pr(c)$
0	542		0	463		0	395	
1	339	881	1	366	829	1	378	774
2	099	980	2	135	964	2	169	943
3	018	998	3	031	995	3	047	990
4	002	1,000	4	005	999	4	009	999
			5	001	1,000	5	001	1,000

	$p = .07$			$p = .08$			$p = .09$	
x	$\Pr(x)$	$\Pr(c)$	x	$\Pr(x)$	$\Pr(c)$	x	$\Pr(x)$	$\Pr(c)$
0	337		0	286		0	243	
1	380	717	1	373	660	1	361	603
2	200	917	2	227	887	2	250	853
3	065	982	3	086	973	3	107	960
4	015	997	4	022	995	4	032	992
5	002	1,000	5	004	999	5	007	999
			6	001	1,000	6	001	1,000

	$p = .10$			$p = .15$			$p = .20$	
x	$\Pr(x)$	$\Pr(c)$	x	$\Pr(x)$	$\Pr(c)$	x	$\Pr(x)$	$\Pr(c)$
0	206		0	087		0	035	
1	343	549	1	231	319	1	132	167
2	267	816	2	286	604	2	231	398
3	129	944	3	218	823	3	250	648
4	043	987	4	116	938	4	188	836
5	010	998	5	045	983	5	103	939
6	002	1,000	6	013	996	6	043	982
			7	003	999	7	014	996
			8	001	1,000	8	003	999
						9	001	1,000

$n = 15$

	$p = .25$				$p = .30$				$p = .40$	
x	Pr(x)	Pr(c)		x	Pr(x)	Pr(c)		x	Pr(x)	Pr(c)
0	013			0	005			1	005	005
1	067	080		1	031	035		2	022	027
2	156	236		2	092	127		3	063	091
3	225	461		3	170	297		4	127	217
4	225	686		4	219	515		5	186	403
5	165	851		5	216	722		6	207	610
6	092	943		6	147	869		7	177	787
7	039	983		7	081	950		8	118	905
8	013	996		8	035	985		9	061	966
9	003	999		9	012	996		10	024	991
10	001	1,000		10	003	999		11	007	998
				11	001	1,000		12	002	1,000

$p = .50$

x	Pr(x)	Pr(c)
2	003	004
3	014	018
4	042	059
5	092	151
6	153	304
7	196	500
8	196	696
9	153	849
10	092	941
11	042	982
12	014	996
13	003	1,000

$n = 20$

	$p = .01$				$p = .02$				$p = .03$	
x	Pr(x)	Pr(c)		x	Pr(x)	Pr(c)		x	Pr(x)	Pr(c)
0	818			0	668			0	544	
1	165	983		1	272	940		1	336	880
2	016	999		2	053	993		2	099	979
3	001	1,000		3	006	999		3	018	997
				4	001	1,000		4	002	1,000

Table A-5 (Continued)

$n = 20$

	$p = .04$			$p = .05$			$p = .06$	
x	Pr(x)	Pr(c)	x	Pr(x)	Pr(c)	x	Pr(x)	Pr(c)
0	442		0	358		0	290	
1	368	810	1	377	736	1	370	660
2	146	956	2	189	925	2	225	885
3	036	993	3	060	984	3	086	971
4	006	999	4	013	997	4	023	994
5	001	1,000	5	002	1,000	5	005	999
						6	001	1,000

	$p = .07$			$p = .08$			$p = .09$	
x	Pr(x)	Pr(c)	x	Pr(x)	Pr(c)	x	Pr(x)	Pr(c)
0	234		0	189		0	152	
1	353	587	1	328	517	1	300	452
2	252	839	2	271	788	2	282	733
3	114	953	3	141	929	3	167	901
4	036	989	4	052	982	4	070	971
5	009	998	5	015	996	5	022	993
6	002	1,000	6	003	999	6	006	999
			7	001	1,000	7	001	1,000

	$p = .10$			$p = .15$			$p = .20$	
x	Pr(x)	Pr(c)	x	Pr(x)	Pr(c)	x	Pr(x)	Pr(c)
0	122		0	039		0	012	
1	270	392	1	137	176	1	058	069
2	285	677	2	229	405	2	137	206
3	190	867	3	243	648	3	205	411
4	090	957	4	182	830	4	218	630
5	032	989	5	103	933	5	175	804
6	009	998	6	045	978	6	109	913
7	002	1,000	7	016	994	7	055	968
			8	005	999	8	022	990
			9	001	1,000	9	007	997
						10	002	999
						11	000	1,000

$n = 20$

	$p = .25$				$p = .30$				$p = .40$	
x	Pr(x)	Pr(c)		x	Pr(x)	Pr(c)		x	Pr(x)	Pr(c)
0	003			0	001			1	000	001
1	021	024		1	007	008		2	003	004
2	067	091		2	028	035		3	012	016
3	134	225		3	072	107		4	035	051
4	190	415		4	130	238		5	075	126
5	202	617		5	179	416		6	124	250
6	169	786		6	192	608		7	166	416
7	112	898		7	164	772		8	180	596
8	061	959		8	114	887		9	160	755
9	027	986		9	065	952		10	117	872
10	010	996		10	031	983		11	071	943
11	003	999		11	012	995		12	035	979
12	001	1,000		12	004	999		13	015	994
				13	001	1,000		14	005	998
								15	001	1,000

$p = .50$

x	Pr(x)	Pr(c)
3	001	001
4	005	006
5	015	021
6	037	058
7	074	131
8	120	252
9	160	412
10	176	588
11	160	748
12	120	868
13	074	942
14	037	979
15	015	994
16	005	999
17	001	1,000

Table A-5 (Continued)

$n = 25$

	$p = .01$			$p = .02$			$p = .03$	
x	Pr(x)	Pr(c)	x	Pr(x)	Pr(c)	x	Pr(x)	Pr(c)
0	778		0	603		0	467	
1	196	974	1	308	911	1	361	828
2	024	998	2	075	987	2	134	962
3	002	1,000	3	012	999	3	032	994
			4	001	1,000	4	005	999
						5	001	1,000

	$p = .04$			$p = .05$			$p = .06$	
x	Pr(x)	Pr(c)	x	Pr(x)	Pr(c)	x	Pr(x)	Pr(c)
0	360		0	277		0	213	
1	375	736	1	365	642	1	340	553
2	188	924	2	230	873	2	260	813
3	060	983	3	093	966	3	127	940
4	014	997	4	027	993	4	045	985
5	002	1,000	5	006	999	5	012	997
			6	001	1,000	6	003	999
						7	000	1,000

	$p = .07$			$p = .08$			$p = .09$	
x	Pr(x)	Pr(c)	x	Pr(x)	Pr(c)	x	Pr(x)	Pr(c)
0	163		0	124		0	095	
1	307	470	1	270	395	1	234	329
2	277	747	2	282	677	2	278	606
3	160	906	3	188	865	3	211	817
4	066	973	4	090	955	4	115	931
5	021	993	5	033	988	5	048	979
6	005	999	6	010	997	6	016	995
7	001	1,000	7	002	999	7	004	999
			8	000	1,000	8	001	1,000

$n = 25$

	$p = .10$			$p = .15$			$p = .20$	
x	$\Pr(x)$	$\Pr(c)$	x	$\Pr(x)$	$\Pr(c)$	x	$\Pr(x)$	$\Pr(c)$
0	072		0	017		0	004	
1	199	271	1	076	093	1	024	027
2	266	537	2	161	254	2	071	098
3	227	764	3	217	471	3	136	234
4	138	902	4	211	682	4	187	421
5	065	967	5	156	838	5	196	617
6	024	991	6	092	930	6	163	780
7	007	998	7	044	975	7	111	891
8	002	1,000	8	017	992	8	062	953
			9	006	998	9	029	983
			10	002	1,000	10	012	994
						11	004	998
						12	001	1,000

	$p = .25$			$p = .30$			$p = .40$	
x	$\Pr(x)$	$\Pr(c)$	x	$\Pr(x)$	$\Pr(c)$	x	$\Pr(x)$	$\Pr(c)$
1	006	007	1	001	002	3	002	002
2	025	032	2	007	009	4	007	009
3	064	096	3	024	033	5	020	029
4	118	214	4	057	090	6	044	074
5	165	378	5	103	193	7	080	154
6	183	561	6	147	341	8	120	274
7	165	727	7	171	512	9	151	425
8	124	851	8	165	677	10	161	586
9	078	929	9	134	811	11	147	732
10	042	970	10	092	902	12	114	846
11	019	989	11	054	956	13	076	922
12	007	997	12	027	983	14	043	966
13	002	999	13	011	994	15	021	987
14	001	1,000	14	004	998	16	009	996
			15	001	1,000	17	003	999
						18	001	1,000

Table A-5 (Continued)

$n = 25$

	$p = .50$				$p = .50$	
x	Pr(x)	Pr(c)		x	Pr(x)	Pr(c)
5	002	002		13	155	655
6	005	007		14	133	788
7	014	022		15	097	885
8	032	054		16	061	946
9	061	115		17	032	978
10	097	212		18	014	993
11	133	345		19	005	998
12	155	500		20	002	1,000

$n = 30$

	$p = .01$				$p = .02$				$p = .03$	
x	Pr(x)	Pr(c)		x	Pr(x)	Pr(c)		x	Pr(x)	Pr(c)
0	740			0	545			0	401	
1	224	964		1	334	879		1	372	773
2	033	997		2	099	978		2	167	940
3	003	1,000		3	019	997		3	048	988
				4	003	1,000		4	010	998
								5	002	1,000

	$p = .04$				$p = .05$				$p = .06$	
x	Pr(x)	Pr(c)		x	Pr(x)	Pr(c)		x	Pr(x)	Pr(c)
0	294			0	215			0	156	
1	367	661		1	339	554		1	299	455
2	222	883		2	259	812		2	277	732
3	086	969		3	127	939		3	165	897
4	024	994		4	045	984		4	071	968
5	005	999		5	012	997		5	024	992
6	001	1,000		6	003	999		6	006	998
				7	000	1,000		7	001	1,000

	$p = .07$				$p = .08$				$p = .09$	
x	Pr(x)	Pr(c)		x	Pr(x)	Pr(c)		x	Pr(x)	Pr(c)
0	113			0	082			0	059	
1	256	369		1	214	296		1	175	234
2	279	649		2	270	565		2	251	486
3	196	845		3	219	784		3	232	717
4	100	945		4	128	913		4	155	872
5	039	984		5	058	971		5	080	952
6	012	996		6	021	992		6	033	985
7	003	999		7	006	998		7	011	996
8	001	1,000		8	002	1,000		8	003	999
								9	001	1,000

$n = 30$

	$p = .10$				$p = .15$				$p = .20$	
x	Pr(x)	Pr(c)		x	Pr(x)	Pr(c)		x	Pr(x)	Pr(c)
0	042			0	008			0	001	
1	141	184		1	040	048		1	009	011
2	228	411		2	103	151		2	034	044
3	236	647		3	170	322		3	079	123
4	177	825		4	203	524		4	133	255
5	102	927		5	186	711		5	172	428
6	047	974		6	137	847		6	179	607
7	018	992		7	083	930		7	154	761
8	006	998		8	042	972		8	111	871
9	002	1,000		9	018	990		9	068	939
				10	007	997		10	035	974
				11	002	999		11	016	991
				12	001	1,000		12	006	997
								13	002	999
								14	001	1,000

	$p = .25$				$p = .30$				$p = .40$	
x	Pr(x)	Pr(c)		x	Pr(x)	Pr(c)		x	Pr(x)	Pr(c)
1	002	002		2	002	002		4	001	002
2	009	011		3	007	009		5	004	006
3	027	037		4	021	030		6	012	017
4	060	098		5	046	077		7	026	044
5	105	203		6	083	160		8	050	094
6	145	348		7	122	281		9	082	176
7	166	514		8	150	432		10	115	291
8	159	674		9	157	589		11	140	431
9	130	803		10	142	730		12	147	578
10	091	894		11	110	841		13	136	714
11	055	949		12	075	916		14	110	825
12	029	978		13	044	960		15	078	903
13	013	992		14	023	983		16	049	952
14	005	997		15	011	994		17	027	979
15	002	999		16	004	998		18	013	992
16	001	1,000		17	001	999		19	005	997
				18	000	1,000		20	002	999
								21	001	1,000

Table A-5 (Continued)

$n = 30$

	$p = .50$				$p = .50$				$p = .50$	
x	Pr(x)	Pr(c)		x	Pr(x)	Pr(c)		x	Pr(x)	Pr(c)
6	001	001		12	081	181		18	081	900
7	002	003		13	112	292		19	051	951
8	005	008		14	135	428		20	028	979
9	013	021		15	144	572		21	013	992
10	028	049		16	135	708		22	005	997
11	051	100		17	112	819		23	002	999
								24	001	1,000

$n = 35$

	$p = .01$				$p = .02$				$p = .03$	
x	Pr(x)	Pr(c)		x	Pr(x)	Pr(c)		x	Pr(x)	Pr(c)
0	703			0	493			0	344	
1	249	952		1	352	845		1	373	717
2	043	995		2	122	967		2	196	913
3	005	1,000		3	027	995		3	067	980
				4	004	999		4	016	996
				5	001	1,000		5	003	999
								6	000	1,000

	$p = .04$				$p = .05$				$p = .06$	
x	Pr(x)	Pr(c)		x	Pr(x)	Pr(c)		x	Pr(x)	Pr(c)
0	240			0	166			0	115	
1	349	589		1	306	472		1	256	371
2	248	837		2	274	746		2	278	649
3	113	950		3	158	904		3	195	844
4	038	988		4	067	971		4	100	944
5	010	998		5	022	993		5	039	983
6	002	1,000		6	006	998		6	013	996
				7	001	1,000		7	003	999
								8	001	1,000

$n = 35$

	$p = .07$			$p = .08$			$p = .09$	
x	Pr(x)	Pr(c)	x	Pr(x)	Pr(c)	x	Pr(x)	Pr(c)
0	079		0	054		0	039	
1	208	287	1	164	218	1	128	164
2	266	552	2	243	461	2	214	379
3	220	773	3	232	694	3	233	612
4	133	905	4	162	856	4	185	797
5	062	967	5	087	943	5	113	910
6	023	990	6	038	981	6	056	966
7	007	998	7	014	994	7	023	989
8	002	999	8	004	999	8	008	997
9	000	1,000	9	001	1,000	9	002	999
						10	001	1,000

	$p = .10$			$p = .15$			$p = .20$	
x	Pr(x)	Pr(c)	x	Pr(x)	Pr(c)	x	Pr(x)	Pr(c)
0	025		0	003		1	004	004
1	087	122	1	021	024	2	015	019
2	184	306	2	063	087	3	041	061
3	225	531	3	122	209	4	083	143
4	200	731	4	172	381	5	129	272
5	138	868	5	188	569	6	161	433
6	076	945	6	166	735	7	166	599
7	035	980	7	121	856	8	146	745
8	014	994	8	075	931	9	109	854
9	005	998	9	040	971	10	071	925
10	001	1,000	10	018	989	11	040	966
			11	007	996	12	020	986
			12	003	999	13	009	995
			13	001	1,000	14	004	998
						15	001	999
						16	000	1,000

	$p = .25$			$p = .25$	
x	Pr(x)	Pr(c)	x	Pr(x)	Pr(c)
1	000	001	10	132	758
2	003	003	11	100	858
3	010	014	12	067	924
4	027	041	13	039	964
5	057	098	14	021	984
6	094	192	15	010	994
7	130	322	16	004	998
8	152	474	17	001	999
9	152	626	18	000	1,000

Table A-5 (Continued)

$n = 35$

	$p = .30$			$p = .40$			$p = .40$	
x	Pr(x)	Pr(c)	x	Pr(x)	Pr(c)	x	Pr(x)	Pr(c)
3	002	002	5	001	001	23	001	999
4	007	009	6	002	003	24	000	1,000
5	018	027	7	007	010			
6	038	065	8	016	026			
7	068	133	9	032	058			
8	101	234	10	055	112			
9	130	365	11	083	195			
10	145	510	12	111	306			
11	142	652	13	130	436			
12	121	773	14	137	573			
13	092	865	15	128	700			
14	062	927	16	106	807			
15	037	964	17	079	886			
16	020	984	18	053	938			
17	010	994	19	031	970			
18	004	998	20	017	987			
19	002	999	21	008	995			
20	001	1,000	22	003	998			

	$p = .50$			$p = .50$	
x	Pr(x)	Pr(c)	x	Pr(x)	Pr(c)
0	000		16	118	368
1	000	000	17	132	500
2	000	000	18	132	632
3	000	000	19	118	750
4	000	000	20	095	845
5	000	000	21	068	912
6	000	000	22	043	955
7	000	000	23	024	980
8	001	001	24	012	992
9	002	003	25	005	997
10	005	008	26	002	999
11	012	020	27	001	1,000
12	024	045			
13	043	088			
14	068	155			
15	095	250			

$n = 40$

	$p = .01$			$p = .02$			$p = .03$	
x	Pr(x)	Pr(c)	x	Pr(x)	Pr(c)	x	Pr(x)	Pr(c)
0	669		0	446		0	296	
1	270	939	1	364	810	1	366	662
2	053	993	2	145	954	2	221	882
3	007	999	3	037	992	3	086	969
4	001	1,000	4	007	999	4	025	993
			5	001	1,000	5	006	999
						6	001	1,000

	$p = .04$			$p = .05$			$p = .06$	
x	Pr(x)	Pr(c)	x	Pr(x)	Pr(c)	x	Pr(x)	Pr(c)
0	195		0	129		0	084	
1	326	521	1	271	399	1	215	299
2	265	786	2	278	677	2	267	567
3	140	925	3	185	862	3	216	783
4	054	979	4	090	952	4	128	910
5	016	995	5	034	986	5	059	969
6	004	999	6	010	997	6	022	991
7	001	1,000	7	003	999	7	007	998
			8	001	1,000	8	002	999
						9	000	1,000

	$p = .07$			$p = .08$			$p = .09$	
x	Pr(x)	Pr(c)	x	Pr(x)	Pr(c)	x	Pr(x)	Pr(c)
0	055		0	036		0	023	
1	165	220	1	124	159	1	091	114
2	242	463	2	210	369	2	175	289
3	221	684	3	231	601	3	220	509
4	171	855	4	186	787	4	201	710
5	087	942	5	116	903	5	143	853
6	038	980	6	059	962	6	083	936
7	014	994	7	025	987	7	040	976
8	004	998	8	009	996	8	016	992
9	001	1,000	9	003	999	9	006	998
			10	000	1,000	10	002	999
						11	000	1,000

Table A-5 (Continued)

$n = 40$

	$p = .10$				$p = .15$				$p = .20$	
x	Pr(x)	Pr(c)		x	Pr(x)	Pr(c)		x	Pr(x)	Pr(c)
0	015			0	002			1	001	001
1	066	080		1	011	012		2	006	008
2	142	223		2	036	049		3	021	028
3	200	423		3	082	130		4	047	076
4	206	629		4	133	263		5	085	161
5	165	794		5	169	433		6	125	286
6	107	900		6	174	607		7	151	437
7	058	958		7	149	756		8	156	593
8	026	985		8	109	865		9	139	732
9	010	995		9	068	933		10	107	839
10	004	999		10	037	970		11	073	912
11	001	1,000		11	018	988		12	044	957
				12	008	996		13	024	981
				13	003	999		14	011	992
				14	001	1,000		15	005	997
								16	002	999
								17	001	1,000

	$p = .25$				$p = .30$				$p = .30$	
x	Pr(x)	Pr(c)		x	Pr(x)	Pr(c)		x	Pr(x)	Pr(c)
2	001	001		3	000	001		15	077	885
3	004	005		4	002	003		16	052	937
4	011	016		5	006	009		17	031	968
5	027	043		6	015	024		18	017	985
6	053	096		7	032	055		19	009	994
7	086	182		8	056	111		20	004	998
8	118	330		9	085	196		21	002	999
9	140	440		10	113	309		22	001	1,000
10	144	584		11	132	441				
11	131	715		12	137	577				
12	106	821		13	126	703				
13	076	897		14	104	807				
14	049	946								
15	028	974								
16	015	988								
17	007	995								
18	003	998								
19	001	999								
20	000	1,000								

$n = 40$

$p = .40$			$p = .40$			$p = .40$		
x	$\Pr(x)$	$\Pr(c)$	x	$\Pr(x)$	$\Pr(c)$	x	$\Pr(x)$	$\Pr(c)$
6	000	001	13	083	211	20	055	926
7	001	002	14	106	317	21	035	961
8	004	006	15	123	440	22	020	981
9	010	016	16	128	568	23	011	992
10	020	035	17	120	689	24	005	997
11	036	071	18	103	791	25	002	999
12	058	129	19	079	870	26	001	1,000

$p = .50$			$p = .50$			$p = .50$		
x	$\Pr(x)$	$\Pr(c)$	x	$\Pr(x)$	$\Pr(c)$			
10	001	001	20	125	563			
11	002	003	21	119	682			
12	005	008	22	103	785			
13	011	019	23	081	866			
14	021	040	24	057	923			
15	037	077	25	037	960			
16	057	134	26	021	981			
17	081	215	27	011	992			
18	103	318	28	005	997			
19	119	437	29	002	999			
			30	001	1,000			

$n = 45$

$p = .01$			$p = .02$			$p = .03$		
x	$\Pr(x)$	$\Pr(c)$	x	$\Pr(x)$	$\Pr(c)$	x	$\Pr(x)$	$\Pr(c)$
0	636		0	403		0	254	
1	289	925	1	370	773	1	353	607
2	064	990	2	166	939	2	240	848
3	009	999	3	049	988	3	107	954
4	001	1,000	4	010	998	4	035	989
			5	002	1,000	5	009	998
						6	002	1,000

Table A-5 (Continued)

$n = 45$

	$p = .04$			$p = .05$			$p = .06$	
x	$Pr(x)$	$Pr(c)$	x	$Pr(x)$	$Pr(c)$	x	$Pr(x)$	$Pr(c)$
0	159		0	099		0	062	
1	299	458	1	236	335	1	177	239
2	274	732	2	273	608	2	249	488
3	164	895	3	206	813	3	228	716
4	072	967	4	114	927	4	153	869
5	024	991	5	049	976	5	080	949
6	007	998	6	017	993	6	034	983
7	002	1,000	7	005	998	7	012	995
			8	001	1,000	8	004	999
						9	001	1,000

	$p = .07$			$p = .08$			$p = .09$	
x	$Pr(x)$	$Pr(c)$	x	$Pr(x)$	$Pr(c)$	x	$Pr(x)$	$Pr(c)$
0	038		0	023		0	014	
1	129	167	1	092	115	1	064	078
2	214	382	2	176	291	2	139	217
3	231	613	3	219	510	3	197	414
4	183	795	4	200	710	4	205	619
5	113	908	5	143	852	5	166	785
6	057	964	6	083	935	6	109	894
7	024	988	7	040	975	7	060	954
8	008	996	8	017	992	8	028	983
9	003	999	9	006	997	9	012	994
10	001	1,000	10	002	999	10	004	998
			11	001	1,000	11	001	1,000

	$p = .10$			$p = .15$			$p = .15$	
x	$Pr(x)$	$Pr(c)$	x	$Pr(x)$	$Pr(c)$	x	$Pr(x)$	$Pr(c)$
0	009		0	001		13	008	995
1	044	052	1	005	006	14	003	998
2	107	159	2	021	027	15	001	999
3	170	329	3	052	078	16	000	1,000
4	198	527	4	096	175			
5	181	708	5	139	314			
6	134	841	6	164	478			
7	083	924	7	161	639			
8	044	968	8	135	775			
9	020	988	9	098	873			
10	008	996	10	062	935			
11	003	999	11	035	970			
12	001	1,000	12	017	987			

$n = 45$

	$p = .20$			$p = .25$			$p = .30$	
x	Pr(x)	Pr(c)	x	Pr(x)	Pr(c)	x	Pr(x)	Pr(c)
1	000	001	3	001	002	4	001	001
2	003	003	4	004	006	5	002	003
3	010	013	5	012	018	6	005	008
4	025	038	6	027	045	7	013	021
5	052	090	7	050	094	8	026	047
6	087	177	8	078	173	9	046	093
7	121	297	9	107	280	10	071	165
8	143	441	10	129	409	11	097	262
9	147	588	11	137	546	12	118	380
10	133	720	12	129	675	13	129	509
11	105	826	13	109	784	14	126	635
12	075	901	14	083	867	15	112	746
13	047	948	15	057	925	16	090	836
14	027	975	16	036	961	17	066	901
15	014	989	17	020	981	18	044	945
16	007	996	18	011	992	19	027	972
17	003	998	19	005	997	20	015	986
18	001	999	20	002	999	21	008	994
19	000	1,000	21	001	1,000	22	004	998
						23	002	999
						24	001	1,000

	$p = .40$			$p = .40$			$p = .50$	
x	Pr(x)	Pr(c)	x	Pr(x)	Pr(c)	x	Pr(x)	Pr(c)
8	001	001	19	114	679	12	001	001
9	002	004	20	099	778	13	002	003
10	006	009	21	079	856	14	005	008
11	012	022	22	057	914	15	010	018
12	023	045	23	038	952			
13	039	084	24	023	975			
14	059	143	25	013	988			
15	082	225	26	007	995			
16	102	327	27	003	998			
17	116	444	28	001	999			
18	121	564	29	001	1,000			

Table A-5 (Continued)

$n = 45$

	$p = .50$				$p = .50$				$p = .50$	
x	$\Pr(x)$	$\Pr(c)$		x	$\Pr(x)$	$\Pr(c)$		x	$\Pr(x)$	$\Pr(c)$
16	018	036		22	117	500		28	031	964
17	031	068		23	117	617		29	018	982
18	049	116		24	107	724		30	010	992
19	069	186		25	090	814		31	005	997
20	090	276		26	069	884		32	002	999
21	107	383		27	049	932		33	001	1,000

$n = 50$

	$p = .01$				$p = .02$				$p = .03$	
x	$\Pr(x)$	$\Pr(c)$		x	$\Pr(x)$	$\Pr(c)$		x	$\Pr(x)$	$\Pr(c)$
0	605			0	364			0	218	
1	306	911		1	371	736		1	337	555
2	076	986		2	186	922		2	256	811
3	012	998		3	061	982		3	126	937
4	001	999		4	015	997		4	046	983
				5	002	999		5	013	996
								6	003	999

	$p = .04$				$p = .05$				$p = .06$	
x	$\Pr(x)$	$\Pr(c)$		x	$\Pr(x)$	$\Pr(c)$		x	$\Pr(x)$	$\Pr(c)$
0	129			0	077			0	045	
1	271	400		1	202	279		1	145	190
2	276	677		2	261	541		2	226	416
3	184	861		3	219	760		3	231	647
4	090	951		4	136	896		4	173	821
5	035	986		5	066	962		5	102	922
6	011	996		6	026	988		6	049	971
7	003	999		7	008	997		7	019	990
				8	002	999		8	006	997
								9	002	999

	$p = .07$				$p = .07$				$p = .08$	
x	$\Pr(x)$	$\Pr(c)$		x	$\Pr(x)$	$\Pr(c)$		x	$\Pr(x)$	$\Pr(c)$
0	027			6	077	942		0	015	
1	099	126		7	036	978		1	067	083
2	184	311		8	015	993		2	143	226
3	221	533		9	005	998		3	199	425
4	196	729		10	002	999		4	204	629
5	135	865						5	163	792

$n = 50$

	$p = .08$			$p = .09$			$p = .10$	
x	Pr(x)	Pr(c)	x	Pr(x)	Pr(c)	x	Pr(x)	Pr(c)
6	106	898	0	009		0	005	
7	058	956	1	044	053	1	029	034
8	027	983	2	107	161	2	078	112
9	011	994	3	169	330	3	139	250
10	004	998	4	197	528	4	181	431
11	001	999	5	179	707	5	185	616
			6	133	840	6	154	770
			7	083	923	7	108	878
			8	044	967	8	064	942
			9	020	987	9	033	975
			10	008	996	10	015	991
			11	003	999	11	006	997
			12	001	999	12	002	999

	$p = .15$			$p = .20$			$p = .25$	
x	Pr(x)	Pr(c)	x	Pr(x)	Pr(c)	x	Pr(x)	Pr(c)
1	003	003	2	001	001	4	002	002
2	011	014	3	004	005	5	005	007
3	032	046	4	013	018	6	012	019
4	066	112	5	029	048	7	026	045
5	107	219	6	055	103	8	046	092
6	142	361	7	087	190	9	072	164
7	157	518	8	117	307	10	099	262
8	149	668	9	136	443	11	119	382
9	123	791	10	139	584	12	129	511
10	089	880	11	127	711	13	126	637
11	057	937	12	103	814	14	111	748
12	032	969	13	075	889	15	089	837
13	017	987	14	049	939	16	065	902
14	008	994	15	029	969	17	043	945
15	003	998	16	016	986	18	026	971
16	001	999	17	008	993	19	015	986
			18	004	997	20	008	994
			19	002	999	21	004	997
			20	001	999	22	002	999
						23	001	999

Table A-5 (Continued)

$n = 50$

	$p = .30$			$p = .40$			$p = .40$	
x	Pr(x)	Pr(c)	x	Pr(x)	Pr(c)	x	Pr(x)	Pr(c)
5	001	001	9	001	001	21	109	670
6	002	002	10	001	002	22	096	766
7	005	007	11	003	006	23	078	844
8	011	018	12	008	013	24	058	902
9	022	040	13	015	028	25	040	943
10	039	079	14	026	054	26	026	969
11	060	139	15	042	096	27	015	984
12	084	223	16	061	156	28	008	992
13	105	329	17	081	237	29	004	997
14	119	447	18	099	335	30	002	998
15	122	569	19	111	446	31	001	999
16	114	684	20	115	561			
17	098	782						
18	077	859						
19	056	915						
20	037	952						
21	022	975						
22	013	988						
23	007	994						
24	003	997						
25	001	999						

	$p = .50$			$p = .50$			$p = .50$	
x	Pr(x)	Pr(c)	x	Pr(x)	Pr(c)	x	Pr(x)	Pr(c)
14	001	001	22	079	239	30	042	941
15	002	003	23	096	336	31	027	968
16	004	008	24	108	444	32	016	984
17	009	016	25	112	556	33	009	992
18	016	032	26	108	604	34	004	997
19	027	059	27	096	760	35	002	999
20	042	101	28	079	839	36	001	999
21	059	161	29	059	899			

$n = 75$

	$p = .01$				$p = .02$				$p = .03$	
x	Pr(x)	Pr(c)		x	Pr(x)	Pr(c)		x	Pr(x)	Pr(c)
0	471			0	219			0	101	
1	357	827		1	336	556		1	236	338
2	133	960		2	254	810		2	270	608
3	033	993		3	126	936		3	203	812
4	006	999		4	046	982		4	113	925
5	001	999		5	013	996		5	049	975
				6	003	999		6	018	992
								7	005	998
								8	001	999

	$p = .04$				$p = .05$				$p = .06$	
x	Pr(x)	Pr(c)		x	Pr(x)	Pr(c)		x	Pr(x)	Pr(c)
0	047			0	021			0	009	
1	146	193		1	084	105		1	046	056
2	226	419		2	164	269		2	109	165
3	229	647		3	210	479		3	169	334
4	171	819		4	199	679		4	195	529
5	101	920		5	149	828		5	176	706
6	049	969		6	091	919		6	131	837
7	020	989		7	047	966		7	083	919
8	007	997		8	021	988		8	045	965
9	002	999		9	008	996		9	021	986
10	001	999		10	003	999		10	009	995
				11	001	999		11	003	998
								12	001	999

	$p = .07$				$p = .08$				$p = .09$	
x	Pr(x)	Pr(c)		x	Pr(x)	Pr(c)		x	Pr(x)	Pr(c)
0	004			0	002			0	001	
1	024	029		1	013	014		1	006	007
2	068	096		2	040	055		2	023	030
3	125	211		3	085	140		3	055	085
4	169	390		4	134	274		4	099	184
5	180	571		5	165	439		5	138	322
6	158	729		6	167	606		6	159	482
7	118	847		7	144	749		7	156	638
8	075	922		8	106	856		8	131	769
9	042	964		9	069	925		9	096	865
10	021	985		10	039	964		10	063	928
11	009	994		11	020	984		11	037	965
12	004	998		12	009	994		12	019	984
13	001	999		13	004	998		13	009	993
				14	002	999		14	004	997
								15	002	999
								16	001	999

Table A-5 (Continued)

$n = 75$

	$p = .10$			$p = .15$			$p = .20$	
x	$\Pr(x)$	$\Pr(c)$	x	$\Pr(x)$	$\Pr(c)$	x	$\Pr(x)$	$\Pr(c)$
1	003	003	3	002	002	5	000	001
2	013	016	4	006	008	6	003	004
3	034	050	5	015	023	7	007	010
4	069	119	6	031	054	8	014	024
5	108	227	7	054	108	9	026	050
6	140	367	8	081	189	10	043	093
7	154	521	9	106	295	11	063	156
8	145	666	10	123	418	12	084	239
9	119	786	11	129	547	13	102	341
10	088	874	12	121	668	14	113	454
11	058	931	13	104	772	15	114	569
12	034	966	14	081	853	16	107	676
13	018	984	15	058	911	17	093	769
14	009	993	16	038	949	18	075	844
15	004	997	17	024	973	19	056	900
16	002	999	18	013	987	20	039	939
17	001	999	19	007	993	21	026	965
			20	004	997	22	016	981
			21	002	999	23	009	990
			22	001	999	24	005	995
						25	003	998
						26	001	999

	$p = .25$			$p = .25$			$p = .25$	
x	$\Pr(x)$	$\Pr(c)$	x	$\Pr(x)$	$\Pr(c)$	x	$\Pr(x)$	$\Pr(c)$
7	000	001	15	068	195	23	054	895
8	001	002	16	085	279	24	039	934
9	003	004	17	098	377	25	026	961
10	006	010	18	105	482	26	017	978
11	012	022	19	105	588	27	010	988
12	021	043	20	098	686	28	006	994
13	034	077	21	086	771	29	003	997
14	049	127	22	070	842	30	002	999

$n = 75$

	$p = .30$			$p = .40$			$p = .50$	
x	$\Pr(x)$	$\Pr(c)$	x	$\Pr(x)$	$\Pr(c)$	x	$\Pr(x)$	$\Pr(c)$
10	000	000	17	001	001	25	001	003
11	001	002	18	001	003	26	003	005
12	002	004	19	003	006	27	005	010
13	005	009	20	006	011	28	008	018
14	009	019	21	009	021	29	013	032
15	017	035	22	016	037	30	021	053
16	027	062	23	024	061	31	030	083
17	059	102	24	035	096	32	041	124
18	055	157	25	048	144	33	054	178
19	071	227	26	061	205	34	066	244
20	085	312	27	074	279	35	078	322
21	095	407	28	085	365	36	087	409
22	099	507	29	092	456	37	091	500
23	099	605	30	094	549	38	091	591
24	092	697	31	091	641	39	087	678
25	080	777	32	083	724	40	078	756
26	066	843	33	072	796	41	066	822
27	051	895	34	059	855	42	054	876
28	038	932	35	046	902	43	041	917
29	026	959	36	034	936			
30	017	976	37	024	960			
31	011	987	38	016	977			
32	006	993	39	010	987			
33	004	996	40	006	993			
34	002	998	41	003	996			
35	001	999	42	002	998			
			43	001	999			

Table A-5 (Continued)

$n = 100$

	$p = .01$			$p = .02$			$p = .03$	
x	$\Pr(x)$	$\Pr(c)$	x	$\Pr(x)$	$\Pr(c)$	x	$\Pr(x)$	$\Pr(c)$
0	366		0	133		0	048	
1	370	736	1	271	403	1	147	195
2	185	921	2	273	677	2	225	420
3	061	982	3	182	859	3	227	647
4	015	997	4	090	949	4	171	818
5	003	999	5	035	985	5	101	919
6	000	1,000	6	011	996	6	050	969
			7	003	999	7	021	989
			8	001	1,000	8	007	997
						9	002	699
						10	001	1,000

	$p = .04$			$d = .05$			$p = .06$	
x	$\Pr(x)$	$\Pr(c)$	x	$\Pr(x)$	$\Pr(c)$	x	$\Pr(x)$	$\Pr(c)$
0	017		0	006		0	002	
1	070	087	1	031	037	1	013	015
2	145	232	2	081	118	2	041	057
3	197	429	3	140	258	3	086	143
4	199	629	4	178	436	4	134	277
5	159	788	5	180	616	5	164	441
6	105	894	6	150	766	6	166	607
7	059	952	7	106	872	7	142	748
8	029	981	8	065	937	8	105	854
9	012	993	9	035	972	9	069	922
10	005	998	10	017	989	10	040	962
11	002	999	11	007	996	11	021	983
12	000	1,000	12	003	999	12	010	993
			13	001	1,000	13	004	997
						14	002	999
						15	001	1,000

	$p = .07$			$p = .07$			$p = .08$	
x	$\Pr(x)$	$\Pr(c)$	x	$\Pr(x)$	$\Pr(c)$	x	$\Pr(x)$	$\Pr(c)$
0	001		9	104	838	1	002	002
1	005	006	10	071	909	2	009	011
2	020	026	11	044	953	3	025	037
3	049	074	12	024	978	4	054	090
4	089	163	13	012	990	5	090	180
5	128	291	14	004	996	6	123	303
6	153	444	15	003	998	7	144	447
7	154	599	16	001	999	8	146	593
8	135	734	17	000	1,000	9	129	722

$n = 100$

	$p = .08$			$p = .09$			$p = .09$	
x	Pr(x)	Pr(c)	x	Pr(x)	Pr(c)	x	Pr(x)	Pr(c)
10	102	824	1	001	001	10	124	712
11	073	897	2	004	005	11	101	812
12	050	944	3	013	017	12	074	886
13	028	972	4	030	047	13	049	936
14	015	987	5	057	105	14	030	966
15	007	994	6	089	194	15	017	983
16	003	998	7	119	313	16	009	992
17	001	999	8	137	449	17	004	996
18	001	1,000	9	138	588	18	002	999
						19	001	999
						20	000	1,000

	$p = .10$			$p = .15$			$p = .15$	
x	Pr(x)	Pr(c)	x	Pr(x)	Pr(c)	x	Pr(x)	Pr(c)
2	002	002	5	001	002	17	091	763
3	006	008	6	003	005	18	074	837
4	016	024	7	007	012	19	056	893
5	034	058	8	015	027	20	040	934
6	060	117	9	028	055	21	027	961
7	089	206	10	044	099	22	017	978
8	115	321	11	064	163	23	010	988
9	130	451	12	084	247	24	006	994
10	132	583	13	100	347	25	003	997
11	120	703	14	110	457	26	002	999
12	099	802	15	111	568	27	001	999
13	074	876	16	104	672	28	000	1,000
14	051	927						
15	033	960						
16	019	979						
17	011	990						
18	005	995						
19	003	998						
20	001	999						
21	000	1,000						

Table A-5 (Continued)

$n = 100$

	$p = .20$			$p = .25$			$p = .30$	
x	$Pr(x)$	$Pr(c)$	x	$Pr(x)$	$Pr(c)$	x	$Pr(x)$	$Pr(c)$
8	000	001	12	001	001	16	001	001
9	001	002	13	001	002	17	001	002
10	003	006	14	003	005	18	002	005
11	007	013	15	006	011	19	004	009
12	013	025	16	010	021	20	008	016
13	022	047	17	017	038	21	012	029
14	034	080	18	025	063	22	019	048
15	048	129	19	036	100	23	028	076
16	064	192	20	049	149	24	038	114
17	079	271	21	063	211	25	050	163
18	091	362	22	075	286	26	061	224
19	098	460	23	085	371	27	072	296
20	099	559	24	091	462	28	080	377
21	095	654	25	092	553	29	086	462
22	085	739	26	088	642	30	087	549
23	072	811	27	081	722	31	084	633
24	038	869	28	070	792	32	078	711
25	044	913	29	058	850	33	069	779
26	032	944	30	046	896	34	058	837
27	022	966	31	034	931	35	047	884
28	014	980	32	025	956	36	036	920
29	009	989	33	017	972	37	027	947
30	005	994	34	011	984	38	019	966
31	003	997	35	007	991	39	013	979
32	002	998	36	004	995	40	008	987
33	001	999	37	002	997	41	005	993
34	000	1,000	38	001	999	42	003	996
			39	001	999	43	002	998
						44	001	999

$n = 100$

$p = .35$			$p = .40$			$p = .45$		
x	$\Pr(x)$	$\Pr(c)$	x	$\Pr(x)$	$\Pr(c)$	x	$\Pr(x)$	$\Pr(c)$
20	000	001	24	000	001	29	000	001
21	001	002	25	001	001	30	001	002
22	002	003	26	001	002	31	001	003
23	003	007	27	002	005	32	003	005
24	006	012	28	004	008	33	004	010
25	009	021	29	006	015	34	007	017
26	014	035	30	010	025	35	011	027
27	021	056	31	015	040	36	016	043
28	029	085	32	022	062	37	022	065
29	039	124	33	030	091	38	030	095
30	049	173	34	039	130	39	039	134
31	060	233	35	049	179	40	049	183
32	070	303	36	059	239	41	058	241
33	077	380	37	068	307	42	067	309
34	082	462	38	075	382	43	074	383
35	083	346	39	080	462	44	079	461
36	081	627	40	081	543	45	080	541
37	076	702	41	079	622	46	078	620
38	067	770	42	074	697	47	074	693
39	058	828	43	067	763	48	066	760
40	047	875	44	058	821	49	058	817
41	037	912	45	048	869	50	048	865
42	028	941	46	038	907	51	039	904
43	021	961	47	029	936	52	030	934
44	014	975	48	021	958	53	022	956
45	010	985	49	015	973	54	016	972
46	006	991	50	010	983	55	011	982
47	004	995	51	007	990	56	007	989
48	002	997	52	004	994	57	004	994
49	001	999	53	003	997	58	003	997
			54	001	998	59	002	998
			55	001	999	60	001	999
			56	000	1,000	61	000	1,000

Table A-5   (Continued)

$n = 100$

$p = .50$

x	$\Pr(x)$	$\Pr(c)$
34	000	001
35	001	002
36	002	003
37	003	006
38	004	010
39	007	018
40	011	028
41	016	044
42	022	067
43	030	097
44	039	136
45	048	184
46	058	242
47	067	309
48	074	382
49	078	460
50	080	540
51	078	618
52	074	691
53	067	758
54	060	816
55	048	864
56	039	903
57	030	933
58	022	956
59	016	972
60	011	982
61	007	490
62	004	994
63	003	997
64	002	998
65	001	999
66	000	1,000

TABLE A-6 Poisson Probability Curves

Probability of Occurrence of c or Less Defects in a Sample of n

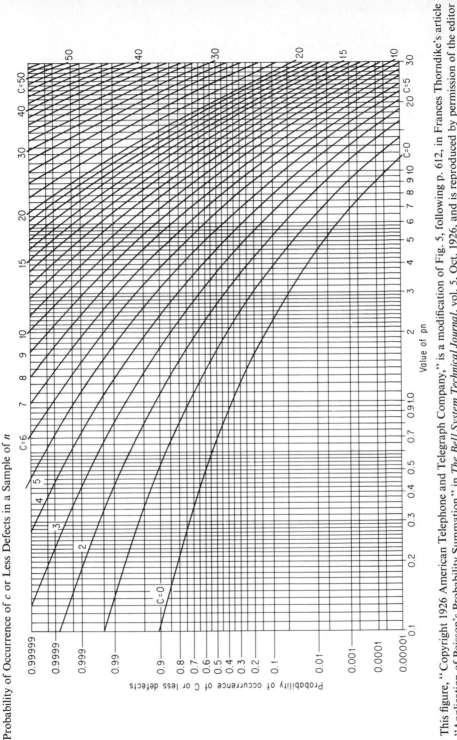

This figure, "Copyright 1926 American Telephone and Telegraph Company," is a modification of Fig. 5, following p. 612, in Frances Thorndike's article "Application of Poisson's Probability Summation" in *The Bell System Technical Journal*, vol. 5, Oct. 1926, and is reproduced by permission of the editor of BSTJ. It appears also as Fig. 2-6 on p. 35 of *Sampling Inspection Tables*, 2nd ed., 1959, p. 35 by Harold F. Dodge and Harry G. Romig, John Wiley & Sons, Inc., and has the permission of the editor to be reproduced here.

TABLE A-7 Nonrandom Variability—
Standard Given: df $= \infty$

k	$Z_{.10}$	$Z_{.05}$	$Z_{.01}$
1	1.64	1.96	2.58
2	1.96	2.24	2.81
3	2.11	2.39	2.93
4	2.23	2.49	3.02
5	2.31	2.57	3.09
6	2.38	2.63	3.14
7	2.43	2.68	3.19
8	2.48	2.73	3.22
9	2.52	2.77	3.26
10	2.56	2.80	3.29
15	2.70	2.93	3.40
20	2.79	3.02	3.48
24	2.85	3.07	3.53
30	2.92	3.14	3.59
50	3.08	3.28	3.72
120	3.33	3.52	3.93

TABLE A-8 Percentage Points for the Studentized Maximum Absolute Deviate in Normal Samples: Nonrandom Variability.   Factors for ANOM.

df	k: 2*	3	4	5	6	7	8	9	10	15	20	30	40	60
	No Standard given: $\alpha = .10$													
4	1.51	2.60	3.03											
5	1.42	2.38	2.74	3.01										
6	1.37	2.24	2.57	2.81	3.00									
7	1.34	2.16	2.46	2.68	2.86	3.00								
8	1.32	2.10	2.38	2.59	2.75	2.89	3.00							
9	1.30	2.05	2.33	2.52	2.68	2.80	2.91	3.00						
10	1.28	2.01	2.28	2.47	2.62	2.74	2.84	2.93	3.01					
15	1.24	1.91	2.16	2.33	2.46	2.56	2.65	2.73	2.80	3.04				
20	1.22	1.87	2.10	2.26	2.38	2.48	2.57	2.64	2.70	2.92	3.07			
30	1.20	1.82	2.04	2.20	2.31	2.41	2.49	2.55	2.61	2.82	2.95	3.14		
40	1.19	1.80	2.02	2.17	2.28	2.37	2.45	2.51	2.57	2.76	2.90	3.07	3.19	
60	1.18	1.78	1.99	2.14	2.25	2.34	2.41	2.47	2.52	2.72	2.84	3.01	3.12	3.27
120	1.17	1.76	1.97	2.11	2.22	2.30	2.37	2.43	2.48	2.67	2.79	2.94	3.05	3.19
∞	1.16	1.74	1.94	2.08	2.19	2.27	2.34	2.39	2.44	2.62	2.74	2.89	2.99	3.12

df	k: 2*	3	4	5	6	7	8	9	10	15	20	30	40	60

No Standard given: $\alpha = .05$ $\qquad H_\alpha = \left[\text{Max} \dfrac{(\bar{X}_n - \bar{X})}{\hat{\sigma}_{\bar{x}}} \qquad \dfrac{(\bar{X} - \bar{X}_1)}{\hat{\sigma}_{\bar{x}}} \right]$

df	2*	3	4	5	6	7	8	9	10	15	20	30	40	60
3	2.25	3.66												
4	1.96	3.07	3.51											
5	1.82	2.77	3.16	3.43										
6	1.73	2.59	2.94	3.19	3.37									
7	1.67	2.48	2.81	3.04	3.21	3.35								
8	1.63	2.39	2.71	2.92	3.09	3.23	3.33							
9	1.60	2.34	2.64	2.85	3.01	3.14	3.24	3.31						
10	1.58	2.29	2.58	2.78	2.93	3.06	3.15	3.24	3.31					
15	1.51	2.16	2.42	2.60	2.74	2.85	2.93	3.01	3.07	3.32				
20	1.48	2.10	2.35	2.52	2.64	2.75	2.83	2.91	2.96	3.18	3.33			
30	1.44	2.04	2.28	2.44	2.56	2.66	2.73	2.80	2.86	3.06	3.19	3.37		
40	1.43	2.01	2.25	2.40	2.52	2.62	2.69	2.75	2.80	3.00	3.13	3.29		
60	1.41	1.98	2.21	2.36	2.48	2.57	2.64	2.70	2.76	2.94	3.06	3.22		
120	1.40	1.95	2.18	2.33	2.44	2.53	2.60	2.65	2.71	2.88	3.00	3.15		
∞	1.39	1.93	2.15	2.29	2.40	2.49	2.55	2.61	2.65	2.82	2.94	3.08		

No Standard given: $\alpha = .01$

df	2*	3	4	5	6	7	8	9	10	15	20	30	40	60
3	4.13	6.52												
4	3.26	4.87	5.56											
5	2.85	4.15	4.69	5.07										
6	2.62	3.74	4.21	4.53	4.78									
7	2.47	3.49	3.90	4.20	4.42	4.60								
8	2.37	3.31	3.70	3.97	4.17	4.33	4.47							
9	2.30	3.18	3.54	3.80	3.99	4.14	4.26	4.37						
10	2.24	3.08	3.43	3.67	3.86	3.99	4.11	4.21	4.29					
15	2.08	2.81	3.12	3.32	3.47	3.59	3.69	3.77	3.84	4.11				
20	2.01	2.70	2.98	3.17	3.30	3.41	3.50	3.57	3.63	3.87	4.02			
30	1.94	2.58	2.85	3.02	3.15	3.25	3.33	3.39	3.45	3 66	3.79	3.96		
40	1.91	2.53	2.79	2.95	3.07	3.17	3.24	3.30	3.36	3.56	3.68	3.84	3.96	
60	1.88	2.48	2.73	2.88	3.00	3.09	3.16	4.22	3.27	3.46	3.58	3.73	3.84	3.97
120	1.85	2.43	2.67	2.82	2.93	3.02	3.09	3.14	3.20	3.37	3.48	3.62	3.72	3.86
∞	1.82	2.39	2.61	2.76	2.87	2.95	3.02	3.07	3.12	3.29	3.39	3.53	3.62	3.73

SOURCE: The values in this table for $\alpha = .05$ and $.01$ are the averages of the upper and lower bounds given by Halperin, Greenhouse, Cornfield, and Zalokar, *J. Am. Stat. Assoc.*, vol. 50, pp. 185–195, 1955. Entries for $\alpha = .10$ are equal to $h_{.10}\sqrt{(k-1)/k}$, where $h_{.10}$ is tabled by Nelson, L.S., "Factors for the Analysis of Means," *J. Qual. Technol.*, vol. 6, No. 4, October 1974, pp. 175–181. *Note*: Factors for $\alpha = 0.10$, $k > 2$ are upper bounds.

* The numbers corresponding to $k = 2$ are appropriate modifications of Student's t table. $k =$ number of means being compared; df = degrees of freedom in estimate of σ.

TABLE A-9   Criteria for Testing for Extreme Mean or Individual

Statistic	No. of obs., k	P_{90}	P_{95}	P_{98}	P_{99}
$r_{10} = \dfrac{X_2 - X_1}{X_k - X_1}$	3	.886	.941	.976	.988
	4	.679	.765	.846	.889
	5	.557	.642	.729	.780
	6	.482	.560	.644	.698
	7	.434	.507	.586	.637
$r_{11} = \dfrac{X_2 - X_1}{X_{k-1} - X_1}$	8	.479	.554	.631	.683
	9	.441	.512	.587	.635
	10	.409	.477	.551	.597
$r_{21} = \dfrac{X_3 - X_1}{X_{k-1} - X_1}$	11	.517	.576	.638	.679
	12	.490	.546	.605	.642
	13	.467	.521	.578	.615
$r_{22} = \dfrac{X_3 - X_1}{X_{k-2} - X_1}$	14	.492	.546	.602	.641
	15	.472	.525	.579	.616
	16	.454	.507	.559	.595
	17	.438	.490	.542	.577
	18	.424	.475	.527	.561
	19	.412	.462	.514	.547
	20	.401	.450	.502	.535
	21	.391	.440	.491	.524
	22	.382	.430	.481	.514
	23	.374	.421	.472	.505
	24	.367	.413	.464	.497
	25	.360	.406	.457	.489

SOURCE: W. J. Dixon, Processing Data for Outlyers, *Biometrics*, vol. 9, no. 1, pp. 74–89. (Reprinted by permission of the editor of *Biometrics*.)

TABLE A-10   Critical Values for Simultaneously Testing the Two Largest or Two Smallest Observations

Compare computed values of $S_{n-1,n}^2/S^2$ or $S_{1,2}^2/S^2$ with the appropriate critical ratio in this table; smaller observed sample ratios call for rejection. $X_1 \leqq X_2 \leqq \ldots \leqq X_n$

Number of Observations	10% Level	5% Level	1% Level
4	.0031	.0008	.0000
5	.0376	.0183	.0035
6	.0921	.0565	.0186
7	.1479	.1020	.0440
8	.1994	.1478	.0750
9	.2454	.1909	.1082
10	.2853	.2305	.1415
11	.3226	.2666	.1736
12	.3552	.2996	.2044
13	.3843	.3295	.2333
14	.4106	.3568	.2605
15	.4345	.3818	.2859
16	.4562	.4048	.3098
17	.4761	.4259	.3321
18	.4944	.4455	.3530
19	.5113	.4636	.3725
20	.5269	.4804	.3909

$$S^2 = \sum_{i=1}^{n}(X_i - \bar{X})^2 \qquad \bar{X} = \sum_{i=1}^{n} X_i/n$$

$$S_{1,2}^2 = \sum_{i=3}^{n}(X_i - \bar{X}_{1,2})^2 \qquad \bar{X}_{1,2} = \sum_{i=3}^{n} X_i/(n-2)$$

$$S_{n-1,n}^2 = \sum_{i=1}^{n-2}(X_i - \bar{X}_{n-1,n})^2 \qquad \bar{X}_{n-1,n} = \sum_{i=1}^{n-2} X_i/(n-2)$$

SOURCE: Frank E. Grubbs, Procedures for Detecting Outlying Observations in Samples, *Technometrics*, vol. 11, no. 1, pp. 1–21, February, 1969. (Reproduced by permission of the author and editor.)

TABLE A-11   Values of Adjusted d_2 Factor (d_2^*) and Degrees of Freedom (df)
To Be Used with Estimates of σ Based on k Independent Sample Ranges of n Each.   (Unbiased Estimate of $\sigma^2 = (\bar{R}/d_2^*)^2$; Unbiased Estimate of $\sigma = \bar{R}/d_2$.)   Also, df $\cong (.9)k(n-1)$.

k	$n=2$		$n=3$		$n=4$		$n=5$		$n=6$		$n=7$	
	df	d_2^*	df	d_2^*	df	d_2^*	df	d_2^*	df	d_2^*	df	d_2^*
1	1.0	1.41	2.0	1.91	2.9	2.24	3.8	2.48	4.7	2.67	5.5	2.83
2	1.9	1.28	3.8	1.81	5.7	2.15	7.5	2.40	9.2	2.60	10.8	2.77
3	2.8	1.23	5.7	1.77	8.4	2.12	11.1	2.38	13.6	2.58	16.0	2.75
4	3.7	1.21	7.5	1.75	11.2	2.11	14.7	2.37	18.1	2.57	21.3	2.74
5	4.6	1.19	9.3	1.74	13.9	2.10	18.4	2.36	22.6	2.56	26.6	2.73
6	5.5	1.18	11.1	1.73	16.6	2.09	22.9	2.35	27.1	2.56	31.8	2.73
7	6.4	1.17	12.9	1.73	19.4	2.09	25.6	2.35	31.5	2.55	37.1	2.72
8	7.2	1.17	14.8	1.72	22.1	2.08	29.3	2.35	36.0	2.55	42.4	2.72
9	8.1	1.16	16.6	1.72	24.8	2.08	32.9	2.34	40.5	2.55	47.7	2.72
10	9.0	1.16	18.4	1.72	27.6	2.08	36.5	2.34	44.9	2.55	52.9	2.72
11	9.9	1.16	20.2	1.71	30.3	2.08	40.1	2.34	49.4	2.55	58.2	2.72
12	10.8	1.15	22.0	1.71	33.0	2.07	43.7	2.34	53.9	2.55	63.5	2.72
13	11.6	1.15	23.9	1.71	35.7	2.07	47.4	2.34	58.4	2.55	68.8	2.71
14	12.5	1.15	25.7	1.71	38.5	2.07	51.0	2.34	62.8	2.54	74.0	2.71
15	13.4	1.15	27.5	1.71	41.2	2.07	54.6	2.34	67.3	2.54	79.3	2.71
16	14.3	1.15	29.3	1.71	43.9	2.07	58.2	2.34	71.8	2.54	84.6	2.71
17	15.2	1.15	31.1	1.71	46.7	2.07	61.8	2.34	76.2	2.54	89.8	2.71
18	16.0	1.15	33.0	1.71	49.4	2.07	65.5	2.33	80.7	2.54	95.1	2.71
19	16.9	1.14	34.8	1.70	52.2	2.07	69.1	2.33	85.2	2.54	100.4	2.71
20	17.8	1.14	36.6	1.70	54.9	2.07	72.7	2.33	89.7	2.54	105.7	2.71
25	22.2	1.14	45.7	1.70	68.5	2.07						
30	26.6	1.14	54.8	1.70								
50	44.2	1.13										
∞		1.128		1.6926		2.0588		2.3258		2.5344		2.7044

SOURCE: Acheson J. Duncan, The Use of Ranges in Comparing Variabilities, *Ind. Qual. Control*, vol. 40, no. 5, February, 1955; no. 8, April, 1955.   (Reprinted by permission of the author and the editor of *Industrial Quality Control*.)

TABLE A-12a   *F* Distribution, Upper 5% Points (F_{95})

df₂ \ df₁	1	2	3	4	5	6	7	8	9
1	161	200	216	225	230	234	237	239	241
2	18.51	19.00	19.16	19.25	19.30	19.33	19.35	19.37	19.38
3	10.13	9.55	9.28	9.12	9.01	8.94	8.89	8.85	8.81
4	7.71	6.94	6.59	6.39	6.26	6.16	6.09	6.04	6.00
5	6.61	5.79	5.41	5.19	5.05	4.95	4.88	4.82	4.77
6	5.99	5.14	4.76	4.53	4.39	4.28	4.21	4.15	4.10
7	5.59	4.74	4.35	4.12	3.97	3.87	3.79	3.73	3.68
8	5.32	4.46	4.07	3.84	3.69	3.58	3.50	3.44	3.39
9	5.12	4.26	3.86	3.63	3.48	3.37	3.29	3.23	3.18
10	4.96	4.10	3.71	3.48	3.33	3.22	3.14	3.07	3.02
11	4.84	3.98	3.59	3.36	3.20	3.09	3.01	2.95	2.90
12	4.75	3.89	3.49	3.26	3.11	3.00	2.91	2.85	2.80
13	4.67	3.81	3.41	3.18	3.03	2.92	2.83	2.77	2.71
14	4.00	3.74	3.34	3.11	2.96	2.85	2.76	2.70	2.66
15	4.54	3.68	3.29	3.06	2.90	2.79	2.71	2.64	2.59
16	4.49	3.63	3.24	3.01	2.85	2.74	2.66	2.59	2.54
17	4.45	3.59	3.20	2.96	2.81	2.70	2.61	2.55	2.49
18	4.41	3.55	3.16	2.93	2.77	2.66	2.58	2.51	2.46
19	4.38	3.52	3.13	2.90	2.74	2.63	2.54	2.48	2.42
20	4.35	3.49	3.10	2.87	2.71	2.60	2.51	2.45	2.40
22	4.30	3.44	3.05	2.82	2.66	2.55	2.46	2.40	2.35
24	4.26	3.40	3.01	2.78	2.62	2.51	2.42	2.36	2.30
26	4.23	3.37	2.97	2.74	2.59	2.47	2.39	2.32	2.27
28	4.20	3.34	2.95	2.71	2.56	2.45	2.36	2.29	2.24
32	4.15	3.30	2.90	2.67	2.51	2.40	2.32	2.25	2.19
36	4.11	3.26	2.86	2.63	2.48	2.36	2.28	2.21	2.15
40	4.08	3.23	2.84	2.61	2.45	2.34	2.25	2.18	2.12
60	4.00	3.15	2.76	2.53	2.37	2.25	2.17	2.10	2.04
100	3.94	3.09	2.70	2.46	2.30	2.19	2.10	2.03	1.97
200	3.89	3.04	2.65	2.41	2.26	2.14	2.05	1.98	1.92
∞	3.84	3.00	2.60	2.37	2.21	2.10	2.01	1.94	1.88

SOURCE: Tables A-12a and A-12b are reprinted with the kind permission of Professor E. S. Pearson. It was published first by M. Merrington and C. M. Thompson, "Tables of percentage points of the inverted beta (*F*) distribution," *Biometrika*, Vol. 33 (1943), p. 73. Several corrections have been made here from *Biometrika Tables for Statisticians*, Vol. 2, Table 5 (1972), E. S. Pearson and H. O. Hartley.

df_2 \ df_1	10	12	16	20	24	30	50	100	∞
1	242	244	246	248	249	250	252	253	254
2	19.40	19.41	19.43	19.45	19.45	19.46	19.47	19.49	19.50
3	8.79	8.74	8.69	8.66	8.64	8.62	8.58	8.56	8.53
4	5.96	5.91	5.84	5.80	5.77	5.75	5.70	5.66	5.63
5	4.74	4.68	4.60	4.56	4.53	4.50	4.44	4.40	4.36
6	4.06	4.00	3.92	3.87	3.84	3.81	3.75	3.71	3.67
7	3.64	3.57	3.49	3.44	3.41	3.38	3.32	3.28	3.23
8	3.35	3.28	3.20	3.15	3.12	3.09	3.03	2.98	2.93
9	3.14	3.07	2.98	2.94	2.90	2.86	2.80	2.76	2.71
10	2.98	2.91	2.82	2.77	2.74	2.70	2.64	2.59	2.54
11	2.85	2.79	2.70	2.65	2.61	2.57	2.50	2.45	2.40
12	2.75	2.69	2.60	2.54	2.51	2.46	2.40	2.35	2.30
13	2.67	2.60	2.51	2.46	2.42	2.38	2.32	2.26	2.21
14	2.60	2.53	2.44	2.39	2.35	2.31	2.24	2.19	2.13
15	2.94	2.48	2.39	2.33	2.29	2.25	2.18	2.12	2.07
16	2.49	2.42	2.33	2.28	2.24	2.19	2.13	2.07	2.01
17	2.45	2.38	2.29	2.23	2.19	2.15	2.08	2.02	1.96
18	2.41	2.34	2.25	2.19	2.15	2.11	2.04	1.98	1.92
19	2.38	2.31	2.21	2.16	2.11	2.07	2.00	1.94	1.88
20	2.35	2.28	2.18	2.12	2.08	2.04	1.96	1.90	1.84
22	2.30	2.23	2.13	2.07	2.03	1.98	1.91	1.84	1.78
24	2.25	2.18	2.09	2.03	1.98	1.94	1.86	1.80	1.73
26	2.22	2.15	2.05	1.99	1.95	1.90	1.82	1.76	1.69
28	2.19	2.12	2.02	1.96	1.91	1.87	1.78	1.72	1.65
32	2.14	2.07	1.97	1.91	1.86	1.82	1.74	1.67	1.59
36	2.10	2.03	1.93	1.87	1.82	1.78	1.69	1.62	1.55
40	2.08	2.00	1.90	1.84	1.79	1.74	1.66	1.59	1.51
60	1.99	1.92	1.81	1.75	1.70	1.65	1.56	1.48	1.39
100	1.92	1.85	1.75	1.68	1.63	1.57	1.48	1.39	1.28
120	1.87	1.80	1.69	1.62	1.57	1.52	1.42	1.32	1.19
∞	1.83	1.75	1.64	1.57	1.52	1.46	1.35	1.24	1.00

TABLE A-12b   *F* **Distribution, Upper 1% (F_{99})**

df$_2$ \ df$_1$	1	2	3	4	5	6	7	8	9
1	4052	5000	5403	5625	5764	5859	5928	5981	6022
2	98.5	99.0	99.2	99.2	99.3	99.3	99.4	99.4	99.4
3	34.1	30.8	29.5	28.7	28.2	27.9	27.7	27.5	27.3
4	21.2	18.0	16.7	16.0	15.5	15.2	15.0	14.8	14.7
5	16.3	13.3	12.1	11.4	11.0	10.7	10.5	10.3	10.2
6	13.7	10.9	9.78	9.15	8.75	8.47	8.26	8.10	7.98
7	12.2	9.55	8.45	7.85	7.46	7.19	6.99	6.84	6.72
8	11.3	8.65	7.59	7.01	6.63	6.37	6.18	6.03	5.91
9	10.6	8.02	6.99	6.42	6.06	5.80	5.61	5.47	5.35
10	10.0	7.56	6.55	5.99	5.64	5.39	5.20	5.06	4.94
11	9.65	7.21	6.22	5.67	5.32	5.07	4.89	4.74	4.63
12	9.33	6.93	5.95	5.41	5.06	4.82	4.64	4.50	4.39
13	9.07	6.70	5.74	5.21	4.86	4.62	4.44	4.30	4.19
14	8.86	6.51	5.56	5.04	4.70	4.46	4.28	4.14	4.03
15	8.68	6.36	5.42	4.89	4.56	4.32	4.14	4.00	3.89
16	8.53	6.23	5.29	4.77	4.44	4.20	4.03	3.89	3.78
17	8.40	6.11	5.18	4.67	4.34	4.10	3.93	3.79	3.68
18	8.29	6.01	5.09	4.58	4.25	4.01	3.84	3.71	3.60
19	8.18	5.93	5.01	4.50	4.17	3.94	3.77	3.63	3.52
20	8.10	5.85	4.94	4.43	4.10	3.87	3.70	3.56	3.46
21	8.02	5.78	4.87	4.37	4.04	3.81	3.64	3.51	3.40
22	7.95	5.72	4.82	4.31	3.99	3.76	3.59	3.45	3.35
23	7.88	5.66	4.76	4.26	3.94	3.71	3.54	3.41	3.30
24	7.82	5.61	4.72	4.22	3.90	3.67	3.50	3.36	3.26
25	7.77	5.57	4.68	4.18	3.86	3.63	3.46	3.32	3.22
26	7.72	5.53	4.64	4.14	3.82	3.59	3.42	3.29	3.18
27	7.68	5.49	4.60	4.11	3.78	3.56	3.39	3.26	3.15
28	7.64	5.45	4.57	4.07	3.75	3.53	3.36	3.23	3.12
29	7.60	5.42	4.54	4.04	3.73	3.50	3.33	3.20	3.09
30	7.56	5.39	4.51	4.02	3.70	3.47	3.30	3.17	3.07
40	7.31	5.18	4.31	3.83	3.51	3.29	3.12	2.99	2.89
60	7.08	4.98	4.13	3.65	3.34	3.12	2.95	2.82	2.72
120	6.85	4.79	3.95	3.48	3.17	2.96	2.79	2.66	2.56
∞	6.63	4.61	3.78	3.32	3.02	2.80	2.64	2.51	2.41

df₂ \ df₁	10	12	15	20	24	30	40	60	∞
1	6056	6106	6157	6209	6235	6261	6287	6313	6366
2	99.4	99.4	99.4	99.4	99.5	99.5	99.5	99.5	99.5
3	27.2	27.1	26.9	26.7	26.6	26.5	26.4	26.3	26.1
4	14.5	14.4	14.2	14.0	13.9	13.8	13.7	13.7	13.5
5	10.1	9.89	9.72	9.55	9.47	9.38	9.29	9.20	9.02
6	7.87	7.72	7.56	7.40	7.31	7.23	7.14	7.06	6.88
7	6.62	6.47	6.31	6.16	6.07	5.99	5.91	5.82	5.65
8	5.81	5.67	5.52	5.36	5.28	5.20	5.12	5.03	4.86
9	5.26	5.11	4.96	4.81	4.73	4.65	4.57	4.48	4.31
10	4.85	4.71	4.56	4.41	4.33	4.25	4.17	4.08	3.91
11	4.54	4.40	4.25	4.10	4.02	3.94	3.86	3.78	3.60
12	4.30	4.16	4.01	3.86	3.78	3.70	3.62	3.54	3.36
13	4.10	3.96	3.82	3.66	3.59	3.51	3.43	3.34	3.17
14	3.94	3.80	3.66	3.51	3.43	3.35	3.27	3.18	3.00
15	3.80	3.67	3.52	3.37	3.29	3.21	3.13	3.05	2.87
16	3.69	3.55	3.41	3.26	3.18	3.10	3.02	2.93	2.75
17	3.59	3.46	3.31	3.16	3.08	3.00	2.92	2.83	2.65
18	3.51	3.37	3.23	3.08	3.00	2.92	2.84	2.75	2.57
19	3.43	3.30	3.15	3.00	2.92	2.84	2.76	2.67	2.49
20	3.37	3.23	3.09	2.94	2.86	2.78	2.69	2.61	2.42
21	3.31	3.17	3.03	2.88	2.80	2.72	2.64	2.55	2.36
22	3.26	3.12	2.98	2.83	2.75	2.67	2.58	2.50	2.31
23	3.21	3.07	2.93	2.78	2.70	2.62	2.54	2.45	2.26
24	3.17	3.03	2.89	2.74	2.66	2.58	2.49	2.40	2.21
25	3.13	2.99	2.85	2.70	2.62	2.54	2.45	2.36	2.17
26	3.09	2.96	2.82	2.66	2.58	2.50	2.42	2.33	2.13
27	3.06	2.93	2.78	2.63	2.55	2.47	2.38	2.29	2.10
28	3.03	2.90	2.75	2.60	2.52	2.44	2.35	2.26	2.06
29	3.00	2.87	2.73	2.57	2.49	2.41	2.33	2.23	2.03
30	2.98	2.84	2.70	2.55	2.47	2.39	2.30	2.21	2.01
40	2.80	2.66	2.52	2.37	2.29	2.20	2.11	2.02	1.80
60	2.63	2.50	2.35	2.20	2.12	2.03	1.94	1.84	1.60
120	2.47	2.34	2.19	2.03	1.95	1.86	1.76	1.66	1.38
∞	2.32	2.18	2.04	1.88	1.79	1.70	1.59	1.47	1.00

TABLE A-13 Critical Values of the Tukey-Duckworth Sum

Approximate Risk	Critical values of the sum $a + b$
.09	6
.05	7
.01	10
.001	13

SOURCE: John W. Tukey, "A Quick, Compact, Two-sample Test to Duckworth's Specifications," *Technometrics*, vol. 1, no. 1, February, 1959, pp. 21–48. (Reproduced by permission.) The critical .09 value was given me by Peter C. Dickinson.

TABLE A-14 Values of H_α $k = 2$, ANOM (Two-tailed Test)

df	$\alpha = 0.10$	0.05	0.01
2	2.06	3.04	7.02
3	1.66	2.25	4.13
4	1.51	1.96	3.26
5	1.42	1.82	2.85
6	1.37	1.73	2.62
7	1.34	1.67	2.47
8	1.32	1.63	2.37
9	1.30	1.60	2.30
10	1.28	1.58	2.24
12	1.26	1.54	2.16
15	1.24	1.51	2.08
18	1.23	1.49	2.03
20	1.22	1.48	2.01
25	1.21	1.46	1.97
30	1.20	1.44	1.94
40	1.19	1.43	1.91
60	1.18	1.41	1.88
∞	1.16	1.39	1.82

TABLE A-15   Distribution of Student's *t*

Values of *t* corresponding to selected probabilities.   Each probability is the sum of two equal areas under the two tails of the *t* curve. For example, the probability is $.05 = 2(.025)$ that a difference with $df = 20$ would have $t \geq |2.09|$

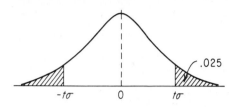

| df | Probability | | | |
	.10	.05	.02	.01
6	1.94	2.45	3.14	3.71
7	1.90	2.37	3.00	3.50
8	1.86	2.31	2.90	3.56
9	1.83	2.26	2.82	3.25
10	1.81	2.33	2.76	3.17
11	1.80	2.20	2.72	3.11
12	1.78	2.18	2.68	3.06
13	1.77	2.16	2.65	3.01
14	1.76	2.15	2.62	2.98
15	1.75	2.13	2.60	2.95
20	1.73	2.09	2.52	2.85
25	1.70	2.06	2.49	2.79
30	1.70	2.04	2.46	2.75
50	1.68	2.01	2.40	2.68
∞	1.645	1.960	2.326	2.576

SOURCE: This table is a modification of the one by Enrico T. Federighi, "Extended Tables of the Percentage Points of Student's *t*-Distribution," *Journ. Am. Stat. Assoc.*, vol. 54, p. 684, 1959.

TABLE A-16 Working Significance Levels for Magnitudes of Quadrant Sums

Significance level (conservative), %	Magnitude of quadrant sums
10	9
5	11
2	13
1	14–15*
0.5	15–17
0.2	17–19
0.1	18–21

* The smaller magnitude applies for large sample size; the larger magnitude for small sample size. Magnitudes equal to or greater than twice the sample size less six should not be used.

SOURCE: Paul S. Olmstead and John W. Tukey, A Corner Test for Association, *Ann. Math. Stat.*, vol. 18, pp. 495–513, December, 1947. Reproduced by permission of the authors and editor.

TABLE A-17   Confidence Belts for the Correlation Coefficient
Chance of Rejecting the Hypothesis When True = .05

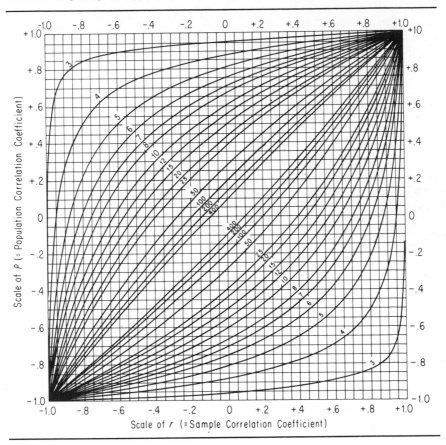

SOURCE: Reproduced by permission from F. N. David, *Tables of the Ordinates and Probability Integral of the Distribution of the Correlation Coefficient in Small Samples,* and E. S. Pearson, Biometrika Office, London, 1938.

TABLE A-18   Non-Random Uniformity, N_α

(No standard given)

	.05					.01			
$k*$	df: 10	15	30		k	df: 10	15	30	
3	.20	.20	.20	.20	3	.09	.09	.09	.09
4	.35	.35	.35	.35	4	.19	.19	.20	.20
5	.46	.46	.46	.47	5	.29	.29	.29	.30
6	.55	.55	.56	.56	6	.37	.37	.38	.38
7	.62	.63	.64	.65	7	.43	.44	.45	.46
8	.69	.70	.70	.72	8	.49	.50	.51	.53
9	.74	.75	.77	.78	9	.54	.56	.57	.59

* k = number of means being compared

SOURCE: Nair, K. R., "The Distribution of the Extreme Deviate from the Sample Mean and its Studentized Form," *Biometrika*, vol. xxxv, 1948, pp. 118–144.

Bibliography

Chapters 1, 2, and 3

American Standard, Z1.3 and ASQC Standard B-3, *Control Chart Method of Controlling Quality During Production,* American Standards Association, Inc., New York, 1958.

American Society for Testing Materials *A.S.T.M. Manual on Presentation of Data, Philadelphia,* 1950.

Burr, Irving W.: *Engineering Statistics and Quality Control,* McGraw-Hill Book Company, New York, 1953.

Duncan, Acheson J.: *Quality Control and Industrial Statistics,* 3d ed., Richard D. Irwin, Inc., Homewood, Ill., 1965.

Feigenbaum, A. V.: *Total Quality Control: Engineering and Management,* McGraw-Hill Book Company, New York, 1961.

Grant, E. L., and R. S. Leavenworth: *Statistical Quality Control,* 4th ed., McGraw-Hill Book Company, New York, 1972.

Juran, J. M. and Frank M. Gryna, Jr.: *Quality Planning and Analysis,* McGraw-Hill Book Company, New York, 1970.

Shewhart, Walter A.: *Economic Control of Quality of Manufactured Product,* D. Van Nostrand Company, New York, 1931.

Tippett, L. H. C.: *Technological Applications of Statistics,* John Wiley & Sons, New York, 1950.

Wilks, S. S.: *Elementary Statistical Analysis,* Princeton University Press, Princeton, N.J., 1948.

Chapter 4

Ott, Ellis R.: Statistical Quality Control: Prepared for the Government of India, U.N. Tech. Assist. Adm., Tech. Assist. Programme, Rep. no. TAA/IND/18 March 25, 1958.

Chapter 5

Batson, H. C.: Applications of Factorial Chi-Square Analysis to Experiments in Chemistry, *Trans. Amer. Soc. Qual. Control*, pp. 9–23, 1956.

Ennerson, Fred, Ralph Fleischmann, and Doris Rosenberg: A Production Experiment Using Attribute Data, *Ind. Qual. Control*, vol. 8, no. 5, March, 1952, pp. 41–44.

Halperin, M., S. W. Greenhouse, J. Cornfield, and J. Zalokar: Tables of Percentage Points for the Studentized Maximum Absolute Deviate in Normal Samples, *J. Amer. Stat. Assoc.*, pp. 185–195, vol. 50, 1955.

Lewis, Sidney S.: Analysis of Means applied to percent defective data, *Proc. Rutgers All-Day Conf. on Qual. Control*, 1958.

Ott, Ellis R.: Analysis of Means—A Graphical Procedure, *Ind. Qual. Control*, vol. 24, no. 2, pp. 101–109, August, 1967.

————: Trouble-shooting, *Ind. Qual. Control, Practical Aids*, vol. 11, no. 9, June, 1955.

Ott, Ellis R.: Achieving Quality Control, *Qual. Prog.* figs. 5-10, 5-12, 5-13, 5-14, May, 1969.

————: Analysis of Means, *Rutgers Tech. Rep. no.* 1, Prepared for Army, Navy, and Air Force under Contract NONR 404(11) (Task NR 042-021) with the Office of Naval Research, Aug. 10, 1958.

———— and Sidney S. Lewis: Analysis of Means Applied to Per-Cent Defective Data, *Rutgers Stat. Cent. Tech. Rep. no. 2*, Prepared for Army, Navy, and Air Force under Contract NONR 404 (11) (Task NP 042-21) with the Office of Naval Research, Feb. 10, 1960.

Schilling, Edward G. A Systematic Approach to the Analysis of Means, *J. Qual. Tech.*, vol, 5, no. 3, pt. 1, pp. 93–108, July, 1973; and pts. 2 and 3, pp. 147–159, vol. 5, no. 4, October, 1973.

Siegel, S.: *Non-Parametric Statistics for the Behavioral Sciences*, pp. 45–46, McGraw-Hill Book Company, New York, 1956.

Vaswani, Sundari, and Ellis R. Ott: Statistical Aids in Locating Machine Differences, *Ind. Qual. Control*, vol. 2, no. 1, July, 1954.

Zahniser, J. Stuart, and D. Lehman: Quality Control at Talon, Incorporated, *Ind. Qual. Control*, pp. 32–36, March, 1951.

Chapter 6

Ott, Ellis R.: A Production Experiment with Mechanical Assemblies, *Ind. Qual. Control*, vol. 9, no. 6, 1953.

————and Frank W. Wehrfritz: A Special Screening Program for Many Treatments, *Stat. Neerl.*, Special Issue in Honour of Prof. H. C. Hamaker, pp. 165–170, July, 1973.

Chapter 7

Mace, Arthur E.: The Use of Limit Gages in Process Control, *Ind. Qual. Control*, vol. 8, no. 4, pp. 24, 28–31, January, 1952.

Ott, Ellis R., and A. B. Mundel: Narrow-limit Gaging, *Ind. Qual. Control*, vol. 10, no. 5, March, 1954.

Stevens, W. L.: Control by Gauging, *R. Stat. Soc. J.*, ser. B, vol. 10, pp. 54–108, 1948.

Chapter 8

Dodge, Harold F.: A Method of Rating Manufactured Product, *Bell Syst. Tech. J.*, vol. 7, pp. 350–368, April, 1928.

———— and Harry G. Romig: *Sampling Inspection Tables—Single and Double Sampling*, 2d ed., John Wiley & Sons, Inc., New York, 1959.

———— and Mary N. Torrey: A Check Inspection and Demerit Weighting Plan, *Ind. Qual. Control*, vol. 13, no. 1, pp. 5–12, July, 1956.

Freund, Richard A.: Acceptance Control Charts, *Ind. Qual. Control*, pp. 13–23, October, 1957.

Frey, William C.: A Plan for Outgoing Quality, *Mod. Packag.*, October, 1962.

Hamaker, H. C.: Some Basic Principles of Sampling Inspection by Attributes, *Appl. Stat.*, vol. 7, pp. 149–159, 1958.

Hill, D. A.: Control of Complicated Product, *Ind. Qual. Control*, vol. 8, no. 4, pp. 18–22, 1952.

United States Department of the Army, Chem. Corps Eng. Agency: *Master Sampling Plans for Single, Duplicate, Double and Multiple Sampling*, Manual no. 2,. Army Chemical Center, Md., 1953.

United States Department of Commerce, National Bureau of Standards, *Tables of the Binomial Probability Distribution*, Applied Mathematics series 6, January, 1950, Superintendent of Documents, U. S. Government Printing Office, Washington, D.C. 20025.

United States Department of Defense: *Military Standard, Sampling Procedures and Tables for Inspection by Attributes* (MIL-STD-105D), U.S. Government Printing Office, Washington, D.C., 1963.

_____: *Military Standard, Sampling Procedures and Tables for Inspection by Variables for Percent Defective* (MIL-STD-414).

_____: *Quality and Reliability Handbook* (*H*53), superseding Inspection (H105) Office of the Assistant Secretary of Defense (Installations and Logistics). Washington, D.C. 20301.

Chapter 9

Dixon, W. J.: Processing Data for Outliers, *Biom.*, vol. 9, pp. 74–89, 1953.

Grubbs, Frank E.: Procedures for Detecting Outlying Observations in Samples, *Technometrics*, vol. 2, no. 1, pp. 1-21, February, 1969.

Proschan, Frank: *Ind. Qual. Control*, pp. 14–19, January, 1957.

Chapter 10

ASQC Standard A1 (proposed), *Ind. Qual. Control*, p. 217, October, 1967.

Dixon, Wilfred J., and Frank J. Massey, Jr.: *Introduction to Statistical Analysis*, 3d ed., Chap. 8 especially, McGraw-Hill Book Company, 1969.

Duncan, Acheson J.: The Use of Ranges in Comparing Variabilities, Reprinted from *Ind. Qual. Control*, vol. 11, no. 5, February, 1965.

Steel, Robert G., and James H. Torrie: *Principles and Procedures of Statistics*, with special references to the biological sciences, McGraw-Hill Book Company, 1960

Wilks, S. S.: *Elementary Statistical Analysis*, Princeton University Press, Princeton, N.J., 1948.

Chapter 11

Merritt, Richard H.: Vegetative and Floral Development of Plants Resulting from Differential Precooling of Planted Croft Lily Bulbs, *Proc. Amer. Soc. Hortic. Sci.*, vol. 82, pp. 517–525, 1963.

Tukey, John W.: A quick, compact, two-sample test to Duckworth's specifications, *Technometrics*, vol. 1, no. 1, pp. 31–48, February, 1959.

Chapter 12

Box. G. E. P., Evolutionary Operation: A Method for Increasing Industrial Productivity, *Appl. Stat.*, vol. 6, pp. 81–101, 1957.

Davies, Owen L. (Ed.): *Statistical Methods in Research and Production*, Hafner Publishing Company, New York, 1958.

Dixon, Wilfred J., and Frank J. Massey, Jr.: (See Chap. 10 listing)

Fisher, Sir Ronald A.: *Statistical Methods for Research Workers*, 14th ed., Hafner Publishing Company, Inc., New York, 1970.

_____: *Statistical Methods and Scientific Inference*, Hafner Press, New York, 1973.

Hicks, Charles R.: *Fundamental Concepts in the Design of Experiments*, Holt, Rinehart and Winston, New York, 1964.

Nelson, Lloyd: Factors for the Analysis of Means, *J. Qual. Techn.*, vol. 6, no. 4, pp. 175–181, October, 1974.

Ott, Ellis R.: Analysis of Means—A Graphical Procedure, *Ind. Qual. Control*, vol. 24, no. 2, pp. 101–109, August, 1967.

——— and Ronald D. Snee: Identifying Useful Differences in a Multiple-Head Machine, *J. Qual. Tech.*, vol. 5, no. 2, pp. 47–57, April, 1973.

Rosenberg, Doris, and Fred Ennerson: Production Research in the Manufacture of Hearing Aid Tubes, *Ind. Qual. Control, Practical Aids*, vol. 8, no. 6, pp. 94–97, May, 1952.

Schilling, Edward G.: A Systematic Approach to the Analysis of Means; pt. I, Analysis of Treatment Effects, *J. Qual. Tech.*, vol. 5, no. 3, pp. 93–108, July, 1973.

Schilling, Edward G.: A Systematic Approach to the Analysis of Means; pt. 2 Analysis of Contrasts, *J. Qual. Tech.*, vol. 5, no. 4, pp. 147–155, October, 1973.

———: A Systematic Approach to the Analysis of Means; pt. III, Analysis of Non-Normal Data, *J. Qual. Tech.*, vol. 5, no. 4, pp. 156–159, October, 1973.

Chapter 13

Baten, W. D.: An Analysis of Variance Applied to Screw Machines, *Ind. Qual. Control*, vol. 12, no. 10, April, 1956.

Halperin, Greenhouse, Cornfield, Zalokar (See Chap. 5).

Nair, K. R.: The Distribution of the Extreme Deviate from the Sample Mean and its Studentized Form, *Biom.*, vol. 35, pp. 118–144, 1948.

Olmstead, Paul S.: How to Detect the Type of an Assignable Cause, pt. 1: "Clues for Particular Types of Trouble"; pt. 2: Procedure when Probable Cause is Unknown, *Ind. Qual. Control*, vol. 9, no. 3, p. 32; vol. 9, no. 4, p. 22.

Ott, Ellis R., and Ronald D. Snee: Identifying Useful Differences in a Multiple-Head Machine, *J. Qual. Tech.*, vol. 5, no. 2, pp. 47–57, April, 1973. This presents an example of ANOM with $r = 1$.

Schilling, Edward G.: (See Chap. 5).

Chapter 14

Dixon, Wilfred J., and Frank J. Massey, Jr.: (See Chap. 10).

Grant, E. L., and R. S. Leavenworth: (See Chap. 1).

Olmstead, Paul S., and John W. Tukey: A Corner Test for Association, *Ann. Math. Stat.*, vol. 18, pp. 495–513, December, 1947, and *Bell Teleph. Syst. Tech. Publ., Monogr.* B-1515.

Ott, Ellis R.: A Scatterdiagram Used to Compare "Before" and "After" Measurements, *Ind. Qual. Control*, vol. 13, no. 12, June, 1957.

Steel, Robert G. D., and James H. Torrie: (See Chap. 10).

Wilks, S. S.: *Elementary Statistical Analysis*, Princeton University Press, Princeton, N. J., 1948.

Chapter 15

Ott, Ellis R., Horace P. Andrews, W. L. Gore, and Kenneth S. Stephens, *Statistical Quality Control, An Aid to Industrial Development*, Final Report to the Government of India of experts appointed under the United Nations Technical Assistance Programme, June 15, 1963.

———: "Achieving Quality Control" (See Chap. 5).

Index